SOCIAL MEDIA ENTERTAINMENT

POSTMILLENNIAL POP

General Editors: Karen Tongson and Henry Jenkins

Social Media Entertainment

The New Intersection of Hollywood and Silicon Valley

Stuart Cunningham *and* David Craig

NEW YORK UNIVERSITY PRESS

New York

NEW YORK UNIVERSITY PRESS
New York
www.nyupress.org

References to Internet websites (URLs) were accurate at the time of writing. Neither the author nor New York University Press is responsible for URLs that may have expired or changed since the manuscript was prepared.

Library of Congress Cataloging-in-Publication Data
Names: Cunningham, Stuart, author. | Craig, David Randolph, author.
Title: Social media entertainment : the new intersection of Hollywood
and Silicon Valley / Stuart Cunningham and David Craig.
Description: New York : New York University Press, [2018] | Series: Postmillennial pop |
Includes bibliographical references and index.
Identifiers: LCCN 2018020900| ISBN 9781479890286 (cl : alk. paper) |
ISBN 9781479846894 (pb : alk. paper)
Subjects: LCSH: Internet entertainment industry—United States. | Internet entertainment—
United States. | Social media—United States.
Classification: LCC HD9696.8.U62 C86 2018 | DDC 384.3/80973—dc23
LC record available at https://lccn.loc.gov/2018020900

New York University Press books are printed on acid-free paper, and their binding materials are chosen for strength and durability. We strive to use environmentally responsible suppliers and materials to the greatest extent possible in publishing our books.

Manufactured in the United States of America

10 9 8 7 6 5 4 3 2 1

Also available as an ebook

In memory of Matt Palazzolo, writer, star, and producer,
Bloomers, *and for all those creators doing good*

CONTENTS

LIST OF FIGURES AND TABLES

FIGURES

TABLES

Introduction

The picture in figure I.1 was taken in spring 2017 of a billboard located on the iconic Sunset Strip, where movie stars have featured on the hoardings since the golden age of Hollywood. The sign promotes a YouTube Red documentary, *This Is Everything*, directed by Academy Award–winning filmmaker Barbara Koppel (*Harlan County U.S.A.*) and starring Gigi Gorgeous. For most Hollywood tourists, or even Hollywood professionals, Gigi's name and face may be unfamiliar. But for 7.2 million global fans and followers across YouTube, Instagram, Twitter, and Facebook (Ifeanyi 2017), Gigi is the new "it" girl—and arguably the world's most famous trans lesbian beauty vlogger. For nearly a decade, long before Caitlyn Jenner or hit series like *Transparent*, Gigi shared her transition from a teenage boy name Gregory to Gigi with her global fan community, who witnessed her progression from a makeup hobbyist to an advertising influencer partnered with global beauty brands. Gigi's trajectory, including her transformation into an LGBTQ activist appearing on the cover of the LGBTQ magazine *The Advocate* with the headline "Trans, Lesbian, and the Face of an Online Movement" (Guerrero 2017).

Gigi was not alone. For the past few years, YouTube has posted campaigns promoting their most prominent "creators." Like their Hollywood counterparts, creators are "next-gen" stars. Unlike their counterparts, these stars are also entrepreneurs, community organizers, and cultural icons populating a brand-new, if brand-focused, parallel media universe we are calling "social media entertainment."

But the social media universe, of course, is not populated only with inspiring uplift. In the aftermath of the 2016 US elections, numerous accounts surfaced of nefarious content creators profiting by posting fake content on social media. This tsunami of fake news may have influenced the outcome of the election as it engaged in "anti-Clinton fervor,"

Figure I.1. A promotional poster for the YouTube Red release of
Gigi Gorgeous: This Is Everything adorns Sunset Boulevard,
Hollywood. Photo by David Craig.

promoting Donald Trump's candidacy and spreading right-wing news.
Buzzfeed described how "Teens in the Balkans" earned up to three thousand US dollars a day "duping Trump supporters." MSNBC and NPR interviewed creators who operate as members of a "new industry" (Craig
and Cunningham 2017).

On the other side of the political spectrum, some of the most prominent US creators spent the election season promoting civic engagement,
advocating for liberal causes, and championing Clinton. The Vlogbrothers, also known as Hank and John Green, launched a "get out the vote"
campaign featuring their fan community—known as Nerdfighters—
through a dedicated YouTube channel, "How to Vote in Every State"
(2016). Prominent beauty vlogger Ingrid Nilsen interviewed President
Obama and attended both political conventions on behalf of YouTube.
Her advocacy resembles MTV's collaboration "Rock the Vote," with the

crucial difference that Nilsen represents a small business entrepreneur, not a multinational media conglomerate.

In turn, these creators risked not only offending fans but also the potential loss of advertising revenue and brand sponsors. LGBTQ creator Tyler Oakley championed Clinton to his nine million YouTube subscribers and six million Twitter followers. Oakley posted an interview with Clinton on the eve of the election entitled "Meeting Future Madam President" (2016). In addition to over sixty-six thousand affirmative responses ("thumbs up"), Oakley received more than ten thousand "thumbs down" from fans who may have unsubscribed from his channel and lost him revenue. In the case of Casey Neistadt, who promoted political topics and insisted that other creators come out against Trump, the BBC considered whether he had committed "YouTube suicide" (Varley 2016).

Since the election, these creators have continued to champion resistance to Trump, progressive concerns, and a healthier Fourth Estate. Nilsen and Oakley promoted and posted videos from the Women's Marches. Neistat attended airport protests against President Trump's immigration ban, and his video garnered over three million views in one day (Gutelle 2017a). Since then, Neistat has partnered with CNN and announced the launch of a YouTube-based news series along with apps aggregating vetted news content while filtering out fake news creators (Jarvey 2017a). Among numerous social media entertainment enterprises, the Greens continue to run Project for Awesome, an annual campaign that encourages creators to raise funds online for their favorite charities and help "decrease world suck" (ProjectforAwesome.com). Their 2016 campaign raised over $1.5 million for Save the Children and the UN High Commission for Refugees. These campaigns align with the topics of numerous Vlogbrother videos about the global refugee crisis and the conflict in Syria, which have been viewed by millions globally. These, and projects like Jerome Jarre's #LoveArmy, which is presently fighting famine in Somalia (Jacewicz 2017), are but a few examples of next-gen creators dedicating their cultural power to global progressive causes.

After the election, Clinton reflected on the pernicious influence of fake news on politics. She described this phenomenon as an "epidemic" with "real-world consequences" (Gambino 2016). In contrast, these progressive creator activists arguably represent a palliative. At the very least, they affirm how this new medium of social media can be harnessed to promote diverse political views. At most, although they did not prevail this past election, these next-gen culture warriors could prove vital to winning the next—while also helping to generate progressive change around the world.

Defining Social Media Entertainment

This is a book about these, and many, many more social media creators. It is a book about current and relatively recent incursions into screen media as we have come to know them over a century and more. It argues that the emerging shape of screen industries in the twenty-first century shows established players, norms, principles, and practices ceding significant power and influence to powerful digital streaming and social networking platforms. Just as notably, these platforms have started to represent a greater value proposition to the advertising industry that has served as the bulwark for main media since the start of broadcasting early in the last century. Creators have harnessed these platforms to generate significantly different content, separate from the century-long model of intellectual property control and exploitation in the legacy content industries. This new screen ecology is driven by intrinsically interactive technologies and strategies of fan, viewer, audience, and community engagement. Combined, these factors inform a qualitatively different globalization dynamic that has scaled with great velocity, posing new challenges for established screen companies, creatives, and regulatory regimes—not to mention media scholars.

The emerging shape of screen industries in the twenty-first century encapsulates deep changes in consumer habit and expectation, technology, and content production related "to a larger trend across the media industries to integrate digital technology and socially networked communication with traditional screen media practices" (Holt and Sanson 2013, 1). This emerging new screen ecology has not only given rise to major challenges to established media but is being shaped by a set of newly prominent online screen entertainment platforms, most prominently Apple, Amazon, and Netflix but also and preeminently Alphabet/Google/YouTube, along with others such as Facebook, Twitter, Instagram, and Snapchat.

Arguably one of the most challenging and innovative elements of this evolving screen ecology is the rise of "social media entertainment," or SME, as we will refer to it for the sake of brevity. We see SME as an emerging proto-industry fueled by professionalizing, previously amateur content creators using new entertainment and communicative formats, including vlogging, gameplay, and do-it-yourself (DIY), to develop potentially sustainable businesses based on significant followings that can extend across multiple platforms. The infrastructure of SME is comprised of diverse and competing platforms featuring online video players with social networking affordances, including YouTube, Facebook, Instagram, Twitter, Snapchat, and Vimeo. These platforms have introduced commercial features that service their own interests but also affordances that entrepreneurial content creators have accessed to cultivate diverse business models and revenue streams.

This "industry" is only a bit more than ten years old, having started soon after the acquisition by Google of YouTube in 2006 and concurrent with the launch of Twitter and their counterparts in China, Youku and Weibo. By 2017, it saw more than three million YouTube creators globally receiving some level of remuneration from their uploaded content and more than four thousand YouTube professionalizing-amateur channels with at least a million subscribers. The top five thousand YouTube channels have received over 250 billion video views in aggregate. But these numbers do not translate into revenue in the same way as Nielsen ratings and television advertiser cost-per-thousand (CPM) rates. And some creators are securing sustainable careers with far fewer views and subscribers but much more engaged fan communities and richer brand deals.

It is important to stress the distinction between social media entertainment content and platforms and Hollywood-like content distributed, and in some cases increasingly produced, by the major "Internet-distributed television" *portals* (Lotz 2017) such as Hulu, Netflix, Amazon Video, and Apple's iTunes. While these portals largely specialize in mainstream long-form premium content supported by sophisticated algorithmic feedback (Hallinan and Striphas 2016), social media *platforms* offer scale, technological affordance, and—especially in the case of YouTube—remuneration and upskilling to previously amateur creators. We argue that SME constitutes a more radical *cultural* and *content* challenge to established media than the digital streamers (or portals).

It would be little overstatement to claim that these dynamics are a huge experiment in seeking to convert vernacular or informal creativity into talent and content increasingly attractive to advertisers, brands, talent agencies, studios, and venture-capital investors on a near-global scale—with implications for content/entertainment formats, production cultures, industry structures, and measurement of audience engagement: "[T]he world has never before seen the likes of YouTube in terms of availability of non-infringing content" (Hetcher 2013, 45).

The book anatomizes this emerging proto-industry, taking an "ecological" approach by investigating the interdependencies among its elements: mapping the platforms and affordances, content innovation and creative labor, monetization and management, new forms of media globalization, and critical cultural concerns raised by this nascent media industry. Our anatomization has been based on deep, ongoing engagement in the field at many levels of the industry, principally through over 150 interviews with creators, platform and intermediary executives and managers, talent agents, technology integrators, and policy makers. While primarily focused on the United States, as that is ground zero of SME, our fieldwork includes interviews conducted in Sydney and Shanghai, Berlin and Beijing, London and Mumbai. We have attended and participated in industry events such as VidCon, the creator-focused trade and fan conferences run by the Greens, and assisted in the development of pop-up YouTube Spaces.

At the same time, our research is informed by similarly deep engagement with a wide range of issues and debates central to media studies, cultural studies, communication studies, and media management. These include the dynamics of participatory culture, minorities and the marginalized in media cultures, digital disruption of media industries, the rise of social media, conditions of creative labor, and new forms of media globalization. This book is the story of a proto-industry that has emerged at the intersection of the cultural, technological, and industrial dynamics tracked in these issues and debates. On the basis of this theoretical engagement, we are able to contribute well-evidenced, revisionist accounts in the political economy of new media (the clash of cultures of globally dominant media and IT corporations); construct an account of short-form commercializing online video culture as a highly normative space driven by appeals to authenticity and community; extend the debate on creative labor to include the precariousness of certain forms of media management; and

Figure I.2. VidCon, the premier SME industry, trade, and fan conference. Photo by David Craig.

assess claims for a new wave of media globalization achieved without IP control.

There are some important caveats to this study. In 2017, it was estimated that one billion hours of YouTube are seen every day as compared to 1.25 billion hours of television per day (Solomon 2017). There were 1.5 billion monthly users, not counting people watching through links, shares, and downloads via other means. There was one hour of YouTube watched per day on mobile alone. This includes user- and professionally generated content. It is estimated, for example, that music makes up as much as 40% of YouTube content, with much of this promotional proprietary content from the big labels. And this is just YouTube. Since our initial research was conducted in 2015, Facebook has grown 25% to over two billion users while its platform partner, Instagram, has doubled in size to over eight hundred million users. But social media networking practices are not at all easily comparable to television viewing. The percentage of native SME creators operating on and across all these platforms is impossible to assess, as we explain in chapter 1. Out of all these statistics, it is clear that SME as yet comprises a small part of the online content universe. Despite much scholarly concern over the "institutionalization" or "formalization" of video sharing, it remains probable that the significant majority of this activity occurs outside the kinds of commercial dynamics that support SME.

In this book, we are driven by a commitment to diverse voices nurturing their owned-and-operated businesses in pursuit of sustainable careers while engaging in media entrepreneurialism that may have profound ramifications for the future of content and cultural production. We are also committed to tracking cultural progressivity where it carves out space within commercializing systems. And, in the wake of the information catastrophe that unfolded around the 2016 US presidential election, it is arguable that the commercial environment within which SME operates inhibits the spread of alternative and fake news—is in fact a safer environment—because most brands and advertisers will not tolerate association with such affronts to civility and democracy.

The Specificity of Social Media Entertainment

This book examines claims for the specificity and distinctiveness of social media entertainment as it has emerged spatially across several industrial dimensions as well as temporally in the context of extraordinarily rapid change.

The Challenge of Online Distribution

The challenge of online distribution calls up the riposte to the oft-quoted saw: if content is king, then distribution is King Kong. The business history of the Hollywood Majors is a history, relatively speaking, of remarkable stability. However, in the decade from the early 2000s, the Majors tried, but largely failed, to establish themselves in online distribution. Instead, this emerging distribution space was occupied by Internet "pure-play" businesses—Netflix, Apple, Amazon, Google, Facebook—many of which are appreciably larger, and have much deeper pockets than the Majors (Cunningham and Silver 2013).

Challenges to media incumbents are, of course, not new. The rise of television in the 1950s threatened the incumbency of film studios, turning cinema audiences into home-bound viewers. Within a decade, however, television co-evolved and converged with Hollywood. The film studios became as codependent on TV for syndication revenue, particularly a newly launched subscription channel called Home Box Office (HBO), as TV had upon the content-generation and talent-management skills of Hollywood. The new screen ecology of home video helped sustain an independent cinema industry throughout the 1980s and 1990s. Similarly, the challenge of cable distribution represented a similar pattern of co-evolution over time, especially in programming. For example, with full distribution across the cable universe, most ad-based networks shifted their programming strategies to embrace Hollywood storytelling to secure larger audiences and higher advertising returns. The former Arts and Entertainment network evolved into A&E, and went from British coproductions to reality programming, while AMC has shifted from libraries of American Movie Classics to complex American TV series like *Mad Men* and *Breaking Bad*.

But this current challenge is not only in distribution. Netflix and Amazon have engaged in very significant investment in original programming, looking to function not merely as a distribution outlet for Hollywood movies and television but increasingly as destinations for their own branded premium content. Global interest in Netflix's *House of Cards*, *Orange Is the New Black*, *Narcos*, and Amazon's *Transparent* and *Mozart in the Jungle* have pundits breathlessly suggesting that "the traditional TV industry should be in panic mode" (McNab 2016). Amazon and Netflix have even emerged as platforms of destination for what was the former independent film market (Siegel 2016).

A crucial distinction lies in the underlying value proposition of these platforms. Amazon's programs function as promotion, to sell memberships for its formidable e-commerce business. Similarly, Apple's iTunes, which is limited to transactional and syndicated distribution while—at least up to 2017—avoiding the messiness of content production, fuels its core business of iProducts. In some respects, this is as it ever was. NBC was to RCA television sets as Disney has been to plush toys and theme parks, as Philco and Texaco were to broadcast, ad-supported television, and as movie theaters are to popcorn and soda. In the professionally generated content (PGC) part of the new screen ecology, media content and distribution operate as means to an end for other higher-margin industries interested in selling products to consumers more than in storytelling for audiences.

Nevertheless, a notable comparison should be made between earlier outsiders engaging with Hollywood, such as the Japanese conglomerates driven by earlier business nostrums of synergy, and the Silicon Valley tech firms:

> Throughout its history, Hollywood has tended to resist outsiders—except when they come bearing money. . . . [T]hey have invariably been parted from their cash by studio executives and talent agents unable to believe their good fortune. . . . Instead of handing over their money to the studios, as some naive international players have done before them, the streaming services have set themselves up as competitors. . . . [T]hey are doing all the things that traditional movie studios do. (Garrahan 2017)

For social media entertainment, the video wars between Silicon Valley and Hollywood saw the rise of hybrid content–social networking platforms, most notably YouTube. These platforms offer open access (to users who can afford to access broadband and mobile systems with enough speed) for unlimited content of multiple modalities (video, photos, text) and innovative formats (vlogs, gifs, memes). In contrast to their digital TV-like competitors, these offer more than increasingly convergent video content players. They also nurture social media networking systems, comment sections and likes, emoticons and shares, friends and followers. And these platforms are appearing in diverse and competitive waves, from web-based platforms like YouTube, Twitter, and Facebook to mobile apps, like Instagram and Snapchat and (the now deceased) Vine. In *The Culture of Connectivity*, Jose van Dijck (2013) has importantly discussed how these platforms have engineered sociality. Here, we also account for how these platforms have facilitated a new mode of enterprise by millions of professionalizing and commercializing users through sociality online.

The SME Creator

We focus our attention on SME creators who started out as hobby-ists with little intention of developing any form of income, let alone a sustainable career. The difference offered by the new screen ecology's provision of potential career opportunity, even celebrity status, through amateur hobbyism and personal expression cannot be gainsaid. These creators disrupted the normative route through which media talent is filtered. YouTubers must be seen as a class of content creators who are able to exercise a higher level of control over their career prospects than in previous models of professionalizing talent. The head of the digital division of a leading Hollywood talent agency sums it up: "A traditional film or television artist—a writer, a director, a performer—has spent a certain amount of their life preparing to be ready for when opportunity knocks. . . . The mentality of a digital creator is the exact opposite. They're not preparing for an opportunity; they're creating it themselves" (Weinstein 2015). The distinctive career pathways and very low barriers to entry have meant that SME is more racially plural, multicultural, and gender diverse by far than mainstream screen media. And YouTubers gave rise to Viners, Snappers, and Grammers—enterprising creators adapting to and harnessing the commercial and technological affor-dances of the later platforms.

The rise of amateur content creators on new media platforms is not in itself new. Early amateur and nonprofit radio operators emerged out of the basements of American households. The development of home movie cameras launched a generation of filmmakers in their back yards. Garage bands and punk rockers began their careers in small venues, playing to friends and family. But the analogy ends there. The amateur broadcasters were "brushed aside" by a federally imposed commercial system (Streeter 1996, 251). To guarantee audiences, the filmmakers were forced to enter the film festival circuit or the studio system to secure dis-tribution. The musicians were inevitably forced to sign with record la-bels, which controlled not only their distribution but also their destinies.

There is simply no comparison with SME creators—across multiple variables, not least of which is access to unlimited distribution across multiple platforms. In addition, the means of digital production af-ford not only low-budget production but virtually no division of labor except at the topmost tier of the ecology. The creator has replaced the writer, producer, director, and actor above the line, as well as the editor, location scout, composer, and visual effects supervisor below. In addition, through the entrepreneurial agency afforded by these platforms, a content creator can operate as his or her own ad sales representative, securing partnerships with the platforms for split revenue. Creators also operate like online community organizers, cultivating a suite of practices—what Baym (2015) calls "relational labor"—to engage their fan communities for commercial and cultural gain.

With personal agency unlike anything in traditional media labor, these entrepreneurs leave their day jobs, if they ever held one, although admittedly for jobs that require operation around the clock. However, working conditions can be as onerous as they are precarious. Recent scholarship, focused less on YouTube creators and more on Instagram and beauty vloggers (Duffy 2015a; Abidin 2016a), describes how aspirational creator labor is often disappointed and creators' livelihoods are often subject to capricious "tweaks" in platform algorithms and regulatory interventions. But such conditions can still bear favorable comparison with the average aspirant in Hollywood, an industry notorious for requiring years of underpaid dues paying and apprenticeship in toxic and demanding positions.

Content Innovation

These creator entrepreneurs are engaging in forms of content innovation that barely resemble that of legacy media. Prominent SME content includes gameplay, DIY/how-to videos, and, most remarkably, the personality vlogger. This content reflects the networked affordances of social media that allow for intense fan engagement and participation. PewDiePie's gameplay featuring his crude and off-color commentaries may reflect a cross between ESPN's *SportsCenter* and Daniel Tosh's US comedy show *Tosh.o*, but is equally grounded in the logics of interactive video games. HGTV, Cooking, and the DIY Channel offer linear accounts of house hunting, food preparation, and home renovation, but still require the production skills of a trained team of videographers, editors, makeup artists, and producers, not to mention the means of distribution afforded by cable. In contrast, the DIY subgenre of unboxing often features, in some instances, a pair of hands, or a voiceover performer, coupled with a musical score, while audiences in the billions watch as toys and electronics are opened and assembled. "Assembly required" has become as simple as a click and play.

The hard-to-define personality vlogger operates at the business and cultural center of this new screen ecology. Perhaps there is a resemblance to the reality show persona, or the talk show guest, or maybe *America's Funniest Home Videos*. But this genre (or format) exhibits far closer affinity with online communication staples such as the blog and features personalities sharing their quotidian experiences who now "own the world of YouTube" (Samuelson 2014). In contrast to the content creators in legacy media, these vloggers excel neither in storytelling nor in what we have come to define as media "talent." But the mistake in evaluating the content innovation with this new industry would be to define their talent solely against norms of traditional entertainment storytelling, production, or performance. Rather, these creators have built a media brand based upon their personalities and through the intensely normative discourses of authenticity around vlogging.

The mediated authenticity of online vlogging, the appeals to the "real," may be comparable to the rise of reality television were it not for the lack of mediators. No camera crews off screen and story editors in post contriving storylines only loosely inspired by the lives of the performers. This is commercialized, mediatized, agentic impression management (Goffman 1959). For these vloggers, YouTube is a stage, but they are more than mere performers. They sell the tickets.

Interactivity

This new screen ecology occupies a fundamentally convergent space between social media communication and entertainment content and is structured by a level of interactivity and viewer- and audience-centricity that is radically distinctive in screen history. The history of the screen audience is one of higher-and-higher-order claims about the industry's responsiveness to viewer behaviors, needs, and wants, from William Goldman's "nobody knows anything" (Goldman 1989) to movie test focus groups to TV viewing diaries to ratings. Fully fledged academic communication theories have been given over to studying viewer "uses and gratifications." More recently, these concerns have come under the aegis of audience and fan studies, stressing audience agency in decoding and using media messages and the deep commitments and creative engagements of fans in their co-creation of meaning with media producers (e.g. Jenkins 1992). Mainstream audience engagement has been preoccupied with creating the "water cooler effect" or "must watch TV" (the antecedents to "binge viewing").

In the present, the PGC component of the new screen ecology (streaming services Netflix and its numerous national imitators, Amazon, and premium brands like HBO decoupled from cable packages) has tended to attract greater attention than the SME component because of its appeal to mainstream viewer demographics, essentially replacing linear broadcast mainstream entertainment options with a la carte options. Much has been made of the streaming services' new affordances for "binge viewing" and hyper-targeting micro demographics (e.g. Anderson 2006). However, busting the tyranny of the linear schedule started decades ago with box sets, and the degree to which the newly dominant streaming services use big data to hyper-target viewer segments but engage in very little interactivity has given rise to critical concern over the power of the algorithm in contemporary entertainment (Hallinan and Striphas 2016).

In contrast, SME is a radical hybrid of entertainment and community development and maintenance. Subscriber or fan engagement is not only critical; it is what triggers the revenue-sharing business model that replaces IP control.

Global Reach and IP Dynamics

It is possible to posit a qualitatively new wave of media globalization based on the global availability and uptake of SME platforms, which is relatively frictionless compared to national broadcasting and systems of film and DVD release and licensing by "windowed" territory. And compared to film and television, there is very little imposed content regulation on the major platforms—some of the world's largest information and communication companies.

For the major PGC streaming services such as Netflix, aggressive global expansion requires them to negotiate with preexisting rights holders in each new territory and often requires them to close down informal means of accessing their popular content, such as VPN (virtual private networks) workarounds, in such territories. While, in the longer term, the streaming giants may well drive territorial licensing to the wall, SME content is largely "born global." This is the case because SME, in contrast to content industries in general and Hollywood and broadcast television in particular, is not primarily based on IP control. Until 2017 and the launch of separate subscription video platforms, YouTube and Facebook elected to avoid the messy and legally cumbersome traditional media model of owned or shared IP. In turn, these platforms also avoided paying fees for content as well as offering backend residual or profit participation. Rather, YouTube entered into "partnership agreements" with its creators based on a split of advertising revenue from first dollar, a business strategy that Facebook, Instagram, Twitter, Twitch, Snapchat, and other platforms have only in 2016–2017 introduced for their own creators.

The key difference between traditional media operating multinationally and YouTube is that the former produces, owns, or licenses content for distribution, exhibition, or sale in multiple territories, while the latter talks of being primarily a facilitator of creator and content.

There are significant reasons for YouTube not taking an IP ownership position, which have to do with its continued status as a platform or online service provider rather than a content company. The US Digital Millennium Copyright Act 1998, in addition to criminalizing circumvention measures and heightening the penalties for copyright infringement on the Internet, created "safe harbor" provisions for online service providers (OSPs, including ISPs) against copyright infringement liability, provided they responsively block access to alleged infringing material on receipt of infringement claims from a rights holder.

* * *

Based on the argument that social media entertainment is a proto-industry, each chapter of the book examines a different, though interrelated, aspect of its emerging industrial status. Each chapter, therefore, can to some extent stand alone, although regular cross-referencing points the reader to the interdependent "ecology" of SME. Each chapter, moreover, engages with a key body of scholarly literature as it seeks to explore more broadly the implications of this proto-industry for the study of media, culture, and communication in the twenty-first century.

Drawing on network economics and production cultures scholarship, chapter 1 frames the political economy of this new proto-industry as the extremely volatile, interdependent clash of cultures between Hollywood (IP-driven entertainment) and Silicon Valley (iterative tech experimentation), rather than as capitalist hegemons conducting business as usual. In chapter 2, we argue that the conditions of creator labor in social media entertainment are empowering at the same time as they are precarious. There is now a very substantial literature calling time on overblown claims for the autonomy and meaningfulness of work in the cultural and creative industries, whereas this chapter asserts that the origins of SME in amateur passion projects that become popular and commercially viable via the affordances of world-spanning platforms represent a qualitatively different scenario.

Regarding the intermediaries (e.g. multichannel networks, data analytics firms) as potentially as precarious as creator careers—perhaps even more so—chapter 3 explores their need to innovate even more rapidly than YouTube and the other digital platforms, and certainly more quickly than established media. Chapter 4, perhaps more than any other in the book, illustrates how different SME is from traditional content industries. Seeking to work with the self-understanding of core discourses of SME, we argue that it establishes its bona fides through differentiating itself from traditional media by highly normative claims to greater authenticity.

In chapter 5, we marshal the evidence that SME is more racially plural, multicultural, and gender diverse by far than mainstream screen media. We argue that online creator entrepreneurs, *precisely because* they are working in a commercializing environment, commit themselves to maximizing their cultural and community reach, and thus must position themselves between subcultural identity politics and broader publics. Chapter 6 treats SME's near-frictionless globality, not as another instance of Western cultural imperialism, but as facilitated by content not governed by standard copyright industry high-control regimes. Concluding, we consider emerging developments that may presage further change and perhaps a new phase in the history of SME. Our final word is a call for creator advocacy in this extremely challenging proto-industrial space that is also replete with opportunity.

Building on current scholarship, we use a critical media industry studies (CMIS) approach that brings the concerns of macro-level political economy and cultural studies closer together. CMIS pays close attention to the political, economic, and social dimensions of popular culture and its production practices. What political economy and cultural studies often see as mass culture fatally compromised by commercialism, CMIS regards as a major focus for representation and contestation, often around marginalized and emerging groups: "Ignoring the logic of representational practices in entertainment production works to reinforce the relative invisibility or misrepresentation of those who often have the least power in the public sphere" (Havens, Lotz, and Tinic 2009, 250).

Havens, Lotz, and Tinic's call for attention to "quotidian practices and competing goals" (2009, 236) is crucial for our project, with its sustained attention to everyday agents (the social media entertainment creators) and deep clashes of business culture (between Hollywood and Silicon Valley). Methodologically, we also align with their emphasis on midlevel fieldwork in industry, including, given the emergent nature of SME, the knowledge of the realities of new media practice acquired through interviews. Our project is to posit the emergence of a new proto-industry, so the relationship of social media entertainment to established media is a key analytical challenge. This means that we will be drawing on a range of research—some of which is new to the field—in social media studies, network economics, media management, and globalization as well as mainstays of media industries research such as political economy, cultural studies, and production studies.

1

Platform Strategy

For critical media industry studies, the key framing background in which to situate social media entertainment lies in the relationship between Hollywood and Silicon Valley.

Analyses of the rate of change of the membership of the Fortune 500 (the largest US companies) show that the velocity of turnover has increased as time has passed (Strangler and Arbesman 2012). In contrast, there has been remarkable stability among the major businesses in the screen industry. Of the original eight companies that dominated film (Paramount, MGM, Fox, Warner Brothers, RKO, Universal, Columbia, and UA) during the first half of the twentieth century, only RKO went, replaced within the oligopoly by Disney during the 1950s. MGM-UA slipped from the annual list of top ten studio distributors during the 2000s. The oligopoly in broadcast television, while somewhat shorter-lived, is even tighter. The big six film studios are joined by CBS, NBC, and ABC dominating the TV landscape for almost seventy years, with Fox the only addition as a major network.

These "Majors" adapted to waves of significant change in regulatory structure, technology, and taste, re-forming into corporate structures that now have reestablished a form of de facto vertical integration through their parent conglomerates: NBC-Universal; Viacom-Paramount-CBS; Time-Warner; Disney-ABC; and Fox. With content and distribution tightly fused, and across film and television as well as music labels, publishers, theme parks, and merchandising fiefdoms, the Majors have formed a dominant oligopoly for decades.

However, they are now confronted by challenges that in some respects are unprecedented. The fragmentation of once-stable viewership means that television's splintering-but-still-big audience remains valuable to advertisers, but industry analysis, as presented in figure 1.1, shows that digital advertising revenue beat out traditional television advertising revenue in 2016 in the United States and globally in 2017 (Slefo 2017;

Poggi 2017). The core North American cinema box office is kept high by increasing ticket prices to offset stagnant attendance, and the cable TV industry, faced with escalating cord-cutting, responds with subscription increases that only contribute to further rates of exit.[1] A new confluence of information technology companies has been able to deliver content to individuals on a broad scale, creating new national and global markets and laying the framework to support new forms of content. This new screen ecology challenges the dominance of legacy media companies, and the companies that have succeeded most in digital distribution are outsiders; they are much larger companies with far larger resources and are employing IT industry business models rather than Hollywood's premium-content and -pricing models.

The fundamental differences between these companies—Apple, Amazon, Google, Facebook, Netflix—and media incumbents are that they are Internet "pure-play" businesses that have large online customer or user populations, generating extensive data on search behavior and purchas-

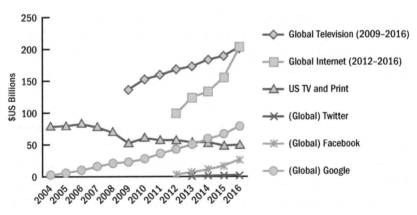

Figure 1.1. SME and Legacy Media Advertising Revenue Comparison.
Source: Outlook segment findings, Global Entertainment & Media Outlook Pricewater-houseCoopers Global, http://www.pwc.com/gx/en/industries/entertainment-media/outlook/segment-insights/internet-advertising.html; Global TV advertising expenditure 2010–2020, Statistica, https://www.statista.com/statistics/273713/global-television-advertising-expenditure/; Investor Relations, Alphabet Inc., https://abc.xyz/investor/; Investor Relations, Facebook Inc., https://investor.fb.com/; Investor Relations, Twitter Inc., https://investor.twitterinc.com/; State of the News Media, Pew Research Center, http://www.journalism.org/media-indicators/local-tv-broadcast-advertising-revenue/.

ing; they share an overriding focus on technical innovation; and they have years of experience marketing directly to their customer base, targeting those most likely to be interested in a particular genre or program on the basis of each individual's past behavior. They have either worked with the Majors or worked around the Majors' content-blocking tactics. They have commissioned new content, facilitating substantial change in the presentation, distribution, and types of content, and lead in controlling the platforms that deliver content to burgeoning audiences across multiple screens. In the United States, Netflix and YouTube now account for more than 50% of primetime Internet traffic, with Amazon Video and Hulu accounting for another 3.96% and 2.47%, respectively (Weiß 2016). People around the globe upload more than five hundred hours of video to YouTube every minute (Robertson 2015). Netflix already refers to itself as the "world's leading internet TV network." Figure 1.2 shows that 2016 incomes of the Majors (with their parent conglomerates) were only 35% of those of the new players (Google, Amazon, Apple, Facebook, Yahoo, Netflix, Twitter)—$29.2 billion versus $83.3 billion.

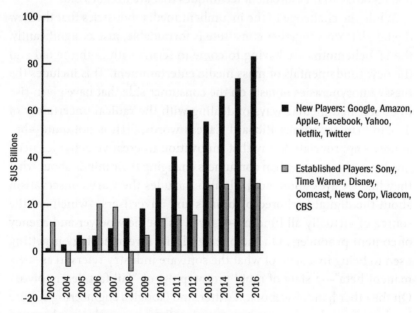

Figure 1.2. Income of New and Established Players.
Source: US SEC 10-K filings 2003–2016, US Securities and Exchange Commission, https://www.sec.gov.

Drawing on the lessons of history, and mindful of the specificity of the new challenges, we propose that the political economy of the emerging shape of social media entertainment is best understood as an *interdependent clash of industrial cultures*. For this reason, we employ the distinction between "NoCal" (or NorCal) and "SoCal," drawing from the "notorious rivalry" in popular culture between Northern and Southern California as evinced in regional accent and degrees of (liberal) politics (Winokur 2004). But our focus is on the fact that this rivalry around cultural geography also maps remarkably to two very distinct, world-leading industrial cultures that are increasingly clashing, converging, and becoming interdependent. "NoCal" business culture deploys information technology strategies, embraces aggressive disruption, and values rapid prototyping and iteration, "permanent beta," advanced measurement, and "programmatics." For its part, "SoCal" business culture is embodied in established screen media, that is, Hollywood, the major broadcasters, and cable interests, with their time-honored business models of talent-driven mass media and premium content and limited recourse to measurement techniques that are decades old.

While the challenge to the incumbent media industries that the new digital platforms together constitute is formidable, just as significantly, the IT behemoths are having to come to terms with both the old and the new fundamentals of mass media entertainment. This includes the messy idiosyncrasies of taste on the consumer side that have given rise to established media's ways of dealing with the radical uncertainty of demand (in economist Richard Caves's words, "[I]t is not quite—but almost—appropriate to say that innovation in creative activities need involve nothing more than consumers changing their minds about what they like" [Caves 2000, 202]). It also includes the wary conservatism about the digital harbored by brands and advertisers—which are the source of virtually all funding—as well as the new power and agency of content producers. On the one hand, the screen ecology is getting used to being in a state of what the software industry refers to as "permanent beta"—a state of rapid prototyping, or "fail fast, learn, pivot." On the other hand, Facebook, Twitter, and Google's engineering culture has been forced to come to terms with influencer marketing, branded content, and other "high touch" commercial realities as revenue generators. This is the challenge of "monetisation after [Google's] AdSense," in the words of digital executive Jordan Levin (2015)—marketing and advertising that cannot be massively scaled up through automation (or programmatics, as it is called in the industry).

Power and Peril

This chapter deals with such oscillatory strategies of the major platforms that provide the affordances for the emergence of social media entertainment. Outline histories of the major platforms are constructed around this clash of cultures and in relation to their variable convergence on video as a driver of platform content. We arrange platform strategy on a continuum. On one side of the continuum are the digital platforms that overwhelmingly play in the PGC space—Hulu, Amazon, Apple's iTunes, Netflix, and its many local imitators. At the other end are pure social media platforms that thrive on scale—Facebook, Twitter, Twitch, Instagram, Snapchat—and seek to leverage user-generated content (UGC) creators and the large audiences network effects afford to them in order to monetize. In the middle is YouTube, which is a huge content platform that nests within a communication platform (Google) with some social media affordance. Our emphasis on YouTube is informed both by its first-mover status for SME and by its proximity and often conflation with television channels and subscription video on demand (SVoD) platforms. The launch in 2015 of YouTube Red, its subscription platform, which features more traditional media IP genres and format and TV-like licensing deals, further supports the claims we are making here about the distinctiveness of YouTube in this new screen ecology. When it comes to social media entertainment content and strategy, it is the social media platforms' variable convergence on video as a driver of monetizable platform content that is the focus of the outline histories presented.

These histories will also provide a counterpoint to the seemingly invincible might of the platforms. Wholesale attacks on the big digital platforms, such as those mounted by Michael Wolff (2015) and Jonathan Taplin (2017), have taken directly divergent positions. On the one hand, Wolff plumps for continuity, arguing against the power of platforms to disrupt the fundamental business resilience of television and dismissing the content produced as commoditized "traffic" rather than quality product. On the other hand, Taplin mounts a full-fledged conspiracy account of the power of the platforms to "move fast and break things," including the time-honored means of producing US screen content. While the tendency to monopoly insisted on by Taplin is real—as we lay out in the following section, which deals inter alia with network economics—such tendencies also have created the conditions for the potential viability of the new voices and new content forms that constitute social media entertainment. There are several reasons to be concerned about platforms and their power, among them tax avoidance, privacy, anticompetitive behavior, and national security (Hart 2013). Many of these are acknowledged fully in our conclusion. But we argue that, in the roiling "creative destruction" that economic historian and theorist Joseph Schumpeter (1975 [1942]) described as the condition of capitalism, the green shoots of social media entertainment are as important to focus on as the brown burn marks on main media.

What follows is as much a story of peril as of power, and less a story of technological determinism than of determined tech cultures pivoting repeatedly in search of sustainability. As Moses (2017) noted, "[N]othing is forever in the world of platforms."

Since its launch in 2005, YouTube has pursued a mix of multilateral and sometimes redundant management strategies. The platform sought out collaboration with Hollywood while competing against it. Simultaneously, the platform partnered with its independent native creators and subsidized their affiliated management firms, only to require creators to sign on to their subscription platform and replace these firms with their own YouTube Spaces and Creator Academy. These backflips and pivots are driven by heightened platform competition from TV-like platforms, like Netflix, Amazon, and Hulu, along with first- and second-generation social media sites, including Facebook, Twitter, Instagram, Twitch, and Snapchat. These latter social media platforms and apps have only recently introduced YouTube-like features, including video players, monetization services, and partnership agreements. In response, YouTube's latest gambit is to launch a networked, multiplatform, multiscreen system operating across desktop, mobile, set-top boxes, and smart TVs, including live streaming for music and video.

Nonetheless, YouTube's profitability remains uncertain, with press claims suggesting that the platform became profitable sometime between 2014 and 2017, comprising a small but growing percentage of the total return on investment for its parent company, Google/Alphabet (Hough 2015; Winkler 2015; Somaney 2016; Rao 2016). Nevertheless, in late 2016, YouTube's CEO Susan Wojcicki declared, "We are still in investment mode," adding, "[T]here's no timetable for profitability" (Rao 2016). Nonetheless, there is little doubt of the massive scale of YouTube, which claims as many as 1.5 billion unique monthly users consuming an average of one hour of video per day (Wallenstein 2017).

Compared to YouTube, Twitter's trajectory has proven much more perilous, leading pundits to anticipate "the Death of Twitter" (Topolsky 2016). Launched the same year as YouTube, Twitter scaled rapidly to over three hundred million users. Rather than introduce new features or launch its own platforms, Twitter spent its first decade purchasing complementary platforms, including the short-form, looping video site Vine and live broadcasting platform Periscope. However, Twitter's management has been riddled with upheaval and employee layoffs, and the firm's revenue and market value have plummeted. Despite securing one hundred million users in record time, Vine atrophied, particularly once its native creators abandoned the platform for more commercial opportunities across competing platforms, and was shuttered in 2016 (Y. Chen 2016).

The Sisyphean struggles of YouTube and Twitter arguably pale in comparison to the Icarus-like fall from grace by Snapchat. By 2015, the latter platform had become the fastest-growing social media platform in history and, in early 2017, garnered nearly $20 billion in IPO (initial public offering) investment. But the platform's success proved as ephemeral as its content, if not illusory and fraudulent. Three months later, after announcing deep losses, the platform lost billions overnight, and became "one of Wall Street's biggest flops" (Tully 2017).

Snapchat's fall may also be attributed to heightened competition from Instagram, which overhauled its features, strategies, and management in 2016 to emulate Snapchat's, launching similar ephemeral "Stories" and photo filters (Shinal 2017a). These shifts helped the platform nearly double its growth to seven hundred million users, surpassing even Twitter (Constine 2017a). Substantial scholarship has focused on Instagram, particularly around its facilitation of female beauty and fashion bloggers (Duffy 2015b; Abidin 2016a). In fact, a subfield of study around this platform and content may have already emerged: a Boolean search in December 2017 revealed over a thousand dissertations featuring both "Instagram" and "beauty." Like YouTube, Instagram features prominently in the SME landscape, particularly by facilitating its creators' engagement with branded content and influencer marketing. But there are vital differences with YouTube. Instagram operates less transparently in partnership with its native creators—more like "the Wild West" (Flynn 2017a) and "influencer marketing's clandestine accomplice" (Hudson 2017). As the *New York Times* noted, Instagram's lack of creator sponsorship has allowed it to flaunt the vagaries of media regulation by the Federal Trade Commission (FTC) around online advertising (Maheshawri 2016).

Instagram's strategies are also a reflection of its integration into its parent company, Facebook, which purchased the platform in 2012. Facebook alone has amassed two billion global users as of mid-2017, but, as with YouTube, as global scale slows, Facebook has been forced to diversify revenue strategies. Facebook has pivoted strategically to compete directly with YouTube, launching comparable content and monetization strategies, including a video player coupled with partnership agreements with native creators (Spangler 2014a).

Like YouTube, Facebook has its sights on traditional media, with plans to launch professionally produced, original programming on its Watch platform by 2017 (Shinal 2017b). Like the endless waltz in Schnitzler's *La Ronde*, this pivoting of the platforms continues, with Amazon placing dual bets on both licensed and original Hollywood content while also targeting native social media creators. In 2014, Amazon acquired the gaming platform Twitch, anticipating what, in 2017, appears to be the launch of the next wave of platforms featuring live broadcasting. Directly competing against YouTube, Amazon launched a separate platform, Amazon Video Direct, in 2016, helping content creators and visual storytellers reach Amazon customers with the same distribution options and delivery quality available to major motion picture and television studios.

These platform strategies and performance serve as the "tell," little clues that reveal big truths. Platform prominence, high growth, and massive scale may not represent dominance, or even sustainability. This chapter argues that, while these platforms and their associated affordances shape the structure and operations of social media entertainment, they do not supervene over or control content, creator, and online community in the manner theorized for traditional media by critical political economy. The capitalist imperatives that drive platform strategy, because of platforms' incommensurate and often directly clashing cultures, have more in common with Scott Lash and John Urry's (1987) "disorganized capitalism" than the superordinate powers, and majestic continuities, attributed to platform capitalism and its antecedents by, for example, Nick Srnicek (2016), Christian Fuchs (2014), or Dal Yong Jin (2013).

In turning now to our key conceptual frameworks—a revisionist notion of power in the political economy of media, network economics, production cultures, and theories of affordances—we look to account for the proliferation, differentiation, and iterative evolution of these platforms. Subsequent chapters will deal with how these conditions have provided the space for a rapidly enlarging community of creator entrepreneurs and multiplying and diversifying management, production, and tech intermediaries. Combined, these platforms, firms, and creators—including the innovative content they generate and the networked communities they harness—form the pillars of the new screen ecology we call social media entertainment.

Theoretical Frameworks

We first offer, in dialogue with political economy theory, a revisionist understanding of media power. In our account of network economics, we consider how the digital age and networked technologies have generated tremendous disruption, not only within the industry but also within scholarly accounts of media power. The consequence of this disruption includes a clash of industrial, corporate, management, and production cultures between the tech and content industries reflected by theories emerging within the field of media production studies. Finally, theories of affordances inform the underlying impulse for the proliferation, differentiation, evolution, and convergence of tech and commercial potentialities.

Our understanding of political economy emanates from a *revisionist account of power*.[2] The notion of power underpins the very notion of the term "political economy"—the idea that the economy, rather than existing as an autonomous domain, is inextricably tied to processes, intent, and actors that are always already political. The fundamental assumption of political economy of media is that large-scale economic actors in the media field exercise great, possibly supervening, power over what is produced, how it is produced, and, possibly also, how it is received. At its core, critical political economy assumes that power emanates from the ability to control the means of production and accumulation and flows from the top echelons of society to the bottom. It also posits stronger or weaker versions of the alignment among economic, political, and cultural power, assuming that economic power results in the ability to exercise political and cultural power.

Scholars of critical political economy have identified, for example, how media conglomerates have engaged in oligopolistic strategies to secure media power (McChesney and Schiller 2003). These strategies include seeking to "capture" regulatory bodies to have them accede to industrial consolidation, lifting caps on ownership, and diminishing competition and diversity. While content may be subject to taste cultures, costly financing, and skilled expertise, the structure of the entertainment industry has been dependent upon distribution scarcity, dictated by a handful of studios or television networks. Media scholar and activist Ben Bagdikian has decried that 90% of American media is owned by six companies, down from fifty companies in 1983 (Bagdikian 1983, 2004). These formations hold true even in the multichannel era of cable and satellite television, since the majority of these networks are owned by the same conglomerates that own film studios and broadcast networks. Media concentration proceeds inexorably.

It is possible to agree with much of the factual basis on which these perspectives rely while reframing the account they give of power, and imply of agency, within media industry cultures. Critical political economy's concept of power is what Michel Foucault (1991) would call "domination." Foucault defines power more generally, with domination as a subset. And the alignment between economic, political, and cultural power can never be decided in advance, and with particular reference to media industries undergoing such fundamental change, we tend to side with Foucault's understanding that power is inherently relational and unstable, and resistance is a necessary corollary of, and inherent in the exercise of, power.

This overarching theoretical orientation is supported by insights provided by *network economics*. Pieter Ballon (2014) has pointed to how much media economics continues to be impacted by technology changes arising from Moore's Law and Metcalfe's Law. Moore's Law states that the number of transistors on integrated circuits doubles approximately every two years and has been an accurate description of the logarithmic increase in processing capacity. Metcalfe's Law states that "the systemic value of compatibly communicating devices grows as the square of the number" (George Gilder, quoted in Ballon 2014, 85). The value of a communication network rises quadratically with the number of users, while costs rise in a linear fashion.

For Ballon, these "laws" draw him to the conclusion that "in the Internet economy the largest economic gains would arise from the production and distribution of digital content . . . instead of from the commoditized hardware and transmission networks carrying this content" (Ballon 2014, 84). Ballon argues that professionally produced content has not (because of IP rights, falling production costs, and consumer reluctance to pay) succeeded in becoming the main engine of economic activity over the Internet. Instead, "new media companies have to build a business upon the low-cost or even 'free' provision of large quantities of easily navigable content and applications that are often produced and/or put online by the end users themselves," and, despite overstated claims, Moore's Law has "come to represent the continuing oversupply of new media" (Ballon 2014, 85).

If Moore's Law leads us toward the idea that attention is king, Metcalfe's Law suggests that connectivity is king. Metcalfe's Law "reinforced the general assumption during the height of the Internet boom that, once a critical mass of users was reached, these effects would ensure very rapid growth and equally large profits" (Ballon 2014, 86). In hindsight, this was a hazardous prediction. A key indirect network effect is that digital media create an additional dependency of users of a certain platform upon producers of complementary goods and services—these are called lock-in strategies. And even though entry barriers have been lowered (Moore's Law), concentration worries are far from over—market domination and new media companies have been a recurrent theme in policy debates over the past twenty years. Metcalfe's Law has been criticized as an overstatement of the value of communication networks. Ballon writes that only a part of the total number of connected users may meaningfully interact with each other; the value of a network may decline as information overload/spam come into play; and affinity among users, rather than simple number of connections, needs to be considered. Also, it favors business models that exploit user involvement and interaction by collecting very detailed user data to enable more targeted advertising strategies based on the more accurate estimation of individual willingness to pay.

Network economics provides insights into both the complexities of platform dynamics and the ways producers and audiences use the platforms. The advantage of the size and scale of these big digital platforms is further compounded by their first-mover advantage, while their dual "born digital" and "network native" status means that they dominate the network economy more effectively than earlier forms of capitalist oligopoly have done. Yet network economics also tells us that there is inherent potential for far better connected, networked possibilities for horizontal, grassroots, peer-to-peer connectivity. The same network economics that gives platforms "lock-in" power also enables peer-to-peer organizational capability and therefore gives creators greatly enhanced communicative opportunities. Thus, while there may be a greater tendency toward oligopoly, there is an also expansive opportunity for at least demotic and possibly also democratic voices and self-expression. Metcalfe's Law, that connectivity is king, allows us to argue that, while it promotes oligopoly and winner-takes-all outcomes at the level of platform ownership and strategy, it equally produces the conditions under which new forms of peer-to-peer communicative empowerment take place. If everyone is using Google or Facebook, there is relatively frictionless communicative affordance available to anyone with a connection—for free.

The implications of these trends in network economics and the dialectics of power for creator culture and opportunity are captured well by "Vlogbrothers" online creator and thought leader Hank Green:

> There is and will continue to be a ton of consolidation. A few legacy media companies will really, deeply get it and they will gain a lot of market share. A few native media companies will also become big players controlling a huge swath of the online media landscape. But the great thing about the Internet (I hope) is that barriers to entry will be much harder for those large companies (and government regulators) to erect, and so there will constantly be smaller organizations or just individuals who will be doing popular new things. Some of those things will be really great, and some of them will only be popular because of how base and disturb-

ing they are. That's the most significant disruption of online media, the inability of consolidated corporations to form barriers to entry. They'll try, but hopefully the culture of Internet freedom and the popular good will keep it from happening. (Green 2015a)

These theoretical perspectives are bolstered by a staple of critical media industry studies—the growing scholarship around *production cultures.* (We also look to this body of scholarship in chapter 3). John Caldwell (2009), reviewing the import of his major work *Production Culture: Industrial Reflexivity and Critical Practice in Film and Television,* and mirroring what we have seen Havens, Lotz, and Tinic (2009) argue, remarks that far less work has been conducted on Stuart Hall's "media encoding" (production cultures) than on his "decoding," that is, textual practice and consumption cultures. But the industry is far from being a monolithic black box of corporate cultural capitalism:

> In fact, as fewer and fewer media conglomerates seem to own everything in sight, the actual work-worlds intersecting the super-companies now churn with an incredibly complex array of production modes, social interactions, cultural practices, and contention. Far from being a hardened monolith, therefore, "the industry" is actually a very porous political economic phenomenon, comprised of hundreds of very different work sectors and conflicted social communities, locked in temporary alliances of willed affinity. Cultural studies would do well to acknowledge the complex, heterogeneous nature of these new risk averse, flexibility-focused media conglomerates. Doing so would allow scholars to study industrial communities (not just audience or fan communities) "from the ground up" as lived, cultural phenomena. Far from being antithetical to political-economic approaches, studying media industry as a set of micro-social "cultures of production"—rather than as the engine behind the macroscopic "production of culture"—actually provides a complex array of evidence that supports many macroscopic political-economic critiques. (Caldwell 2009, 68)

Caldwell's work presciently anticipated the disruption created by digital media. As early as 2009, in describing uploading culture, Caldwell accounted for how "alternative media producers" are capable of disrupting the cult of technical superiority within traditional entertainment. "The Internet and digital media now provide optimum conditions for realizing the culture-jamming imperative, since access to the master's 'machine' is now ostensibly available to everyone" (Caldwell 2009, 77). In fact, Caldwell's recognition of the greatly enhanced access to digital media by creators, both for production and distribution, represents but one of several affordances that distinguish SME platforms.

Differentiating Platform Affordances

Vital to grasping the significance of SME is understanding how social media entertainment platforms operate as both content delivery systems and networked communication technology. This dual nature of SME was assumed when prominent creator and SME thought leader, Hank Green, spoke to us:

> These days "new" media isn't so new and it's hard to argue that it isn't part of the mainstream. But there are still good reasons to differentiate between the two, so I suggested "new mainstream," which really is only going to work for a few more years until this really does all blend into being just "media" again. To me, the technology is just the systems that allowed the new mainstream to exist, while what really matters is that humans constantly find new ways to communicate with each other, and that's fun to engage with and talk about. (Green 2015a)

Here, we set out the conceptual and industrial distinctions between TV-like linear, closed digital media portals and interactive social media platforms. The latter are distinguished by features that, in turn, foster an array of affordances harnessed by users, among these commercializing and professionalizing creators.

In our conceptual framing, digital media platforms like Netflix, Hulu, and Amazon comprise closed platforms that distribute syndicated and original traditional media content. This content has been prelicensed from and financed and produced by traditional media firms and producers, often featuring Hollywood talent. Although distributed and curated differently from traditional television, these platforms emulate the same genres and textual features of traditional PGC (professionally generated content), whether scripted or documentary, animation or live-action, comedy or drama. Previous terms used to describe these sites include "Web TV," "OTT" (over the top), and "VOD" (video on demand), as these terms are limited in mapping these distinctions from traditional television. Amanda Lotz (2017) has proposed the term "portals" to describe those sites that feature Internet-based protocols "to distinguish the crucial intermediary services that collect, curate, and distribute television programming via internet distribution."

Lotz further distinguishes TV-like media portals from social media platforms that feature amateur or user-generated content (UGC), which she describes as an "emerging internet-distributed television industry that utilizes the dynamics of social media and is based on personalities that cultivate a community of followers . . . but distinct enough to require its own focus" (Lotz 2017).

With the exception of Burgess and Green's (2009) volume on YouTube, early social media scholarship had little to offer about content or creators, but rather focused on their communicative features. In their seminal paper, boyd and Ellison (2007) first defined these "social network sites" as "web-based services that allow individuals to (1) construct a public or semi-public profile within a bounded system, (2) articulate a list of other users with whom they share a connection, and (3) view and traverse their list of connections and those made by others within the system" (boyd and Ellison 2007, 211). At the time their article was published in 2007, numerous social network sites had already been launched and disappeared, including Friendster and MySpace—a pattern that foreshadows the rapid evolution of NoCal-based SME platforms. As these sites have changed, so have the terms scholars and practitioners have used to describe them. As Bucher (2015) notes, "[W]e now commonly group [social network sites] under the term social media" (Bucher 2015, 1).

Subsequent scholarship has consolidated an emerging subfield of platform studies, focused on "social media logics" (van Dijck and Poell 2013) of networking, connectivity, and datafication. Twitter users could post, share, and like text-based tweets among their followers. Facebook users provided status updates on walls to like, comment, and share among a network of "friends." Second-generation social media platforms offered further distinguishing features, including photos (Instagram), ephemeral content (Snapchat), and short-form video (Vine). In time, as we will see through this chapter's platform history, these social media platforms have converged to offer similar features, creating a highly competitive landscape distinguished mostly by interface design, mobility, and user demographics. These patterns have been anticipated by Burgess (2014), who presciently described an emerging "platform paradigm" in which a handful of tech companies own platforms that are dominating the way online users communicate and interact, including the SME variation in which platforms converge social networking with content creation and media consumption.

Centrally in the evolution of SME, YouTube has operated as a hybrid of a TV-like content portal and social media platform, although with limited success at integration. Initially launched as a "video content repository" and later promoted for users to "Broadcast Yourself," YouTube's core feature allows users to upload, watch, and share videos. Throughout the evolution of the platform's interface, the video content player remained central while social networking features were placed—literally—underneath. Like Netflix, the platform delivers video content curated across various programming verticals. Like Facebook and Twitter, the platform features share and like buttons and space for comments and replies but has struggled to successfully integrate these features with its player. YouTube has attempted to integrate social networking features through a mixed strategy of acquisition and in-house innovation.

As platforms proliferated, creators have been afforded the means to operate across and take advantage of their differentiated features. When they do so, new uses are found for these features. Psychologist James Gibson (1977) first coined the term "affordances" to describe the "actionable possibilities" in an environment that an individual has the actual capability to deploy. A key binary has emerged in studies of affordances that parallels the tension in ICT (information and communications technology) between the intended purpose of the platform's design and user interface and the actual and agentic user experience. The digital turn in communication technology studies has generated much discussion of affordances (Hutchby 2001; Hsieh 2012; Postigo 2016; Nagy and Neff 2015) and social media has generated still further discussion. danah boyd (2010) describes the structural affordances of social media that foster the creation of networked publics. As we will encounter in chapter 2, SME creators have been able to convert their networked publics into both committed fan communities and the source of diverse revenue streams. Similarly, commercial affordances, "wherein financial and social economies can co-exist" (Humphries 2009, 1), sit within the "logics" of social media (van Dijck and Poell 2013), including programmability, popularity, connectivity, and datafication. Van Dijck and Poell argue that "[t]he logic of social media, as was previously the case with mass media logic, is gradually dissipating into all areas of public life, the cultural and commercial dynamics determining social media blend with existing commercial and advertising practices, while also changing them" (van Dijck and Poell 2013, 30). In keeping with our focus on the agency of creators, we emphasize their engagement with the industrialization of SME while co-evolving with and reverse engineering traditional entertainment and media advertising.

Whereas the shifting features of platforms serve their corporate interests to grow in scale and revenue, a mix of technological and commercial affordances allows creators to harness these platforms to attract, engage, and aggregate communities to serve their own interests.

These affordances are quite different from those offered by traditional film and television distributors, including digital TV portals. Studios and networks, including Netflix and Hulu, either own or license the content they distribute. In contrast, YouTube introduced programmatic advertising features and split revenue partnership services for its creators. Consequently, YouTube's features and services *afforded* creators outright ownership of their content, nonexclusivity across multiplatforms, and the ability to engage in multiple revenue streams, including influencer marketing, crowd-sourcing, virtual goods, subscription plays, and licensing, among many. In other words, platforms design technological features and offer commercial services that, in contrast to traditional media conditions, afford creators multiple commercial opportunities, whether intentional or otherwise.

In addition, *between* SME platforms, another set of distinguishable technological and commercial affordances exists. YouTube has struggled to successfully integrate social networking features into its video content platform; nonetheless, creators have been afforded the means to harness platforms like Twitter and Instagram to more efficiently engage with and aggregate their fan communities. Despite these latter platforms having neither programmatic advertising nor partnership services, creators have been afforded the means to monetize their content through influencer marketing campaigns, with or without video content or a YouTube channel.

Different technological features of platforms such as Vine (short-form, loops, on-screen editing) and Snapchat (ephemerality, filters, Snap stories) have afforded creators the means to engage in alternative forms of content innovation (for example, digital illusionist Vine star Zach King and Snapchat prankster Jerome Jarre). The most prominent variation on video as affordance may be Instagram, which combined social networking and mobility with photo-sharing capabilities, but has since incorporated video as part of its multimodality. Yet, the convergence of video across all SME platforms, including Twitter and Instagram, contributes to less differentiation but greater commercialization for creators across multiple platforms. As we will see in chapter 2, affordances can also empower, as witnessed with the flight from Snapchat to Instagram because the former refused to afford creators the means to generate more revenue while building scale for the platform. "YouTube and Instagram cultivated social stars. But Snapchat seems to take the view that catering to influencers, who are often hawking brands' wares, could hurt the app's appeal to its core users" (Chen 2017). These affordances have contributed to the professionalization and commercialization of creators, albeit not necessarily through the intentional design of the platforms themselves. As Hank Green (2015b) observed,

> Suddenly, it wasn't just a culture of economically productive creators; there was an industry being layered on top of us. . . . It feels very weird for that business to have been constructed on top of an economy that has been, for me, nothing more than a pleasant surprise. It's especially strange how YouTube seems to have enabled this shift completely unintentionally. Weird. (Green 2015b)

As Tom Streeter (1996, 2011) has noted, there is precedence in this phenomenon of alternative, disruptive, and innovative deployment of affordances in media history. Like telegraphy, telephony was initially designed for transmitting entertainment and news content. The early development of radio broadcasting was designed initially for maritime communication until adopted for person-to-person use, but then taken over by corporate interests. Early ICT technology featured military or industrial design with little recognition of their transformative affordances, economically, communicatively, or culturally. Media historian Michelle Hilmes (1997, 2010) has also noted that emerging media industries co-evolve with their predecessors while sometimes reverse engineering their designed features and perceived affordances.

Historicizing SME Platforms

The emergence and evolution of SME platforms evidence parallels with earlier turning points in media history. At least initially, the challenge of television to movies represented significant peril to Hollywood's century-long dominion over content sourcing and distribution. There are parallels with the clash of cultures between broadcast and cable television and that among digital portals like Netflix and social media platforms like YouTube and Facebook. Corporate conglomeration may look eerily similar to the Majors' stabilized oligopoly. Furthermore, the cross-ownership of media and tech industries is not unknown in Hollywood. Sony's consumer electronics is partnered with its filmed entertainment and game software business, much as Comcast's cable, telephony, and broadband service benefits from ownership of NBC Universal. Likewise, Apple to iTunes, Amazon to Amazon Prime, Google to YouTube.

But the comparisons end there, while the distinctions prove vital to our understanding of this new screen ecology. The rate of industry evolution is unprecedented. Understood through network economics, disruptive tech culture, and iterative platform affordances, in one decade, these platforms have emerged from early adoption to emulate the structural foundations of the entertainment industry, which took decades to build. Drawing on the theoretical and conceptual frameworks in the previous sections, we map the history of the platforms, accounting for their massive scale and scope in contrast to the limitations of traditional media at the national, geographic, and cultural levels. While network economics helps to explain the dialectical effects of abundance, platform affordances underpin the potential for commercial viability, for example by creating artificial scarcity in a superabundant offer. The panoply of technological features distinguishes channels and website, website and applications, portals and platforms, but the strong convergence around video for every platform reflects the attractions as well as limits of programmatic video advertising.

Our emphasis here is on SME platforms featuring convergent affordances that provide the features of shareable content and social networking, creating the conditions for a new proto-industry, while reverse engineering practices of both Hollywood and Madison Avenue. More broadly, this history of platform strategy affirms the disruptive and transformative "power of platforms—a new business model that uses technology to connect people, organizations, and resources in an interactive ecosystem in which amazing amounts of value can be created and exchanged" (Parker, Alstyne, and Choudary 2016, 4). Fueled by network effects, platforms provide access and opportunity for industry entrepreneurs, partners, and users, foster new economies (sharing economy), feature alternative management strategies, and require distinctive regulatory oversight and governance. These building blocks of a new proto-industry will be teased out over the course of the book.

We argue that the core driver explaining how SME has evolved is the clash of cultures inherent in the interdependence and negotiated convergence of, on the one hand, the new "NoCal" platforms (with their information technology strategies and cultures, including rapid prototyping and iteration, permanent beta, advanced measurement, and programmatics) and, on the other, established "SoCal" screen media (Hollywood, broadcasters, and cable interests, with their time-honored business models of talent-driven mass media and premium content).

YouTube features centrally throughout this platform history for a variety of reasons. In contrast to other SME 1.0 platforms, Facebook and Twitter, YouTube appeared most closely to both emulate and threaten television primacy with its streaming video player and advertising initiatives. YouTube was launched and quickly engaged in competing with Hollywood film and television for audiences and advertisers through a mix of professionally generated (PGC) and user-generated content (UGC) strategies. But YouTube encountered competition from emerging PGC video portals, like iTunes, Netflix, Amazon, and Hulu, and turned to fostering the rise of creators through partnership agreements and programmatic advertising. This was the SME 1.0 period.

In SME 2.0, YouTube faced impending peril from fellow NoCal social media platforms, most notably Facebook and Twitter, followed by the proliferation of second-generation social media platforms, including Vine, Instagram, Snapchat, Twitch, and Periscope. Nonetheless, YouTube has continued to iterate, experiment, and scale globally, and, after a decade, perhaps is in the black. In this period, platform evolution continues as YouTube and other first-generation platforms have developed into multiplatform, multiscreen systems, converged around video content while introducing multiple revenue streams split with their native creators. The consequence is a fiercely competitive platform landscape for which premium content and advertising represents the new scarcity and, in turn, creator empowerment.

If the past decade is any indication, disruption, iteration, and the precarious pursuit of scale and sustainability have become normal operating procedure for SME platforms. The evolution of SME platforms represents a powerful, if temporal, alignment of competing and powerful digital and social corporate media interests that imperil Hollywood. SME platform networks may threaten traditional media industries but, as Henry Jenkins (2006) and many others remind, media industries do not go away. Rather, they adapt to assume new cultural values and commercial strategies, engage in alternative content innovation and audience formations, and evolve to represent new value propositions. In addition, Hollywood's incumbency has proven resilient throughout its history, which is filled with the detritus of former competitors, either acquired or usurped. While the scale of the challenge may be formidable, the outcome of these video wars is by no means a foregone conclusion. Despite massive capitalization and market-fueled valuation, Twitter is for sale, its subsidiary, Vine, is gone, and Snapchat is a shadow of its former self. Continued technological disruption such as virtual reality and holographic technology may make for many more "burning platforms."

SME 1.0: YouTube History

In his account of the platform's history, Hank Green claimed that "[a] decade later, YouTube remains a mystery, especially to itself" (Green 2015b). A mystery indeed, as YouTube's evolution features as much failure as success. The platform has failed to compete with other video portals and Hollywood for premium PGC and experimented with multiple attempts to integrate social networking platforms to no avail. The platform has engaged in constant and rapid iteration of features and affordances that have facilitated and frustrated a wave of entrepreneurial creators and intermediaries—although YouTube has not necessarily been the beneficiary of their successes and has often had to bear the opprobrium of their failures. As we will see in chapter 6, the variegated media regulatory systems worldwide continue to complicate the global frictionlessness of the platform and its ability to get into the black. While the platform has secured over 1.3 billion users, it represents only modest returns for its corporate owner, Google (now Alphabet). And yet, numerous social media firms have had to attempt to emulate YouTube's strategies to compete for audiences, subscribers, advertisers, and returns by converging on video.

YouTube's origin story is the subject of much debate and dissent. The nature of communal and noncommercial (or precommercial) content on the platform has become a key topic in media, communication, and cultural studies scholarship, alternatively described as "vernacular creativity" (Burgess 2006), "produsage" (Bruns 2008), and "amateur media" (Hunter et al. 2013). In the first critical monograph on YouTube, Jean Burgess and Joshua Green spoke of its meaning and uses being "underdetermined" in its early days: "YouTube's ascendancy has occurred amid a fog of uncertainty and contradiction around what it is actually for. YouTube's apparent or stated mission has continuously morphed as a result of both corporate practices and audience use" (Burgess and Green 2009, 3).

Where this debate has turned to YouTube's "formalization" (which references, in Ramon Lobato and Julian Thomas's [2015] framework, the movement from amateur video into monetization and the market), it has tended to center on the loss of the communitarian, originating amateur spirit of the early days of the platform. Earlier scholars have mapped YouTube's early history more critically to describe a "fall from grace" narrative that structures an account of social media platforms whose originating communal visions have been fatally compromised by the encroachment of commercialism. These scholars have been unequivocal about YouTube being seemingly poised to become yet another cog in the media content industry. Jin Kim (2012) describes this shift as the "institutionalization of YouTube from user-generated to professional-generated content" (53). Similarly, José van Dijck (2013) describes YouTube's evolution from homecasting to broadcasting and "toward viewer-based principles and away from community-oriented social networking" (2013, 117). In the wake of these changes, according to van Dijck, "A far cry from its original design, YouTube is no longer an alternative to television, but a full-fledged player in the media entertainment industry" (van Dijck 2013, 127).

In a significant piece of historiographical revision, Patrick Vonderau (2016) has shown that YouTube was from its earliest plans always envisaged as a commercial proposition as the former PayPal employees and engineers behind its beta iteration sought to develop a scalable project capable of rapidly growing an audience comprised of millions, with revenue-generation opportunities designed as part of its core functions. Notwithstanding this strike at the heart of the "fall from grace" narrative, there is still massive civic space available on YouTube, with millions of citizens the world over using such space for noncommercial purposes. But it does underline the need for a critical history that deals with the internal contradictions and inherent tensions of a major commercial platform significantly built around the value of originally amateur content and content makers. This is our task.

The history of YouTube since Google's takeover can be written as a history of Google seeking to come to terms with the SoCal fundamentals of entertainment, and content and talent development, from its NoCal base as an IT company dedicated to scale, automation, permanent beta, rapid prototyping, and iteration. These efforts reflect both continuities and contestations with traditional media models, particularly business models. And they demonstrate the constitutive limits on the exercise of domination—in Foucault's sense of the term. The results, especially for creators and multichannel networks (MCNs), have been decidedly mixed. YouTube tried to operate as a digital distribution platform, but was not able to compete successfully with established media companies and models that favored copyright and scarcity. Their efforts to professionalize UGC creators created enormous opportunity and laid the basis for SME, but the NoCal obsession with scale led to the collapse of the SME 1.0 business model—shared revenue from programmatic advertising. The consequences were to force content creators and MCNs to seek out new sources of revenue such as licensing, merchandizing, TV deals, and live appearances—all well-established SoCal strategies for revenue generation.

YouTube's monetization strategies have exposed the faltering code-pendency between media and advertising, reflecting the inefficiencies of traditional media advertising while highlighting the affordances and targeted efficacy of online analytics. In marked contrast to traditional film studios and television networks, YouTube elected to avoid the messy and legally cumbersome traditional media model of owned or shared IP. YouTube also avoided paying fees for content as well as offering backend residual or profit participation. Rather, YouTube entered into "partner-ship agreements" with its content creators based on a split of advertising revenue from first dollar. This strategy has proven effective. In the years since the partner plan launched in 2007, YouTube has "partnered" with over three million creators worldwide.

Following established practice in broadcast media, Google adopted the traditional advertising algorithm based on cost-per-thousand views (CPMs); however, Google was able to introduce targeted advertising based on the wealth of data provided by Google Analytics. Building on this NoCal twist, in 2007, Google introduced its AdSense technology to the YouTube platform, which allowed content creators to feature advertising on their YouTube pages, including semitransparent banner ads overlaid on top of the videos. In 2008, Google's purchase of DoubleClick introduced programmatic (automated) ad buying to YouTube's platform. Combined, these technologies helped YouTube achieve virtually frictionless commerce on their platform and scale it precipitously.

In the wake of these initiatives, while precise data is curtained behind its parent company's firewall of limited corporate reportage, YouTube may have finally turned a profit, with revenue of $9 billion globally in 2015 (Hough 2015). Although this figure constitutes only 10% of Alphabet's total revenue—estimated in 2015 at $86 billion (Somaney 2016)—as YouTube viewing keeps rising and ad dollars continue to shift to digital, figure 1.3 shows, these numbers are predicted to rise significantly, to an estimated 36% of total corporate revenues by 2023. Figure 1.4 tracks the growth in digital video ad spending, showing that while spending on TV advertising will increase by 12.5% over the period 2014 to 2020, spending

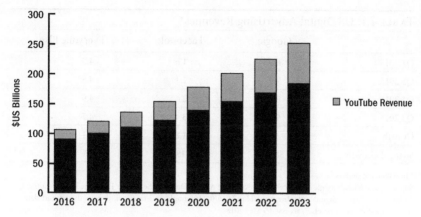

Figure 1.3. YouTube as a Component of Alphabet Revenue, Estimate 2016–2023.
Source: Base Case: Google, Trefis Forecasts, Trefis, https://www.trefis.com/stock
/GOOG/model/.

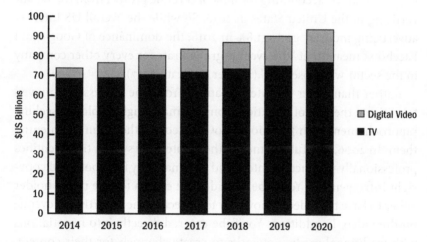

Figure 1.4. Projected TV and Digital Video Advertising Spend, 2014–2020.
Source: Digital Video Advertising to Grow at Annual Double-Digit Rates, *eMarketer*,
https://www.emarketer.com/Article/Digital-Video-Advertising-Grow-Annual-Double
-Digit-Rates/1014105.

on digital video advertising will increase by 218.5% over the same period. YouTube has become a viable competitor to traditional television
advertising, hoping to lure up to 24% of television's advertising revenue
to the platform (O'Reilly 2015). Table 1.1 shows that together Google and
Facebook captured a combined 72% of gross spending in 2015, increasing

TABLE 1.1. US Digital Advertising Revenues*

	Google	Facebook	Everyone Else
Q1 2015	6.9	1.6	4.6
Q3 2015	7.9	2.1	4.6
Q1 2016	8.3	2.6	4.9
Q3 2016	9.5	3.4	4.7
Growth	2.6	1.8	0.1
Share of Growth	58%	41%	1%

* in billions of dollars.
Source: Jason Kint, "Google and Facebook Devour the Ad and Data Pie: Scraps for Everyone Else," *InContext*, 16 June 2015, https://digitalcontentnext.org/blog/2016/06/16/google-and-facebook-devour-the-ad-and-data-pie-scraps-for-everyone-else/, accessed 5 May 2018.

to 77% in 2016—accounting for 99% of revenue growth from digital advertising in the United States in 2016. So while the overall US Internet advertising industry grew 21.8% in 2016, the dominance of Google and Facebook meant that "the average growth rate for every other company in the sector was close to 0" (Wieser in Heath 2017).

Rather than suffer the fate of Napster, YouTube aggressively moved to mitigate the risk of litigation from the major rights holders, seeking rapprochement with traditional SoCal media rather than threatening them. In 2006, YouTube launched the Content ID system that identifies professionally produced content and automatically flags potential copyright infringement. YouTube provides the option for the rights holder either to have the video removed or to collect all the advertising revenue on the video. In addition, YouTube entered directly into negotiations with traditional media networks to create channels for their content. Because of this strategy, YouTube managed to avoid most litigation with the major players, except for Viacom, which would eventually settle its suit against YouTube for copyright infringement in 2014.

While YouTube's response may have thwarted expensive lawsuits, and potential state-based intervention by the FCC, the Content ID system has been very much a two-edged sword. As Zapata-Kim (2016) points out, YouTube "unfairly favors copyright holders and YouTube itself at the expense of content creators and the greater Internet community" (Zapata-Kim 2016, 1847). While potentially inhibiting their own creativity and content innovation, creators risk losing monetization on their YouTube videos if they contain any elements of protected Hollywood IP. From the inception of Content ID through to the "Adpocalypse" of 2017 (numerous creators' revenue streams were lost when Google and Facebook overreacted to major premium brands withdrawing their advertising when it was revealed that it had sometimes been placed programmatically beside extremist content), this platform continues a reactionary pattern of overcorrection—designed to preempt state-based intervention and thwart legal redress—at the expense of creators. We go further into the Adpocalypse in later chapters.

In short order, YouTube had gone from a safe harbor for pirated Hollywood content to partnering with Hollywood media companies and professionalizing their own talent. Through their channel initiatives, YouTube seemed to be emulating television, in terms of both its search for premium content and its dependence upon advertising revenue. As we have seen, for many industry pundits and academic scholars, YouTube seemed poised to become yet another media content industry. José van Dijck was clear: "[T]he distinctiveness of YouTube as an alternative to television was no longer defensible, particularly when we look at the site's content" (van Dijck 2013, 118).

However, the SoCal makeover was decidedly incomplete, and has in many ways been abandoned. There remain stark differences in structural, organizational, and material interests between traditional and online media, not least of which is the lack of distribution scarcity online leading to an abundance of content and low barriers of entry for content creators. The sheer, unprecedented scale of the ramp-up of both content creators generating substantial subscriber/fan bases, and the engagement with advertisers to generate the revenue has resulted in an overwhelming emphasis on volume, which is now in crisis.

This crisis is highlighted by the collapse of YouTube CPMs, even as overall online advertising revenue has continued to grow. The "programmatic" advertising model is an "extremely limited economic model," according to one of the most successful online entrepreneurs, Hank Green (2014), becoming less and less viable as a sustaining revenue base for both creatives and intermediaries like MCNs. Partners signed up to share AdSense revenue and the content inventory grew exponentially. AdSense income could not keep pace with the exponential growth of content seeking advertising support. Thus, according to Andrew Baron of Tubefilter, "YouTube has literally DESTROYED—with a capital DESTROYED—the video ad market. What started out as a standard and relatively reasonable benchmark of $25CPM for both broadcast sales and online video sales just a few years ago, is down now to around a $2 take home this year" (Winkler 2015).

It is worth contemplating the depth of the "clash of cultures" this situation represents. As fierce critics of digital's claims to innovation, such as Michael Wolff (2015), point out, the structural tendency of digital platforms to apply downward pressure on advertising prices creates corresponding pressure to produce greater amounts of lower-quality content that in turn intensifies the compression of advertising revenue in an inevitable downward spiral: the "race to the bottom" feature familiar in many digital content critiques. Wolff argues that the NoCal focus on audiences as commodity leads to a focus on "traffic" rather than quality product and environment. This focus worked best when high CPM rates meant advertising revenue surpassed the costs of buying the traffic, but the documented decline of CPMs has destroyed the arbitrage model. Wolff argues that while the new digital platforms have increased competition, at the same time they provide traditional networks with new distribution and monetization opportunities. New distribution platforms are providing new forms of content and new audiences for archives that grow the market rather than cannibalizing it.

It is important to stress the multiple ironies in this history. YouTube's leading position in incubating social media entertainment began because it failed to consolidate its prior strategy of attracting Hollywood premium content. Pivoting to Plan B, YouTube managed to build alternative commercial value by simultaneously offering copyright/IP deals that do not seek ownership rights from original creators while also developing a robust original content strategy. That strategy, however, as we shall see in chapter 2, is structurally volatile, based as it is on extracting maximum surplus value from creators who cannot rely on what YouTube offers alone. YouTube's revenue earnings have been significantly bolstered through partnership agreements with creators of original content, who split advertising revenue with the platform typically 55 (creator)/45 (platform). Google's development of Content ID—whereby video uploads are automatically scanned for material matches—was initiated in order to avoid "Napsterization" and attract premium Hollywood content, but was then turned into a key strategy for circumventing the difficult and cumbersome traditional media model of owned or shared IP and largely avoiding paying fees for content while simultaneously offering residual profit sharing with copyright holders.

"NoCal" tech culture is clearly very comfortable with regularly "rebooting" (starting again), "iterating" (trying again), or "pivoting" (changing direction). YouTube's ability to iterate rapidly reflects its NoCal ethos of "pivot or die," although its latest moves regularly borrow from SoCal business models. Over the past few years, YouTube has repeatedly changed its partnership plan. Revenue splits have shifted from a high of 70/30 in favor of its premium creators to a standardized split of 55/45. In addition, to improve its analytics for advertisers, YouTube routinely changes its algorithms, which has resulted in the mysterious—mysterious, that is, to creators who depend on the constant connectedness to their viewers—disappearance of millions of subscribers overnight for some creators. These shifts in agreements and analytics have contributed to creator-partner disgruntlement, driving a great many creators to alternative platforms such as Facebook, Instagram, and Vine (when it existed). In response, YouTube has begun to fund film and television ventures under the banner of YouTube Originals featuring their top content creators, for example PewDiePie, Smosh, the Fine Brothers, RoosterTeeth, Lilly Singh, and Joey Graceffa. These "SoCal" initiatives have helped YouTube thwart defections to other platforms, including a raft of first- and second-generation social media platforms that have emerged to compete with YouTube for creators and content, audiences and advertisers. We will come back to what this constant pivoting has led YouTube to later in the chapter.

SME 1.0: TV.com

YouTube's attempts to attract premium content from traditional media were thwarted by the rise of transactional, subscription, or even advertiser-based TV-like portals (Lotz 2017) offering more lucrative deals, such as iTunes, Amazon, Netflix, and Hulu. Then premium and basic cable, as well as broadcast networks, launched their own portals, including HBO, which allow subscribers to watch content on mobile or online, with or without cable or satellite packages. Even sports franchises and leagues, for example, major league baseball, have launched their portals, extending the value of their brands and content into digital.

The clash of cultures between NoCal and SoCal extends across the panoply of digital platforms, creating highly variable conditions for content production. Maintaining and sharpening our distinction between digital (PGC) and social (UGC), we now turn to those digital platforms focused on professionally generated content, analyzing them in comparative perspective to YouTube strategies, with a view subsequently to further contrasts with social media platforms converging on video. While Amazon, iTunes, and Hulu operate prominently in this industry, our analysis focuses on Netflix, whose similarities to and differences from YouTube help us to understand some of the distinctive nature of social media entertainment.

The old Hollywood saw, "content is king," occludes the political economy truism that, if content is king, then distribution is King Kong (Cunningham and Silver 2013). And the two biggest online content distribution gorillas are Netflix and YouTube. Together, they constitute more than 50% of primetime US online viewing. Netflix and YouTube are alike in numerous ways. Both are world-spanning platforms. YouTube's platform is uploaded to and streamed around the world, with the exclusion of China, North Korea, and at any one time some countries in the Middle East and northern Africa. Netflix is available in almost every country in the world, aided by many accessing the brand via VPN technology.

But there are also big differences. Rather than pivoting constantly between NoCal and SoCal strategies, Netflix fuses them into a single uniform offer. It is by and large a mainstream video store, just online, and is populated uniformly by professionally generated content (PGC). It refers to itself as the "world's leading internet TV network." It has NoCal state-of-the-art recommendation algorithms driving consumer navigation and a great deal of resultant consumer satisfaction. Apart from its innovative binge-watching distribution strategies promoted for its original content, in many regions outside North America, its back catalogue can be quite limited. Nevertheless, it has global brand recognition and attracts much entertainment media attention.

A further fundamental distinction goes to the question of intellectual property and the modes of global reach. Netflix's aggressive global expansion requires it to negotiate with preexisting rights holders in each new territory and often requires it to attempt to block informal means of accessing its popular content, such as VPN workarounds, in such territories. While, longer term, the streaming giants (Amazon, Apple's iTunes, as well as Netflix) may well drive territorial licensing to the wall, SME content is largely "born global." This is the case because it is not primarily based on IP control, in stark contrast to content industries in general and Hollywood and broadcast television in particular. YouTube elected to avoid the messy and legally cumbersome traditional media model of owned or shared IP. YouTube also avoided paying fees for content as well as offering backend residual or profit participation. Rather, YouTube entered into "partnership agreements" with its content creators based on a split of advertising revenue from first dollar. While Netflix's formidable branding and direct challenge to broadcast and cable attract most media and scholarly attention, YouTube's platforming of social media entertainment may constitite a deeper, longer-term challenge to mainstream media than Netflix as it has viewer demographics on its side and draws from a much more diverse global production and participation base.

Netflix has built an enviable IT architecture—with one piece of reportage famously claiming to explain "How Netflix Reverse Engineered Hollywood" (Madrigal 2014)—a platform for delivery of long-form content that sets a benchmark for scalability, adaptability, and flexibility. Netflix—along with Amazon and Apple—strives to fuse NoCal and SoCal strategies. It exemplifies NoCal algorithmic culture at the service of customer-centric digital delivery of entertainment and information consumer goods and services, while its commitment to professionally produced, premium screen content exemplifies SoCal values and priorities.

Fusing NoCal and SoCal strategies means that certain critical affordances characteristic of social media entertainment are squeezed out. The accumulation and interpretation of viewer data reveals extensive information on viewing patterns, social values, and consumption experiences, but the ways such data is utilized by PGC digital distribution companies remains—in the main—"wired shut" under patent laws, nondisclosure agreements, noncompete clauses, and other legal instruments. Blake Hallinan and Ted Striphas (2016) argue that such algorithmic information processing intervenes in "the conceptual foundations of culture" (2016, 118) as engineers and algorithms become arbiters of culture. Their analysis looks at the recommendation systems belonging to NoCal organizations such as Amazon, Facebook, Match.com, Twitter, and other technology-driven companies with special focus on the way the Netflix Prize opened the process to partial, expert scrutiny.

But arguably the effects on culture of Netflix's recommendation system are of less concern than the echo chamber effects on public life of algorithmic culture on news and current affairs. Of more immediate critical concern should be Netflix's treatment of the producers of its content, which goes to the limits of its SoCal ethos. Netflix does not release information—which it of course has in spades—about ratings, about who watches what and how much, and this especially inhibits producer interests. Compared to Netflix, information on broadcaster and cable company program performance reaches the heights of transparency, and YouTube's openness to creator/producer interests is of another order. As Jason Mittell (2016) argues,

> Currently, [Netflix] functions more like a tech company than a media brand, meaning its key assets are its user base, its hype, and the vast bank of data it has related to its customers. Actual revenue and profits are secondary to building that base. In the coming years, Netflix will likely be forced to decide whether to more closely mirror the media business (where content and monetized viewers are key assets), to try to carve an identity for itself as a hybrid media/tech company (a balance that Apple and Amazon are both struggling with), or to follow the path of most tech companies: acquire, or be acquired by, other companies. (Mittell 2016)

SME 2.0: The Upstart Startups

Roughly encompassing the years 2010–2014, the emergence of numerous second-generation, web-based platforms and mobile applications further heightened platform competition in the SME landscape. The key players include Instagram, Snapchat, Twitch, and Periscope. These second-gen platforms scaled at speeds in some instances faster than their first-gen predecessors. Over the past decade, YouTube has secured 1.3 billion users and Facebook has 1.7 billion while Twitter has plateaued at a little over 300 million users during 2017. In a little over six years, Instagram secured 500 million users. Twitch (a relaunched and rebranded Justin.tv) has grown to over 313 million users. Vine secured over 200 million users in its first four years before the platform was shut down overnight by its owner, Twitter. The most recent platform, Snapchat, was dubbed the "fastest growing platform" in 2015 with over 200 million users, surpassing Twitter in daily usage (Morrison 2015).

The differentiation of technological affordances on these platforms helped lure users, although their allure is not a zero-sum game. Rather, as Heidi Cohen (2014) notes, "[S]ocial media is no longer one size fits all," and over 50% of US adults use multiple platforms. Most notably, second-generation social media platforms have achieved rapid scale while featuring differentiation of video players and modalities, while their user interfaces provide better integration of content players with social networking, differentiating them from first-generation platforms, most notably YouTube. This second-mover advantage has helped lure users and audiences, and in turn, advertisers and revenue, away from their predecessors.

Like their antecedents, these platforms featured rapid iteration of technological and commercial features, most notably convergence around video. Video is what optimizes platform monetization and therefore potential sustainability beyond venture capital investment rounds. Mobility features prominently as well, as Instagram, Periscope, and Snapchat are applications that have user interfaces that harness the mobility and tech affordances of mobile phones.

Other distinctive affordances were ephemeral and live broadcasting, although the precursor of the latter was launched years earlier in 2005. Originally developed to feature online reality programming, Justin.tv pivoted in 2009 to allow users to integrate their own live broadcasting channels. The platform soon became the home for gameplay, a genre of content that allows viewers to watch as their favorite e-gamers comment and demonstrate strategy to play video games online (see chapter 4). By 2011, Justin.TV rebranded itself as Twitch.tv and introduced more features that allowed video game streaming alongside a companion chat room for fan comments. This innovation arguably features the most effective integration of single-screen integration of video players and social networking.

Following YouTube's partnership model, Twitch enacted its partner program in July 2011, allowing Twitch creators who stream at least three times per week with average video views over five hundred to share in the advertising revenue generated from their streams. By 2014, Twitch had become the fourth-largest source of Internet traffic during peak times in the United States (Aisch and Giratikanon 2014). Twitch further anticipated the launch in 2014–2015 of multiple live broadcasting mobile applications, including Periscope, Meerkat, Streamly, and YouNow, among others.

Most notable among these second-gen platforms are Snapchat and Instagram. In contrast to YouTube and live broadcasting, Snapchat content is short-lived, disappearing from view after twenty-four hours. In addition, the platform integrated social networking limited to invited users only. As Gary Vaynerchuk (2016) notes, Snapchat provided affordances that rapidly lured teen users, a separate platform walled off from their parents, who had started to use Facebook, featuring content that evaporated every day. Such features, as one might imagine, were considered valued affordances.

Although initially limited to images, like their platform predecessors, Snapchat has pivoted to include ephemeral and live video. In addition to adding new technological affordances, Snapchat has entered into partnerships with advertisers and brands through its Discover interface. This section features sponsored and branded content from major digital publishers including BuzzFeed, CNN, ESPN, Mashable, and Vice. Snapchat has introduced a "freemium" model for some of its features, offering users the chance to purchase branded filters for photo and video. While Snapchat has no revenue-sharing deals in place with its creators, savvy Snapchatters seeking to monetize their content can still earn significant income on branded content deals. Nonetheless, Snapchat's viability may prove as short-lived as Vine's, and that of numerous other social media predecessors like MySpace and Friendster—most notably because of the threat posted by Instagram.

According to Mediakix (2017), a media marketing firm, "Instagram commands a $1B influencer economy," which is projected to be a $5–10 billion market by 2020. Indeed, the rise of Instagram has situated this

platform centrally among SME platforms. Instagram's photo-sharing capacity has lent itself more readily to the image-oriented and "brand-safe"
verticals of beauty, lifestyle, and design. This close alignment of affordance and content type has seen waves of Instagram creators engaging
in influencer marketing sponsored by Madison Avenue brands, products, and services. Steeped in the tech culture of constant iteration, the
platform has pivoted repeatedly to update user interfaces, tweak user
and creator affordances, and monetize the platform in lock-step with
Facebook. These changes included the introduction of a short-form
video player dedicated to lure Vine users. In addition, the platform introduced its version of Instagram stories coupled with ephemerality to
more effectively compete with Snapchat. As we see in the next section,
as YouTube is to Google, Instagram has become to Facebook, part of
a convergent, integrated, multiplatform ecology designed for optimal
commercialization of content and communication.

While social networking affordance promotes spreadability, video
players promote higher CPMs than mere text or image. However, SME
advertising still takes the approach of the traditional TV "pipe model,"
in that it targets consumers only through monetizing eyeballs. While
1.65 billion eyeballs is by no means insignificant, the pipe model fails to
recognize that social media are "platforms" not "pipes," and that social
media advertising therefore needs to simultaneously support brands,
creators, and consumers. The strategy of monetizing eyeballs on social
media is likely to fail (Choudary 2014).

SME 2.0: Multiplatform Wars

In response to the launches of the second-gen platforms, first-gen
platforms employed a diverse array of NoCal and SoCal strategies
in response to the increased competition. Well-capitalized through
investment, advertising, and IPOs, Facebook and Twitter engaged in
multiplatform acquisition and accelerated feature enhancement. Nonetheless, these efforts have achieved varying levels of integration and
degrees of success, and have not guaranteed sustainability.

Two years after Instagram launched, Facebook purchased the platform in 2012 for $1 billion, before the platform had generated any rev-
enue. At the time, the purchase was mocked, but by 2014, the platform

was estimated to be worth $35 billion (Gelles 2014), turning Zuckerberg's folly into fortune. Facebook's purchase signaled a value-added content play by Facebook emulating Google's purchase of YouTube. Facebook has since acquired other platforms like the messenger service Whats-App. Facebook's acquisition strategy signals its ability to "build multiple products at the same time" (Wagner 2017).

Facebook and Instagram operate as separate platforms but are partially integrated. A dual platform system creates economies of scale and also offers a suite of technological features that appeal to separate groups of users and, in turn, creators. Partially protected under the Facebook corporate umbrella, Instagram has operated like a startup despite securing massive global scale approximating eight hundred million by late 2017. Facebook hired a new management team that relaunched Instagram in 2016 with the purpose of directly emulating the features of its competitors. The platform introduced short-form video like Vine and an ephemeral Insta-stories feature that erased content every day along with branded photo filters like Snapchat. The result has contributed to Instagram's accelerated growth and Snapchat's precipitous decline.

Facebook itself continues to add new features and foster affordances that emulate YouTube video content, partnership, and advertising strategies. In 2014, Facebook embedded its own video player, featuring an autoplay mechanism that causes videos to play while scrolling down the Facebook wall. Since 2015, Facebook has solidified its convergence on video with the launch of Facebook Live. The platform's acquisition of virtual-reality headset manufacturer Oculus VR for $2 billion is indicative of its long-term plans for the development of live video content. In mid-2015, Facebook launched its Suggested Videos to feature branded content videos from an array of main media companies like CNN and the *New York Times*, sports leagues like the NBA, as well as film studios and television networks. Gradually, these partnerships have included new digital and social media intermediaries, like Tastemade and Funny or Die, along with a limited array of premium content creators. With advertising partnerships available or imminent, for most creators and intermediaries, Facebook has emerged as another viable video platform in addition to its social networking capacities that have always contributed to fan aggregation and generated additional influencer marketing revenue.

Due to these video-driven, content-oriented initiatives, Facebook claims that its users watch four billion video views per day, with brands uploading more videos directly to Facebook than to YouTube (James 2015). However, a key controversy has ensued over what actually counts as a Facebook video view, and its importance for content creators and advertisers. Online leader Hank Green, in a 2015 blog post titled "Theft, Lies, and Facebook Video," noted that Facebook measures anything longer than three seconds as a "view" (regardless of sound), including those videos that have played automatically in someone's news feed as they scroll past. "This might seem a little like this is a victimless crime, but it fundamentally devalues the #1 metric of online video. The view is the thing that everyone talks about and it's the thing creators sell to advertisers in order to make a living" (Green 2015c). Green's critique was confirmed when the platform revealed that, for two years, it had dramatically overestimated platform watchtime between 60 and 80%, leading to a backlash from overcharged advertisers and brands (Vranica and Marshall 2016). (We discuss this further in chapter 4.)

Another complaint leveled at the platform is its pernicious practice of "freebooting," where Facebook partners rip videos from YouTube and upload them to Facebook without the original creator's permission for which they derive potential revenue. Freebooting differs from sharing a link to a YouTube video in which all views, credit, and revenue are returned to the original publisher. Rather, the revenue goes to Facebook and the freebooter, with little accountability. As George Strompolos, CEO of Fullscreen, wrote in a Twitter post,

> I love FB video but getting very tired of seeing our videos ripped there with no way to monitor or monetize. I now regularly see our videos with 50M+ view counts that are stolen by individuals on FB . . . sometimes by other media companies. It costs us a lot to hunt them down one by one. I'm a huge DMCA [Digital Millennium Copyright Act] proponent, but this has to improve fast. Frankly, I'm shocked that a rights holder with deep pockets has not sued yet. (Strompolos in Dredge 2015a)

Facebook responded to these concerns in early 2016, launching its own video rights manager—a version of YouTube's Content ID system. A year later, the platform also allowed original video creators to profit from pirated content on their platform (Constine 2016). The devil, however, lies in the details, or rather, definitions of creators. Facebook's emulation of YouTube's content strategies includes similar unintended or poorly executed consequences of navigating between a content and a communication platform. Platform rights management systems support the IP of traditional media companies but do little to protect the noncopyrighted content of creators emerging natively off, and more dependent upon, the commercial affordances of these platforms (J. Johnson 2017). In other words, Facebook is making a play for the SoCal model of premium content that is typically accompanied by premium advertising. Meanwhile, its native creators remain unsupported and partnerless, but not without agency that includes harnessing the commercial and communicative affordances of Facebook. This is analyzed further in chapter 2.

Amazon's history emulates Google/YouTube by offering multiplatform services through launch and acquisition that competed with digital portals like iTunes and Netflix for PGC and social media platforms like YouTube and Facebook for UGC. These also were value-added services that complemented Amazon's core value proposition as the world's largest e-commerce sales platform and were successfully integrated into their parent platform. In 2006, Amazon launched Amazon Unbox, its first video platform, which was later renamed as Amazon Instant Video (and later just Amazon Video). The service initially provided transactional video on demand (TVOD) to compete with iTunes before adding a streaming subscription video on demand (SVOD) service like Netflix. Over the ensuing years, Amazon has engaged in an original content strategy to more effectively compete with native and traditional media portals like Netflix and HBO. Amazon's original series, like *Transparent*, have secured great critical acclaim, including several Emmy Awards. The platform has expanded into films by the likes of Woody Allen as well as reality formats, including the acquisition of the world's most successful format reality series, *Top Gear*. These strategies have positioned Amazon as one of the most powerful, deeply capitalized tech firms with the potential to threaten Hollywood incumbency.

Meanwhile, Amazon has also pivoted to compete with its NoCal counterparts and even its Chinese equivalent. In 2014, Amazon paid $1 billion for Twitch, which had grown to over one hundred million users in the interim. Although Twitch evolved into a destination for game players, the platform represents arguably one of the most sustainable arrays of technological and commercial affordances. The platform integrates a live broadcasting player with a chatroom interface, coupled with multiple monetization strategies, from advertising and subscription to e-commerce and virtual goods. In 2016, Amazon pivoted directly to compete with YouTube with the launch of its UGC-oriented Amazon Video Direct Service and entered into deals with YouTube MCN partners, including Machinima and Stylehaul (Spangler 2016a).

As a value-added service, Amazon is integrating e-commerce across all these platforms that encourage audiences and viewers, fans and communities to click through and purchase products featured in the video content. This strategy emulates the successful e-commerce strategies of Chinese platforms like Alibaba, which owns the YouTube-like Youku platform. Youku creators have been able to monetize their channels' content by launching their own e-commerce stores on Alibaba-owned T-mall and Taobao platforms. These strategies affirm how Chinese SME may have developed even more sustainable models than their Western competitors. We discuss global models of social media entertainment in chapter 6.

Like Google/YouTube and Facebook/Instagram, Twitter engaged in an even more aggressive multiplatform acquisition strategy, but with less successful integration or monetization. Before the actual platforms were launched, Twitter purchased Vine in 2012 and Periscope in 2015. However, in contrast to Google/YouTube, Facebook/Instagram, or even Amazon/Twitch, these platforms were not value-added services to their parent company. Rather, these were simply competing social media and content players that offered alternative technological affordances—short video (Vine) and live broadcasting (Periscope)—without clear monetization strategies. During this same acquisition period, Twitter added images and video, but none of the commercial affordances that would contribute to greater revenue or encourage native content creation. As a result, Twitter stopped growing users at around three hundred million and has yet to return a profit to investors. Market shares have plummeted from a high of sixty dollars per share to less than ten dollars. As a consequence, the Twitterverse is in peril, with numerous apocalyptic accounts circulating (e.g. R. Meyer 2015; Newton 2016a).

Reports of Twitter's imminent death, as they say, may be premature, or the platform may become victim to the next wave of platform consolidation tectonics. In late 2015, Twitter cofounder and start-up wunderkind Jack Dorsey returned as CEO. Dorsey has tried to make up for years of platform stagnation, integrating numerous initiatives to quickly emulate YouTube's video and advertising strategies. The platform even introduced a live video player and has secured deals with the likes of the NFL to air live games on what was once a 140-character, text-based messenger service.

These rapid, if dizzying, pivots may prove to be too much or too late. In September 2016, the press reported that the platform was up for sale. A month later, Twitter shut down its Vine platform. This telling account from Verge.com, based on interviews with multiple executives, revealed

> a portrait of a company whose cultural impact far outstripped its strategic benefits to Twitter. Working a continent apart from their parent company, Vine's small, New York–based team struggled to grow its user base or find ways to make money. While Vine once boasted a commanding lead over other social video apps, it failed to keep pace as competitors added features—something that ultimately drove its biggest stars away. The app generated more beloved memes and cultural moments than most apps with twice as many users—but Twitter's mounting core business problems this year all but ensured it would eventually be sold off or shuttered. (Newton 2016b)

Twitter's history exemplifies how the fast-moving, disruptive NoCal strategy of constant iteration, including platform aggregation, without a solid SoCal content and monetization strategy, is a royal road to unsustainability.

For first-gen platforms, their incorporation of second-gen platforms and video content comes late for Twitter and highly variably for the other platforms. Despite many differences, the YouTube monetization model is enticing, even forcing, convergence on similar video content and advertising strategies to those of YouTube as they seek ways to stabilize as businesses by capitalizing on their massive audiences through monetization. Steeped in the NoCal ethos of constant iteration, experimentation, and disruption, YouTube has responded to these competitive pressures with a decade of resilient experimentation, albeit heavily supported by Google's very deep pockets, which has produced mixed results, while exhibiting little sign of ceding its first-mover advantage.

SME 2.0: YouTube(s)

Like its first-generation competitors, YouTube continues to pivot at a rapid pace, integrating and evolving new features, including several, mostly failed, attempts at integrating social networking affordances, while launching multiple platforms, effectively morphing into its own multiplatform ecology: YouTube(s). These strategies are multilateral, designed to compete with the PGC portals of Netflix and Amazon, while also trying to thwart the competition from social media–focused platforms, such as Facebook, Twitter, Snapchat, and Twitch. It should always be kept in mind that this constant experimentation is possible because of the deeply capitalized support of its corporate owner—a luxury not shared by some other competitors. As Hector Postigo (2014) ironizes, "YouTube (or any platforms that invite UGC for its inventory) is not unlike a bettor at a roulette table who is in the happy position of betting on all the numbers, where the payout though low in aggregate outweighs what appears to be an otherwise wild investment." While many of its moves may appear reactive and often unsuccessful, they have helped YouTube remain the central player in the rapidly evolving and competitive SME platform landscape. A good amount of its experimentation can be said to have benefited creator labor, offering enhanced affordance for sustainability through platform monetization, content innovation, and fan engagement and aggregation.

Over the past decade, YouTube has engaged in several failed efforts to integrate social networking affordances with its content player. It is fair to suggest that this has been YouTube's hamartia—its central failing. These efforts started with the parent company Google's launch of Orkut in 2004 (discontinued in 2014), Google Friend Connect (launched in 2008, retired in 2013), and Buzz (launched in 2010 and discontinued in 2011). Google Plus was launched in 2011, and YouTube users were forced to sign up for the service in order to subscribe, comment, or like videos. After voluble criticism by creators and users, this forced integration with YouTube was discontinued in 2015. In fall 2016, YouTube integrated its latest social networking effort, a "community" button embedded on YouTube channels. This service is designed to finally offer the networking affordances that other platforms offer and inhibit the multiplatforming practices of its users and creators (Perez 2016b). These strategies and outcomes confirm the rule in the NoCal world that users' adoption, adaptation, or invention of affordances may determine success as much as intentional design by platforms.

On the SoCal side, YouTube has engaged in a multilateral multiplatform strategy to compete with Hollywood and digital media portals for traditional entertainment content. In a major move that apes PGC platforms, YouTube Red, an ad-free subscription service claiming to enable access to 95% of existing platform content, was launched in late 2015. Red helped address a series of concerns faced by YouTube. It was designed to thwart the new windowing strategies offered by subscription platforms like Vessel and Vimeo Plus. Windowing emulates a traditional media licensing practice, effectively offering subscribers a "sneak peek" without advertising, typically for the span of a few days or weeks. This service also created another revenue stream for creators who, after an unspecified amount of time, could make their content available on their original platform with advertising. In mid-2015, YouTube also hired former MTV programming executive Suzanne Daniels to develop, finance, and produce original content generated by its native creators. Once more, we see NoCal conceding to SoCal content management expertise.

In addition, as a separate subscription platform, YouTube Red can "work around" Digital Millennium Copyright Act safe harbor provisions that prohibit YouTube from emulating Hollywood without liability for its content. As a "walled garden" behind a subscription interface, YouTube Red can more reliably compete with PGC portals like Netflix, Amazon, Hulu, and traditional television to incubate and exploit its own intellectual property. To do this, it engages the services of top-level creators who conceive, develop, and produce the content in exchange for split revenues and paid fees. For those creators interested in pursuing a premium PGC model with more traditional genres of content and narrativity, this becomes their back door to Hollywood. However, as we have heard repeatedly in field interviews, most creators are not writer-director-producer wannabes. Rather, they are communicators engaging programmatically in alternative content from that of main media, less interested in building IP libraries than engaging with a global community—albeit one that can also be commodified.

YouTube Red has received mixed reception from creators, users, and the press fraught with the skepticism that YouTube Red may be cast into the dustbin of platform history—like the record of its Original Channel initiatives that have since been erased from YouTube's platform like a Snapchat Moment. Most worryingly, to support the claim to enable access to up to 95% of existing platform content, YouTube has flexed its muscles with its creators in a very traditional corporate fashion. At best, Red represents a nominal, value-added service to incentivize creators not to leave by offering them subscription revenue and the chance to engage in more sophisticated storytelling.

YouTube has also ventured into competition with streaming music platforms like Spotify, Pandora, and Apple Music. YouTube Music is included with a subscription to YouTube Red, a bundling strategy comparable to cable television packages and Amazon Prime. This strategy recognizes the preeminence across YouTube of music content, which constitutes as much as 40% of its content. However, in doing so, YouTube may have fallen into Napster-esque territory, attracting wrath and retaliation from music rights holders and performers currently "lining up to lobby" regulators to contain YouTube's disruption of the music industry (Forde 2016).

Subscription music and video, coupled with original content, is only one of an ongoing array of strategies at YouTube's disposal. In an effort to thwart Amazon's Twitch, YouTube launched a separate YouTube Gaming platform. This platform provides recorded let's-play videos, trailers, and reviews from the top gaming channels, along with live streaming of console, computer, or mobile device gaming. YouTube has integrated a Live button on its platform to compete directly with the wave of new live platforms like Twitter's Periscope. Whereas YouTube's web-based platform reflects only subtle changes in user-interface design, YouTube's mobile application emulates user design and technological affordances of second-generation social media platforms, including the push-button record and upload features of Vine, Instagram, Snapchat, and Facebook.

Finally, the YouTube Kids app represents a curated, child-friendly platform designed to lure younger viewers while offering greater parental supervision. More importantly, the platform allows YouTube to be seen to respond to various children's media policy regulations, such as the Children's Online Privacy Protection Act (COPPA), designed to protect children's privacy and inhibit exploitation. Through YouTube

Red, parents can also turn off advertising on the platform. However, the platform continues to indulge the questionable content innovation of children's unboxing, which blurs the line between YouTube's online socialization potential for children and overt consumerism and promotion of children's toys sponsored by manufacturers. These concerns are canvased in our concluding chapter.

Having said all this, it is instructive to consider the level of maturation in the YouTube content market—the culmination of ten years of (often unintentional) empowering and enriching SME creators. When Google acquired YouTube in 2006, the site was registering about sixty-five thousand video uploads and one hundred million video views per day. Since its acquisition by Google, YouTube has implemented a range of strategies in its transformation to a site of increasingly professional and professionalizing content, including—on the back of calls for the removal of copyrighted content—the development in 2007 of a robust Content ID system that by 2016 had paid over $2 billion to rights holders who had chosen to monetize, and the development of a revenue-sharing program that enables creators to monetize their content through advertising revenue. The "YouTube for Creators" benefits program is available in ninety-six countries. Access to the program has shifted over time from invitation by the platform only to free to all users—provided the content meets YouTube's eligibility criteria (original material, non-copyrighted, advertising friendly, compliant with Terms of Service and Community Guidelines)—to the introduction of minimum levels of viewership before monetization starts. As creators accrue scale, they are rewarded with an array of benefits increasing in tandem with tiered subscription levels (Graphite level 0–1000, Opal level 1000+, Bronze level 10,000+, Silver level 100,000+, Gold level 1 million+, Platinum 10 million+). YouTube has invested heavily in working with content creators through its dedicated creator "Spaces" (in Los Angeles, London, Tokyo, New York, São Paulo, Berlin, Mumbai, Paris, Toronto, and Dubai), numerous pop-up spaces around the world, and programs such as the 100 Channel initiative and the Next Up competition. Of all the SME platforms, YouTube is best able to provide viable advertising split-revenue partnerships through pre-roll and other browser-based advertising and sponsored content.

Outro

We have seen how the advantage of the size and scale of these big digital platforms is further compounded by their first-mover advantage, while their combined "born digital," "network native," and "mobile friendly" status means that they dominate the network economy even more effectively than standard forms of capitalist oligopoly. Yet network economics also tells us that despite the lock-in advantages, these platforms remain inhabited by far better connected and networked possibilities and potentialities for horizontal, peer-to-peer connectivity and community that are not under direct platform control. The kind of capitalist power exercised by SME platforms is a textbook example of revisionist Foucauldian understandings of power. Such platforms are constantly trying to deal with the special vagaries of information economics. They are seeking to monetize in an environment that is built on scale, free access, aggregation of other people's IP, and leveraging of social networks.

Yet as we will see in the next chapter, for the creators, less and less advantage can be drawn from the size and scale of any single SME platform, while increased platform competition makes their jobs harder. From the creators' point of view, engaging with audiences on multiple platforms is a necessity for the success of their businesses and communicative strategies, with content creators using Facebook and Twitter to aggregate their audience as part of paid influencer marketing campaigns wherein brands pay them to promote across all platforms regardless of remuneration on any particular platform.

While interactive, communicative, and networking affordances facilitate the social interaction that underpins the utility of each of these platforms, each platform has different starting points and serves different user needs, particularly when it comes to video content. Twitter, for example, is much more a core social media platform than YouTube ever was or ever will be, while Facebook traffic remains resolutely "news" about family and friends. At the same time, in comparison with YouTube, neither Facebook nor Twitter has had to deal with traditional media copyright industries challenging its content. The dilemma for both advertisers and creators seeking advertising revenue is that, despite its massive scale, the Facebook feed remains beyond their control. If users want to connect with their family and friends via Facebook, then those same family and friends will inhabit their wall and their feed in ways advertisers and creators cannot control. The Facebook feed is very different from that of the curating videographer or content creator on YouTube. That YouTube started as "broadcast yourself" remains still a critical point of platform affordance. So even though it retains high-touch interactivity, it remains the case that an individual creator can still create and maintain his or her own channels and no one can (apart from posting comments, which can also be blocked or filtered) take control of the creators' feed.

The evolution of the SME platform landscape currently features a highly competitive, globally scaled, deeply capitalized array of companies. Their dizzying experimentation and pivoting, and birth and sometimes eclipse, affirm that deep capitalization, high market valuation, and global scale may not guarantee sustainability. Their competitiveness, scale, and affordance have incubated the structural and material conditions for creator labor to make its own history, albeit not under conditions of its own making.

2

Creator Labor

In chapter 1, we described how the network economics of social media, the innovation culture of Silicon Valley firms that own the platforms, and the technological and commercial affordances of platforms have created the structural conditions for the creator economy. In doing that, we proposed a revisionist account of political economy, emphasizing the deep conflicts and creative tensions arising from the clash of industrial cultures of the two major forces in media and tech in the world, Hollywood and Silicon Valley. Our main revisionist effort in this chapter concerns a debate equally central to media, communications, and cultural studies—creative labor. We argue, through attention to key literature in the debate, through exploring the contrasts between SME and main media, as well as through the voices of creators themselves, that creator labor is both empowered *and* precarious. One distinguishing feature of creator labor that requires attention is that it, by necessity, works within an algorithmic culture—which engages another key debate in the discipline. Much of the scholarship in these debates is designed to reveal precarity and platform control masked by industry boosterism, rhetoric, and spin. We are animated more by seeking to trace the elements of empowerment in comparison to main media labor.

First, though, turning our attention to the distinctive nature and value of creators, we outline the scale of SME and consider terminological conundrums that often get in the way of analytical clarity. After establishing the theoretical frames for the chapter, we break down the conditions of creator labor into their component parts. Then we examine the problematics of the business models that underpin, as well as threaten, the sustainability of creator careers.

Defining and Mapping Creators

The rapid emergence of social media entertainment has contributed to a new industrial lexicon, with nomenclature almost as evanescent as a Snapchat post and considerable opaqueness about reliable data. YouTube used to release its revenue-sharing partner statistics every year, until it changed its policies and permitted every user to become a partner and thus no longer released such data. SME intermediaries, like multichannel networks and talent representatives, are no more forthcoming with their client data, emulating Hollywood's notorious accounting practices. As *Adweek* declared, the industry is "secretive and lacks transparency" (Talavera 2015).

Third-party data sites, like Social Blade, offer limited accounts of the scale of the creator universe. It is estimated that, in mid-2018, the top five thousand YouTubers globally had at least one million subscribers; more than two hundred had ten million subscribers; and more than one hundred had a billion lifetime video views. Figure 2.1 tracks the rapid expansion of the most popular YouTube channels—those with over one million subscribers. Across other platforms, the top five hundred Twitch streamers have a minimum of two hundred thousand paying subscrib-

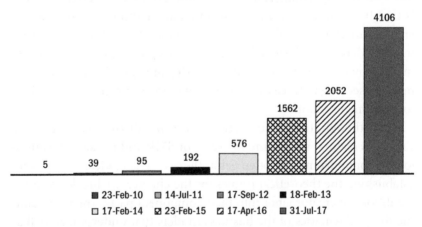

Figure 2.1. YouTube Channels with over One Million Subscribers.
Source: Top 100 most subscribed channels, Vidstatsx, http://vidstatsx.com/youtube
-top-100-most-subscribed-channels; Top 5000 Subscribed YouTube Channels
(sorted by subscriber count), SocialBlade, http://socialblade.com/youtube/top/5000
/mostsubscribed.

ers, the top one hundred Instagram users have a minimum of twenty million followers, and the top one hundred Twitter users have twenty million followers and up. These figures might impress, but they fail to distinguish native online or commercializing users from traditional media and celebrities, much less noncommercial users sharing cyberspace with their millions of socially mediated friends around the world. Arguably, creator scale correlates only as much with commercial value as a nation's land mass converts into GDP.

SME publicity and influencer agencies generate research reports that add some further insight. Tubular's State of the Influencer Economy Report (Stern 2017) claims that 57% of all consumers have purchased products based on influencer recommendations. Linqia's "Value of the Influencer Content 2017" (Linqia 2017) claims that 86% of marketers have incorporated influencer marketing into their advertising campaigns. Tailored for diverse clients, including platforms, advertisers, and creators, these reports provide as much spin as substance while conflating influencers with creators.

Terminology employed in social media studies and SME itself struggles with the proliferation of a "medley of half-neologisms" (Duffy 2015a). SME terms build on earlier understandings of the blurred distinctions among producers, consumers, and users in the digital space. There is a long genealogy (see Hartley et al. 2013) of terms building on Alvin Toffler's concept of prosumers (1980), which was later adopted as a marketing concept to describe the rise of Web 2.0 technologies in the early 2000s. Later, Axel Bruns (2008) coined the term "produsers," about which José van Dijck (2013) remarked, "[T]he problem with overly optimistic re-conceptualizations of the audience as 'users' or 'produsers' is that many professionals as well as scholars ignored the role of technologies, business models, and governance structures in the construction of social media platforms" (Moe, Poell, and van Dijck 2016).

Studies of SME creative labor employ a multiplicity of terms. Denise Mann (2014) refers to "YouTube talent partners," Brooke Duffy (2015a) alternates among "creative workers," "bloggers," and "content creators," and John Caldwell (2009) calls them "alternative media producers," whereas Crystal Abidin (2016a) uses the term "influencer." None of these uses means the scholars' positive endorsement of their implications. In particular, "influencer" has become a term that marks the commercial value to advertisers who are engaging with these creators in the commercial practice of what they call "influencer marketing," which will be described in greater detail later. However, in our field research, we found that creators often rejected this term as pretentious or insulting, overwriting the cultural and communitarian value of their work.

Theresa Senft (2008) coined the term "micro-celebrity," which Abidin (2016b) also uses. Alice Marwick and danah boyd (2014) say this term "involves viewing friends or followers as a fan base; acknowledging popularity as a goal; managing the fan base using a variety of affiliative techniques; and constructing an image of self that can be easily consumed by others" (Marwick and boyd 2014, 140). Anne Jerslev (2016) takes issue with the term "micro-celebrity" as distinct from traditional media celebrity which, she argues, are often conflated. "Attention-creating performances of a private authentic self are the most valuable commodity in social media celebrification" (Jerslev 2016, 5240). As discussed in chapter 4, discourses of authenticity represent a core claim about the traits distinguishing SME content from that of traditional media.

Industry use also proliferates terms. Platform-specific terms like "YouTubers," "Tweeters," "Grammers" (Instagram), "Chatters" or "Snappers" (Snapchat), and "Viners" (on the now defunct platform, Vine) belie the multiplatform practices of creators. While our research has primarily focused on those who started (and continue) on YouTube, first-generation creators also entered this new screen ecology on Facebook and Twitter. Although these platforms did not provide partnerships for creators until recently, in SME 1.0 creators found alternative ways to harness the commercial affordances of the platforms. In those countries where broadband and mobile speeds and access are slow and technology like computers and cameras are prohibitively expensive, text- and image-based platforms have often been preferred over video. As technological and economic conditions improve, creators have gradually migrated to video-based content. As second-generation platforms have emerged, a second wave of creators has used the newer platforms, like Instagram, Vine, and Snapchat. They often avoid the first-generation, highly scaled SME platforms to appeal to more defined demographics and take advantage of alternative affordances, like ephemerality on Snapchat and the brand-safe marketing ability and mobile accessibility of images posted on Instagram. Most recently, live-streaming has added more titles to the mix: "live-streamers," "showroom hosts" (China), or "online," "digital," "mobile," or "social" "broadcasters."

The multiplatform practice of creators often means multimodalities, whether text-based tweets, images on Instagram and Snapchat, or multiformatted video across all these platforms, including YouTube. This means that bloggers (text and image), podcasters (audio), and vloggers (video) are all meaningful distinctions in SME.

There is no question that our use of the hyphenated "professionalizing-amateurs" may be confusing. We do not mean to suggest that creators are morphing into next-gen Hollywood talent, which we found repeatedly contradicted in interviews with creators. Laura Chernikoff, the then executive director of the Internet Creators Guild, an organization "dedicated to promoting the interests of people making a living creating content online" (internetcreatorsguild.com), asserts that drawing distinctions between amateur and professional creators has proven increasing challenging (Chernikoff 2016).

Further afield, Korea refers to "VJs" or "video jockeys," with an etiology that dates back to the rise of MTV's on-air hosts. The subsequent rise of live broadcasting, particularly across the popular Korean platform, AfreecaTV, has introduced the new term, "BJs," or "broadcast jockeys." These terms curiously refer to the technological affordance of platforms (archived versus broadcast video), coupled with performance, as implied by the term "jockeys."

In China's "parallel universe" SME industry, the term "KOL" (key opinion leader) is dominant; however, the rise of influencer marketing has led to the use of "influencers" as industrial markers of their commercial value. The Chinese sometimes refer to creators as "Wang Hong," the literal translation of which is "Red Internet," but the term is more often used to describe online celebrities. A more pejorative translation would be "pretty girls," which implies a lack of talent among the female fashion and beauty creators and live streamers that dominate their platforms. There must be some talent involved as some of these Wang Hong are generating nearly $50 million per year (Tsoi 2016).

Having reviewed this terminological profusion, we use the term "creator" and define this as commercializing and professionalizing native social media users who generate and circulate original content to incubate, promote, and monetize their own media brand on the major social media platforms as well as offline. This is consistent with broad industry use and connotes both the status of originator and the fact that SME is largely generated without the divisions of labor seen in main media. We look to avoid the pejorative connotations in terms like "influencers" or "micro-celebrity." When we use them, it is under advisement.

Precarious Labor

A rapidly burgeoning literature has developed around the notion of precarious labor—much of it focused on the specific condition of creative labor in the cultural and creative industries (for example, McRobbie 2002; Terranova 2004; Deuze 2007; Scholz 2008; Rossiter 2007; Gill and Pratt 2008; Ross 2002, 2007, 2009). This debate has largely been conducted in the mode of a wide-ranging ideology critique. Criticisms of the presumed overly celebratory accounts of the increased significance of creative labor in contemporary economies have focused on ostensibly neoliberal concepts of human capital and of labor that inform Panglossian endorsements of glamorous and attractive, but volatile and precarious, forms of work.

Indeed, in his panoramic overview of the state of play in media and cultural studies, Toby Miller (2010) characterizes the future of media, communication, and cultural studies as lying in just such a focus on labor. Characterizing the dominant paradigms as "misleadingly functionalist on its effects and political-economy side" and "misleadingly conflictual on its active-audience side," Miller argues that "[w]ork done on audience effects and political economy has neglected struggle, dissonance, and conflict in favor of a totalizing narrative in which the media dominate everyday life. Work done on active audiences has over-emphasized struggle, dissonance, and conflict, neglecting infrastructural analysis in favor of a totalizing narrative in which consumers dominate everyday life" (Miller 2010, 50). Miller's third mode "should synthesize and improve" the dominant paradigms by its analytical concentration on the status of labor. He reminds us in the most ringing of tones, "There would be no culture, no media, without labor. Labor is central to humanity" (Miller 2010, 50).

Mark Banks and David Hesmondhalgh (2009) summarize the growing body of work on precarious creative labor with an emphasis on lower- and midlevel media professionals operating within dominant, powerful, consolidated, and integrated creative industry firms. The "consistent findings" of this work are that

> creative work is project-based and irregular, contracts tend to be short-term, and there is little job protection; that there is a predominance of self-employed or freelance workers; that career prospects are uncertain and often foreshortened; that earnings are usually slim and unequally distributed, and that insurance, health protection and pension benefits are limited; that creatives are younger than other workers, and tend to hold second or multiple jobs; and that women, ethnic and other minorities are under-represented and disadvantaged in creative employment. All in all, there is an oversupply of labor to the creative industries with much of it working for free or on subsistence wages. (Banks and Hesmondhalgh 2009, 420)

The negative critique of creative labor arises largely in response to the overly sanguine accounts given of it in earlier work to establish the provenance of the role of creativity and the place of creative industries in the modern economy. Charles Leadbeater's (1999) *Living on Thin Air* and John Howkins's *Creative Economy* (2001), for example, were early paeans of praise for creative labor, as indeed was Richard Florida's (2002) very influential account of the so-called creative class, which was held to comprise fully one-third of the US workforce. Howkins's spin is full-on: "For these people, betting their creative imagination against the world may appear a more secure proposition, and certainly more fun, than becoming a little cog in a big organization or another bit in the information society" (Howkins 2001, 125). Leadbeater's language is more measured, but it is still about the normalization of the working life of the independent knowledge worker: "self-employed, independent, working from home . . . armed with a laptop, a modem and some contacts" (Leadbeater 1999, 1). Partly this is a matter of genre: these are "business" books that, according to their genre, are breezy reads with lashings of what Adorno would scorn as "affirmative" culture thrown in. (It is also partly because Florida is a genre bender—mixing his business pitch with straight academic social science research—that he has attracted more academic criticism.)

But it is important not to lose sight of the fact that even some of the most strident critics also affirm the potential for "good work" that creative labor represents in the modern economy and the undeniable attraction of (relatively) autonomous labor that it promises (Banks and Hesmondhalgh 2009, 419; Banks 2010; Hesmondhalgh and Baker 2010). This is a recurring theme, registered as a paradox by some (e.g. Arvidsson, Malossi, and Naro 2010) but unfortunately often downplayed as false consciousness by others (hopeful entrants can be "seduced"; critical social science must "expose": Banks and Hesmondhalgh 2009, 418, 419). We will build on such congruity, balancing critique and affirmation, in our account of SME labor.

Conditions of Digital and Social Labor

The debate on labor precarity has been extended into the newer tech, digital, and social media industries. In their account of fashion and new media workers, Gina Neff, Elizabeth Wissinger, and Sharon Zukin (2005) set forth claims around the rise of "entrepreneurial labor," which blurs the line between media work and practice and personal identity. Entrepreneurial labor encourages risk taking and greater levels of flexibility, with entrepreneurs "lured by the possibility of sharing in the profits of risk" (Neff, Wissinger, and Zukin 2005, 309). The authors claim that the opportunity for "cool jobs in hot industries" more often resulted in limited rewards and discrimination, which "does not bode well for either social justice or upward mobility" (Neff, Wissinger, and Zukin 2005, 331). With somewhat more critical ambivalence, Rosalind Gill (2007) studied fifty web workers in Amsterdam, asking whether these were "Technobohemians or the new Cybertariat." Gill's analysis considered how the stratification of labor and management in these firms contributes to greater job insecurity, but she also registers the appeals to greater forms of creativity, autonomy, and informality that motivate workers.

Since these earlier accounts, critical accounts of digital labor have proliferated within research around media production. As well summarized by Duffy (2015a),

Recent interest in media work is also a product of digital media theorists seeking to conceptualize new patterns of productivity emerging in the fuzzy space between production and consumption; between labor and leisure; and between professional and amateur. In just the last few years, a medley of half-neologisms—among them, digital labor (Fuchs, 2010; Scholz, 2013), co-creative labor (Banks and Deuze, 2009), passionate labor (Postigo, 2009), hope labor (Kuehn and Corrigan, 2013), venture labor (Neff, 2012) and playbour (Kücklich, 2005)—has emerged as scholars attempt to understand the implications of new forms of digital and social production. A central line of inquiry connecting these various conceptual dots is whether emergent forms of productivity fit within Marxist-inflected notions of exploitation and alienation—or, instead, if digitally enabled modes of content creation and distribution "empower" audiences. (Duffy 2015a, 444)

As scholars have redirected their focus from digital to social media, new distinctions of social media labor have been identified. Sam Srauy (2015) argues that corporate-owned platforms are exploiting the expressive practices of social media users, without considering that creators exercise agency as they engage in these same conditions. Mann (2014) raises concerns for how platforms and social media firms convert their users into consumers and "invisible labor as their consumer preferences are aggregated and sold to advertisers" (Mann 2014, 33). Mann advocates for state-based intervention, regulation, and worker protections, which anticipates the formation of the Internet Creator's Guild (ICG), launched by Hank and John Green in 2016. We discuss ICG in our conclusion; here, we note that it is a direct response to such concerns and the first signs of organized creator labor in this proto-industry.

In addition to highlighting labor precarity, critical and feminist scholars have fostered concerns around the heightened personal, emotional, and gendered nature of digital work, including accounts of "affective labor" (Hesmondhalgh and Baker 2011) and "self-branding"

(Banet-Weiser 2012; Marwick 2013; Marwick and boyd 2014). Duffy's account of "aspirational labor" (2015a) maps the discordance between the promise and uneven rewards afforded female beauty vloggers, often underpaid for "doing what they love." Duffy suggests how appeals to entrepreneurism and creative autonomy represent a kind of labor ideology that masks the "problematic constructions of gender and class subjectivities" (Duffy 2015a, 443). Our account of the representational practices of Asian American and LGBTQ creators in chapter 5 engages with these concerns around gender and class.

Recent scholars have contributed vital new perspectives in the ongoing project of articulating the distinctiveness of digital and social labor, most notably the spatial and mediated relations between artists and celebrities and their fans and followers. In her account of "relational labor," Nancy Baym (2015) considers the social and economic relationship established between artists and fans through communicative and networked affordances of social media platforms.

The concept of "relational labor" abuts "emotional labor," "affective labor," "immaterial labor," "venture labor," and "creative labor" but offers something new by emphasizing the ongoing communicative practices and skills of building and maintaining interpersonal and group relationships that are now so central to maintaining many careers (Baym 2015, 20).

Like Duffy, Abidin focuses on the gendered space of practices of female fashion influencers and followers on Instagram, and like Baym, highlights the dynamic of the relationship between creators and communities as compared to the traditional celebrity-fan construction in traditional media and culture. Referencing earlier scholarship around parasocial relations, Abidin describes how social media foster "perceived interconnectedness—a model of communication in which influencers interact with followers to give the illusion of intimacy" (2015, 1). Influencers can appropriate this intimacy for commercial, interactive, reciprocal, and disclosive value. In her account of "visibility labour" (2016a), Abidin considers the practices of co-creation conducted by influencers and followers from which influencers may profit considerably but that may also represent "tacit" and "insidiously exploitative" labor on the part of followers.

Algorithmic Culture

Another element that further differentiates online culture from its predecessors is the digital trace that every action leaves and the consequent algorithmic culture that has been spawned. This debate is less concerned with precarity and more concerned with control. Critical algorithm studies has become a burgeoning field. As of July 2017, there were 239 items on Tarleton Gillespie and Nick Seaver's (2016) "Reading List" of critical algorithm studies, and it is growing rapidly. As Greg Elmer et al. (2015) point out, big data analytics can give us authoritative pictures of global warming and the effects of armed conflicts. Nevertheless, the focus in the field is very much on the power of the algorithm as "a tool of predictability and therefore as a tool for social and economic control" (Elmer et al. 2015).

But we need to qualify claims around the quantified self and the quantified audience in relation to the conditions of SME labor and production. SME creators are a significant cohort working at the heart of algorithmic culture, and we need to specify better how they are impacted through surveilling algorithmic cultures. Consistent with our approach to precarity, we steer between positions of celebration and critical suspicion, offering an immanent critique of the limits of data analytics in shaping SME and controlling its participants. Our theoretical framework, like that in chapter 1, draws on Foucault's (1991) distinction between power and domination. Power is relational, contingent, unstable, and reversible, and the exercise of power produces resistance to it, whereas there is a tendency in critical algorithm studies to view the power of agents in algorithmic culture such as the platforms as domination—one-way, supervening, and controlling.

Based on this framework, an "immanent" approach to social and industry critique works within the terms set by the object of critique in order to expose its own internal contradictions. We offer an immanent critique of the limits of data analytics and a broader algorithmic culture in shaping SME from within the industry on both the creator (bottom up) and the platform (top down) side. This is a limited, but strongly evidenced, critique of the tendency to totalize notions of surveilling power and therefore treat resistance as standing outside of such power.

As we have seen in chapter 1, the IT behemoths are having to come to terms with some of the fundamentals of SoCal media entertainment. Indeed, the ten-year history of YouTube since Google's takeover can be written as a history of Google seeking to come to terms with the non-scalable fundamentals of entertainment, notoriously fickle consumer taste, and content and talent development, from its base as an information technology/engineering company dedicated to scale, automation, permanent beta, rapid prototyping, and iteration. In this chapter, we show how creators manage the relationship between, on the one hand, the quantitative feedback generated by the data analytics stream from Google's AdSense and many multichannel networks' suites of business analytics, and, on the other, the qualitative feedback offered freely by the fan base. Creators spend at least half their working week interacting directly with their cross-platform communities and cannot rely on data analytics alone for either management of their channels or adequate revenue derived from programmatic advertising. Single-platform analytics (such as the standard dashboard available to YouTube partners) are not sufficient and often induce information overload without real analytical insight. Managing community interaction across platforms—vital for maintaining authenticity and maximizing promotion—significantly extends creators' workload. Unlimited word counts on Facebook often mean trying to limit the workload by attempting to direct engagement to Twitter, for example.

There is a range of nonscalable practices essential to success. A "trial and error" approach is prevalent; lots of time is spent "tweaking" various elements to ensure that content is able to find a place in a crowded cultural space across numerous countries. This means ensuring that creators' work is contextually relevant, which is in turn dependent on mastering metadata, video tagging, and copywriting for search engine optimization, including understanding different cultural nuances and modes of engaging in multiple national contexts simultaneously. Creators spend much time in trial and error, learning when work should be uploaded and amplified, while working in seasonal, regional, and national references targeting key viewerships in dozens of countries.

At the same time, the massive growth in scale of SME content has destroyed value—the click-per-thousand rate that drives AdSense revenue sharing on YouTube has bottomed out, driving creators into further nonscalable engagements to restore value (brand deals, merchandising, television and cable options, live appearances, and licensing content).

Entrepreneurialism and the Labor of Spreadability

Critical perspectives such as those canvased thus far need to be balanced with accounts of entrepreneurialism and the labor of "spreadability" that theorize agency, innovation, and reform. In their study of pre-SME online production culture, Adam Fish and Ramesh Srinivasan (2011) attempt to "bridge the ethical challenges of labor exploitation as well as the promises of social entrepreneurship in the digital economy." They describe how "in related video entrepreneurial firms, such as Google's YouTube and Next New Networks, we see business models emerging that are profitable for both the freelance producer and the hosting firm" (Fish and Srinivasan 2011, 149).

Fish and Srinivasan's claims parallel early scholarship by Jean Burgess and Joshua Green at the onset of SME 1.0. In their article about "Agency and Controversy in the YouTube Community" (2008), the authors describe how YouTube operates as a "cultural system . . . co-created by users. Through their many activities, the YouTube community forms a network of creative practice" (Burgess and Green 2008, 2). In subsequent research, Burgess and Green (2009) identified the distinctiveness of "entrepreneurial vloggers" on YouTube, which operates as a "key site where the discourses of participatory culture and the emergence of the creative empowered consumer have been played out" (Burgess and Green 2009, 89).

The concept of participatory culture has been developed most fully by Henry Jenkins in work that started with *Textual Poachers* in 1992. That book analyzed the active participation between traditional media fans and producers that can contribute to co-creative content and cultural meaning. In *Spreadable Media* (2013), Jenkins's collaboration with Sam Ford and Green translates the concept of participatory culture for the cultural and industrial conditions of social media. "Previous work on participatory culture stressed acts of reception and production by media audiences; this book extends that logic to consider the roles that networked communities play in shaping how media circulates" (Jenkins,

Ford, and Green 2013, 2). Like Burgess and Green, Jenkins, Ford, and Green describe YouTube vloggers who "are entrepreneurial in the sense that they don't just produce video blogs, but they use the trappings and practices of vlogging to court YouTube viewers, rather than just serve viewers content" (Jenkins, Ford, and Green 2013, 93). These authors describe how community engagement and meaningful participation have the potential to generate greater value than passive attention from media audiences measured in terms of size and demographics. They further describe the diverse strategies deployed in the development, production, and circulation of content in social media, including knowing when and where audiences want it and its relevance to multiple audiences, as well as its frequency—part of a "steady stream of material" (Jenkins, Ford, and Green 2013, 197–98). This scholarship contributes to our account of the strategies, practices, management, and working conditions of creator labor, including creator entrepreneurialism. Jenkins, Ford, and Green engage fully but critically with the commerciality of content and strategy, divorcing themselves from the techno-speak of virality. "Spreadable"—a term that grounds us in the stuff of human labor—is the concept by which they displace virality.

Approaching Creator Labor

Like *Spreadable Media*'s authors, we look to compare SME creators' labor with that in traditional media. All labor is precarious, but, as we see it, there are critical distinctions to be made, driven by the need to avoid the "idealized, oppositional binaries" that Fish and Srinivasan found in accounts of networked (or social) digital labor. Like Fish and Srinivasan (2011), we have interviewed numerous creators in an effort "to provide a view on digital labor that is grounded less in speculation but in narratives from the producers of the platforms and content of the digital economy" (Fish and Srinivasan 2011, 14).

Of the more than 150 interviews conducted for this book, nearly a third were with creators. Befitting the main focus of the book, most were in the United States, but they also included creators in England, Germany, India, China, and Australia. These creators included those who have worked on a number of the main platforms; those who have worked across many platforms; those who specialize in the main modalities (video, photo, text); and those who specialize in diverse formats and content verticals—beauty influencers, science geeks, toy unboxers, sketch comedians, or personality vloggers. Our primary focus was locating diverse creators who manage a YouTube channel, although every creator we interviewed was operating across multiple platforms. However, as discussed in chapter 1, as a competitive landscape of second-generation platforms emerged, like Instagram and Twitter, so too have enterprising creators. In the case of the demise of Vine, Vine-based creators like Zach King have since launched channels on YouTube and other platforms. As discussed in chapter 6, outside the United States, creators were drawn to the technological affordances and accessibility of Facebook and Twitter that did not require video editing software limited primarily to desktop computers. Whereas chapter 4 focuses on creators at the top of their respective online formats—those who have received the greatest notoriety, success, and presumptive sustainability—in this chapter, our focus includes a mix of low-, mid-, and high-range creators. We include views ranging from those of relatively new entrants struggling to create a sustainable business to those of some of the most successful creators and thought leaders who have helped define the emerging practices of creator labor.

With the massive scale of online content, our sample is by no means offered as representative. There are billions of users on YouTube alone, accumulating millions of subscribers and billions of views, and SME is one small part of that universe. Privilege and success notwithstanding, we would consider all creators to be aspirational and perpetually precarious. As we saw in chapter 1, a platform like Vine—with three hundred million users—can disappear overnight. Similarly, Instagram creators feature centrally in SME because image-based content fosters optimal affordances for brand-safe influencer marketing—and photos are simpler and cheaper to upload than video. In chapter 3, we describe the ephemeral history of SME intermediaries who have secured millions in investment and acquisition only to vanish in less than a decade. Here, and in chapter 4, we canvas creator failure, as Brooke Erin Duffy does more extensively in *(Not) Getting Paid to Do What You Love* (Duffy 2017). But we seek to maintain a dynamic balance, with accounts arising from grounded engagement with creator sustainability, empowerment, agency, and opportunity.

Once Were Amateurs

There is a recurring career trajectory. Unlike mainstream screen industry professionals, creators with sustainable careers—they measure success not only in terms of monetization but also in growing audiences and subscribers, building extensive video catalogues, securing brand deals or leveraging further opportunities off-platform—mostly started out as hobbyists and online aficionados with little intention of developing any form of income, let alone a career. For most, the early experience was of a noncommercial, participatory culture (Jenkins 1992).

Depending on platform, many creators started out simply posting their status updates on Facebook and Twitter, or images on Instagram, or filming their hobby or passion and uploading to YouTube (as with YouTube's very first video, each now sees his or her first work as a terrible early version of his or her craft) "just for fun" or "to see what happened." They were surprised to note audience growth and engagement and, inspired by this initial success, started to steadily increase their output. All tell the story of how, as their channels grew, their workloads grew and—through trial and error—their production quality and professionalization improved, with incremental expansions to include better-quality cameras, microphones, and studio lighting, advanced editing programs, more capable computers, in one instance some professional training, and a work ethic that sees maintaining a community of engagement through various social media as an integral component of the "job."

As Brent Weinstein, a prominent talent agent for SME creators at United Talent Agency remarked, "[T]he first real YouTube stars were not talented artists, in most cases. They were people who created a meme, or did something silly, and became popular as a result and they became the digital media equivalent of what one-hit-wonders in music are" (Weinstein 2015). Midlevel beauty vlogger Tati Westbrook mentioned,

> I started as a performer but I didn't even know how to plug in the camera. I didn't know editing. At first, when I sat down to edit, it would be

a twelve-hour process. I didn't know where to make the cuts or how to move things. Beauty tutorials still take a long time but I've been able to get this down to three hours. (Westbrook 2015)

Not all creators began as outright amateurs. For Phillip Wang of Wong Foo Productions, YouTube became an option because pursuing a career in formal entertainment was not an option for cultural reasons. First-generation Asian migrants would not regard entertainment as a viable career path: "[I]t's not safe and our parents don't encourage it, because they want something secure for us" (Wang 2015). Some were trained media talent who honed their craft on these platforms until their online practice morphed into revenue-generating businesses. The no-to-low barriers to entry facilitated a level of diversity suppressed in main media. (We pursue this in much greater detail in chapter 5.) For Chrissy Chambers of Bria and Chrissy,

> We were both just so burnt out on the traditional route, and I was so tired of going to auditions and hearing people say, "Well, you look too Hispanic" or, "Your nose is too big." Whatever it was, I was really tired of having to depend on other people to give me opportunities for a creative outlet or talent. YouTube started as a way for us to pursue our entertainment goals. (Kam and Chambers 2015)

Indian American and LGBTQ creator Krishna the Kumar studied acting at UCLA before discovering how to produce his own videos on YouTube. His videos were initially designed as contributions to his "acting reel" but, after discovering viral success, he began to monetize his channel, featuring "high quality sketch comedy based on relatable humor." Although a low-level performer with a little over fifty-two thousand subscribers on YouTube, according to our interview, he pays his rent from his proceeds from YouTube while securing other part-time jobs. While he remains interested in traditional acting, and worries that he may be described as a "YouTuber," he no longer goes out on casting calls. Instead of a traditional media agent, he has a manager at Big Frame, a social media firm dedicated to creator representation.

Similar to Krishna, Matt Palazzolo, creator of the scripted online sitcom *Bloomers*, also studied filmmaking at UCLA. He created the series with acting friends in pursuit of traditional media roles, until the series "developed an audience" and commercialization across multiple platforms (Kumar 2015). Similarly, Brent Rivera, a prominent second-generation creator, began using Vine, and later Instagram and Snapchat, in his early teens out of an interest in performing. "It was not about being a big celebrity. I like acting. I did auditions in seventh grade for commercials and TV shows, and I always liked performing in front of the camera, but I didn't enjoy being in the producer's hands. I wanted to make my own content" (Rivera 2015).

But, as a general rule, creators were not trained or experienced in their craft. Indian stand-up comedians Aditi Mittal and Atul Khatri from East India Comedy had no background in their craft. The former was an out-of-work advertising executive (Mittal 2016) and the latter, a computer engineer running his own successful business (Khatri 2016), until they discovered how to use SME platforms to develop their own comedy brand, promote their appearances, and eventually generate revenue. In the case of Khatri, his hobbyism began pre–Web 2.0 in a series of e-mails filled with jokes circulated among his family, friends, and fans.

Other creators became successful sideways. Indiana "Indy" Neidell was hired to host *The Great War*, a one-of-a-kind interactive YouTube series produced in Berlin about World War I, told in real time one hundred years on. He landed the job and became centrally involved in the interactive design and production of the series after he was discovered on his own YouTube channel, WatchSundayBaseball, a channel dedicated to the "weirdness and coolness of 150 years of professional baseball history" (Neidell 2016). (*The Great War* is profiled in chapter 6.)

Adolescence marks the entry point for the typical creator we interviewed. This remarkably youthful demographic profile mitigates the fear of failure and almost demands risk taking and experimentation, but also leaves many unprepared for success. Regarding SME 1.0 creators, Big Frame manager Byron Austin Ashley notes, "[M]any of them never worked elsewhere and never went to college" (Ashley 2015). Ashley's comment is not about privilege but about age, since most of them started when they were still living at home and in school. Early success often meant they never had to pursue work or attend college. Beauty vlogger Ingrid Nilsen, who incubated her YouTube career in the bathroom of her Berkeley university dorm, mentioned, "Had I gone the traditional 9-to-5 route, I would have sat there with regrets. By then, I was already making more money than I would at an entry-level job" (Nilsen 2015). Contrast Nilsen's account with the average aspirant in Hollywood, an industry notorious for requiring years of underpaid dues paying and apprenticeship in toxic and demanding positions.

Big Frame's Ashley continues by noting that sudden fame can overwhelm young creators. "A lot of them turn to religion because they can't explain what happened and why they can no longer go out in public" (Ashley 2015). Although Ashley did not specify, he might have referenced Kevin Wu, aka KevJumba, one of the earliest and most successful Asian American creators who disappeared suddenly from YouTube in 2013 with over three million subscribers and two hundred million views on YouTube. He has since returned in early 2017 with videos promoting his faith in Buddhism and describing his recovery from a car accident, and an original satirical rap music video called "Internet Power" that criticizes social media celebrity. We also profile Michelle Phan's career, which bears similarities to Wu's, in chapter 4.

Training and the Division of Labor

Very few creators have had formal education or training in video production. Older creators, if they hold formal qualifications, tend to have had IT or business backgrounds. Creator skills are often learned in situ and through experimentation. But the communicative affordances of social media have also introduced a set of more communal, supportive, mentoring, and collaborative labor practices. These practices suggest distinctively new forms of power relations within creator labor in contrast to the notoriously competitive conditions of Hollywood that require years of apprenticeships, dues paying, and networking before receiving tenuous acceptance into the "club."

Creators frequently mentioned the support garnered from their mentors, usually more experienced creators. This "pay it forward" mentality extends to recent creators, many of whom were initially the most engaged members of the first-gen creators' fan communities. Boone Langston, a low-level toy unboxing creator, said,

I do find value in talking about the workings of YouTube to explain how it works to seek and give advice. . . . It might have been Shay Carl [a prominent YouTuber and cofounder of Maker Studios] who said, "I came through a really big door . . . I'm going to bring as many people with me . . . to find success with me." That would be why a group like that works . . . because everyone on there believes they have as much a shot at a million views as the next person. (Langston 2016)

The mentoring relationship between high-achieving creators and emerging creators can often lead to on-screen collaborations. Beauty vlogger Westbrook described how these practices are very welcome but not without risk: "YouTubers are going to gravitate to one another. You go to events, you meet people, you say, 'Let's collaborate.' If you love the same things, then it makes sense. I did one forced collaboration once and it was horrible. My audience hated it, her audience hated it. Today, I only collaborate with friends" (Westbrook 2015).

In the course of the brief history of this industry, various organizations have integrated creator pedagogy as part of their service offering. As we will see in chapter 3, SME intermediaries like multichannel networks offered tutorials early in SME 1.0. These low-touch and programmatic resources were designed to assist their signed creators with developing their brands, channels, content, and communities and boosting their commercial return, from which these firms also benefited. In the SME 2.0 phase, platforms have begun to offer their own versions, harnessing deeper capital and resources, designed to encourage greater platform loyalty while undercutting the value offered by these intermediaries. YouTube, for example, has put in place a global network of "Spaces," often in partnership with formal media training schools, along with an extensive online training regime called the Creator Academy (also discussed in chapter 3).

Some aspects of creator training, particularly in the better-resourced YouTube Spaces, would look familiar to film schools: industry standard cameras, green screen technology, and attention to scriptwriting, performance, and editing. But what differentiates this training is the way it is wrapped completely in an entrepreneurial ethos and platform and community management—Spreadability 101. Video courses offered in the

Figure 2.2. YouTube Space (Los Angeles). YouTube Spaces offer resources and training to foster platform and community management. Photo by David Craig.

Creator Academy, with titles like "Build Your YouTube Community—Featuring Kalista Elaine" (2017) and "How Collaboration Can Help Your YouTube Channel Grow (ft. LaToya Forever & King of Random)" (2017) are typical.

Media production was neither a skill these creators had mastered nor one they spent large sums of money to learn. Compared to traditional media talent, many of whom honed their craft in school or local theater, these amateurs were often self-taught, sometimes using the tutorials they watched on YouTube delivered by other creators. Joey Graceffa, who had been rejected by film schools, started off making short films and sketch comedy before he joined YouTube with little concern for an audience. He "would make these random, stupid videos for myself" (Graceffa

2015). In our interview with Bria and Chrissy, a midlevel lesbian creator couple who have featured their sexual orientation, relationship, music, and activism in their content, Bria Kam admitted,

> I'd never been behind the camera, really. . . . And neither of us had any knowledge about the industry, like how to make a video. We didn't even know people who were YouTubers! We had a Flip camera. Our first couple of videos were on a Flip camera. And it's grainy, and horrible, and the audio is just ridiculous. (Kam and Chambers 2015)

As we discovered with numerous creators, Bria and Chrissy developed their self-taught production skills and, until recently, did all the work themselves. The lack of formalized education may prove fortuitous as creators may be less inhibited in developing their own production practices not taught, and possibly discouraged, in traditional media programs. As Big Frame's Ashley described, they have to "get their hands dirty," including collaborating with other creators and continuously testing their production values until these practices become more "turnkey." The downside of cultivating SME production values is that the core Hollywood skills of acting, screenwriting, or directing remain underdeveloped if they were to attempt the transition to main media.

The means of creation and production afford not only low-budget production but virtually no division of labor except at the top tiers of the SME. The creator has replaced the writer, producer, director, and actor above the line, as well as the editor, location scout, composer, and visual effects supervisor and other craft laborers below the line. As Gigi Gorgeous commented, "I'm in front of the camera—makeup, hair, glam. I definitely love the producing aspect, I love directing" (Gorgeous 2015).

Even as producing skills become more sophisticated, and a division of labor is embedded, the challenge is to keep from emulating traditional media content. (We argue in chapter 4 that this is one of the hallmarks driving claims to authenticity in SME.) According to Barry Blumberg, manager for Smosh,

> [W]hen you're on YouTube and you watch a Smosh video, especially a Smosh video from six or seven years ago, we hired actors. We wrote scripts. We had full-scale productions. But we didn't want it to look like

a television show or movie. We wanted it to look just slightly out of reach from what the audience does. . . . And when I watch a guy play video games on YouTube for hours on end. . . . [I'm] not watching the professional gamer who's so great and never fails. [I'm] watching the guy who's kind of a little better than [I am]. . . . There's a relationship. (Blumberg 2015)

Nonetheless, invisible forms of labor operate in both traditional media and creator labor. The former is reflected in the work of network and studio creative executives who have been denied producing credit on their projects while sharing many of the same creative and producing responsibilities as creative producers. The latter is reflected in the lack of credits on most creator videos that acknowledge little other production assistance.

Early creators, particularly those producing scripted fare, were quick to launch and pivot towards more traditional production companies, albeit with mixed results. Freddie Wong created the successful *Videogame High School* series that appealed to large gamer audiences that helped Wong secure YouTube subsidization, project-based crowd funding, and Lionsgate investment. Wong subsequently launched Rocketjump.com—"a weird hybrid/studio production company"—but with great caution. Wong warns, "Hollywood production is too expensive, you can't spend as much on content. At Rocketjump, we run a lean operation and look at the world as platform agnostic" (Wong 2015).

Similarly, along with Felicia Day, Kim Evey was part of the successful team that created *The Guild*, another gamer-oriented scripted web series that was bought by Xbox. Evey and Day launched their own production company, Geek and Sundry; however, Evey soon left the company to return to her own producing and performing roots. "I didn't want to be an executive behind a desk. I wanted to be in the mix, actively participating in all aspects of production" (Evey 2015).

As the far-less-traditional, non-IP or format-oriented vlogger creators have emerged successfully in SME, they have hired production teams and signed up for representation. In numerous interviews, creators not only mentioned their assistants, editors, managers, publicists, and agents but brought them to interview as their "partners." This included family members. In the case of beauty vlogger Tati Westbrook, her husband is a partner-producer. For prominent Viner Brent Rivera, who has run his business while living at home and attending high school, his father screened our phone call approaching him for an interview as well as our followup call. However, for these vloggers, the discourses of authenticity and direct appeals to community, as featured in chapter 4, limit growth. As Wong (2015) pointed out, "For YouTube stars, Vine personalities, and Tencent celebrities, the value is in personality and taking a community-oriented approach and, with more platforms, more personalities are finding success. However, scale is difficult with that kind of video." In the quest for sustainability, creators may represent the apotheosis of start-up precarity and further indicate the need for strategic media management, as discussed in chapter 3. As creator publicist Tess Finkle warns, "If they are cute now, they should bank the money, buy real estate, get the right team to manage their career" (Finkle 2015).

At the top level, large enterprises like Hank and John Green's Vlog-brothers represent what Blumberg, Smosh's manager, refers to as the "biggest economic stars to come out of YouTube" (Blumberg 2015). The complexity of production depends on format and distribution platform, according to Hank Green (the Greens are profiled in chapter 4):

> We have around thirty people working for us, mostly producing SciShow, Crash Course, and our other shows. Vlogbrothers is still just me and John. These people are grouped into teams that occasionally branch off and help each other or help start new shows when someone has a good idea. We also have an events team that works on VidCon and our new event, NerdCon: Stories. And we have our merchandise company, DFTBA Records, which has three on-staff people but scales to have as many as fifteen people working during the holiday season. (Green 2015a)

Production assistance also varies depending on the content and format but also extends to assistance throughout all dimensions of production labor. According to Graceffa, his creator team is "pretty big," including up to five members of his producing team, coupled with a business manager, a lawyer, an assistant, and an editor. Scripted fare requires greater collaboration whereas "vlogging and social media are both more independent" (Graceffa 2015). Graceffa's comment goes to the more complex nature of scripted production, which demands much more up-front capital and several stages of script development, talent packaging involving actors and directors, more diverse craft skills, and post-production. In contrast, for less complex content like vlogging, creator labor can require little more than a camera, light kit, audio, and editing skills.

Working Conditions

The vast majority of creators, however, run their YouTube channels in a full-time sole-trader capacity (or with intimate partners or other family members). Most spend between fifty and sixty hours a week on their channel or channels. Production times for each video will vary depending on set arrangements, and the degree of simplicity or complication involved (especially in cooking and makeup videos) but on average a creator might spend between three and seven hours filming a video. Editing is generally more time consuming, and takes between five and eight hours per video. Depending on the channel, a number of hours are spent researching and trialing new ideas before filming, shopping for necessary associated products and/or ingredients, and managing the business side.

These conditions can be as onerous as they are precarious. As Duffy's (2017) research shows, aspirational creator labor is often disappointed. Yet, in all our encounters with creators, even as working conditions may be worsening, none were looking for an exit strategy and all emphasized the creative rewards of their careers:

> I work constantly, whether it is filming, editing, e-mails or social media. It is a lot of work and I spend the majority of my time dedicated to it. Sometimes I don't feel like I'm actually working when I'm working, and that makes it difficult to keep track of how much work I am putting in. I love it so much that I don't even have a regular schedule. I just want to be able to access it whenever I feel inspired. (Maroun 2015)

For other creators, the demands of creator labor are carefully weighed against other lines of work. Brian is the father of Gabe and Garrett, the stars of their own toy unboxing channel. (To ensure privacy, the family's last name was withheld in our interview and throughout all publicity for the channel.) Brian described how his family videos stored on You-Tube turned into "passive residual income." He could pursue his dream of running a family business from home, albeit not without recriminations that signal another set of concerns regarding working conditions for underage creators.

> A lot of people will just say, "You are using your kids just to make money." They don't get it. Would it be better for me to work forty, fifty, sixty hours a week away from them to make money? Or we could work together as a family on something that just happens to be an income source and we get to spend all this time together having fun? (Gabe and Garrett channel 2016)

These work conditions operate in stark contrast to those of traditional media and other industries. For some, the opportunity to work from home and spend more time with their families while still managing to sustain an income is a dream come true. Jason Pinder, who runs the Simple Cooking Channel, was very happy to give up a counseling job and yet be able to support a growing family, be at home more, and pursue a passion without needing to become a celebrity (Pinder 2015). However, there is, for some, a sense of culture shock as they move into a career that sees them work constantly, within a massive online community, but also essentially alone. According to beauty and fashion and lifestyle creator Rachel Anderson, "[O]ur phone numbers are the only personal connection we have to the people that are part of our real lives" (Anderson 2015). Similarly, beauty and lifestyle creator Wendy Huang remarks that her work "gets very lonely, you don't know who to talk to and no one really understands what it is you're doing. All your other friends have regular jobs and regular lives" (Huang 2015). For some creators hoping to take time off, managing a break from the routine means developing an inventory. For Jason Pinder of the SimpleCookingChannel,

> I have eight or nine things up my sleeve at any given time so that I can have some time off if I am unable to work or have a holiday. When we were expecting a new baby I knew I was going to take a month off, but I had a library of about forty videos ready to upload. (Pinder 2015)

Community Engagement as Relational Labor

The SME business is a radical hybrid of production and community development and maintenance. These are diverse, constantly iterative practices that vary from creator to creator and are dependent upon the communicative affordances of the different platforms that are also constantly changing. A short list of these practices includes liking, sharing, posting and responding to comments, visiting the sites of other creators and members of the fan community to interact, featuring behind-the-scenes content on channels or platforms, and more. These practices are vital to the success and sustainability of a creator's brand. As noted by United Talent Agency (UTA) agent Brent Weinstein,

> The biggest thing is understanding the nature of community building and maintenance. In the past, actors, writers, directors, producers—they only had to focus on making something, and there were always these marketing guys who would handle the digital distribution, the awareness angle. Your digital stars today have to not only be really great content creators, they have to know how to build and maintain community. (Weinstein 2015)

Across any single platform, creators spend an inordinate amount of time interacting with their community, managing comments, and exploring new opportunities for fan engagement. For a mother, Simone Kelly, overseeing the careers of her children in Charli's Crafty Kitchen, managing comments on YouTube is a complicated and involved process of quarantining trolls amid the hundreds of daily comments, maintaining a professional look ("You do not want a brand looking at your channel and seeing inappropriate comments or anything like that" [Kelly 2015]) but also allowing the children to answer some questions.

These practices reflect creators' deep knowledge of the features and affordances of these platforms. Big Frame manager Ashley claims, "[I]t doesn't require much effort to teach them on fan engagement. They are 'naturally gifted'" (Ashley 2015). However, as found in multiple interviews, like their production-oriented skills, these practices were developed through years of trial and error and experimentation, including the communal pedagogy of the creator community.

Community engagement may or may not be commercialized. YouTube and, to a limited degree, Facebook are the only platforms that provide partnership agreements and programmatic advertising. Other platforms like YouTube Red, Twitch, and Vimeo offer subscription fees. However, the lack of commercial features does not mean a lack of commercial affordances, and these practices may be communicative and commercial, particularly if featured as part of an influencer marketing campaign (to be explained in the next section).

Community maintenance may or may not be deemed content. In these practices, the lines between content and promotion is admittedly blurred, at some times more conspicuously than at others. For example, numerous creators have second YouTube channels or live-streaming channels that feature behind-the-scenes footage of their preparation for creating and producing content that will air later on their monetized platforms. Tweets and comments often encourage their community to tune in to their monetized content on YouTube channels. Instagram photos may tease audiences about upcoming video fare. In this regard, there is some continuity between traditional media content and promotion, particularly with the rise of social media marketing for film and television.

The fact that responding to fan feedback is largely nonscalable and can occupy easily 50% of working life applies no matter how high one climbs in the SME universe. Joey Graceffa agreed that he spends probably an equal amount of time vlogging and responding to comments. "For the first hour that I post a video. Then I'm replying to probably one hundred to two hundred comments [on YouTube]. And then after that, I'll go to Twitter and respond on Twitter. It's a lot of work to do that on a daily basis" (Graceffa 2015).

As the number of platforms grows and technological features change, so do the array of community management practices. Over time, creators develop more formalized production and programming management strategies, including a schedule for regularly uploading content. Whereas in traditional media, the production company may have little say over when the film or television series premieres, scheduling falls within the purview of the creator's practice. With the help of her assistant, beauty vlogger Nilsen generates a production report featuring a design, preproduction, production, editing, and uploading schedule. In her case, as a brand ambassador for multiple beauty products, her content must integrate the product and coordinate with the brand's schedules, creating a complicated array of concerns for programming management.

These practices create a set of expectations for their fan community and advertising partners but also are difficult for creators to manage around the clock. German game player and prominent SME thought leader Fabien Siegismund described the challenges he faces with managing community expectations, which can sometimes turn about in unexpected ways.

> The last couple of weeks I have pretty much ignored YouTube as I had so many different jobs and no time to do that. But my community knows that and I have trained them . . . told them: "Guys, this is a hobby. If for two weeks there's no videos, don't unsubscribe. Don't hate. It's just the channel." I can't change it, and they are fine with that. Actually, if I do a lot of videos people will say "Slow down, think about your family and give yourself a break." (Siegismund 2016)

Siegismund's comment reflects the deeply relational nature of the creator-community bond that makes the affective labor of creators more demanding and more foundational to their identity and business than with traditional media celebrity and fandom.

As Baym (2015) proposed, relational labor blurs the line between the social and the economic, extending beyond pure self-promotion and demanding that artists "connect with their audiences." The relationship between creators and their communities is even more intimate and dialogical. As publicist Leila Marsh described, "The talent doesn't refer to it as an audience; instead, [the audience is] community, they're fans, they're viewers, they're friends" (Marsh 2015). The interactive and communicative practices of community management feature unique appeals to community and authenticity, as described in chapter 4. These practices also create a kind of virtual production loop in which the community's interests and feedback inform the design and production of creators' content.

SME 2.0 and Multiplatform Practice

In March 2017, Snap, the parent company for Snapchat, went public and, on its first day, was valued at $34 billion, which was three times higher than Twitter, which was twice as old. This valuation was driven by the platform's rapid growth, particularly among young users worldwide, driven in part by the way SME creators have used this platform. Nonetheless, as reported in Buzzfeed, prominent Snapchat influencers earning as much as eighty thousand dollars per brand campaign felt neglected by the platform and abandoned it for Facebook-owned Instagram. According to a social influencer manager, "Where it [Snapchat] used to be the primary platform they were making content for, now it's like a secondary platform where they'll make content for other platforms and repost it on Snapchat" (Kantrowitz 2017).

One of the hallmark features that distinguishes the first and second phases of SME is that spreadability has gone into overdrive; production and uploading take place across multiple platforms. The multichannel and multiplatform practices of creator labor contribute to complex and exhausting labor conditions but also inform risk-management strategies to avoid platform precarity. These practices include the design, production, and circulation of several formats, depending on the affordances of the platform. The same video content is not simply posted across platforms, since content players vary in length, as do reception practices between laptop platforms and mobile applications. Creator Zach King started his career making YouTube videos but migrated to Vine, which allowed him to develop his "digital magic" format. King says, "That's what I love about different platforms. They give you different rules and boundaries" (King 2015). Like most creators, King does not rely solely on one platform, even if that platform provides specific affordances to generate his content, especially when platforms continue to experience precarity. King subsequently added Snapchat as a platform for his content, only to determine that the platform did not afford him the opportunity to be as creative as Vine did. With the demise of Vine, King migrated over to Instagram, where he has eighteen million followers, as well as to Twitter and Facebook.

Similarly, Covergirl glambassador and LGBTQ activist Ingrid Nilsen describes a set of platform practices that reflect strategic design:

> Facebook is just to announce a video. Instagram and Snapchat are my sacred platforms where brands do not enter, unless there's some kind of grandfathered deal like Covergirl. There are no brands on my second

channel, TheGridMonster, which consists of me talking about more personal topics. The Ingrid Channel is for DIY and lifestyles, which is where I can't fully have a conversation, but it will spark a conversation that I'll post on Gridmonster, which serves as an extra outlet for me. I have a private Tumblr account that allows me to see what others are posting, and then I'll discuss them in my videos. I like to be the observer on Tumblr. (Nilsen 2015)

Nilsen's strategic multiplatform practice was often evidenced in our interviews with creators and recalls well the circulation practices Jenkins and colleagues describe in *Spreadable Media* (Jenkins, Ford, and Green 2013).

For some creators, platforms include not only social media but film and television, for which distinctions are drawn with regard to the design, production, and circulation of content. These represent multiple challenges as well as opportunities for these creators. Premier creators Rhett McLaughlin and Lincoln Neal (Rhett & Link) own multiple channels on YouTube that feature several formats, but they have also operated cross-industry, starting with earlier work on the IFC channel and forthcoming scripted work for web and television.

> The vast majority of content is on Good Mythical Morning [GMM] and Good Mythical More. On and off we also have weekend series; right now we're doing an animated series based on a live series where we did song biscuits. GMM is the beast that is constantly being fed; when we do release on GMM, that's our core audience who needs to know about it and take action on it. What started as a side project to make a connection with our fans back in 2011 when we were doing our scripted IFC series started as an experiment that quickly turned into something that people wanted. We have no interest in turning off GMM, but we are continuously interested in doing other things. Break it down, half our time on GMM, half on other projects. . . . [W]e really want to get into comedic narrative scripted content, whether web series, features. (McLaughlin and Neal 2015)

Across a single platform, creators often feature several playlists, formats, and verticals and operate multiple channels. The Greens have cre-

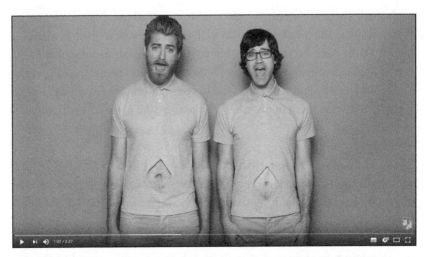

Figure 2.3. Rhett & Link, YouTubers who work successfully across both SME and traditional media industries. Rhett & Link, https://www.youtube.com/watch?v =TO8gAvl59Kw.

ated many formats on their Vlogbrothers channel, where they feature mostly vlog posts discussing contemporary topics and events. They also have other YouTube channels like Crash Course, on which colleague creators discuss educational topics. In addition to their own personal channels, Ian Hecox and Anthony Padilla of Smosh have another nine channels, including two comedy channels, a channel for cartoons, gameplay, French- and Spanish-language channels, and more. Similarly, Graceffa has his main vlog channel but also a gameplay channel.

These practices serve several purposes that belie the normative conventions of "typecasting" experienced in traditional media. They allow creators to experiment with more or less potentially monetizable forms of content. But these channels also allow the creator to explore other forms of expression. As we have seen, beauty vlogger Nilsen has her main YouTube channel for makeup and lifestyle tutorials but also a separate channel under a different name (TheGridMonster). This second channel is often voluntarily demonetized and often features political topics, such as her interview of President Obama. Musician and vlogger Louna Maroun manages three independent channels that focus on musicianship, makeup tutorials, and vlogging, and views the work involved in managing three channels as comparable to that of managing one, while her additional channels allow her to focus on different aspects of her online personae.

The increasing competition in the creator community, especially with the more prominent and distinctive content verticals on platforms, places added pressures and precarity on creator labor.

> If you're a gaming YouTuber, you're competing for a share of voice with every other single gaming YouTuber. And the more popular the game, the more people you compete with. There are a lot of people who have made it big on YouTube in gaming, and the majority of them are Minecrafters. And those that have made it big are now very influential. So to start a YouTube channel on Minecraft now is really hard, unless you have something ridiculously different or new to show. (Kouvchinov 2015)

Competition does not only come from other YouTubers, with a growing range of creators gaining significant followers on platforms like Instagram and Periscope that, while they may not offer creators Ad-Sense revenue, have gained the attention of brands seeking to reach target audiences. And creators are increasingly competing with the brands themselves, who are able to significantly outspend them in terms of promotion on social media. For example, one YouTuber interviewed uses Facebook to connect with her thirty-five thousand followers in hopes of driving them to her YouTube channel. On viewing her analytics she found that only twenty-two hundred of her followers had seen her post, with only 154 actively responding. She then used Facebook's "Boost Post" paid promotion feature, paying around two thousand dollars for her post to appear prominently on eighty-one thousand (fan base plus "friends of friends") people's pages. (This carries no guarantee against AdBlocking software.) But, she argues, she is competing with brand producers who regularly spend upwards of fifty thousand dollars on a single Facebook status post on a promotion that may run for more than a week (Grimstone 2015).

Working within Algorithmic Culture

We noted earlier in the chapter the doubts raised by critical theorists about the presence of progressive or alternative voices in social media because of its pervasive algorithmic culture. There is no question that the power that the platform holds is asymmetrical. An elaborated early instance is the plangent account of "what it's like being sacked by a Google algorithm" (Winter 2011). This is the story of Dylan Winter, an English freelance journalist and filmmaker, and it reveals rare details of the financial interactions with Google of the then ninety-seventh biggest "reporter" on YouTube globally and seventh in the UK. Despite being a very successful contributor to YouTube and a valuable generator of attention to the ads placed next to his content by AdSense, Google's advertising placement company, he infringed a contract that was "designed so that it was almost impossible not to break the Google rules" (Winter 2011).

What algorithmic culture usually means for creators, however, is just more work resulting from having to manage the relationship between the quantitative feedback generated by the data analytics stream from Google's AdSense and many multichannel networks' suites of business analytics, and the qualitative feedback offered freely by the fan base. For many creators, the extra work is often not justified by the enhancements offered by the data feed.

Given the critical role of high-touch community management, creators cannot rely on data analytics alone for either management of their channels or adequate revenue derived from programmatic advertising. Single-platform analytics (such as the standard dashboard available to YouTube partners) are not sufficient and often induce information overload without real analytical insight. Managing community interaction cross-platform—vital for maintaining authenticity and maximizing promotion—significantly extends creators' workload. Unlimited word counts on Facebook often mean trying to limit the workload by attempting to direct engagement to Twitter, for example.

The network affordances of platforms facilitate a highly iterative design and development process by creators, supercharged by algorithmic feedback. For some creators, like Kumar, the demands of algorithmic culture are like a virtual gilded cage. He laments that he has become about the "numbers" and "analytics"—a practice that generates resentment and conflict with the demands of authenticity (which we analyze in chapter 4). "I don't want to be tailoring my creative to reach my numbers. I want it to remain more organic" (Kumar 2015). For others, like

Australian creator Sarah Grimstone, algorithmic practice can be more diagnostic than prescriptive, which contributes to confusion over clarity.

> It's just information overload. When you get analytics that tell you your retention rate is 35%, or your clickable link rate is 65% . . . what are the factors that play into that? I go away from analytics going, "I need to improve my retention rate," but what does that mean for YouTube videos? Does that mean I talk about a different topic? Does that mean I change the editing? Do I go shorter or do I go longer? What is it? Ultimately, it is just trial and error. (Grimstone 2015)

The communicative affordances of different platforms also pose unique and precarious challenges for creators. Managing interaction across several social media accounts—vital for maintaining authenticity and maximizing promotion—significantly extends their workload:

> Facebook is one of the hardest mediums to respond to. I have about two hundred Facebook messages sitting unanswered because every time I look at it I get overwhelmed. But often if I don't respond people get angry at me. The thing with Facebook, compared to Twitter, is because of the unlimited word count you get people that write really long essays about their life and you feel like you need to respond with a lengthy reply as well. You can't reply to a follower spilling their heart with a quick one sentence. You want to sit down, read through it, reflect, and respond. Times that by fifty to a hundred a day and it becomes an overwhelming task. Now I just ask people to tweet at me—140 characters, short and sharp, I can keep on top of that. (Huang 2015)

As we have already said, the dispersal of SME reception around the world complicates life even as it can be highly remunerative for creators. As we note in chapter 6, it is estimated that 80% of YouTube traffic comes from outside the United States, and 60% of creators' views come from outside their home country. Australian creators, for example, are at the very high end of this dispersal. Because English affords relative ease of international passage, about 90% of Australian-originated content is consumed outside the country. This has meant a disproportionately high per capita number of high-end (one million-plus subscribers) creators, but it also means that Australian creators work in a regime of flipped hemispheres, needing to embed their community management practices into the rhythms of overwhelmingly northern hemisphere seasons, major holidays, language vernaculars, and product ranges.

SME Business Models

In October 2016, *60 Minutes* aired a segment called "The Influencers" featuring interviews with SME creators, including Kim Kardashian. When prompted, Kardashian acknowledged that social media was most responsible for her fame and success. The interviewer demurs, suggesting that she has no appreciable "talent," in comparison to other influencers who can do comedy, sing, or dance. Nonetheless, the interviewer mentions, Kardashian has created an "empire worth in excess of $100 million." Kardashian responds, "I would think that involves some kind of talent" (Whitaker 2016).

Thus far in this chapter, we have explored the distinctive characteristics of SME production practices. We now turn to the business models on which the possibility of sustainable careers may be built.

But first, given the fundamental nature of this distinction, it is worth outlining the IP ownership model in traditional media. IP rights ownership can be split among an often complicated, contested, and unwieldy array of stakeholders and participants. These can include financing, production, and distribution partners coupled with underlying literary, brand, or life rights holders. In addition, the collaborative nature of traditional media production has resulted in complex formulas for providing residual payments to writers, producers, directors, and actors, who have earned their piece of the pie through guild-backed bargaining agreements.

Over the last few decades, Hollywood has been distinguished by its ability to extract maximum value in the age of vertically and horizontally integrated media conglomerates that pursue ownership and market share of media content and distribution. With some variation, Hollywood conglomerates create entertainment intellectual properties (IP) from which diverse forms of commercialized transmedia content can be generated, including multiple films, television, books, music, and more. For some firms, the value lies outside media, in merchandising and licensing. For example, while the film and television sectors of Disney generate the highest revenue, more than 75% of Disney's profit growth comes from its consumer products and parks and resorts. Disney films, which generate only 16% of corporate profits, operate as IP incubators, half-billion-dollar advertisements for selling plush toys and theme park rides.

This SoCal IP-ownership model, which is designed to create scarcity through copyright to monetize by controlling and sequestering scarce and premium content, contrasts markedly with NoCal's spreadability model. YouTube initially sought neither to finance, produce, license, nor purchase creator content. As described in chapter 1, steeped in Silicon Valley values of scalable technological innovation and driven by the safe-harbor protections of the DMCA, SME platforms tried to bypass the messy and complicated IP ownership and control model. Even with the shared commercial practices of advertising, platforms have cut out the proverbial middleman by introducing fully automated programmatic advertising with the added advantage of social analytics capable of delivering more targeted viewers to advertisers. An index of the strength of the spreadability model in creator culture was in evidence when the Fine Bros tried to trademark and license a popular video format in 2016. They are producers of one of the biggest reaction video formats and sought to trademark the term "react"—a term that is widely used by other creators. They were called out by other creators, and at one point they were losing ten thousand followers an hour (Foxx 2016). Strongly normative assumptions about spreadability in SME restrict core aspects of SoCal wealth creation.

As we have outlined in chapter 1, YouTube's business proposition from 2007 was based on partnership agreements and programmatic advertising and offered the first array of commercialization prospects to previously amateur creators. Talent agent Weinstein captured this: "[T]hat first generation really introduced the power of YouTube to the world [SME 1.0], but it was the next generation [SME 2.0] that figured out how to leverage YouTube into lasting brands and powerful careers" (Weinstein 2015).

The carrot-and-stick architecture of "partnerships" and revenue sharing generated by an algorithm under Google's control was both the first mover in commercializing online video content and the source of greatest precariousness. There is a history of "tweaking" partnership agreements, the algorithm itself, as well as the rates of return through AdSense based on the traditional advertising metric of CPMs. (Cost per mille, where mille is French for thousand, often becomes clicks per mille in SME.)

For the platform, the economics of scale have generated repeated gains in advertising revenue over time. For the creators, programmatic advertising has turned out to be a false promise or, as Hank Green refers to it, "a kinda shitty model" (Green 2015a). The visibility of the creator is often in inverse relation to his or her viability. In Gaby Dunn's heartfelt lament, "Get Rich or Die Vlogging: The Sad Economics of Internet Fame" (2015), she argues that "[m]any famous social media stars are too visible to have 'real' jobs, but too broke not to." Chapter 1 shows that, as YouTube continues to scale globally and more advertising is driven over from traditional media, the platform has continued to witness revenue growth. On the back of creator labor, YouTube is now well placed to contribute to, rather than draw on, Google's coffers. But for individual creators, the CPMs that were promised at twenty-five dollars with initial partnerships have since collapsed to around two dollars or less, depending on the nature of the content. The massive growth in scale of SME content has destroyed value even as the CPM rate on YouTube has bottomed out. Except for top creators, the best AdSense can do is provide some "bread and butter" (Pinder 2015).

The platform has sought to accommodate to the collapse of CPMs by packaging high-end and brand-safe creators into their Google Preferred advertising programs. While this policy benefits certain creators, this pattern also emulates the scarcity model of cable television advertising. (As cable networks reached full distribution and caps on potential subscription fees, they were forced to change programming to attract larger audiences and secure premium advertising.)

Meanwhile, YouTube partnership agreements have also changed over time. Although creators are subject to nondisclosure agreements, it is well known that some premium creators secure higher revenue participation from the platform. Through their Google Preferred plan, YouTube can secure higher CPM programmatic advertising rates by bundling "brand-friendly, premium creators" to advertisers. For low-level and emerging YouTubers, the path towards success grows more challenging over time as they encounter obstacles placed by the platforms themselves. Continuing to shift features, services, and requirements for creators, in 2017, YouTube established a floor of ten thousand views before ads will run and creators can earn money. This policy change was deemed an attempt to "weed out bad actors," like nonlegitimate creators uploading other creators' content, but it also reintroduced barriers of entry for newcomers (Popper 2017).

YouTube's technological innovations can have a cascading effect through its ecology, often affecting certain creators more than others. YouTube's IP control software Content ID has been effective in making the platform less cluttered with infringing content and therefore more welcoming to brands and advertisers. But it has also produced overkill for creators. The collapse of AdSense revenue has been doubly impacted by the Content ID algorithm sending all revenue from flagged content back to the rights holder and leaving the creator on his or her own to appeal a decision that bespeaks little due process. An aspiring musician covers a popular song in the hope that it will lead viewers to their own original content. However, in one case, over a period of twenty-eight days, one such creator received 815,000 views, which equated to only thirteen dollars through AdSense. Her top five videos—being cover versions of copyrighted material—earned zero dollars, with only her eighth-most-watched video, which gained thirteen thousand views, paying one dollar for ten thousand views (Grimstone 2015).

YouTube's Content ID system is not the only technology that makes algorithmic judgments on content while generating concerns for YouTube creators. In 2010, the platform introduced their Restricted Mode feature that allowed viewers, particularly parents and schools, to restrict certain forms of content. In early 2017, LGBTQ creators discovered that their content was being censored and deemed "potentially objectionable" for those channels in restricted mode. This limits not only audience but also advertising for prominent creators, although YouTube rushed out a response claiming to correct this problem. This rapid response underlines the value of the LGBTQ community to YouTube, which is further discussed in chapter 5.

Perhaps the greatest precarity faced by YouTube creators is the repeated changes in algorithms. These changes can sometimes generate a steep and sudden loss of viewers and revenue with little recourse by creators. Repeated efforts to reverse engineer YouTube's algorithm have proven fruitless, particularly since the algorithm was revealed to be controlled by "Deep Neural Networks" or, rather, artificial intelligence (Covington, Adams, and Sargin 2016). This advanced technology has created a black box in which the platform's computers engage in "distributed learning" to develop sophisticated recommendation systems that not even their engineers understand.

SME 2.0 Business Models

SME 2.0 ushers in a period of greater creator entrepreneurialism—in Weinstein's words, this is when creators "figured out how to leverage YouTube into lasting brands and powerful careers" (Weinstein 2015). The rise of competing platforms with other affordances has contributed to new forms of commercial prospects, although only Facebook and Twitch offer revenue-sharing partnerships, often limited to their premium creators. In addition, advertisers have developed new practices that exploit the intimate but nonetheless transactional relationship between creators and their communities. Creators have dealt with this rapidly changing landscape by engaging a wide range of business models using but not limited to the IP exploitation strategies of traditional media. Weinstein speaks of this creator entrepreneurialism and innovation: "The mentality of a digital creator is not about preparing for when opportunity knocks, they're creating the opportunity themselves. Digital stars are more proactive and more aggressive about taking their careers into their own hands than any generation we've ever seen before in the video business" (Weinstein 2015).

SME 2.0 business models start with revenue derivable from single platforms, including programmatic advertising, subscriptions, transactional downloads, and virtual goods. In addition, operating across multiple platforms is the basis for the more lucrative practices of influencer marketing and sponsorship. More recognizable IP ownership and licensing models include content and format packaging, sales and distribution across social and traditional media platforms in domestic and international markets, and licensing and marketing of products, brands, and services, especially through e-commerce sites that create higher return with limited risk. Fees and royalties can be earned in traditional media whether as a performer, writer, director, host, contestant, or reality star, or through book or music sales. Live performance fees, whether touring or paid appearances, are also very significant, as are crowd funding and subscriptions through platforms like Kickstarter and Patreon.

Necessity is the mother of invention: the constant disruption by YouTube's NoCal pivots has long since demanded that creators pursue other revenue-generating opportunities, starting with other platforms, including YouTube-owned platforms. We have noted in chapter 1 that YouTube has launched sister platforms featuring other forms that vary the AVOD business model, including YouTube Red's subscription platform, which Green regarded as "good for independent creators" (Green 2015a). Other platforms like Vimeo and the short-lived Vessel have also offered subscription plans to premium content creators. Amazon's Video Direct platform has made available to all creators its partnership plans, which feature multiple revenue models, including advertising, subscription, rental, or purchase with an advertiser split of 55/45 like YouTube.

Platforms have introduced other commercial features that are generating revenue opportunities for creators. Twitch, a live broadcasting and gaming platform purchased by Amazon for $1 billion in 2014, is closely aligned with the videogame industry, including Amazon-owned Blizzard entertainment, and has focused on the online game content sector. This sector includes "recorded gameplay, reviews, and anything that engages the gaming community" (Brouwer 2015b). As a result, the game industry helps fund Twitch creators through sponsorship and advertising, which totaled nearly $1.6 billion in 2015. In addition, Twitch offers its creators revenue-generating features from subscriptions to donations via their Twitch Tip Jar feature that allows fans to send virtual goods to their favorite gamers. Twitch Tips generates far more revenue than what creators are earning either on YouTube Live or on Facebook Live (Le 2016). The development of live-streaming may presage a new stage, SME 3.0, which we contemplate in the conclusion.

Influencer Marketing

We regard the term "influencer" the same way that Jenkins, Ford, and Green regard the term "viral" (2013). It is a marketing term that connotes a one-way relationship, precisely of influence *on* a relatively passive receiving audience. We use it—under advisement—as it has widespread legibility.

As we have seen, Instagram features prominently in the development of influencer marketing and a larger "influencer economy." Instagram does not share advertising revenue with its creators like YouTube's partner program; rather, its "partner program" refers to its B2B platform connecting advertisers with influencer marketing firms and tech companies. However, the platform offers a form of passive or complicit partnership by creating the brand-safe affordances for influencer marketing. In the ongoing evolution of the platform, Instagram introduces features that facilitate influencers while also circumventing potential regulatory concerns. In mid-2017, the platform introduced a "paid partnership" feature that fosters greater transparency by the creators for their sponsored content. According to the platform, this design was instigated by and for the creators. "We want to make a product that serves the creators, the brands and also the community," said Charles Porch, creative program director at Instagram (Flynn 2017b). Like the addition of the Community button on YouTube's channels, Instagram appears to be catering better to its creators, who have become vital stakeholders in the platform's success.

Influencer marketing represents a major shift in advertising practices and has been a sustaining source of revenue for even midlevel creators—but can also be the fateful apple that sees them expelled from the Garden of Eden. (This latter possibility is taken up in chapter 4.) Gone in this ecology are the ad sales divisions of the television networks and the creative agencies and media buyers who crafted the thirty-second spots and bought the airtime. Creators can field direct inquiries from advertisers extending influencer marketing deals at significant CPMs. The closest analogy to traditional media commercialization would be product placement, celebrity endorsement, social media marketing, and word of mouth.

The creator enters into a "creative partnership" with a brand. Some creators receive a flat fee whereas others are paid CPMs. Recent accounts reveal that advertisers can pay up to $75–100 CPMs for influencer marketing deals as compared to the $1–2 CPMS for programmatic advertising. As with product placement, some creators feature the brand's product in their video without mention, but include a link to the product website in the video description box. The creators are paid more revenue for every time their followers click on these links ("click-thru rates"), and even more if their community purchases the brand, product, or service ("conversion rates").

Not all creators and their content are created equal when it comes to influencer marketing. More brand-friendly creators, such as DIY beauty and lifestyle vloggers, have benefited most from these new advertising instruments. And they exploit these opportunities with sophisticated agency. Nilsen is a "glambassador" for Covergirl, although she describes this partnership as providing a service to the brand, which aligns with her own. In fact, as she noted in our interview, "I turn down brands all the time. I'm either not interested in the product or it doesn't fit with what I'm doing or I worked with them before and it didn't work out" (Nilsen 2015). Similarly, in our interview with Westbrook, aka GlamLife Guru, she confided that

> [a]ll of the offers come to me. I don't go to them. If it's scripted, I pass. If they have an idea about what they want me to focus on, or if they have ideas about the story, that's OK as long as it fits with my voice. But I turn down 99 for each one I accept. It has to be the right fit. If I lose trust with my audience, I lose everything. (Westbrook 2015)

Influencer marketing opportunities are not limited to only brand-friendly or high-level players. For advertisers, engagement matters as much as scale (the number of platforms, channels, subscribers, and views). In some accounts, niche creators are up to six or seven times more valuable to advertisers than top creators. According to CEO Kyla Brennan of influencer marketing firm HelloSociety, "Engagement goes down once you reach a certain threshold of followers, which is almost counterintuitive" (Brennan, quoted in Main 2017). This is another sense in which the classic A list/B list celebrity phenomenon (Caves 2000) in the traditional entertainment industry does not apply in SME.

Midlevel lesbian creator couple Bria and Chrissy acknowledged that "we already know that we're putting something on our viewers by doing a branded integration, but they also already know that we have to make a living, and YouTube ad sales alone is just not going to do it" (Kam and Chambers 2015). Creators' reputation for authenticity is the core of their community management and commercial capacity; brand identification and integration demand transparency. SME thought leaders Hank and John Green have avoided influencer marketing because of the dangers it carries. Chapter 4 is preoccupied with this fundamental tension in SME.

Other influencers have violated the implicit terms of their community relations and suffered the consequences. Talent manager Ashley affirmed that influencer marketing can "be a trap . . . where creators feel exploited and their fans feel betrayed" (Ashley 2015). Some creators have lost their entire business because they were either not transparent or their brand deals were misaligned. Ashley described a female YouTuber who had created a community invested in how she navigates her newfound freedom working near the beach while still struggling to make a living. When she posted an image of her new Mercedes on Instagram, her community fled. Ashley notes wryly, "At nineteen, a million dollars is great. It's not great if it's the last check you will ever cash" (Ashley 2015).

Having said that, creative agency can come to the fore when it is liberated from platform interference or advertising middlemen. In their account of one influencer deal, Bria and Chrissy described making a skit (for NuMe) entitled "Get Ready with Us in the Morning":

> We had so much fun doing it, and people loved it. And then [we] got the points across at the end, and kind of made fun of the product a bit, but in a light way, because the product works. It was very smart on their part [to give us creative freedom] because a lot of companies, for so long, have wanted to have so much control, trying to treat it like traditional advertising, which takes out the complete essence and beauty of why you're doing a YouTube-invested brand integration. (Kam and Chambers 2015)

Crowd Funding

Created by Hank and John Green, Patreon offers subscription revenue to creators that totaled over $150 million in 2017 (Constine 2017b). Similar crowd-funding platforms like KickStarter and IndieGoGo have allowed creators to fund specific projects that may be more ambitious than their traditional fare, like scripted web series and films. The list of other platforms continues to expand every year. A short list includes revenue transactional and streaming audio platforms (iTunes, Spotify, Soundcloud), as well as merchandising platforms like District Line. Interviewing Meredith Levine, SME researcher and self-proclaimed "fanthropologist," we learned about the "economics of asking." When it comes to crowd or fan funding, creators depend upon "people who love you who will pay what they can afford because you are asking them to. Sometimes that works" (Levine 2015).

Hollywood Calling?

As we have seen, Freddie Wong's RocketJump was the result of early success in scripted web series in SME that afforded him the chance to strategically pivot into Hollywood. However, the early track record for most of these early creators using SME as a back door to Hollywood has proven unsuccessful. Creator Grace Helbig had a short-lived talk show on E! Entertainment that was canceled after only a brief run. Saba Hamedy from the *LA Times* regarded this as an "experiment," and questioned whether "YouTube stardom equals ratings" (Hamedy 2015). This comment bespeaks traditional media ignorance; creators are engaging in mutually exploitative commercial practices by appearing in traditional media. While E! continues to struggle to secure ratings and revenue, Helbig's SME business was valued at over $5 million in 2016, according to Forbes. com. Meanwhile, she has continued to secure roles in feature films and television series on YouTube Red as well as through traditional film studios, like Lionsgate. Similarly, LGBTQ vlogger Tyler Oakley has appeared in reality shows like *The Amazing Race*, has hosted award shows either on stage or on the red carpet, and has launched his own web-based talk show on Ellen DeGeneres's digital network (Spangler 2016b). Less than a year later, that series has also been canceled (Burch 2017).

For premier and even midlevel creators, Hollywood often proves neither an ambition nor a viable revenue stream. For those content creators who might be earning six- or seven-figure sums from other revenue streams, traditional film and television fees can be uncompetitive. Other content creators are less willing to give up the virtually absolute control they have over their own work. Meanwhile, the time required to write or perform in traditional media, including protracted periods of development or simply waiting around on set for the lighting to change, can cost the creators valuable time better spent creating their own proprietary content and fostering further engagement with their fans. Vine star Brent Rivera mentioned numerous Hollywood offers that he rejected for the reasons cited here, even as he is still completing high school.

> I was dealing with a television network for a long time last year for an upcoming TV show, and the character they wanted me to play was dramatic

Figure 2.4. A New Literary Age? Photo by David Craig.

and super nerdy. We've seen that character a lot. It's so different from my Vines and YouTube videos. There have also been some radio opportunities, so we discussed some stuff like that. I'm just waiting for the right opportunity. I do like radio and can see myself having a radio show. But I want to make my own thing and then sell it off. I don't want to work under someone. (Rivera 2015)

For creators located with little proximity to traditional media industries, "going Hollywood" is neither viable, necessary, nor even desirable. Prominent game player Seth Bling harnesses his massive and lucrative online gamer community from his apartment in Seattle. Gabe and Garrett are the child stars of their own toy unboxing channel produced and distributed by their parents, Brian and Lori, out of their suburban home in San Bruno, California. According to the parents, the family has no interest in television or films, although according to Brian, "an animated film based on [Gabe and Garrett's] series *Sidewalk Cops* may be in the works" (Gabe and Garrett channel 2016).

A Literary Age?

Perhaps the most successful commercial practice by creators in traditional media has been the remarkable success of creator books. Since 2014, creators have secured numerous lucrative publishing deals. Beauty and lifestyle creators like Michele Phan have published books that translate their video tutorials into how-to and self-help nonfiction. Other personality-driven creators have published bestselling memoirs, like Connor Franta and Graceffa, despite their extreme youth. Other creators have been able to convince their community to purchase their original fiction, including the least likely of creators like beauty vloggers Zoe Sugg and Elle and Blair Fowler (Votta 2015).

A Harbinger of SME 3.0: YouTube's Adpocalypse

The question of a further phase in SME history beyond SME 2.0 is raised for consideration in our conclusion. YouTube's Adpocalypse may play a central role in this "new regulatory era." Here, we focus on the deep and ongoing impact it has had on creators.

Despite the proliferation of SME 2.0 business models, YouTube continues to offer core value for most creators, particularly in markets where broadband and mobile access is affordable and accessible and video-level speeds viable. As platforms like Vine faltered, YouTube became home, and big names, like Zach King, quickly pivoted to long-form video fare. Even as other SME platforms have integrated video players, the global scale, commercial affordances, and centrality of creators to YouTube's ongoing viability make it one of the most obvious platforms on which to launch careers. Yet, as we have seen, perhaps no greater threat to creator sustainability has been posed by YouTube itself than in a rolling series of crises coined "the Adpocalypse."

In 2017, investigating journalists revealed that multinational and national brand advertising was appearing programmatically alongside YouTube videos featuring terrorist organizations, antisemitic clips discussing a "Jewish World Order," and Swedish neo-Nazi groups (Mayes 2017). The backlash from over 250 major advertisers, like Walmart, who pulled their advertising from the site was met swiftly by a response from Google/YouTube vowing to crack down immediately on this flagrant failure of programmatic advertising to maintain baseline community standards. YouTube introduced a set of filters to promote more "ad-friendly content." Creators were charged with indicating whether their content fit a list of categories that advertisers had the option to delete from their advertising inventory. If left unmarked, these videos would remain demonetized and undergo a human review process—a kind of purgatory—by anonymous censors hired by the platform. Even if the video was later cleared for monetization, most creators reported losing up of 90% of the revenue they might have earned under the filterless system.

YouTube's filtering process revealed the limitations of the machine learning affordances of NoCal low-touch automation. John "totalbiscuit" Bain, a leading Youtuber, explained,

> Right now, the problem is that the machine isn't operating in a logical way. It's demonetizing videos that don't seem to have any logical reason behind the demonetization, and their communication with partners is next to zero. We don't know what they want us to do, and if they want

us to fix things, they can't expect us to just guess what exactly those things are. (Kain 2017)

For example, one of the most successful video games, and in turn, game-play sources of revenue, is the popular *Assassin's Creed*. Any content with the term "assassin," however, was immediately demonetized.

Google/YouTube's behavior in the Adpocalypse—very well disposed towards leading brands and well intentioned in response to community standards—risks violating the core value proposition of YouTube as an open access content and social media platform protected by safe harbor laws. Left with a Solomon's choice between creators and advertisers, some predict the Adpocalypse is here to stay (Snell 2017), although it hardly impacts some creators in more brand-safe and child-friendly verticals.

Beyond the commercial implications, YouTube's overreaction appeared to contradict its longstanding support of certain marginalized and alternative creators and communities. As we note in chapter 5, these automated filters cut deep into the return on investment of creators producing culturally progressive content. For LGBTQ creators, any representation of their identity could be deemed sexually suggestive and ad-unsafe (Weiss 2017). For communities supporting these creators, typically poorly represented throughout legacy media, these conditions appeared to perpetuate deeper underlying social discrimination by the very platform that had given them voice and means.

Outro: Creators Creating Value

In *TV Is the New TV*, Michael Wolff (2015) argues that the scale of the Internet has destroyed the value of media content. Media scarcity has been replaced by a dehumanizing algorithmic culture that is dictated and controlled by platforms that exploit users, converting their techno-presence into target practice for a culture of hyperconsumption. This chapter, on the other hand, has argued that building and maintaining a sustainable career—a concern with the bottom line—is a very human dimension of SME content production and is inextricable from the struggle to create meaning and value. Beyond survival and monetary value, the community and cultural value so generated are explored in chapters 4 and 5.

Our theoretical framework has sought to balance critiques of creative labor and algorithmic culture with more agentive frameworks of entrepreneurialism and spreadable media. Our field approach, grounded by interviews with a relatively large and diverse creator set, has pointed to the potential for empowered agency relative to traditional media labor. Not in any way wishing to downplay the precariousness of SME labor conditions, nevertheless we have argued that it has been possible for the more successful creators to carve out a level of agency that is distinctive and may—as we note in chapter 3—underpin greater longevity than the intermediary companies that were brought into being to manage SME.

3

Social Media Entertainment Intermediaries

Shortly after YouTube started its creator partnerships and programmatic advertising in 2006–2007, it also facilitated the emergence of a raft of so-called multichannel networks, or MCNs, to manage the proliferation of content that it found itself auspicing. In exchange for a percentage of creators' advertising revenue, these YouTube-affiliated firms signed creators for the purpose of maximizing value from their content and communities. Of these, the largest and most prominent firm was Maker Studios, which was launched in 2009 by a team of prominent YouTubers: Danny Zappin, Lisa Donovan, Scott Katz, Kassem Gharaibeh, Shay Butler, and Ben Donovan. Ryan Lawler (2013) described Maker Studios as "a creator-friendly multichannel network on YouTube that would help individual producers to create better videos, collaborate with each other, and boost the number of subscribers and views they all had. It also hoped to help them all monetize those videos a little bit better" (Lawler 2013).

Maker Studios drew quick comparison to United Artists, or UA, a Hollywood film studio launched in 1919 by leading film talent D. W. Griffith, Charlie Chaplin, Mary Pickford, and Douglas Fairbanks. UA produced numerous Oscar-winning films, launched franchises like the Bond series, and became a media corporation with record labels and television divisions. Since the fiasco of *Heaven's Gate* (Bach 1985), the most expensive movie bomb in history at that time, UA experienced a series of mergers and acquisitions that became self-inflicted wounds. Today, UA only exists as a brand name. Whereas the rise and fall of UA took almost a century, Maker Studios has experienced a similar "story arc" in just a few years.

Early on, Maker secured over $70 million in investment from a mix of venture capitalist firms and traditional media companies like Canal+ and Time Warner. In 2011, through their Original Channel Initiative, YouTube paid Maker Studios millions to launch and/or manage thousands of original channels. By 2014, Maker was managing over 55,000 channels and secured talent deals with premium creators like

PewDiePie (see chapter 4) and the format producers of Epic Rap Battles. These channels were reportedly generating over 5.5 billion video views a month and attracted over 380 million subscribers. That same year, Disney beat out rival investors to acquire Maker for a deal worth up to $1 billion, a deal *Wired* labeled "the future of TV" (Tate 2014).

Three years later, all the partners had cashed out of the business, along with most of its senior executives. Maker had experienced numerous rounds of layoffs, the network had been pared down to a thousand creators and channels, and the organization folded into Disney's digital division (Spangler 2017). In the wake of a series of scandals, Disney/Maker severed ties with their SME superstar PewDiePie, jeopardizing their access to his fifty-million-plus subscribers (Roettgers 2017). Maker's fall from grace signals how the firm has been transformed from a "princess into a pumpkin" (Patel 2017). Maker's fate illustrates the challenges faced by all MCNs. UTA digital agent Brent Weinstein, one of those intent on taking business from MCNs, says, "MCNs have played an important part of the digital content ecosystem . . . but, as quickly and consistently as the digital landscape evolves, MCNs must continually evolve so that they align with the needs of the community" (Jarvey 2017b).

Precarious Media Management

Our argument in this chapter is that SME management may be as precarious as creator labor, perhaps even more so. These intermediaries operate in the middle of the convergent space between NoCal and SoCal that we have traced in chapter 1. MCNs' placement sees them needing to innovate on both the NoCal and the SoCal side. On the NoCal side, MCNs attempt to provide value-added services superior to basic YouTube analytics, with multiplatform data integration and pioneering attempts at management of scale and volume. On the SoCal side, they seek to manage a quite different class of entry- to midlevel talent, who bring to the relationship an empowered track record of successful audience development and clear ideas about the roots of their success with them. The MCNs face Clayton Christensen's (2000) "innovator's dilemma"—the dangers of first-in-line innovators.

Despite these intermediaries' track record of accelerated innovation, they have been "squeezed" from above and below. From "above," an ever-increasing array of competing NoCal platforms and tech firms strive to reclaim the value—and revenue—previously ceded to MCNs by launching their own creator management strategies. "Below" them, successful MCN-mentored creators are poached by mainstream talent agencies, move across the numerous platforms on offer, and/or negotiate much better terms of trade for themselves.

To remain viable, these firms and professionals have needed to innovate even more rapidly than YouTube and the other digital platforms, and certainly more quickly than established media. This innovation involves a ramifying array of NoCal and SoCal management services that integrate the low-touch automated affordances of technology with the high-touch management strategies of Hollywood and Madison Avenue. Even then, as Mickey Meyer, cofounder of Jash, affirmed, "It's more complex than a digital versus traditional dichotomy; there is some blending going on between the two" (M. Meyer 2015).

The history of SME intermediaries we offer in this chapter aligns with the accelerated evolution of this new screen ecology. As described in chapter 1, these firms have emerged prior to the YouTube era of SME 1.0, pivoted to accommodate the multiplatform landscape of the 2.0 era, and struggled with sustainability in the 2.0 era of networked platforms offering competing services. As reflected in our account of the diversification of creator labor in chapter 2 around platforms, content, community, and commercialization, these firms innovated constantly in their suite of management services. Yet, each service required dealing with challenges distinct from its traditional media counterparts. Our analysis of intermediaries deepens the themes of previous chapters: the tension between NoCal and SoCal corporate, management, and production cultures, the rapid evolution of this industry from SME 1.0 to 2.0 and after, and the increasingly complex nature of professionalizing creator labor. Before the history, however, we need to define what we mean by "intermediaries" and frame our discussion in the context of contemporary accounts of strategic media management.

Defining Intermediaries

We define SME intermediaries as firms and professionals operating between SME creators and platforms and, more broadly, between SME and other industries, including traditional media and advertising. In exchange for a piece of the action, these intermediaries look to extract greater commercial value from assisting creators, platforms, advertisers, and traditional media throughout this industry. Intermediaries include MCNs, which originated as YouTube-certified entities aggregating, affiliated with, and/or managing YouTube channels by "offering their assistance in diverse areas, ranging from production to monetization, in exchange for a percentage of the ad revenue" (VAST Media 2014). Prominent MCNs include Fullscreen, Machinima, AwesomenessTV, Stylehaul, Kin Community, DanceOn (US), BroadbandTV (Canada), UUUM (Japan), AIR and Yoola (Russia), and Channel Flip, Gleam Futures, Diagonal View, and Brave Bison (UK). Other firms include influencer marketing agencies (the Marketing Arm, ViralArm), talent representatives and publicists (Big Frame, Addition), data firms (Social Blade, Tubular Labs), live touring (MagCon, DigiTour), crowd-funding sites (Patreon, Kickstarter), creator merchandise and product lines (DFTBA), and more. This list includes the digital and social divisions of traditional media production firms, including studios, networks, and talent agencies, like the division run by UTA's Weinstein.

Mapping the scale and scope of SME intermediaries proves as challenging as mapping the breadth of the creator economy. In contrast to SocialBlade's list of the top 250 YouTube networks, YouTube's Creator Services Directory only lists 230 firms. These are only "YouTube-certified," which means they have passed vetting by the platform. Yet the lists also feature far greater diversity than SocialBlade's networks, including categories of Audience Development, Content Strategy, Livestreaming, Monetization, Music, Production, Talent Management, and Video Development (https://servicesdirectory.withyoutube.com). Facebook features its own directory of "vetted Marketing Partners" (https://facebookmarketingpartners.com/), as does Instagram, which is owned by Facebook (https://instagrampartners.com/) and Twitter (https://partners.twitter.com/en.html). None of these platforms' lists account for firms operating across multiple platforms or distinguish native firms from social media divisions of traditional media management organizations like production companies or talent and advertising agencies.

"SME intermediaries" applies not only to firms but also to new classes of SME professionals operating independently or hired by SME and traditional media firms based on their ability to generate revenue within this new screen ecology. A short list of titles bears witness to their distinctive status and expertise, e.g., influencer partnerships (Stylehaul), content architect (Google), Audience and Platforms (Kin Community), and engagement manager (Tubular Labs). Our favorite is self-appointed "fanthropologist" Meredith Levine, who has been hired by SME firms to conduct trend studies about creators and fan communities. She told us the term came from Kris Longfield (who runs her own firm called Fanthropology): "I took that job title. About a dozen people call themselves fanthropologists now" (Levine 2015).

Framing SME Management

Early scholarship around television production, emerging media industries, and production studies offers background frameworks for our analysis of SME intermediaries. Television scholars Horace Newcomb and his co-authors (Newcomb and Hirsch 1983; Newcomb and Alley 1983) drew on the anthropology of liminality developed by Victor Turner to explain how television producers function as cultural intermediaries. Vicki Mayer, Miranda Banks, and John Caldwell (2010) show how television production executives operate at the intersection of creative labor and brand management. Timothy Havens and Amanda Lotz (2011) have brought these insights into mainstream textbook discourse, considering how media managers have "circumscribed agency" within the structure of media organizations.

There has been a welcome increase in the study of talent representatives. A benchmark was talent agency historian Tom Kemper's *Hidden Talent: The Emergence of Hollywood Agents* (2009). Kemper traces the emergence from the 1920s of talent agencies and the growth of their considerable power and influence in Hollywood. Jump ahead a century and, in the wake of traditional media conglomeration and vertical and horizontal integration, Hollywood agencies have evolved into major firms with complex divisions of labor and diversification across ramifying sites of cultural production, including sports, news, marketing, advertising, art, politics, and digital and social media. Violaine Roussel and Denise Bielby (2015) describe how contemporary talent agents and managers have morphed into "middlemen and women" engaging in diverse forms of cultural brokerage. Roussel (2016) further analyzes how "structural changes have reorganized the agency business and redefined talent representation" (Roussel 2016, 75).

Roussel (2015) describes the vital "relational work" of talent agents and managers along with production executives operating within the highly networked structures of media industries:

> The triangular relationship between artists, talent representatives, and production professionals is at the heart of the making of cultural products and artistic careers. But agents are more than a hub connecting the production side to talent by procuring work for their clients. In Big Hollywood, they tend to act as *de facto* producers by orchestrating and coordinating entire film and television projects from an early stage through the practice of packaging. (Roussel 2015, 104)

Roussel's concept of *relational work* shares properties with Nancy Baym's concept of *relational labor* (2015), which we discussed in chapter 2. Both concepts reference the vital and collaborative dynamics of media industries that belie notions of auteurship. For Roussel, Hollywood is an industry fueled by the creative, if codependent, alliances forged among writers, producers, directors, and actors as well as network and studio production executives—alliances that are vitally facilitated by intermediary talent representatives. In the same sense, as creators professionalize and engage in more sophisticated labor, they can outsource the relational work to SME intermediaries. These firms, publicists, and managers serve a comparable function to their traditional counterparts, which is why there has been greater overlap in management between traditional media and SME. They assist the creator with securing funding, developing his or her brand and content, and brokering deals between the creators and traditional media networks and studios, book publishers and music labels, advertisers and brands. In Baym's account, social media have cut out the intermediaries; rather, media *are* the intermediary through which artists have the means to interact directly with fans and audiences, nurturing relationships that are vital to their success. In this instance, Baym's reference aligns with the community practices of creators, the nonscalable, time-consuming work of engaging with fans across many platforms, through multiple strategies, including live performances. As further discussed in chapter 4, this labor and practice cannot be outsourced without risk of appearing inauthentic and crippling the vital relationship between creator and community.

Despite operating prominently in Hollywood for most if its history, these media firms and professionals have attracted little interest in media studies. In part, this was a consequence of limited access and their occult practices. Kemper (2009) refers to these media professionals as "hidden talent" (Kemper 2009), and Roussel (2015) describes their work as "invisible labor." But media studies' inattention to intermediaries is also in part a lack of interest in media management practice per se, and in part a reflection on the relatively dour state of early media management scholarship, described by Alan Albarran (2008) as "descriptive in nature" (Albarran 2008, 185).

Recent critical media scholarship has developed new frameworks for understanding media management, suggesting how distinctions between media and creative labor, management, and ownership increasingly blur. In field-defining volumes such as *Managing Media Work* (2011), Mark Deuze and Brian Steward map media management at the macro, meso, and micro levels. Their differentiation of the field of study is designed to

> suggest a new focus for media management research and teaching, considering what may be the new networks emerging through the creative industries, not necessarily tied to specific companies, products or places, that define new and evolving constellations of skill sets, practices and beliefs that could provide a road map through the morass of contemporary creative industries. (Deuze and Steward 2011, 10)

In *Making Media Work,* Derek Johnson, Derek Kompare, and Avi Santo (2014) proposed that "management should be framed not merely as a work category responsible for overseeing labor, but as a kind of labor— and a way of creating meanings and values from labor—that takes diverse forms within the media industries" (Johnson, Kompare, and Santo 2014, 19). In the same volume, Havens (2014) ties together management and agency work, describing how media intermediaries are "operating as prime focalizing sites for the transaction between industrial and representational practices" (Havens 2014, 39).

In the management discipline, Albarran (2010) and Lucy Küng (2008) have argued that normative assumptions in standard business management cannot apply in efforts to understand the imperatives around collaboration, creativity, and innovation in media management. In the second edition of Küng's book, *Strategic Management in the Media* (2017), the "ascendency of technology in the media" (Küng 2017, xv) forced her to conduct major revisions in her theoretical base. Borrowing from the adaptive school of management studies, Küng now sees management strategies as "an evolutionary process where change takes place progressively as firms undertake a series of strategic readjustments in responses to a changing environment" (Küng 2017, 66). Process-oriented strategies inform management responses to technological change, a heightened understanding of the nature and vitality of creativity and innovation in management, embrace of risk-taking leadership, and more fluid forms of organizational structure and strategy.

None of this literature, of course, engages with specific issues in SME intermediary management. Such management operates with a radically blurred division of labor and under conditions of constant platform pivoting. SME intermediaries, including management firms and professionals, are affiliated with but increasingly in competition with the platforms and in consort with but limited in their capacity to manage and extract value from creators.

Nonetheless, some critical scholarship has emerged regarding the rise and influence of MCNs. Denise Mann's (2014) study of the "Unregulated Wild, Wild, Digital West" is squarely focused on labor and regulatory concerns:

> As media industry scholars, we need to be mindful of the exploitative practices on display in these new media practices. We should question user-generated-content creators who have been trained by YouTube and its MCN partners to focus on achieving celebrity by any means necessary in order to increase their user count, and hence, their share of AdSense dollars. (Mann 2014, 33)

Patrick Vonderau (2016) argues that MCNs consolidate the *asymmetric* relationships between users and the YouTube infrastructure. In the context of his work—discussed in chapter 1—that reveals YouTube's original commercial motives, he emphasizes MCNs' close affiliation with YouTube, providing scarcity to offset YouTube's scale, operating as a "prosthetic device or prolongation of YouTube's own content filtering systems" to identify creators with the greatest revenue potential.

Drawing on cultural studies' reference points Pierre Bourdieu (1984) and Raymond Williams (1981), Ramon Lobato (2016) reinforces the framing of YouTube-certified MCNs as cultural intermediaries. The industry formalization process is emphasized—these firms provide a "new layer of professional management around YouTube producers" (Lobato 2016, 349), a layer "actively constructed and defined" exclusively by Google (Lobato 2016, 353). "The MCN," Lobato says, "reminds us that the history of media is not just a history of creative producers but also, inevitably and especially, a history of middlemen" (Lobato 2016, 358).

An account of SME intermediaries must start with the fact that traditional media intermediaries were already contributing to the early commercialization of the Internet. Consequently, these firms were pre-positioned to enter SME once platforms introduced commercial features and users morphed into creators, securing commercial and cultural value. Many, if not most, of these firms, it should be emphasized, are active through to the present. This period is followed by the rapid, subsidized scaling of MCNs that proved unsustainable, contributing to the "post-MCN" period featuring strategies of diversification and acquisition.

Pre-MCN Era

Companies that predate SME platforms and often became SME intermediaries include publicity and social media marketing firms that later morphed into influencer agencies, third-party data firms already mapping data across early online content and social media platforms, talent management companies already established in Hollywood, and early web and digital studios and video production companies. Operating within traditional media and advertising industries, some of these firms were already assisting with the commercialization of early digital and web technologies. These firms were poised to engage with SME as soon as YouTube launched its advertising programs and creators engaged in strategies of career development and sustainability. The arrival of other SME intermediaries like MCNs offered, at first, strategic partnerships for these firms, as did second-generation platforms in the SME 2.0 era. However, as the value of these firms increased, so, rapidly, did the competition.

Influencer Marketing Agencies

As we have seen in chapter 2, influencer marketing has proven to be a much more sustaining source of revenue for creators than programmatic advertising; however, the concept of influencer marketing is as old as marketing itself. Throughout their history, advertising firms have hired celebrities and public figures as pitchmen and spokespersons, often paying exorbitant fees for them to endorse brands or feature product placement in their radio and television programs.

In the digital age, each new era of technologically advancing and commercializing platforms has precipitated a corresponding wave of marketing firms, from online and digital to social and mobile. These firms adapted old marketing strategies to the affordances of platforms and cultivated new ones. The advent of SME 1.0 was no different. As platforms afforded creators the means to monetize their fan communities, advertisers pivoted rapidly to secure deals with these micro-celebrities and their mass appeal, or rather, as the industry preferred, *influencers*. So-called influencer marketing agencies appeared, ruled by twenty-first-century Mad Men tailoring new advertising instruments for Gens X, Y, and Z.

These firms were a mix of incumbents and upstarts as diverse as the advertising industry itself. Some firms represented the newly launched division of major global consolidated firms like WPP, Omnicon, and Publicis (Bruell 2016). This sector also featured a new generation of native firms, often described as both social-media talent agencies and social-media marketing agencies. A list of these would include vaguely luxurious- or ominous-sounding names like IMA, IMF, Moda Creative, Viral Nation, and Ministry of Talent. Although still dependent upon creators to get to consumers, some brands have cut out their ad agencies and are "using influencers like ad agencies" (Pathak 2017).

Industry and platform reports often lack support or accuracy. Sites like often-cited Mediakix interpreted Google trend data to conclude that the value of the market would reach between $5 and $10 billion by 2020

(Mediakix 2015). Nonetheless, NoCal and SoCal firms have taken notice. Native influencer agency FameBit was bought by Google, as was Hello-Society by the *New York Times*. Neither existed in 2011.

Contemporary influencer marketing continued traditional practices of marrying advertisers and brands with potential spokespersons and advocates, but with some vital distinctions. As Larry Weintraub, a veteran advertising executive from Fanscape, told us, this is a new form of advertising rife with distinctive challenges and undernourished strategies:

> "Influencer marketing" is the jargon—the term we use to describe an influencer with a significant fan base on social media who engages in forms of brand amplification or activation. [The strategy is to] ask who is the product right for, who has that audience, who can talk about it authentically and organically, and in a way that is endemic and not overt. The goal is to find ten to twenty top-notch influencers and pay them thousands to integrate the message we want into their content, although this practice doesn't scale well and some don't know what they are doing. They can't do "authentic" with a brand. (Weintraub 2015)

Unlike programmatic advertising, influencer marketing is nonscalable and labor intensive. SME creators are also not like traditional celebrities, whether actors or public figures, nor are they virtual pitchmen. Their influence, and agency, are not limited solely to their relationship to their global communities but can be exerted over their brand deals in highly irregular ways. Interviewees told us of creators walking away from six-figure offers out of the belief that the brand was not aligned with their content. To go forward with a brand that contradicts their brand would be a breach of trust between creator and community. Creators understand that sustaining their relationship with their fans represents the only long-term commercializable value. (We canvas the always-ready capacity to fail this authenticity test in the next chapter.)

Talent Management Firms

While social media marketing agencies sometimes referred to themselves as "talent agencies," these firms were primarily interested in the nexus between SME creators and Madison Avenue. These firms bore little resemblance to traditional talent agencies and management firms that have spent decades representing entertainment talent and intellectual properties in Hollywood. As we have seen, scholars like Roussel have shown how these firms have diversified, brokering every conceivable deal throughout the cultural economy.

These agencies pose direct competition for advertising agencies, although they were relatively delinquent in identifying the value of creators. For these Brahmins of Hollywood, creators often lacked the traditional media skills, like writing, directing, and starring in scripted content, that might signal crossover potential to these firms. An exception was United Talent Agency, self-described as a more client-focused firm, which launched a digital division as early as 2003 with junior agent Weinstein, which predates the SME 1.0 era. From 2007 to 2009, Weinstein ran 60 Frames, an experimental digital studio dedicated to producing branded content and original IP in this new industry. With UTA's support, Weinstein shifted back to representation, signing some of the earliest and biggest SME creators like Shane Dawson and Michelle Phan. UTA's digital division also brokered deals for their traditional media clients securing investment to launch SME firms, including Hollywood producer Brian Robbins's AwesomenessTV.

While the remaining Hollywood talent agencies sat out SME 1.0, a small number of SME talent management firms were launched by old agents, like the Collective. Alternatively, firms like Big Frame were comprised of native SME professionals who lacked experience in traditional media deal making but arguably better understood how to manage their creators and translate their community value into traditional media value. As with all the intermediaries we examined, these firms pivot to incorporate emerging strategy, angle, and opportunity, whether engaging in traditional media representation, aggregating channels like MCNs, or securing advertising opportunities like influencer agencies. In the wake of YouTube's channel initiatives, these firms quickly diversified, including production and programming operations.

Founded in 2005, the Collective was a talent agency servicing traditional film, television, and music talent before representing emerging digital talent. Launched by a former music and film agent, the firm was the first to recognize the commercial value of early YouTube channels like Annoying Orange and early native YouTube stars like Fred Figglehorn. The trajectory of Fred's career proved to be a bellwether for the distinctive nature of SME creators and the precarity of their managers. In contrast to most creators, who based their channels on their own lives, Fred was a pseudonym for a character created by Lucas Cruikshank, who for comic effect emulated a small child with a high-pitched voice. The agency helped Fred translate into a traditional media figure in his own television and movie projects. According to Fred's agent, Evan Weiss, "We believed that Fred was an authentic, great comedy brand, and that if we developed the right script, it was going to be a great movie. And, equally important, we believed in the audience . . . and the power of technology and social media to aggregate audiences—this person had done it" (Weiss 2015). Cruikshank subsequently outgrew his audiences and, particularly after he came out of the closet, lost interest in his Fred character. This created ethical concerns for his young-skewing audiences and, in turn, his management. The Fred channel on YouTube was franchised, featuring other child creators emulating the Fred comedic style, while Cruikshank has attempted to resurrect his creator career on his own channel while appearing in branded web series.

Despite its old-school media expertise, the Collective would undergo repeated and rapid transition from one business model to another and back. In 2011, in the wake of YouTube's original channel initiatives, the agency launched a division called Collective Digital Studios (CDS), a multichannel network that also managed talent and provided production facilities for its creators. In the SME 2.0 era, after YouTube shuttered its original channel initiatives, CDS returned to its primary function as a talent management firm servicing digital content creators operating across platforms, aware, as most MCNs had become, that being tied exclusively to one platform was unsustainable. CDS agent Joe Hodorowicz, referring to his services as a "white glove experience" (very high touch), added that

> [w]e refer to ourselves as a multiplatform network. We're not YouTube-only by any means. We're going to grow with the content and the artist. . . .
> The creator is now in more power than they've ever been and should be

focusing on their art. They should be focusing on and be mindful of their business and how it's growing. They shouldn't be the ones negotiating all the time. (Hodorowicz 2015)

In July 2015, the German media company ProSieben invested $85 million to acquire a controlling interest in the company. ProSieben partnered with two other European media conglomerates, TF1 and MediaSet, to merge CDS with multiple MCNs, rebranding the merged companies as Studio 71, which focused on deals with traditional, SVOD, and SME platforms.

Big Frame also started as a talent agency, managing the careers of early digital creators like Philip DeFranco, although the founders, Sarah Penna and Steve Raymond, were former television executives, not talent agents. YouTube's channel initiatives impelled Big Frame, like CDS, to become an MCN with programmed channels featuring a suite of "verticals." A vertical is a single themed set of channels, comparable to but distinguishable from TV genre or format, with a focus on particular market segments that are at the same time potentially cohesive online communities. Digital media have introduced alternative concepts and terms from legacy media around the aesthetic conventions of content, form, and narrative. Scholars have discussed the distinctiveness of Internet memes (Shifman 2013) and gifs (Miltner and Highfield 2017). In chapter 4, vlogging is posited as a format rather than a vertical or a genre.

Big Frame's early verticals were channels catering to women creators (Wonderly), fashion-lifestyle (Polished), LGBT (Outlandish), and urban (Forefront). However, in 2011 Big Frame was acquired by a larger MCN, AwesomenessTV, which assumed programming management of these channels. Big Frame subsequently returned to being a digital talent management firm, including creators signed with other MCNs. In 2015, AwesomenessTV was acquired by Dreamworks Animation, which was subsequently acquired by Comcast NBC Universal. Shortly after AwesomenessTV became a subsidiary, the cofounders, Penna and Raymond, along with other senior managers, left the company. Their decline prompted a second generation of talent representation firms, including management companies and publicity firms, to rise in their wake. This includes Addition LLC, which represents YouTubers Justine Ezarik (iJustine) and Joey Graceffa, and Select Management, which represents YouTubers Gigi Gorgeous and Eva Gutowski (*My Life as Eva*).

Data and Technology Firms

The explosive growth of social media platforms contributed to the rise of third-party data and technology firms like Tubular Labs, VidStats X, and Social Blade. These firms developed their own proprietary technology and data analytic services initially for advertisers and then later for MCNs and creators. Launched in 2006, Social Blade initially mapped data on sites like Digg.com before pivoting to YouTube in 2010 once it reached massive scale. Some of these firms, including Bent Pixels and Zefr Media, also provided content-rights management services for social, digital, and traditional media firms across SME platforms. Zefr's customers include Universal Pictures, Paramount, Warner Bros., Lionsgate, MGM, the Weinstein Co., NBCUniversal's Bravo, Broadway Video's Saturday Night Live, Sony Music, and Warner Music Group and, by 2014, it managed more than 375 million online videos and tracked over 31 billion video views a month (Spangler 2014b). As Social Blade's Vak Sambath explained to us, "We are the back office providing software for MCNs and platforms that manages workflow—everything from recruiting talent and talent management to brand campaign to assist MCNs and platforms with matching brands with talent" (Sambath 2015).

As creators have grown in importance in the evolving ecology, these firms have begun to focus more on the creators; in fact, Social Edge was renamed Creator IQ in 2017. As with all intermediaries, there are distinct challenges that these firms have in providing their services. Services to creators and brands alike, such as their data integration from multiplatforms, are vital but are not necessarily welcomed by individual platforms, which treat other platforms as competitors. Most notably, they are dependent on access to platforms' data and their APIs. Some platforms are more open, like YouTube and Twitter, although creators must subscribe to these services and provide them access to their platforms, channels, and passwords, which the services use to help aggregate their numbers. Other platforms like Facebook and Snapchat do not offer much information at all, although (Facebook-owned) Instagram is more forthcoming. Nevertheless, in the SME 2.0 multiplatform era with new apps emerging constantly, these firms have become even more vital in this ecology. As evidence, Tubular Labs generates industry reports like the "State of the Influencer Economy" and "Online Video" that are circulated widely and for free.

The Prototype MCN?

A notable precursor of multichannel networks, Next New Networks (NNN) was launched in 2007 by a mix of veteran traditional and digital media executives, including Herb Scannell, a senior Nickelodeon and MTV executive who went on to run BBC Worldwide productions. NNN described itself as "a new kind of media company"—one that produced multiplatform web video content for Web 2.0 platforms like AOL and MySpace as well as YouTube (Podell 2016). In 2011, NNN was purchased by YouTube and became a division called the Next Lab and Audience Development Group. Numerous NNN executives have migrated to senior positions at YouTube, including NNN partner Timothy Shey, who now runs YouTube's scripted programming division. Similarly, former NNN executive Lance Podell is global head of YouTube Spaces, which oversees the creator production facilities that have been launched around the world. Since their acquisition, this division helped launch the Original Channel initiatives that subsidized numerous affiliated MCNs. As a prototype MCN, what happened to NNN bespeaks precariousness: YouTube not only acquired NNN but subsequently shuttered its operations, borrowed its business model for aggregating creators and programming channels, and then disbanded or subsumed its management. NNN would be the first and last of these new media firms specializing in creator management services to be acquired by YouTube. Rather, the platform chose to create an affiliated relationship with a new crop of SME intermediaries. These were the MCNs.

The MCNs

In the wake of YouTube's partnership program and channel initiatives in 2007, a raft of firms began to launch their own channels as well as sign creators to help them grow and monetize their own. YouTube also directly facilitated and subsidized many of these firms, seeing them as a way of managing the explosion of online "partners." These became known as multichannel networks, or MCNs. We have noted some of the difficulty in accurately counting MCNs, made more challenging by the rapidity with which names have disappeared, merged, or changed.

(Three years after a list of YouTube MCNs on Playsquare [Higgins 2014] was published, a large percentage no longer existed.)

The larger MCNs operate globally, signing creators regardless of nationality because their communities are global. Prominent US-based firms that dominated this space initially include Maker Studios, Fullscreen, Machinima, AwesomenessTV, Stylehaul, Kin Community, DanceOn, Mitu, ScaleLab, and dozens more. Outside the United States, even larger MCNs have more recently emerged, including BroadbandTV (Canada), UUUM (Japan), as well as AIR and Yoola (Russia), although many have added US branches or acquired and integrated US-based firms. As further discussed in chapter 6, English-language firms feature prominently, including those based in the UK. A short list includes Channel Flip, Gleam Futures, Diagonal View, and Brave Bison, which is the merger of earlier firms Rightster and Base 79.

Bounded but also protected by national cultural, market, and regulatory conditions, other MCNs cater to more domestic or regional audiences. Germany features a number of MCNs tailored to German-speaking and Eastern European creators and communities, including MediaKraft and Studio 71—the latter also acquired and renamed US-based Collective Digital Studios. Other European firms include Zoomin TV (Amsterdam) and Studio Bagel (France). Outside of the United States and Europe, MCNs have emerged across other regions, catering to non-Western cultures and languages, including Thoughtful Media (Southeast Asia), Diwan (Middle East), and UltimaLimited (Nigeria), with more appearing regularly. Although "India is difficult for [non-Indian] YouTube MCNs to accommodate in terms of multi-lingual and multi-ethnic genres" (Vardhan 2015), an array of Indian MCNs have stepped into the gulf, including Culture Machine, Qyuki, Ping Digital, One Digital, and Whackedout Media.

MCNs were initially channel aggregators, seeking to stabilize runaway growth and respond to "glocal" dynamics, but leveraging their aggregated scale and value to advertisers across their network. As UTA agent Weinstein pointed out, the core value proposition of MCNs is mutually constitutive for creators and MCNs:

A multichannel network plays a unique and important role in the careers of creators, especially around channel optimization and growth, and large-scale brand deals that take advantage of an MCN's scale. Certain brands and media planners require access to the billions of annual video views that an MCN can deliver, in order to unlock the larger sponsorship opportunities. (Weinstein 2015)

All MCNs sign creators and aggregate channels, although with significant variation in terms of scale, content, culture, and category. Horizontal aggregators are scale driven. According to Social Blade, as of June 2017, Broadband TV (based in Vancouver) had over 230,000 members that aggregated over 23 billion views per month, and was the largest MCN (Social Blade 2017). Midsized networks include Fullscreen with over 60,000 creators. Russian-based MCN Yoola is the former VSP Group and the consolidation of a number of early MCNs, including Russian-based QuizGroup. Its website claims over 72,000 creators and 7 billion video views, although Social Blade indicates that it now has little over 40,000 members. In contrast, vertical aggregators target niche markets, genres of talent, and verticals of interest defined by culture, language, and community. Tastemade is to food as StyleHaul and Kin Community are to lifestyle as DanceOn is to dance culture. Los Angeles–based MiTu features Latino creators from several countries with cross-cultural content prominent, including Cholos (a term with multiple meanings, including Latino gang members), Latina Moms, and Abuelas (Grandmothers). Dubai- and Cairo-based Diwan Group features Middle Eastern and African creators like Ameer Aladabi from Iraq with over 1.3 million YouTube subscribers and 319,000 Instagram followers as of 2017.

At point of entry, the criteria for creators signing with MCNs are variable, depending upon a range of factors that ensure greater brand alignment of the creator and the services provided by the MCNs. These variables are constantly changing as these firms pivot, but include the quality of data regarding the scale and scope of the creators' fan communities on multiple platforms, the creator's content and style, traditional demographics around age, gender, location, etc., and cultural factors, including location and language. Most of the larger MCNs operate multinationally. However, these criteria may be applied inconsistently, particularly as these creators mature and create other forms of content. For example, the biggest creator at the lifestyle-oriented Stylehaul is Joey Graceffa, who is better known for his scripted fare, music parodies, gameplay, and personality blogging, which features LGBTQ topics, than for traditional beauty or style vlogs. Although known as a gameplayer, PewDiePie became famous for his bawdy and sometimes scandalous humor, which led Disney to fire him from its Maker Studios as it morphed into a "family friendly" division.

MCNs also look for the recent rate of growth in subscribers and video views, and the alignment between the creator and community demographics. The latter, for example, could mean that older creators with younger audiences represented a misalignment that posed challenges for the agent with regard to monetization, especially brand integration. In addition, creators deemed "brand safe" or "G-rated" are more likely to appeal to MCNs than subversive, political, or edgy creators. These practices support Vonderau's (2016) analysis of artificially reintroduced scarcity designed to regain control over pricing and contribute to establishing a cultural repertoire across which risks can be spread (Vonderau 2016, 367).

But the creator yields as much agency in joining MCNs as these firms yield to sign them. Even first-generation YouTubers with little training and few qualifications came into the orbit of the MCN with at least some degree of success already established and seemingly abundant clarity about their relationship with their "fan base." As a consequence, these young, but empowered, creators have the ability to come and go from the embrace of MCNs. While MCNs contract for exclusivity, as talent grows in power and agency, the MCNs lose the ability to sustain these relationships. As a result, talent flight is common, whether a consequence of poor management, competition from other MCNs, or youthful whimsy.

The value of MCNs to creators has been a point of contention, particularly by disgruntled creators who have publicly voiced their concerns over "exploitative" MCNs. One of the most notorious was Ray William Johnson, one of the biggest early-generation creators. Launched in 2009, his YouTube series, *Equals Three*, featured his own commentary about viral videos on YouTube, and became the first YouTube channel to reach five, and later ten million subscribers. However, after signing with Maker Studios in 2011, Johnson entered into contract disputes, which he discussed openly on his YouTube channel. By 2012, Johnson left Maker to launch his own production company, Equals Three Studios, and, by

2014, resigned as host of his own *Equals Three* series. As of June 2018, Johnson's channel had a little over three million subscribers and Johnson had migrated to Facebook, where he was reportedly earning over two hundred thousand dollars a year to produce live videos (Seetharaman and Perlberg 2016).

Another example of MCN malfeasance and conflict of interest involved the company My Damn Channel and Grace Helbig, one of the biggest SME creators. My Damn Channel posed as both a production company generating its own content and an MCN signing creators who arguably owned their own content as well as their community. As with Johnson, "contract disputes" led Helbig to leave the company, although she was forced to leave her own channel, Daily Grace, behind, which led to community and creator outrage. According to Fruzsina Eördögh, "[B]y populist accounts, My Damn Channel is now an evil corporate villain" (Eördögh 2014). Like Johnson, Helbig has found subsequent success on her new channels, including YouTube with over three million subscribers, landed her own eponymous E! talk show, appeared as the lead in feature films, developed podcasts that appeared at the top of iTunes, published *New York Times* bestsellers, and is listed as having a net worth of $5 million. Backed by the relational labor of their own communities, Johnson and Helbig have developed more sustainable careers than either Maker Studios or My Damn Channel.

As creators become more viable and valuable, and the forms of creator labor become more complex and expansive, MCNs could provide management assistance across their content, community, commercialization, and platforms. To justify their additional stake in the revenue stream, MCNs began to provide a creole mix of scalable management services. Arguably, these firms helped creators cultivate new divisions of labor, but this strategy was not as easy to emulate as in traditional media, with its divisions of labor above and below the line, and craft categories. According to Amanda Taylor, CEO of DanceOn,

> The biggest ones do [have division of labor], and I think that's why they get so big, like Grace Helbig, Hannah Hart. There are YouTube stars with big teams around them, and in some cases, production companies. But I think part of it [resistance] is stage fright, too, to be honest, because a lot of these guys started in their bedrooms or basements [and to hire

management means to] have to perform in front of people, and manage [them] and maybe lose a little bit of control. (Taylor 2015)

In providing these services, MCNs encountered another management dilemma, notably the critical role of authentic engagement between creator and fan community (further analyzed in chapter 4). Barry Blumberg, who helped develop and manage the SME comedy duo Smosh, told us about the challenge with maintaining their "voice" as their channels, content, and community grew:

> Me and this guy who had his PhD in German literature from Berkeley sat in an office and created Smosh content. What we realized was that there's a language and a cadence, a vernacular and a rhythm to not just what the Smosh guys did but how people spoke to each other visually and orally, or using the written word, online. It was always changing. You had to be very mindful of what was going on and how quickly it was migrating to something else. Then there were some things that were very specific to Smosh, and you had to learn how to talk about Pokemon or meme. It was learning another language. (Blumberg 2015)

As they diversified their services, MCNs also became competition for first-generation, especially influencer, agencies, as MCNs bid to help facilitate and manage advertising integrations. Rather than compete, AwesomenessTV acquired Big Frame, for example, and restored it to its original value as a creator talent management firm. Particularly in the SME 2.0, multiplatform era, numerous MCNs like Maker and Fullscreen went head to head with third-party data firms. They launched their own proprietary software that they claimed could provide superior analytics and royalty reporting. If you can't beat them, join them.

Particularly for the massive horizontal aggregators, MCN services concentrate on scale, creating the kind of artificial scarcity referred to by Vonderau (2016). While providing automated, low-touch services to their lower-tier creators like online video tutorials and data analytics, these firms offer more services featuring greater levels of direct interaction. As premium creators aggregate more subscribers, likes, and followers, secure higher levels of revenue, and require more complex practices of creator labor, these firms provide higher levels of management assistance in kind. This approach combines the hands-off, NoCal strategies of tech culture and the high-touch content-development and talent-relations services provided by SoCal firms in Hollywood. For lower-level creators, MCNs provide online tutorials for how to more efficiently create content, boost viewership, and secure higher CPMs through programmatic advertising. Most of these firms offer what they claim is proprietary software that their signed creators can use to obtain higher-level analytic insights across all their platforms. Only for their premier creators do these firms offer "white glove," less scalable services. These include influencer brand deals and talent representation, as well as assistance with content development and access to production resources, including studio space, wardrobe, casting, visual effects, and editing equipment.

In addition to channel aggregation and creator management, some MCNs provide production studios and facilities for creators, including Maker Studios, Machinima, and AwesomenessTV. These provide training and access to better equipment, production resources, and sophisticated editing practices. These services reflect the old media approach of studios and backlots, providing production facilities that date back to when studios primarily financed their own content and most production happened on a sound stage. The services provided by MCNs are quite different. MCNs do not own the content but also do not charge fees to the creators, as the aim is to produce content that will generate higher revenue split with the MCNs. In addition, these spaces provide as much pedagogy as production value, helping the creators learn more sophisticated ways to create content. These spaces, furthermore, facilitate collaborations with other content creators, orchestrated with the help of the MCNs. These "collabs" help introduce new creators and/or aggregate communities for both creators. This further reflects NoCal, ideal social media values, as distinct from the more competitive world of traditional media. However, as mentioned in chapter 2 with toy unboxer Boone Langston (2016), geographical proximity is no hindrance in this space as collaborations can happen virtually as well.

MCNs venturing into production services can also create more complications and conflicts of interest. Numerous creators told us (and we further analyze this in chapter 4) that the risk with crafting more sophisticated content is creating further distance between creator and community, inhibiting engagement and even generating a backlash. Emulating their traditional studio counterparts, MCNs with production facilities can often morph into digital studios creating their own branded content and launching their own channels—often with little understanding of the distinctiveness of creator labor. Consequently, creators may find themselves competing with their own management for brand deals and production assistance. Accustomed to owning and crafting their own content, creators may be less inclined to work for fees-only or relinquish creative control on an MCN's project. As we will see, in the post-MCN era, YouTube Spaces began to offer similar production resources to YouTuber creators, with far fewer strings attached, in an emerging array of sites all around the world.

As creator labor diversifies, so have the MCNs, launching ancillary divisions to ensure that they retain a piece of all the creator's commercial action. There is no greater example than AwesomenessTV, the closest equivalent to a vertically and horizontally integrated SME corporation, although very little integration has occurred through traditional media infrastructure. But it sits directly across the NoCal/SoCal divide: as CTO Jenn Robinson defined it for us, Awesomeness is a "tech-enabled media company" (Robinson 2015). The firm is a multiplatform network, servicing as many as ninety thousand creators and channels focused on the thirteen- to seventeen-year-old teen demographic. As we have seen, Big Frame is their in-house 360 talent management firm that brokers deals for creators across all the culture and media industries. Their TV production division develops, pitches, and produces series starring their own creators and appearing on networks like Nickelodeon. The division also develops and produces sponsored and branded series-like content airing on its YouTube channels, like its Royal Caribbean Cruises teen romantic drama, *Royal Crush*. According to Robinson, "Teenagers are the most important decision makers for family vacation. The shows were effectively a walking tour of the boat, showing off all the features, but disguised as a love story." Other divisions include sales and distribution repackaging content for international platforms and television, even where YouTube is available, as well as selling content for subscription platforms willing to pay for first window or exclusive fare like YouTube Red and Vimeo. Then there is AwesomenessTV film production and a book and music label.

Other intermediaries service live touring, including MagCon, Vans-Warped Tour, Amity Fest, and DigiTour. In 2014, Fullscreen launched InTour as "a vehicle for our Fullscreen talent to be with fans, experiment and create" (Fullscreen SVP Larry Shapiro in Bloom 2014). Similarly, AwesomenessTV has its own live tour business, which includes the Fifth Harmony tour. These tours are also occurring around the world, like the nonaffiliated YouTube FanFests, produced in association with the platform but run by an outside management firm, and operating in Mumbai, Rio, Bangkok, Ho Chi Minh City, Hong Kong, Tokyo, Seoul, and Jakarta. MCNs may also assist creators with developing a line of consumer products or merchandise lines, like the Fullscreen Shop or Maker Shop or AwesomenessTV's retail store in Los Angeles. But as we have seen in chapter 2, creators are increasingly likely to secure their own deals with ancillary merchandise websites devoted to creators and their communities, like the Creator Shop, District Lines, and DFTBA (Don't Forget to Be Awesome).

Some MCNs represent more than a media company; rather, a more apt description might be a lifestyle brand, much as MTV emerged to represent more than a music channel. Taylor described how dance represents a community that appeals to diverse values and interests, well beyond choreographers, dancers, and their fans. DanceOn's community engages with certain forms of art and music, healthy living and diet, and forms of fashion and style. Access to these communities allows these MCNs to pursue not only broader audiences and revenue streams but also larger and more diverse advertisers. In referring to her pitch to advertisers, Taylor noted, "This is a category where there are [dance] stars, and oh, by the way, have you thought about how positive this category is, and how brand-safe it is? It's aspirational, inspirational, physically active" (Taylor 2015). This may all be spin, perhaps in anticipation of MCNs' ephemeral status in the post-MCN era.

Post-MCNs

The early SME intermediaries, and the MCNs proper, have experienced similar trajectories. These firms scaled rapidly, pivoted often, and diversified their suite of management services for their stakeholders. But by 2017, these firms encountered even greater competition and more heightened precarity. The competition was not only from other SME intermediaries but also from their former platform "partners," coupled with new digital divisions of traditional media management firms. Consequently, these firms and professionals have been forced to pursue alternative strategies for sustainability, with very mixed results.

As MCNs pivoted, they created as many fractures as opportunities for creators and partners, particularly as these firms desperately sought out new forms of content, funding, and revenue. A leading case was Machinima. Machinima was the name of a format created in the 1990s that combined videogame assets (characters, action) and voiceover scripts into narratives, often without legal permission from the videogame companies. Around 2000, a website called machinima.com was launched that aggregated these videos and later emerged on YouTube. A decade later, the company had evolved into one of the largest-scaling (fifty thousand–plus) MCNs affiliated with and subsidized by YouTube and featuring content beyond the original format, including gameplay. Just as rapidly, Machinima was accused of poor management and unfair contract demands by even its biggest creators, many of whom soon left the company. PewDiePie, the leading creator in the world, who had previously sued to get out of his Machinima contract, claiming that "[i]t was managed in such a terrible way," said of Machinima, "During the time I was a member of their network, I grew into the world's biggest YouTuber—and they didn't even know I was with them! They didn't get in touch a single time, except when I wanted to leave—then their CEO e-mailed me once" (Tassi 2014). The company also pivoted in the direction of Hollywood, trying to migrate its creators and content over to, or to compete with, film or television. This turn included hiring seasoned production executives like Ralph Sanchez, who came from Warner Brothers, Disney, and MTV. This proved a disastrous turn, as Sanchez told us, "When you grow so fast sometimes you forget what got you there in the first place. And what got Machinima there . . . was inside gaming and personalities . . . and doing gameplay" (Sanchez 2015). In the post-MCN era, Machinima has struggled for sustainability, experiencing numerous changes in management, rounds of layoffs, abandonment by creators, falls in rankings, failed attempts to rebrand itself, and minimal investment from venture capitalists and traditional media. By 2017, like Maker Studios, the firm operated as a production company within a division of Warners Brothers Digital Networks. In contrast, Warner bought Machinima for less than $100 million, nearly a tenth of what Disney paid for Maker (Weiss 2016a).

The post-MCN period has been further characterized by the pivot back towards a traditional legacy model of IP creation. "They have, in essence, become digital-first production companies" (Csathy 2016). However, these efforts have placed these upstarts into competition with legacy players and professionals—with limited success. In late 2017, former leading digital-first content firms like Buzzfeed, Mashable, and Vice Media who never played the creator card have missed revenue targets, experienced waves of layoffs, and/or been the subject of fire sale acquisitions (Sherman 2013). The IP model has proven as precarious as the creator model.

As we saw in chapter 1, YouTube regularly "pivots" its platform, partner, and channel strategies. This includes shuttering its original channel initiatives that temporarily subsidized creators and SME intermediary firms, most notably MCNs. YouTube erased these initiatives from the site as if they had never existed (Gutelle 2013). What better evidence of the ephemerality of this iterative NoCal tech culture than treating expensive management strategies like Snapchat posts? Simultaneously, the SME 2.0 era saw the rise of numerous competing platforms, including Vine, Instagram, Snapchat, and Periscope. As described in the CDS case study, these platform conditions transformed MCNs into multiplatform networks, or MPNs.

As MPNs, these firms seek to craft management strategies for pursuing alternative revenue streams across numerous platforms and offer creators platform integration strategies and analytics superior to YouTube's. For some, this strategy is simply a reflection of their talent-centric management model, following their clients wherever they migrate. For others, this strategy helps thwart an untoward dependency on YouTube. As Taylor noted,

> I think that if you were to launch a company strictly saying, "We're just going to aggregate a bunch of channels and that's going to be our business model on YouTube," you're vulnerable. . . . YouTube has way too much power over you. When people say, "MCNs don't work," that's what they're thinking, but really, with any of these companies, I think that you

either have to be multiplatform or combine with a media giant to survive in some ways, but also to flourish. Every powerful media company is a combination of a variety of different companies. (Taylor 2015)

Not only did YouTube abandon its original channel initiatives, but the platform no longer provides a list of affiliated MCNs. In their Creator Services Directory, out of 235 firms, only 22 are listed as multichannel networks, or MCNs. Prominent MCNs are missing from the directory, including Maker Studios, Machinima, and AwesomenessTV. A YouTube executive confirmed that numerous MCNs initially opted out of the directory; however, some firms, like Fullscreen and Broadband TV, have recently been certified and added to the directory. Most revealing is YouTube's help page, which provides an overview of MCNs for creators and describes key aspects of MCNs and best practices by these firms. But there is also this:

> Joining an MCN is an important choice for any YouTube creator. Before you join, make sure you understand what services and/or results the MCN will deliver in exchange for your payment. While some creators may choose to partner with an MCN, you don't need to join an MCN to be successful on YouTube. Make sure you know how to get help as a YouTube Creator and use YouTube's support options, which are available to you whether you're in an MCN or not. Every YouTube Creator is eligible for the YouTube for Creators Program, which provides resources like workshops, meetups, channel consultations, production access to the YouTube Spaces, and more—all free of charge and based on your channel's specific needs. (YouTube Help 2017)

Considered as business poker, this proviso represents more than just the "tell"—a subtle clue as to YouTube's management strategy. This serves as a declaration that the age of MCNs has passed. Google/YouTube, having invited in, nurtured, certified, and licensed MCNs, is now encroaching on their basic business model by developing its own branded content R&D through direct engagement with top brands in its in-house agency the Zoo and launching YouTube Studios worldwide and their online Creator Academy. Chapter 1 outlined how YouTube built both a soft and a hard infrastructure around professionalizing SME creators. In the age of SME 2.0, with ongoing platform competition, YouTube has been forced to pivot to a SoCal model, fashioning incentives, support, and services for its creators, with whom it remains as codependent as ever as SVOD platforms like Netflix and Amazon lured away PGC from Hollywood.

YouTube has devoted significant resources to this end. YouTube Spaces have been established in major hot spots of creator activity globally. They can be stand-alone YouTube-owned and -operated facilities, as found in Los Angeles, New York, Paris, Tokyo, and London; joint ventures with existing training organizations (Toronto, Berlin, Sao Paolo, Mumbai); or pop-up ventures engaging with local interests (for example, Sydney and Brisbane). New spaces are appearing constantly, including surprising locations like Dubai. Codified as "Learn, Connect, Create," the YouTube Spaces experience provides a suite of services from basic training to meet-ups with other creators to production facilities to create more professionalized content. Through interviews and observation at a number of YouTube Spaces and pop-up training events, we noted the standardization of the components of basic training: pursue your passion, upload regularly, learn to use basic YouTube analytics, develop your individual brand, use thumbnails and metadata efficiently and effectively, and practice community engagement and interaction strategies at best-practice level.

The Creator Academy and YouTube Spaces represent a kind of "McDonaldization" of the professionalizing amateur trajectory. They are designed to create a more seamless experience for creators and viewers alike. While the training is rigidly normalized at the lower levels, it is also carefully tiered such that the training becomes more customized as the creator becomes more popular—and presumably professionalized. In other words, YouTube leaves the foundational popularity to the market, while retaining the high-touch customized development work to those already on a success pathway. Emulating the scalable practices of MCNs, these studios provide clear tiering opportunities. The higher the subs, the greater the services. And with success comes an array of framed oversized YouTube "play" buttons—these are, variously, the Graphite, Opal, Bronze, Silver, Gold, and Diamond Creator Awards, with the latter recognizing ten million subscribers.

Further competition has emerged from traditional media agencies, including Creative Artists, William Morris Endeavor, and United

Talent, along with other boutique firms. As agencies, they can technically partner with the SME management companies, who arguably provided a different array of services, provided the creators are willing to pay both firms a portion of their fees. More strategically, these venerable Hollywood firms have cherry-picked the top SME clients since these agencies come with more specialized and diverse expertise in traditional media and throughout all forms of cultural brokerage. As with influencer agencies, talent management is radically different for creators than for traditional talent, according to Weinstein in our interview: "[O]ur jobs are to both create and respond to opportunities, to help an artist achieve their career goals. For digital stars, this means focusing not only on digital opportunities but also opportunities across film, television, publishing, live events, licensing, merchandising, and more" (Weinstein 2015).

Fostered over years of relational work, these traditional agencies confer the power of their networks throughout traditional media to broker deals for these creators. The value of these deals to traditional media can exceed that for the creator. For example, UTA helped convince Razorbill, an imprint that is a division of Penguin and Random House, to launch a line of creator books that have landed at or near the top of bestseller lists. Their success is the reason why the *Los Angeles Times* asked, "Can YouTube Stars Save Publishing?" (Kellogg 2015). Yet, for top creators, the revenue from book sales as well as advances may only comprise a small portion of their total revenue. Rather, the book sales often lead to book tours that afford creators a more intimate opportunity to interact directly with their community—in situ and all expenses paid. In support of her bestselling book, *How to Be a Bawse* (2017), creator Lily Singh (aka Superwoman) had over thirty-four tour dates in the United States, Canada, the UK, Australia, New Zealand, Singapore, India, the Philippines, and Trinidad Tobago.

As evidenced by our earlier account of the Fred Figgelhorn–Lucas Cruikshank story, SoCal-style talent-management services' strategy to move clients from the farm to the big league is fraught with complication and viable for only a small subset of creators. Traditional media have less value for creators, who have never cultivated the core Hollywood skills of acting, screenwriting, or directing. Only a small percentage of content creators recognize the value of working in Hollywood, whether for lack of adequate remuneration, lack of control, or lack of time. For the more successful content creators, some of whom are earning six- or seven-figure sums from several revenue streams, traditional film and television fees can be uncompetitive. Other content creators are less willing to give up the virtually absolute control they have over their own work. As we saw in chapter 2, the time required to write or perform in traditional media can cost creators valuable time creating their own proprietary content and maintaining community engagement.

Increasingly, the way forward for many MCNs is being bought out. As previously indicated in the Maker, CDS, and Big Frame examples, acquisition is considered an increasingly safe harbor for MCNs exposed at the vortex of SME evolution. There have been over $1.4 billion in acquisitions or investments by traditional media of MCNs-turned-MPNs. In October 2013, Dreamworks Animation launched what has become a proverbial land grab by traditional media for MCNs. They spent $33 million to buy and merge AwesomenessTV and Big Frame; a year later, Hearst paid $81 million for a 25% stake in the company, now valued at $325 million. Dreamworks Animation's acquisition was followed by other traditional media players' moves to acquire, partner with, or invest in MCNs. Most notably, Disney acquired Maker Studios for a staggering $500 million (with an additional $450 million on offer against performance targets). In addition, in 2014, Fullscreen was acquired by Otter Media, a joint partnership between the Chernin Group and AT&T, for between $200 and $300 million. European media group RTL purchased beauty vertical Stylehaul for $150 million and invested in Canadian-based Broadband TV, which allowed them to launch RTL's Digital Hub.

Table 3.1, current in 2017, reflects the ongoing acquisitions and investments involving SME intermediaries. Less apparent is whether the value of these firms has been enhanced through acquisition and, more often, integration into the existing divisions of their new owners. Maker Studios fared poorly seeking refuge through Disney, although the cofounders landed a significant payday, as have the various executives who have since come and gone from the firm. Ynon Kreiz, who became the CEO of Maker Studios in 2012, was described by the *Hollywood Reporter* as the second most powerful man in Silicon Beach (The Hollywood Reporter 2014). Four years later, after orchestrating the Disney deal, Kreiz

TABLE 3.1. MCN Acquisitions and Investments

MCN	Acquired by	Price	Date
Next New Networks	Google	Undisclosed	March 2011
Channel Flip	Shine Endemol Group (News Corp)	Undisclosed	January 2012
Alloy Entertainment	Warner Bros. Television	Undisclosed	June 2012
BroadbandTV	RTL Group (51% stake)	$36M	June 2013
AwesomenessTV	DreamWorks Animation	$33M	December 2013
Stylehaul	Bertelsmann/RTL Group	$107M	February 2014
Maker	Disney	$500M (up to $950M if milestones met)	March 2014
Fullscreen	Otter Media	$200–300M	September 2014
Culture Machine (India)	The Aleph Group (Singapore)	Undisclosed	2015
Studio 71 (Collective Digital Studio)	ProSiebenSat.1	$83M	July 2015
Zoomin.TV	MTG (Sweden)	Undisclosed	July 2015
Curse Inc./Union for Gamers	Twitch	Undisclosed	August 2016
Machinima	Warner Bros.	"slightly under" $100M	December 2016

MCN	Major Investments	Stake	Date
Kin Community	Corus Entertainment	Undisclosed	September 2014
Tastemade	Scripps Networks Interactive	$25M	February 2014
Defy	Zelnick (31%), ABS Capital (31%), Lionsgate (31%)	Undisclosed	October 2013–June 2014
Whistle Sports	Sky TV, NBC Sports	>$28M	October 2014–March 2016
MediaKraft (Germany)	M. DuMont Schauberg	>€16M	September 2014

stepped down. Six months later, as part of a larger management team, Kreiz attempted a takeover of *Time* magazine and has since been elected to the board of Mattel, Inc. Kreis's trajectory represents the contradictions within this space. Whereas intermediary firms themselves may operate precariously, for senior management the media business can offer remarkably sustainable careers—even if the firms on their business cards change as frequently as the fortunes of those firms.

Outro

Precarity can also be generative, as evidenced by the highly innovative management strategies engaged by these intermediaries in pursuit of sustainability within this new screen ecology. The value of these services, as witnessed by early intermediaries, had been established by some traditional media and early Internet and digital commercialization before their services were extended into the SME 1.0 era. For those firms native to SME, value had to be generated from scratch, often from their living rooms, which, for example, is where Sarah Penna launched Big Frame. Early differentiation helped establish value that would often prove limited and perilous, especially as new competition entered the fray. The swirl of disruption throughout this industry demanded constant and iterative expansion of services, often placing these firm in direct competition with former allies. The alternative strategy was to merge or consolidate, especially as platforms—new and old—introduced even more opportunity and peril. What YouTube giveth, it taketh away.

SME intermediaries' liminal status between Silicon Valley and Hollywood initially offered benefits. Tech-oriented venture capital (VC) firms for whom precarity is baked into their portfolio strategy contributed to numerous rounds of investments. As it had done in the early formations of SVOD platforms, Home Video, cable, and broadcast television, Hollywood hedged its bets. Some networks and production companies joined VCs by offering modest investment. But as these firms went from value-generating to potential competition, true to form, Hollywood went on a buying spree like an anticompetitive industrial junkie.

The rise and fall of MCNs and other intermediaries signal their struggle to identify and measure the value of this creator-driven industry. As we argue in chapter 4, this value is centered less upon content or distribution and more upon the creators' discursive appeals to authenticity and community. The business task to capture this is formidable. Since 2011, Forbes has posted year-end lists of top influencers, aka creators. As their lists have evolved in number and diversity, so too have their methods to try to determine commercial value, evolving beyond initial assessments of YouTube programmatic advertising to include revenue generated across all platforms and business models.

Over time, Forbes has relied upon an evolving array of data firms claiming to have cracked the algorithm for measuring "influence." In 2011, Forbes relied upon a "social media audience" metric developed by a firm called PeekYou (Shaughnessy 2011). Forbes's most recent lists are now divided into a dozen verticals (e.g., Fashion, Pets, Parenting) and released year-round and continue to reflect methodological imprecision. The latest list features partnerships with multiple data firms, including influencer analytics firm Traackr and social insight platform Captiv8, combined with lists of endorsements and product lines, while also factoring in consultation with platform executives, talent managers, and other SME professionals (O'Connor 2017). Comparable lists by the likes of Vogue and LinkedIn have also been explicit in describing, if problematizing, their own methodology strategies. The challenge is summed up by digital marketing firm Contrevo: "[I]t has become clear that the quality of the followers now carries more value than the quantity" (Cravo 2016).

Without fully engaging the elusive but distinctive value in SME—built off creators and their ability to leverage their communities for commercial value—many of these firms were unmade. We need now to turn to the discursive foundation through which this distinctive value is captured. In the next chapter, we explore the relationship among creator claims to a greater authenticity than traditional media, which relies on their relationship with their community, and the claim that this relationship is facilitated, but can never be dominated, by commercial brand involvement.

4

Authenticity, Community, and Brand Culture

SME thought leader Hank Green (2014)—whom we meet numerous times in this book—says that, for video creators online, there are only three kinds of content that viewers "really, really love." He distinguishes these three from drama web series, stunt comedy, reality TV, and game and talk shows. All these can be found online, but they each have clear precedents in broadcast television and are therefore not content innovations central to SME:

> I want to point out the tremendous variety and quality of content that has been created within this extremely limited economic model. YouTube has helped people create at least three massive genres of cheap-to-produce, high-quality content that viewers really, really love. Video game "Let's Plays," style tutorials, and direct-to-camera monologues (which we in the biz call "vlogs") all fill those requirements and all score billions of views per month.
>
> Other content has been nearly impossible to make work. Narrative content has existed mostly as aspirational, money-losing, pre-pilot pilots for TV shows. Even content that TV people consider dirt cheap (like game shows, talk shows, and reality shows) is hard to produce with online video budgets.
>
> I was the executive producer for the *Lizzie Bennet Diaries*, which won an Emmy. I'm even more proud of the fact that it is one of the only narrative projects in online video to ever turn a profit, mostly because we did it on a shoestring.
>
> Possibly the only genre that efficiently converted from TV to YouTube/ Vine is sketch comedy, which has always had more to do with the skills of its creators than its budgets. (Green 2014)

These three native-to-online social media entertainment content types embody the fundamental modes of address that constitute the powerful discourses legitimizing the appeal of SME. This chapter develops an analytical framework to understand these modes of address, which differ sharply from established film and television, and are constituted from intrinsically interactive audience-centricity and appeals to authenticity and community in a commercializing space. In terms of cultural value, SME content can be, and popularly is, dismissed as self-absorbed vlogging and beauty tips, addictive gameplay, and sophomoric stunt comedy, and concerns about its popularity can rehearse the iron law of cultural history that sees every new era of popular culture considered as evidence for a new moral panic. But we argue instead that social media entertainment is governed by quite strict norms that put the highest value on authenticity and community, and these governing "rules of the game" have developed rapidly to shape and discipline creators and the commercial environment in which SME creators work.

Green's analysis stresses the Darwinian-like economic selection pressures that have shaped the SME content universe. As we saw in chapter 2, the massive growth in scale of SME content has destroyed value (Green 2014)—the cost-per-thousand rate that drives Google's AdSense revenue sharing on YouTube has bottomed out, driving creators into further nonscalable engagements to restore value (brand deals, merchandising, television and cable options, live appearances, and licensing content). But there are countervailing, powerful discourses of authenticity and community legitimizing the positive appeal of SME. As we will show, these practices are rigorously differentiated from established professional media by both creator and fan and mark a stark contrast to the production, content, and marketing strategies of traditional media industries.

First, however, we need to attend to a definitional issue. As noted previously, Internet and digital content has generated new forms of screen aesthetics, along with new terms to describe them, like "verticals," "memes," and "gifs." However, Green's reference to "vlogging" as a genre may be somewhat misleading, since gameplay, DIY, and other SME content all feature creators speaking directly to camera. Rather than a genre, we treat vlogging as a core SME format that deepens the effect of intimacy between creators and their community. The closest comparision in legacy media would be broadcast journalists speaking to camera to address their audience or counterparts in the studio. However, there are major rhetorical and strategic distinctions. Journalists perform a role to deliver the news. In contrast, as described by You-Tube's Creator Academy tutorial, vlogging is about "talking to viewers in an authentic way on camera" and "is often what makes the difference between gaining an audience, and creating a community. . . . Vlogging gives your fans access to the real you" (https://creatoracademy.youtube .com/page/lesson/vlogging). In this chapter, therefore, when we turn to detailed profiles of leading creators in the three native SME genres, we refer to the Vlogbrothers as exemplars of "civic entertainment." In vlog format, their content is designed to foster a more active citizenry, featuring overt appeals to civic engagement, including encouraging their community, the Nerdfighters, to consider their role as agents of social change.

Authenticity and Brand Culture in Critical Studies

Critical studies of online culture hone in on claims around authenticity and community as vitally contestable domains of value. Alice Marwick's *Status Update: Celebrity, Publicity, and Branding in the Social Media Age* (2013) makes a major contribution to these debates in her uncompromising critique of claims for authenticity and entrepreneurship in social media industrial culture as "really myths" (Marwick 2013, 16) generated by "modern neoliberal market capitalism":

> The focus of this book is how, and why, social media . . . produces subjects. In other words, what types of selves are people encouraged to create and promote while using popular technologies like Facebook, Twitter and YouTube? Strategic online self presentation plays an enormous role in increasing one's social status, how one is viewed both online and off. . . . For neoliberal market policies to operate properly, people must adopt actions, ways of thinking, and discourses that are congruent with neoliberalism. Neoliberalism, or the infiltration of market logic into everyday social relations, requires a willing subject and is far more effective when consensual and dispersed through micro-interactions than when imposed from the top down. This book argues that Web 2.0 models ideal neoliberal selves, and rewards those who adopt such subjectivity. (Marwick 2013, 5–6)

Marwick studied the "center of the social media world," the Bay Area tech companies and the people who worked for them, between 2006 and 2010. While this group of tech producers is quite different from SME creators, their preparedness, in Marwick's words, to "fully integrate advertising and marketing practices into the ways they view their friends and themselves" (Marwick 2013, 16) certainly aligns them with the labor practices of creators. "'Authenticity' and 'being yourself,'" she says, "have become marketing strategies that encourage instrumental emotional labor" (Marwick 2013, 17). Marwick reads the cultural and identity superstructure off the base of the economic and the technological without remainder. For her, there is a direct, homologous alignment among techniques of subjectivity, technological affordance, and commercial practice, all "tied in with" neoliberal capitalism.

Brooke Duffy (2015b) also challenges the "social construct" of authenticity that underpins the three "interrelated myths" of amateurism, creative autonomy, and collaboration that inform the aspirational labor of female fashion bloggers. These myths serve to "conceal the hierarchical, market-driven, quantifiable, and self-promotional realities of the blogosphere" (Duffy 2015b, 61). Jose van Dijck (2013) is more nuanced but still unequivocal in her account of *The Culture of Connectivity*. Seeking to shift the governing metaphors in debate on the social effects of the online world, she clinically pursues the implications of shifts from "the communalist jargon of the early utopian visions of the Web as a space that inherently enhances social activity" to the processes "turning connectedness into connectivity. . . . Besides generating content, peer production yields a valuable by-product that users often do not intentionally deliver: behavioral and profiling data. Under the guise of connectedness they produce a precious resource: connectivity" (van Dijck 2013, 16).

Social media anthropologist Crystal Abidin (2015) takes a more graduated approach, distinguishing the way influencers "appropriate and mobilize intimacies in different ways (commercial, interactive, reciprocal, disclosive)," developing a model termed "perceived interconnectedness, in which influencers interact with followers to give the impression of intimacy." How "instrumental" emotional labor is should be mapped on a much broader continuum than Marwick's direct, even causal, alignments allow.

Underlying much critical debate is the assumption that commercial dynamics and pressures always conflict with, and either fatally undercut or compromise, claims to authenticity and community. Hector Postigo's (2016) studies of the gameplay genre give us a handle on a more nuanced, creator-centered account of these tensions. He traces the delicate dance of authenticity, independence, and small-business savvy in these commercial environments: subscribers/fans and game commentators "live in the same normative environment where sharing and community must be prioritized." They also "live in the life world where capital accumulation is important and so have sometimes conflicting values" (Postigo 2016, 14).

Dealing with these questions across a wide range of contemporary online commercial and not-for-profit culture, Jenkins, Ford, and Green (2013) are clear that participatory culture cannot be reduced to "consumptive behavior by a different name":

> [I]f we see participatory culture, though, as a vital step toward the realization of a century-long struggle for grassroots communities to gain greater control over the means of cultural production and circulation—if we see participation as the work of publics and not simply of markets and audiences—then opportunities to expand participation are struggles we must actively embrace through our work. (Jenkins, Ford, and Green 2013, 193)

Most centrally, Sarah Banet-Weiser (2012) has put what Theodor Adorno called the "jargon" of authenticity on the agenda for contemporary cultural and media studies. Drawing on an intellectual history that includes traditions from Rousseau to Marx to Thoreau, Banet-Weiser first acknowledges that authenticity is "tricky" to define. Rather than attempting to be definitive, Banet-Weiser positions herself relationally between the anticonsumerism of Naomi Klein and the consumer-as-agent position occupied by Henry Jenkins, Clay Shirky, and Yochai Benkler. She is

> thinking about how, and in what ways, the concept of authenticity remains central to how individuals organize their everyday activities and craft their very selves. Moreover, in a culture that is increasingly under-

stood and experienced through the logic and strategies of commercial branding, and in a culture characterized by the postmodern styles of irony, parody, and the superficial, the concept of authenticity seems to carry even more weight, not less. (Banet-Weiser 2012, 10)

Banet-Weiser has immersed herself in the supply or production side of brand culture, coming to—albeit ambivalently—appreciate the degree to which the search by brands for ways of authentically and thereby more effectively engaging with particularly millennials and other young people has led at times to genuine social and cultural surplus value as well as innovation in advertising and marketing. Equally, she has engaged on the demand or consumption side, talking to those for whom the famous Dove campaign for "Real Beauty" worked, and with proponents of user-generated postfeminist content online.

The importance of Banet-Weiser's work is that she rejects the binary logic that equates the commercial with inauthenticity, and the noncommercial with authenticity, as "too simple" (Banet-Weiser 2012, 11), just as she similarly refuses the "fall from grace" narrative that a citizenship culture has been transformed or disintegrated into a consumerist culture (Banet-Weiser 2012, 133). Brand culture is first and foremost *culture*; it is foundational, rather than the epiphenomenon thrown up as the byproduct of a singular, supervening capitalist hegemony—as the anticonsumerists would have it. As such, it is fundamentally productive yet ambivalent, holding out the "possibility for individual resistance and corporate hegemony simultaneously" (Banet-Weiser 2012, 12). Deeming the anticonsumerist left critique to be "nostalgia for authenticity," Banet-Weiser recognizes that "individual resistance within consumer culture is defined and exercised within the parameters of that culture; to assume otherwise is to believe in a space outside consumerism that is somehow unfettered by profit motive and the political economy" (Banet-Weiser 2012, 12–13).

Ambivalence is the pivotal concept for Banet-Weiser as she seeks to work with the concept of brand culture as deeper than and quite different from commercialization or marketing: it is "deeply, profoundly cultural" (Banet-Weiser 2012, 14), with all the competing power relations and specifics of individual production and practice that any media culture carries. "Such an explanation is largely missing from scholarly discourse on consumption and branding, and allows us to analyze the cultural meanings of branding without resorting to a binary that is often unproductive" (Banet-Weiser 2012, 13). For Banet-Weiser, contemporary brand culture is characterized by the blurring between the authentic self and the commodity self, and "this blurring is more *expected* and *tolerated*" (Banet-Weiser 2012, 13, original emphasis). It is also characterized by a relationship between individuals and commodity culture that is constructed as "authentic" (Banet-Weiser 2012, 14).

Creator, Community, and Brand Culture

When we turn from these general debates on authenticity and brand and commodity culture to the specificity of social media entertainment, we are immediately struck by not only the applicability of such general debates but also three irreducible characteristics of SME. The first is that the claims to authenticity that animate native SME content are established through comparisons with the presumed inauthenticity of established fictional screen formats. The second is that the distinctive mode of address of SME is constituted in the relationship *between* discourses of authenticity and community. The third is that there is a discursive logic that attempts to render brand relationships subordinate to the dominant discourses of authenticity and community.

Comparisons between the "really real" nature of online content and the inauthenticity of established entertainment formats are a constant and contain a trace of the spirit of youthful rebellion expressed in a compilation video of young people's attitudes to YouTubers: "YouTube is, like, a nerd behind a camera. . . . He's really real with it. . . . He has more of a personality whereas, like, actors, they're almost, like, a body with a script" (Pittman 2015). Or consider the remark of Christopher Willey, vice president of development for Defy Media, in a personal communication with one of the authors, that "[t]raditional audiences go into a theatre. Our audiences would rather hang out in the green room with the talent" (Willey 2016). Or the precision of this calibration of quality from a creator: "[W]e don't want to be a bit worse than television, we want to be a bit better than amateurs" (Cohen 2012).

These discourses serve in stark contrast to the production, content, and marketing strategies of traditional media industries. Whatever we finally make of "self-absorbed" vlogging and beauty tips, "addictive" gameplay, and "sophomoric" stunt comedy, there can be no denying the centrality of SME's freshly minted claims to authenticity. These arise from millennials and other young people's rigorous differentiation of SME from established professional media, with its heavy legacies of intermediation, fictionalized abstraction from the everyday, and encrusted barriers to entry. Social media entertainment, for a great many of its creators and their fans, is a fully fledged critique of legacy media, striking at its core of well-imagined stories, well told, following established narrative-fiction conventions, produced, written, and acted by appropriately trained professionals. The type of authenticity expected from SME creators and their content breaks through all of these artifices and marginalizes all those artificers.

But it is not such claims to breakthrough authenticity on their own that make for the particularity of social media entertainment. The unparalleled degree of interactivity between creator and fan community leads to the second defining characteristic: the relationship *between* discourses of authenticity and community defines the distinctive mode of address of SME. Every SME creator is subject to a level of fan and subscriber response and feedback that in its almost real-time intensity and transparency is without parallel in screen entertainment. The creator's distinctiveness—in a massively crowded field—is his or her claim to authenticity, whether that be the individual's highly personal real-time life in the vlog, the inner as well as outer beauty discourse of the DIY beauty format, the way gameplayers show their virtuosity, commitment, and responsiveness to their followers, or the rough reality and lack of production values of the stunt.

But the only way to validate these repeated authenticity claims is to be tested constantly by the community the creator calls into being as a result of the intense level of interactivity intrinsic to the SME business model and to digital platform affordances. The normative weight carried by the first characteristic (discourses of SME authenticity are constructed in radical contrast to traditional television and to actorly fictions) is now wedded to the second characteristic (an expectation of peer-to-peer equality and easy access between creator and fan). Authenticity is not established in a monadic relationship but in a dialogic relationship with the fan base generated by the creator, through his or her "affective" (Papacharissi 2015) and "relational" (Baym 2015) labor. Any and all claims to authenticity are tested continuously in a call-and-response rhetorical field.

The third particularity that characterizes SME is the way these discourses of authenticity and community are placed in relation to brand culture. The critical point here is that brands, by definition, only enter the picture *after* the establishment of this dialogic relationship between authenticity and community. Brands' interest lies in marketizing that established relationship, while creators look to reinforce the brand relationship as a *secondary* relationship as they negotiate their authenticity status with their community. And just as there is this irreducible temporality to the relationship among authenticity, community, and brand, so the testing of claims to authenticity by the fan community happens over time—with brand relationships with SME creators waxing and waning at least partly as a factor of the dynamics of the dialogic relationship between authenticity and community.

We can now see more clearly the ways in which we build on Banet-Weiser's account in *AuthenticTM* in order to develop our analytical framework. Instead of a binary between authenticity and commerciality being *blurred*, there is a temporal topography to be *mapped*. And instead of discourses of authenticity tracking across a bilateral relationship between individuals and commodity culture, the relations are trilateral among the "authentic" creator, the fan community that validates all such claims to authenticity, and the brand that is seeking to buy into, and leverage, that primary relationship.

This is not to claim that the authenticity-community-brand dynamics we trace in this chapter embrace all SME content formats in every culture. Variations on the DIY vertical, such as kids unboxing (touched on in chapter 2 and the conclusion), cannot be analyzed using claims to authenticity as the proponents are too young to dissemble (be "inauthentic"). This should be differentiated from adult product review/unboxing.

And, as we will see in chapter 6, the cultural and industrial systems underpinning SME in China and India, for example, are distinct. The three core verticals as defined by Green are very much Western- and US-centric; all in a sense pivot on the individuated personality of the creator, and thus performances of authenticity are all-important. Western psychological notions of authenticity figure little in Chinese SME.

In India, the most promising SME genres are those underrepresented in dominant film, television, and music: youth-oriented web series, non-Bollywood music, and regional cooking.

Breakdowns in the Authenticity-Community-Brand Relationship

It is important to stress that the authenticity-community-brand relationship requires constant work and is very unstable, particularly over time. Our arguments can be tested by looking at examples of failure to maintain the authenticity-community bond, where the community has disciplined creators, and/or where brand relationships have destroyed the bond. Such breakdowns occur regularly and usually with great fanfare, and underline the inherently volatile, friable nature of this triangular relationship.

Issues of authenticity and inauthenticity have been endemic for online creators before monetization and professionalization. "YouTube's first viral sensation" (Cresci 2016), teenage vlogger Bree—lonelygirl15—an amateur with no media training, armed with only a digital webcam and an Internet connection—attracted over thirty million views and became the fifth most subscribed YouTube channel at that time, by simply and honestly discussing the problems and anguish of teenage life such as schooling, controlling parents, and fights with her boyfriend, through a typically amateurish vlogging style. However, as the series developed, the narrative began to focus on the more bizarre aspects of Bree's life, and questions about Bree's authenticity started to emerge in the comment sections of her videos and on her personal MySpace page (through which she interacted with her fans). After much speculation—and a great deal of fan labor—it was revealed that Bree was the creation of Californian filmmakers Mesh Flinders, Miles Beckett, and Greg Goodfried, whose character was played by aspiring New Zealand–born actress Jessica Rose. After the exposé, creators Beckett and Goodfried formed the media and technology company EQAL, raising $5 million in venture capital, through which they developed lonelygirl15 into an ongoing franchise (Buckman 2008).

In a commercializing space where lifting the lid on untoward practices can have direct consequences for creators, UK vlogger Dorothy Clark's *Brand Deal Rant* (2015) is unusual, if not rare. While she is careful to assert that "[b]rand deals can be so wonderful if they are done correctly. There is nothing wrong with a brand deal if it's done well. A creative and entertaining video letting people know about a product that they may be interested in using," her post is a grievance about brand deals that had gone wrong. She warns creators that brands try to feed creators insincere catch phrases or artificial scripts that turn audiences off; do not understand social media (but claim to), while creators do; and want their product showcased in the first ten seconds of the video (which are the most important in terms of holding a viewer's attention). The "rant" goes further: there is a lack of trust between brands and creators, and brands do not undertake adequate research around creators and their communities.

Scott Disick (most famous for having dated a Kardashian) accidentally revealed to his 18.6 million followers how little involvement he had in promoting brand products. In one Instagram campaign (for which he receives up to fifteen to twenty thousand dollars per post), Disick posted a photo of himself with a Bootea shake, but regretfully included not only the caption the company told him to paste but also the instructions telling him to paste it. Instead of posting "keeping up with the summer workout routine with my morning @booteauk protein shake!" he wrote, "Here you go, at 4pm est, write the below. Caption: Keeping up with the summer workout routine with my morning @booteauk protein shake!" Disick quickly deleted the post, but not in time to stop screenshots and ridicule circulating across social media (Beale 2016).

In another example, Chriselle Lim, a fashion model and blogger known for publishing "authentic" lifestyle photos of travel, fashion, and beauty trends alongside her photogenic family, posted a photo with a Volvo car that stood out to her community as inauthentic. Her community noted that amid her usual posts about fashion, beauty products, family, and travels, her only previous mention of a Volvo was that she was attending a sponsored event. Discussion among her followers turned to the obvious staging of the photo and the buttoned-up caption that touted a variety of hashtags focusing on message points established by Volvo. The post ignited anger within her community to the point where Lim had to add more context to her caption to support the image and the message she was trying to convey.

Creators' communities often call on creators to justify their need to generate additional income from their creative endeavors. Anna Akana's video *Why I'm a Sell Out* (2015) responds to the heartache over her community's backlash over branding deals: "If a sellout is someone who puts high value on their work, then sure. If a sellout is someone who recognizes that money frees up your time to work on non-paying passion projects, awesome. If a sellout is someone who loves what they do, but also wants to make a living at it, then yeah."

We now turn to the counterfactual—those who have been able to manage the authenticity-community-brand relationship over time. Sustained analytical profiles of major creator representatives of the three native SME content types—PewDiePie (gameplay), Michelle Phan (DIY beauty), and the Vlogbrothers (civic entertainment)—now illustrate these arguments. These profiles are all of outliers—they are three of the most prominent SME creators worldwide. We highlight these creators because they have been operating for most of the decade-long history of SME, so that the question of how authenticity-community-brand relationships are managed over time becomes answerable. Also, their notable prominence brings the tensions among authenticity, community, and commercialism/brand culture into very sharp relief. Even at the mezzanine level, however, the discipline of keeping the three balls in the air has led to burnout and flameout.

Gameplay: PewDiePie

Gameplay features videogame and e-sports players recording and commenting on their game play. By far the most popular SME creator among those approximately three million globally who derive some income from their video uploads, PewDiePie (Felix Arvid Ulf Kjellberg) reached fifty-three million subscribers in 2017, boasts the most video views (15.2 billion), and earns $15 million annually from declared revenue streams (advertising) and much more from merchandising, appearances, and now an episodic television show (*Scare PewDiePie*). PewDiePie's YouTube story begins with his enrolling in industrial economics and technology management at Gothenburg's Chalmers University of Technology in 2010. Finding he gained greater enjoyment in making and sharing his gaming videos, he left university and took part-time employment in a hot dog stand (and briefly as a port captain) while building his channel. Typifying the narrative of the SME creator we traced in chapter 2, he started out as a hobbyist with no notion of career, incurring the disapproval of his parents for dropping out of university to play games. This informal beginning is mirrored in the story of how the nom de plume "PewDiePie" came about. "Pew" is the sound of shots fired in a shooter game; "die" is what happens in such games. "Pie" got added because he forgot the password to his "Pew Die" account. While relatively late to the platform compared to other major YouTubers, PewDiePie's arrival coincided with the rapid proliferation of videogame commentary, horror games, and Let's Play videos on YouTube. Yet PewDiePie was one of the first to turn the burgeoning genre into something far more creative, and he was certainly the most successful.

PewDiePie has deftly managed the community relationship with his now fifty-three million "bros," while at the same time churning out over thirty-two hundred videos (by 2017) at the rate of sometimes two per day. Textual analysis of the historical development in the very substantial body of content available at https://www.youtube.com/user/PewDiePie evidences considerable change and adaptation. His original video, "Minecraft Multiplayer Fun" (2010), is pure gameplay walkthrough, while off-screen two people laugh and goof around, talking between themselves in Swedish with occasional swearing in English. The video offers no "Felix," no personified interaction or reflexive discussion, no signature sign in or sign out, and no video or sound editing for quality. Embarking on a period of prolific content output, PewDiePie rapidly evolved his channel through the integration of now-familiar YouTube initiatives such as enticing thumbnails and multitrack backing music, while developing a distinct gameplay identity through humor and vulgar satire that soon galvanized a following. His schtick—brash, over-the-top humor offset by genuine, but at times exaggerated, emotions—set him apart from the bulk of "Let's Play" YouTubers who showcased their gaming skills with obdurate seriousness. PewDiePie continued to evolve his own style in conjunction with a rapidly increasing following, soon branching out through an eclectic mix of Let's Play videos interspersed with live-action and animated comedy shorts. From the time he reached a paltry twenty-five hundred subscribers, he developed an ability to address each viewer as if he or she were already part of his community.

PewDiePie reflected on the changes in his style, noting, "I kind of feel that these aren't commentaries anymore, they are more like vlogs," and commenting that while his early gameplay videos were enjoyable, his newer vlog style is more personally rewarding and fun. The vlog approach also allowed him to act as though he was always spending time with a friend, simply "sharing moments on YouTube with my bros." By 2012 PewDiePie had evolved his channel to incorporate ways *within* his "Let's Play" genre for audience comments and subscriber requests, collaboration videos with his girlfriend Marzi Bisognin (fashion beauty YouTube channel CutiePieMarzia) and other YouTubers, and more traditional vlog videos centered around his home and family life. Within four years of launching his channel, PewDiePie had secured twenty-four million subscribers.

Some have attributed PewDiePie's success to his physical location, arguing that the YouTube algorithm, in favoring locally produced content, has contributed to an artificial inflation as localized users subscribed and followed PewDiePie as he relocated from Sweden to Italy to Los Angeles and to Brighton (Baker 2014). Others suggest that his Swedish heritage gives him an international appeal, helped further by his fluency in English and a hip Swedish accent (Willman 2016). It also helps that PewDiePie is primarily a gamer, and that gaming—the second most

Figure 4.1. Prominent YouTuber PewDiePie (Felix Kjellberg) reflects on his YouTube career. PewDiePie, https://www.youtube.com/watch?v=dtAuAu3nI_0.

popular type of content on YouTube after music—steals a significant slice of the YouTube demographic, and that the financial success of the channel allows PewDiePie access to the most relevant, popular games that many of his subscribers either cannot afford to buy or do not have time to play. But the greatest contributing factor is his work ethic, the seriousness with which he takes his address to his community of "bros," and his facility with native-to-online profiling and navigation strategies such as his enticing thumbnails. PewDiePie maintains a rigorous schedule even when he is traveling or under the weather (Willman 2016). His regular and consistent uploading sees him following the YouTube categorical imperative: Thou must upload at all times.

The workload is even more impressive when one considers that he insists on doing as much of it as possible by himself. In 2014, PewDiePie addressed comments suggesting he could lighten his workload through hiring labor, stating in the video that he does not

> want to make the business of PewDiePie anything much bigger than myself. My goal is not to make money, I just want to do this. I want YouTube to be YouTube. There are so many channels now that are just big companies. . . . I'm just one guy and I still manage somehow and I hope that can inspire people. If Pewds can do it, you can do it. Go chase your dreams, Bros. ("Take Your Pants Off! [Update Vlog]" 2014)

While a large part of PewDiePie's success springs from community management, engaging such an enormous follower community takes enormous energy. PewDiePie has always tried to actively engage his community, talking directly to viewers as though they are assumed to already be part of his "Bro Army" and inviting them to interact with him further. At times this has proven to be an overwhelming task, and on several occasions PewDiePie has acknowledged the difficulties managing such accessibility amid overwhelming work pressures. Several times he has turned off the comment stream on YouTube that, he claims, is filled mostly with provocation, spam, and self-advertising, and chosen instead to interact with core "Bro" respondents through Twitter, Reddit, Tumblr, and his own custom forum "broarmy.net." When necessary, PewDiePie will tend to deal with trolls and negative commentary through self-deprecatory humor.

He does not directly do brand deals. PewDiePie does play well-known and popular mainstream video games, and is thus fully engaged with brand culture, but he not only makes a point of regularly playing and promoting indie and nonbranded games; he is also open to criticizing brands when he feels it necessary. When gaming giant Nintendo announced its "Creators Program"—a scheme requiring YouTubers to register with Nintendo in order to share advertising revenues from specific videos (a 60–70% revenue share in comparison to Nintendo's previous policy, which was to keep 100% of advertising revenue), PewDiePie demonstrated his managed independence of brands:

> First of all, they have every right to do this and any other developer/publisher have as well. There'd be no "let's play" without the game to play. And we (YouTubers) are humble to this fact. But what they are missing out on completely is the free exposure and publicity that they get from YouTube/YouTubers. What better way to sell/market a game, than from watching someone else (that you like) playing it and enjoying themselves? (PewDiePie 2015)

Further, he suggested that in many instances the YouTuber is more important than the game when it comes to popularity on YouTube: "If I played a Nintendo game on my channel most likely most of the views/ad revenue would come from the fact that my viewers are subscribed to me, not necessarily because they want to watch a Nintendo game in particular" (PewDiePie 2015).

Despite the distance he keeps from brand deals, in 2015 PewDiePie was named in a Federal Trade Commission complaint that alleged he and other creators did not properly disclose a paid sponsorship deal with Warner Bros. when promoting the game *Middle-Earth: Shadow of Mordor* (2014) on their channels. PewDiePie was not charged with any wrongdoing by the FTC, who accused Warner Bros. of failing to adequately disclose the payments. Warner Bros. agreed to do so in the future (Spangler 2016c, 2016d; McCormick 2016; Grubb 2016). In a video released following the findings, PewDiePie defended himself and his actions, pointing out that he had disclosed that the original video was sponsored (in text on the YouTube website, but not in the video itself), and arguing that the FTC did not release its guidelines for sponsorship disclosure until 2015, after the video was made:

> This is two years ago. A lot of YouTubers were involved in this spon-sorship but since I'm the biggest YouTuber, my name is the only one that pops up. We weren't required to disclose. I still did it. Some other YouTubers actually didn't disclose it, but I'm getting all the shit for it. The FTC didn't release guidelines to YouTube until 2015. And this video was in 2014. Because of this back then YouTube paid promotion was a bit of a grey area. Nevertheless, I still disclaimed it. ("The PewDiePie 'Scandal'!!" 2016)

This candid video, which involved reading and responding to critical tweets, forum posts, and video comments, is classic PewDiePie com-munity management, incorporating honesty, humor, and authenticity in his response.

PewDiePie has moved from many instances of saying he cannot af-ford to play certain games in the early years to now positioning himself as offering a service generating strong vicarious community engagement through playing games that are often out of the financial reach of his community. While there are always subscribers who call him a sell-out, overwhelmingly, he has managed the transformation from gameplay enthusiast to the most popular online creator through finding ways to deal directly with his base and managing commercial relationships with strategic ambivalence. "It's never been about the money."

Yet as his content changes, he risks alienating his earlier fans. In early 2015, a subreddit post made by a fan, TheFlyingMarlin, stated, "I miss the old PewDiePie" before launching a two-thousand-word post detailing all the things he dislikes about the "new" PewDiePie. TheFlyingMarlin calls out PewDiePie for selling out, being childish ("Now he is immature in a stupid way"), and snubbing fans, and says that generally "his new videos just aren't as good." TheFlyingMarlin complains that PewDiePie is play-ing flash games and doing "pointless" nongaming videos such as Marzia collaborations, and expresses disappointment with PewDiePie's increas-ing distance from fans. "Now he seems to be just pandering. Seems less like a friend and more like some guy thousands of miles away" (Red-dit.com 2015). Before PewDiePie commented and linked his fans to the post, the post had over 90% "upvotes" with the majority of commenters agreeing with TheFlyingMarlin. PewDiePie commented to defend himself, calling TheFlyingMarlin an "Unfair Nagger." "Feel free to not watch my videos. I think my content has improved drastically." "I'm a person. You're basically telling me to act the same for 5 years. Because you liked it better. . . . You call me a sellout, but give no good reason why. You don't explain." "Watch my older videos . . . they are waaaaaay more immature." PewDiePie concedes that he has reduced his connection with fans. "This may be true, but I never once stopped trying to. I can't please everyone" (Reddit.com 2015).

In the video "Catering to Your Audience—PewDiePie" (2016) PewDiePie again discusses how fans are mad because he is no longer the guy they fell for. The gist of the video is that he is no longer an amateur enthusiast, offering expletive-laden commentary alongside footage of his videogaming exploits, sitting home alone in front of his computer, talking about upcoming titles he wanted to play but could not afford, and that while the old PewDiePie was a "character" his fans could relate to, his fans are so diverse now (no longer just gamers), he wants to enjoy his success and experiment with new ideas. In other words, PewDiePie is growing up and leaving youthful things behind. PewDiePie has to mature; he is YouTube's tentpole channel. And as YouTube matures, he has too.

Maturing also means apologizing for previous misdemeanors and, he claims, effecting personal change in line with community standards. A leading example of this came in 2012–2013 after the posting of his video "It's Raping Time," which included the song "Shut Up (and Sleep with Me)"—a song about the "deception of rape"—by German musician Sebastian Roth. PewDiePie took down the "It's Raping Time" video, his video "I'm Sorry [VOSTFR]" (2013) acknowledges that his catalogue of rape jokes is offensive, and in a subsequent Tumblr post he vowed not to continue. "I just wanted to make clear that I'm no longer making rape jokes, as I mentioned before I'm not looking to hurt anyone and I apologize if it ever did" (PewDiePie 2012). Mainstream media such as the Canadian *Globe and Mail* have since acknowledged that "unlike many young gamers, he listened when fans and critics alike pointed out their harmful nature, and resolved to stop making rape jokes" (Woolley 2014). Yet while PewDiePie has similarly expressed regret for his use of words like "gay" or "retard," he continues to use "slut" as an insult.

This extended *cri de couer* in his video "Reacting to Old Videos (45 Mil Subs) (Fridays with PewDiePie—Part 118)" (2016) is instructive:

> Obviously, I've undergone a massive change from my first video to my last. I am very happy where I am right now, but it still seems that many people are stuck in the old days. I still make kind of stupid jokes that I shouldn't make, but I feel like back then I didn't understand. I was so immature, and I just thought things were funny just because they were offensive. So I would say a lot of stupid shit. I'm not proud of it, I'm really not. But I'm also glad that I've grown past it. I was probably better at being more engaging with my audience, but to be fair, my audience was a lot smaller back then. I feel like it has been a struggle for me to adjust from being so small to being so big and still have a close relationship with the audience. To me the improvement is clear. To me, I've grown so much as an entertainer, as a comedian, but also as a person. I feel like back then I was very childish and very confused. I didn't know what I was doing, but I know I enjoyed it. And it really is thanks to you Bros. I always read the comments, I always listen to feedback and criticism and I feel like that's an important part. Criticism has really helped me grow and I'm very happy about that. And more than anything I am very proud of who I am today and I'm also excited to keep improving for the future. It's not a secret, I make a great living doing YouTube. But I am confident I would not have invested this much time on YouTube if it wasn't for you Bros. There's no way. I really do work a lot, because I love doing it. I love doing it because you Bros are here and supporting me. Even though it's gotten out of hand.

Nevertheless, in a further demonstration that even the most sustained management of the creator-community-brand relationship can fail, in January 2017 PewDiePie pushed his vulgar satire strategies too far, posting videos featuring antisemitic comments or Nazi imagery, including the video "I've Discovered the Greatest Thing Online . . ." (2017). In this video PewDiePie attempts to "show how crazy the modern world is, specifically some of the services available online" by highlighting the absurdity that people on Fiverr (an online marketplace predominantly used to buy and sell digital services including writing, translation, graphic design, video editing, and programming by freelancers for between five and five hundred dollars) "would say anything for 5 dollars." PewDiePie navigates the Fiverr user interface through categories "Writing & Translating," "Music & Audio," "Programming & Tech," etc., before pausing on the "Fun & Lifestyle" category—a category whose discovery he claims was a "blissful moment" "because it's basically just become 'I'll do anything you want for five bucks.'" After introducing two men who will produce a video of them dancing in the jungle with a message painted on their bodies, PewDiePie walks us through other available services, including a message delivered by a Jesus Christ impersonator and a Donald Trump impersonator making phone calls and solicits a handful of services for himself before editing the video to a few days forward when his requests have been fulfilled. The video culminates with the two aforementioned semiclad men dancing and laughing in the jungle before unveiling a banner reading "Death to all Jews." That the video is not live and that it was edited to show PewDiePie partially typing the controversial message clearly shows his intent.

Following the publication of the video, the *Wall Street Journal* reported that PewDiePie had posted nine videos featuring antisemitic comments or Nazi imagery, including the aforementioned Jesus Christ impersonator who says, "Hitler did nothing wrong" ("I'm Banned" 2015), a video with PewDiePie wearing a "Make America Great Again" cap while watching a Hitler speech ("The YouTube Heroes!" 2016), multiple videos featuring swastikas, videos containing audio of the Nazi Party anthem, and archival "Sieg Heil" voiceovers. In response to the videos and the related media coverage, both YouTube and Maker Studios swiftly ended their commercial relationship with PewDiePie, with YouTube canceling the release of *Scare PewDiePie Season 2* and removing the PewDiePie channel from Google Preferred (the program that aggregates YouTube's top creators into higher-priced packages for advertisers).

PewDiePie's response was to claim that his content must be "understood as entertainment, and not political commentary," and that he in no way supports racism or "any kind of hateful attitudes" (PewDiePie 2017). Nevertheless, the community has fractured: his video content has been both championed by the white nationalist blog the *Daily Stormer* and criticized by the Anti-Defamation League for normalizing racism and racist attitudes, and deeply opposing voices clash within the comment sections of his videos. PewDiePie's content has skirted the platform's rules before, with homophobic slurs and jokes about rape and rape culture. The rush of racist material in his commentary feed increases the likelihood that YouTube will further pressure PewDiePie to adhere to its conduct rules, which ban any video that "promotes or condones violence against individuals or groups based on race or ethnic origin or religion" (YouTube Help 2018).

DIY Beauty: Michelle Phan

The DIY or do-it-yourself category includes online creators discussing beauty, style, and fashion tips. It also includes "how-to" videos, which cover a welter of SME material from popular science to practical repair hints. The most well-known beauty vlogger, and one of the most successful, is Michelle Phan, who in early 2017 had over 8.79 million YouTube subscribers, 3.16 million Facebook likes, and 2.1 million Instagram followers. Impressive figures, but an increasingly small part of her overall business profile.

While no longer among the highest-ranked YouTubers in terms of either output, subscribers, or video views, Vietnamese American Michelle Phan remains prominent among the burgeoning field of DIY/how-to beauty vloggers. The beauty-vlogger-turned-multimillionaire-beauty-mogul's success helped spawn a new generation of YouTube talent that has already surpassed Phan's subscriber and page view numbers, while simultaneously laying the groundwork for the turn to influencer marketing that both brands and creators now seek. While Phan's success owes a great deal to her self-determination and work ethic, she also enjoys first-mover advantage.

Phan is the original beauty vlogger, having started as early as 2007. In a field that now yields over 1.3 million channels if one searches for "beauty" on YouTube, having first-mover advantage has conferred considerable commercial momentum despite SME's extremely low barriers to entry. This is the case not only because DIY beauty is the most amenable to brand alignment of any native SME format but also because variations on the theme of applying makeup and wearing style/fashion accessories constitutes a narrow field. PewDiePie can play with indie games as much as Nintendo products, but there are few if any "indie" makeup companies. And as *the* original, she was able to "patent" a style of straightforward, artful, and well-edited videos that present audiences with easy-to-follow titles and clear voiceover instructions. With this unparalleled degree of brand alignment, Phan has laid out a template for how contemporary influencer marketing seeks to operate in the online space.

Michelle Phan's business empire is now orders of magnitude greater than the revenue she generates from online video. To her L'Oreal makeup line, Em, can be added book sales and her e-commerce/online community site Ipsy, which has over a million subscribers—Forbes has valued it at over $500 million. She has launched a network of online channels called ICON through her partnership with Endemol Beyond.

Phan has gone beyond relating to and managing her community; she has consistently mentored followers into the business. She is no longer preeminent in beauty vlogging. In terms of all YouTube channels, Michelle Phan, at the time of writing, is 91st in terms of subscriptions (8.77 million) and 462nd in terms of views. However, it should be noted that all three dedicated beauty channels that rank higher than Phan—YuYa (lady 16makeup) (16.4 million), Zoella (11.2 million), and Bethany Mota (10.2 million)—hold her as a beacon to their success. In an interview in 2014, Bethany Mota claimed to have stumbled upon Michelle Phan's videos and was "instantly hooked." "I thought, 'I finally have something to make videos about!' So I created an account and a couple of weeks later, uploaded my very first video" (Mau 2014). In 2012, after four years and two hundred videos, Phan was offered $1 million to create twenty hours of content by Google, enabling her to launch FAWN (For All Women Network), a YouTube multichannel network representing other influential beauty and style experts, including Jessica Harlow, Bethany Mota, Promise Phan, Daven Mayeda, and Chriselle Lim (PRWeb 2012). (Lim, we saw earlier, was called out for her inauthenticity.) Her company Ipsy claims more than 140 employees, including many beauty vloggers. Beauty vloggers who now outrank her in online hits (YuYa, Zoella, Bethany Mota) always acknowledge that Phan has created opportunities for them. The ICON venture represents many YouTubers and facilitates their profile on multiplatforms as well as on TV.

Phan's key self-narrative is the articulation of authenticity through the Cinderella story. Well established by 2013 and following the pattern of creators' staged self-revelation (akin to bringing Goffman's [1959] "back region" and "front region" together), she began to build the blocks of her Cinderella narrative. In the video "Draw My Life" (2013), Phan claims that at the time her first YouTube video was produced, she was keeping a personal online blog in which she depicted herself as the girl she wanted to be—one with sufficient money and a perfect family—while in reality she was struggling both financially and personally with insecurities gathered during her "unstable childhood." Phan reveals that her natural father was a problem gambler, and she and her family were often forced to move. At one point, her father disappeared and she did not see him for ten years. Phan's mother remarried, and the family's relationship with her stepfather, while good at first, eventually broke down, forcing the family to relocate again. At age seventeen, Phan, her mother, her brother, and her younger sister were living in a single rented room. Phan started work as a hostess to supplement her mother's income and, with some help from her extended family, enrolled at Ringling College of Art and Design, in Florida, in 2006. Upon enrollment Phan received the same laptop given to all incoming students, and joined YouTube.

Having always been interested in makeup (Phan's mother is a beauty technician), Phan applied for a job at a nearby Lancôme counter, and while she "nailed the demonstration," she was rejected because she did not have sales experience. Phan decided to repeat the demonstration online, and after initially uploading tutorial vlogs to her Xanga blog, she uploaded her first YouTube video—"Natural Looking Makeup Tutorial" on 20 May 2007. The self-edited, seven-minute tutorial pulled in a, for the time, huge forty thousand views within a week. (This video debuted the same month that YouTube first introduced its partner program. To date, it has garnered over 11.7 million views.) Phan was encouraged enough by the viral "hit" she had produced to quit her job as a hostess and turn her hand to YouTube as an additional means to supplement her family's income.

Despite her initial media success, Phan long maintained that her real "Cinderella moment" came when L'Oréal (with whom Phan was already making videos for their Lancôme imprint) gave her her own makeup line (Glamour 2013). Phan continued to build her beauty and lifestyle empire. A 2013 *Cosmopolitan* article on Phan claimed she was earning over $5 million a year (Sherman 2013). Realizing in 2015 that Em was not reaching sales expectations, due to both high prices for Phan's audience and lack of support from L'Oréal, Phan retook the brand and assumed control. As well, there were book sales (*Make Up: Your Life Guide to Beauty, Style, and Success—Online and Off*, 2014) and her e-commerce/ online community site Ipsy—which in addition to selling makeup and beauty products runs a "glam bag" program offering subscribers personalized selected monthly beauty products for a ten-dollar monthly membership fee. Phan claims Ipsy is sending out 1.5 million glam bags per month and boasts more than 140 employees, including other beauty vloggers hired to create content promoting the business. And Forbes. com reported that in 2015 Ipsy raised $100 million, with Forbes valuing the company at over $500 million (Robehmed 2015). Ultimately, Phan recognizes that the value in Ipsy resides in continued development of relationships and partnerships with brands. Phan says Ipsy has pulled in over one million candid product reviews—a veritable gold mine of data for the beauty and fashion industries.

In 2015, Phan launched ipsy Open Studios (ipsyOS)—a dedicated studio space for beauty vloggers—and partnered with Endemol Beyond USA to relaunch FAWN as a new premium lifestyle network named ICON. This was Phan's global outlet for "premium content, conversation, and community," serving a "multi-cultural demographic featuring original programming in beauty, fashion, wellness, DIY, food, human-interest stories, and travel" (http://icon.network). Phan's new ICON venture represents YouTubers like Ann Le, Cassey Ho, Charis Lincoln, and Anisa Noor through its own YouTube channels and on rival online video service Dailymotion, set-top box Roku, various connected TV services and TV syndication deals with AOL and Scripps Networks, and, of course, the full range of social media platforms Facebook, Twitter, Instagram, Snapchat, Pinterest, and Tumblr. In 2015 Phan also cofounded a music company called Shift Music Group, which will license tracks for use in online videos.

Creatively, Phan has scripted changes in her profile based on discourses of inner as well as outer beauty, and around the personal journey themed as the Cinderella story. She initially experimented with narrative in "Catch My Heart" (2011), a video she wrote and directed as a "love story meshed with a makeup tutorial" that includes a long line of acting, cinematography, and assistant credits along with disclaimers of sponsored products used. Her narrative videos continued, with her video "Underneath Your

Love" (2012) offering a "modern take on the Cinderella story"—a recurrent theme across large swaths of Phan's content—wherein the heroine will always emerge triumphant after finding *inner beauty*. "I believe that our insecurities can become our evil stepsisters. Learning to love and accept who you are can truly free you from your gilded cage. My mother always told me, that 'a beautiful heart will take you far'" ("Underneath Your Love" 2012). More recently, Phan has expanded her repertoire of videos to include content that is less focused on beauty and more on "life advice." "I see myself going more towards the storytelling element. My brand is going to evolve. I can't do the same thing every day, it gets boring" (Mau 2014). In this regard, Michelle Phan has been described (Yi 2016) as an "Oprah Winfrey for millennials" as she is growing her brand beyond beauty to female empowerment, and this suggests ways in which SME creators might learn strategies of brand extension, evolution, and sustainabilty over time from mainstream personality/lifestyle trajectories.

Critics have noted that Phan has adopted a "New Age" philosophy in both her more recent beauty, well-being, and travel vlogs and her public persona. For example, when prompted about her views on religion in a recent interview, Phan stated, "I believe if religion brings you to a sense of peace, that's beautiful. But I also believe if religion's not your thing, that's fine too, just so long as you're a good person and you find that one thing that leads you to peace and teaches you to have harmony with yourself and other people around you" (Marotta 2015). Her response led the journalist to ponder how Phan remains authentic in the beauty and makeup industry, suggesting that if someone is more aligned to root vegetables than Lancôme, isn't using and promoting concealer a little fake? Phan replies "Well, let me ask you this—what's considered fake? Brushing your teeth is not natural, right? Yet even a cat grooms itself *every* day" (Marotta 2015).

Phan's career—which outpaces PewDiePie's business scale by many orders of magnitude—and the DIY beauty vertical as a whole raises real questions around authenticity and "truth in advertising" when virtually every video is, at least on the denotative level, an exercise in multiple, explicit product placements. This has led critics such as Jayme Cyk (2015) to argue that, while beauty vlogging has become so pervasive and powerful within SME culture, its basic premise serves up contradictory messages that can strain credibility. Cyk suggests that while beauty vloggers

Figure 4.2. Beauty vlogger Michelle Phan has built an empire promoting inner beauty and branded cosmetics. Michelle Phan, https://www.youtube.com/watch?v=5_hTn9 STHB0&t=76s.

put forth their honest opinion on specific beauty products, an increasing number of them seek work from brands in order to draw a paycheck, raising questions around truth and bias in sponsored advice. Nevertheless, beauty vloggers like Phan insist that they remain unbiased in their viewpoint, even while on the corporate payroll. Phan maintains that she has always been up-front to her community about sponsorship and brand deals and, like most YouTube beauty vloggers, claims she maintains creative control and will not endorse products that she does not believe in herself, stating, "If there's a brand I don't like, I normally don't even talk about it or feature it. If someone is going to pay for something, it has to be a product that I really enjoy" (Cyk 2015).

These criticisms continue to play out for Phan, who has suffered anxiety and depression as a result of balancing her own celebrity amid high-profile business setbacks. In mid-2016 Phan took a year-long hiatus from all social media, deleting a large portion of her video back catalogue and changing her profile picture to a black box. Her online hiatus coincided with her buy-back of Em, the makeup line that L'Oréal produced and developed with her over a three-year period. Em was not well received, and poor sales, negative reviews, and accusations that Phan had "sold out" and that the product price was too high for her community demographic impacted her. Sternly disciplined in this way by her community, when Phan returned to YouTube in June 2017, with the animated video "Why I Left" (2017), she explained that she undertook a break as she no longer gained enjoyment or happiness from her achievements, suggesting that the price of fame had left her feeling "broken."

> Who I was on camera and who I was in real life began to feel like strangers. Money can bring out the worst in people, and I was no exception. My insecurities got the worst of me. I became imprisoned by my own vanity, and I was never satisfied with the way I looked. The life I led online was picture-perfect, but in reality, I was carefully curating the image of a life I wanted, not had. ("Why I Left" 2017)

A 2015 Defy Media study found that more than 60% of thirteen- to twenty-four-year-olds said they would try a product suggested by a YouTuber (Defy Media 2015), echoing Phan's suggestion that "the millennial generation grew up with TV commercials and got tired of seeing a 22-year-old model trying to sell us anti-aging cream. That's why we went online—to see the real story" (Spector 2015). But the "real story"— the claim to authenticity—can also increasingly be about anti-haul videos that strike out against overpriced product. This increasing element in the haul genre, and the community discipline it registers, is exactly what led Phan to take back her Em brand and take her channel dark (Gutelle 2017a). For high-end vloggers like Phan, the business is no longer, and perhaps never was, about being the most talented makeup technician and beauty stylist, but about the high-wire act of being able to engage a following while representing explicit product placement as an acceptable component of a wider journey into self and success.

Civic Entertainment: The Vlogbrothers (Hank and John Green)

Together, John and Hank host the popular YouTube channel Vlogbrothers, which is itself a part of a much larger portfolio of SME outlets and online communities. The Greens are the thought leaders of, and largest creative and social entrepreneurs in, the SME space. They exemplify the claims made in this chapter about authenticity and community. But given their highly principled communitarianism and commitment to civic activism, where are the brand relationships that we have argued challenge and complicate but also financially sustain online creator careers? As we have argued, this question comes into frame once the dynamics of authenticity and community are understood.

The Vlogbrothers story began in January 2007 (also the year of Michelle Phan's debut, the year YouTube introduced its Partners program) when the brothers launched the "Brotherhood 2.0" project, in which they pledged to cease all text-based communication between each other for a year, keeping in touch only via publicly accessible vlogs. (John had recently relocated from New York to Indianapolis, and Hank was a twenty-five-hour drive away in Missoula, Montana.) The project was made available on YouTube, as well as through the brothers' own Brotherhood 2.0 website. Following the conclusion of Brotherhood 2.0 at year's end, the brothers evolved the project into the Vlogbrothers channel, with John posting a video every Tuesday and Hank posting on Fridays, and set up a public website for their growing community of Nerdfighters.

Good morning, John.

Good morning Hank, it's Tuesday!

Figure 4.3. Brothers Hank and John Green together host long-running YouTube channel Vlogbrothers. Vlogbrothers, https://www.youtube.com/user/vlogbrothers.

The key portfolios that have been developed by, or in close collaboration with, the Green brothers include centrally the Vlogbrothers YouTube channel. This is their main channel, boasting 2.9 million subscribers, 652 million views, and 1,468 video uploads. The channel sells merchandise (clothing, posters, music) and is supported by Tumblr, Twitter, and Facebook accounts.

Included also are Nerdfighters (where the Greens engage and empower "nerds" like them in social and community causes); Crash Course (a project aimed to educate high school students through short-format educational video series); SciShow (videos showing that science is approachable); and Sexplanations (vernacular sex knowledge produced by Hank). There are many other YouTube channels produced by the Greens: for example, Animal Wonders Montana; the Brain Scoop (Natural Museum); Hank Games (gaming); Healthcare Triage (medical); Mental Floss (popular knowledge); and the Warehouse (merchandise tours).

In addition to video channels, there is DFTBA (Don't Forget to Be Awesome) Records, an e-commerce merchandise company and record label whose main focus is on music generated by prominent YouTube stars. The company represents top YouTubers, including Hank Green himself, Rhett and Link, Hannah Hart, and several others. The main annual conference and festival for the SME creator community is VidCon, created by the Greens in 2010. In 2013 YouTube signed a deal to become the principal sponsor of VidCon for two years. VidCon has evolved into a major industry conference for people and businesses working in the field. The 2016 VidCon drew twenty-five thousand attendees. In 2017 VidCon is going global with three separate conferences: Amsterdam in April, Anaheim in June, and Melbourne in September. Project for Awesome (P4A) is an annual two-day online event in which YouTubers create videos about their favorite charities and nonprofit organizations to encourage individual donations for perks like signed merchandise. In 2013, they launched Subbable, a subscription-based crowd-funding platform that facilitates subscribers pledging a small monthly donation to creators in exchange for certain perks. In March 2015 Subbable was acquired by Patreon, a competing and better-capitalized subscription-based crowd-funding platform.

Through their honed creator practices of vlogging and community engagement, the Vlogbrothers have effectively harnessed the participa-

Figure 4.4. VidCon, created by the Greens, is the industry's major conference. Photo by David Craig.

tory nature of SME to connect with like-minded youth where they meet (that is, online), tapping into a gestalt in which many young people feel disenchanted and disenfranchised with mainstream politics. The sense of belonging in a community is central for Nerdfighters, who are mostly in their formative years—a time when peer relationships are a central preoccupation. Nerdfighters offer like-minded youth an interest-driven friendship group, and for "nerds"—stereotypically introverted, shy, or awkward—an online community like Nerdfighters (with real-life on- and off-line social opportunities) provides a place where they can be themselves and make friends with like-minded others. This ethos ex- tends also to their commitment to charity, such as their involvement in developing and promoting "This Star Won't Go Out," a charity that offers assistance to the families of children diagnosed with cancer that was founded in memory of Ester Grace Earl—a Nerdfighter diagnosed with thyroid cancer in 2006 who remained active in the community until she died in 2010—the inspiration behind John Green's *The Fault in Our Stars* (2012).

The Vlogbrothers' many projects and supervening ethos exemplify everything that is positive about participatory culture. In *Textual Poach- ers* (1992), Jenkins discusses fandom as "a participatory culture which transforms the experience of media consumption into the production

Figure 4.5. Merchandise available to supporters of the Nerdfighter community. Vlogbrothers, https://store.dftba.com/collections/vlogbrothers.

of new texts, indeed of a new culture and a new community" (Jenkins 1992, 46). Jenkins defines participatory culture as participation contrasted with spectatorship, positioning fans not only as consumers of media but as a creative social community that uses popular culture as a raw material, which they reappropriate for their own goals. Youth-driven participatory culture spaces provide an opportunity to explore identity, connect with like-minded others, and develop skills necessary for participation in causes and communities. The content they produce connects young people with "everyday politics" (Highfield 2016).

The Greens define a Nerdfighter as "a person who, instead of being made of bones, skin and tissue, is made entirely of awesome," and the "barriers of entry" to being a Nerdfighter are kept intentionally low. As the Vlogbrothers explain in the video "How to Be a Nerdfighter:

A Vlogbrothers FAQ" (2009), "If you want to be a Nerdfighter, you are a Nerdfighter." The Nerdfighters community resides under the umbrella of two overarching goals—to "decrease world suck," and "don't forget to be awesome." The deliberately broad definitions of "world suck" and "awesome" leave a great deal of space for interpretation of what this means to Nerdfighters, from an individual doing something at a personal level to the collective engagement in projects such as Project for Awesome (P4A).

As mentioned, the Vlogbrothers' content prompts Nerdfighters to consider their own role as agents of social change. While the lead status of the Greens within the Nerdfighter community is central to their ability to mobilize their community, it differs significantly from the model of celebrity activism in which the celebrity's influence is derived mostly from the attention he or she commands. Neta Kligler-Vilenchik (2016) writes that "the successful translation of Nerdfighters' participation into civic influence cannot be attributed simply to the size of the VlogBrothers' following." If that were the case, she argues, we would see much larger mobilization by fans of, for instance, Katy Perry, who has ninety-four million Twitter followers. This highlights a difference between the efforts of celebrities to mobilize a fan base around their "pet causes" and the grassroots work of communities who pull on popular culture resources and interpersonal connections to energize their social change efforts (Kligler-Vilenchik 2016). The Vlogbrothers can mobilize their community because they have invested heavily in maintaining ongoing, authentic communication with their community through a mix of regular videoblogging, direct interaction with individuals through social media, and offline Nerdfighter gatherings and events.

Jenkins's continuing work on participatory culture, now extending over decades, has focused recently on concrete examples of the movement from participatory culture to participatory politics. He comments (Jenkins 2016, 47), apropos the Nerdfighters,

> Most forms of activism reach the same core group of participants, who already are politically engaged, and redirect them toward new issues. But the . . . Nerdfighters . . . often target young people who are engaged culturally, who may already be producing and sharing fan art, and help them to extend their engagement into politics, often by deploying existing skills and capacities in new ways.

Many of the Vlogbrothers' videos start by positioning a current event or issue within its broader historical or political context, assisted by behind-the-scenes research and production work. Their core body of videos sutures informal vlogging to wider civic and political issues, openly discussing public concerns pertinent to young people (e.g. environmentalism or LGBT rights) and broader civic and democratic processes (e.g. importance of voting, paying taxes), global issues (e.g. the Arab Spring, the Zaatari refugee camp) alongside of, and often enmeshed within, "everyday" blogging topics such as "16 sports that should be in the Olympics" and "The time I fell asleep with an M&M in my mouth." A now canonical example within the Vlogbrothers catalogue is their "peanut butter face" video of 2008 ("Peanut Butter Face [while discussing the Georgia-Russia War]" 2008). In the video, John provides a detailed account of the war between Russia and Georgia while slathering peanut butter over his face, proclaiming, "[E]veryone knows the only way to get the internet to pay attention to news is via peanut butter face." Their videos maintain a standardized YouTuber/vlog aesthetic—self-deprecation, slapstick humor, the familiar rapid-fire speech, jumpy and stylized editing, "insider" jokes, community shout-outs and collaborations—but put at the service of civic politics.

* * *

Because they eschew all direct relations with brands, the Vlogbrothers may appear not to fit appropriately in the analytical framework we have set up. They never do direct brand promotions. That said, they work in a thoroughly commercial framework—brands are prominent at VidCon, and John Green's earnings in 2014 were estimated at $9 million, largely due to the film adaptation of his 2012 novel, *The Fault in Our Stars*. Merchandising and entrepreneurial ventures such as Subbable and VidCon add considerably to their revenue streams. Nevertheless, their approach to revenue generation through advertising and branding remains different from that of most YouTubers, with pre-roll advertising against their videos only finally enabled in 2015. In mid-2015 Hank Green asked the community if they should enable pre-roll ads, and if so, where the money from the revenue should go (Brouwer 2015c). The community decided that the Greens should give half of their pre-roll revenue to the Foundation to Decrease World Suck, and half to the Vlogbrothers' Sponsorship program. The result has seen the Vlogbrothers accepting applications from YouTubers working on an "an online educational/informational/ super awesome project," and recipients have included the antiviolence/ antiharassment nonprofit Uplift, the *Yeah Maybe, No* documentary about consent and sexual violence, and the Physics Girl YouTube channel. Their overall approach to income generation is philosophically consistent with statements John Green has made about his own personal wealth:

> When we imagine that people's net worth is directly correlated with their value as a person or professional, I think we give money too much power. . . . My family is incredibly lucky (and privileged) to have financial security. But I'm not sure what money can do beyond providing financial security. Like, I am not in need of a yacht. I feel like owning a yacht would stress me out. (Brouwer 2015c)

The key brand relationship, however—and the key to understanding the Greens' place in the authenticity-community-brand relationship—is actually with YouTube itself. Hank Green's attacks on Facebook's "lies" about the way it counts views (Green 2015b) need to be seen in this context. His interventions, such as this one, which influenced Facebook to change its practice, are in the name of the true state of play ("lies") and are always done in the cause of standing up for the community—which is, to a significantly greater extent than either PewDiePie's or Michelle Phan's, a creator-community. The Greens have recently been given the role of Community Ambassadors for YouTube.

They were key advisors to YouTube in the creation of the "Community button." After its many attempts to build more dynamic social media affordances into the platform—Orkut (2004–2014), Google Friend Connect (2008–2013), Buzz (2010–2011), Google Plus (2011–2015)—YouTube turned in 2016 to the community for advice in integrating its latest social networking effort, the aptly named "community" button/tab that can be embedded on selected YouTube channels (with the promise of full rollout if successful). The YouTube Community tab is an attempt to keep creators from departing to competing platforms (that are increasingly moving toward video, see chapters 1, 2, and 3) by offering more tools for better audience connection and further community development well beyond the videos themselves.

The Greens have been central to the prototyping of the YouTube Community Tab. On their channel, they use the Community Tab to inform their fans about updates to their channels, events, and other fun links and photos they have been collecting, engaging with viewers using text, gifs, images, and live feeds that their community can thumb up or down as well as comment on. Effectively, the tab allows the Greens to run their own mini–social network of sorts within their You-Tube channel (an important issue for the Greens, given their Facebook criticisms), and as John Green explains, "[W]e've always had to build homes off YouTube for the non-video community stuff. . . . YouTube has always thought of itself as being about video, but for many of us, it's mostly been about community. I'd argue that the best YouTube channels aren't just shows you lean back and watch, they're communities you're a part of."

Exemplifying the authenticity-community-brand relationship, he continues:

> I'm really excited about it because one, it means that Hank and I can finally make our YouTube channels the community hubs we always wanted them to be, two, live shows are now easier and better, and three, in our beta testing the quality of discourse in comments in the community tab has been great. I just realized I sound like I'm being paid to say these things, to be clear, I'm not. We have never and will never accept any kind of corporate sponsorship on Vlogbrothers. But we did work closely with YouTube on the development of the community tab and I do think it's awesome. ("YouTube's New Thing [and a New Thing of Our Own]" 2016)

Outro

This chapter has developed an analytical framework to understand the modes of address, or discourses, that characterize three native-to-online content types (gameplay, DIY beauty, civic entertainment). These types of content differ sharply from established screen entertainment, and are constituted from intrinsically interactive audience-centricity and appeals to authenticity and community in a commercializing space that we call social media entertainment. We have argued that there are three key characteristics that, in their interaction, allow us to form the analytical framework necessary to understand the discursive dynamics of social media entertainment.

The first is that the claims to authenticity that animate native SME content are established through comparisons with the presumed inauthenticity of established fictional screen formats. The second is that the distinctive mode of address of SME is constituted in the relationship *between* discourses of authenticity and community. The third is that there is a discursive logic that attempts to render brand relationships subordinate to the dominant discourses of authenticity and community.

The chapter sits in dialogue with those, such as Alice Marwick, Brooke Duffy, Jose van Dijck, Crystal Abidin, Hector Postigo, Henry Jenkins, Sam Ford and Joshua Green, and Sarah Banet-Weiser, who have analyzed the fundamental value claims of online content and its producers. We have offered a revisionist analysis of the shaping and disciplining of brand culture, and of creators, through the twinned discourses of authenticity and community. But there are many related value claims made by SME creators who use the platforms to engage with progressive cultural politics, and it is to these that we now turn.

5

Cultural Politics of Social Media Entertainment

The decades-long struggle over media diversity and representation in entertainment reached a kind of apex in 2016. In January, for the second year in a row, the Academy Awards failed to recognize any person of color in the acting categories. Prior to the Oscars ceremony, a vocal backlash emerged, including an online hashtag activist campaign that went viral called #OscarsSoWhite. After the broadcast, numerous minority activist organizations joined forces, including the National Association for the Advancement of Colored People (NAACP) along with a coalition of Hispanic, Asian American, and Native American activist organizations, "to pressure the big six movie studios for more diversity" (McNary 2016a).

Although the timing was coincidental, a month later, academia joined the chorus. USC Annenberg's Institute for Diversity and Empowerment (IDEA) published its "Comprehensive Annenberg Report on Diversity in Entertainment" (Smith, Choueiti, and Piper 2016), which assessed "inclusion on screen and behind the camera in fictional films, TV shows, and digital series distributed by 10 major media companies (21st Century Fox, CBS, Comcast NBC Universal, Sony, the Walt Disney Company, Time Warner, Viacom, Amazon, Hulu, and Netflix)" (Smith, Choueiti, and Piper 2016, 1). The report was damning; featured in numerous press stories, it quantified the underrepresentation of female, older, Black, Asian, Latino, Middle Eastern, and LGBTQ characters on screen and behind. Their conclusion: Hollywood "still functions as a straight, white, boy's club" (Smith, Choueiti, and Piper 2016, 16).

At the same time, SME diversity was garnering recognition and advocacy. In May, the Coalition of Asian-Pacifics in Entertainment (CAPE) launched its third series in its advocacy #IamCampaign. The series has featured Asian American creators Michele Phan, Phil Yu, Ryan Higa, David Choi, Wong Fu Productions, and Dominix "D-Trix" Sandoval. Similarly, in August 2016, GLAAD announced that Hannah Hart would be the second creator (after Tyler Oakley) to receive the Davidson/Valentini award as "an LGBTQ media professional who has made a significant difference in promoting equality and acceptance for the LGBTQ community" (Weiss 2016c). Hart was recognized for creating a series of videos on YouTube that discussed her coming out along with other LGBTQ topics, which have garnered over 3.5 million views.

Over the summer, the 2016 Streamy Awards, which honor the best in online video awards and creators, announced their nominees,

Figure 5.1. Tyler Oakley and Friends. Tyler Oakley (@tyleroakley), https://twitter.com /tyleroakley.

including Indian-Canadian-Sikh Lily Singh, LGBTQ American Tyler Oakley, African American Viner King Bach, Asian American YouTuber Ryan Higa, transgender beauty vlogger Gigi Gorgeous, and Muslim American Yousef Erakat, aka Fousey. In the "Social Good" category, they recognized the #ProudToLove Campaign on behalf of LGBTQ marriage equality and Tyler Oakley's Birthday Campaign to raise funds for the Trevor Project, an organization that provides crisis intervention for LGBTQ young people.

The global media platform and entertainment industry site Mashable.com published its own Hollywood "Diversity Report Card" that considered representation across the media industries. The film, television, and game industries received grades of C and D, whereas "YouTubers/Digital Entertainment" received an A. According to the editors,

> The online video industry's diversity track record is rooted in online video giant YouTube, which has evolved into the go-to space for creators of all ages, races, genders, and sexual orientations. Such a wide variety of voices and content spawned diversity across the digital entertainment industry, with companies and creators maintaining the all-inclusive philosophy. (Hamedy 2015)

The #OscarsSoWhite "moment" and its aftermath dramatically illustrate the concerns over diversity of media representation shared by industry players, scholars, activists, and journalists. More notably, for the purpose of this chapter, it points to the equally dramatic distinctions between cultural diversity in mainstream and social media entertainment. Within the broader concerns surrounding the cultural politics of media, we focus specifically on media representation and activism within SME, specifically that of Asian American and LGBTQ creators. In contrast to traditional entertainment, both groups have greater visibility and influence in this emerging industry. In our survey of Asian American creators, we consider how they critically account for their representational practices in this industry. In recognition of the distinctive identity work of LGBTQ creators, we offer an account of the *activist trajectories* of most of these creators. These journeys extend beyond coming out and show an increasingly overt political engagement with calls to action in support of the LGBTQ community and other progressive issues.

In this book, we have sought to take full account of structural conditions—huge, globe-spanning online platforms owned by corporations far bigger than the Hollywood majors that have had a dominating influence on global media; a fast-advancing algorithmic culture; and the precariousness of online labor. But the core of our project is a commitment to new voices and new forms of enterprise—professionalizing and commercializing creators pursuing sustainable careers. We are interested in tracking cultural progressivity as it creates space within commercializing systems. There is strong evidence to suggest that we are finding those types of voices, businesses, and careers to a larger extent in the online social media entertainment space than in older, established global media orders.

Specifically, our intention here is to focus programmatically on the progressive potential of SME. For decades, media scholars have articulated a vision of resistance, subversion, and self-definition: "Ultimately, the most effective form of resistance to the hegemony of the mainstream is to speak for oneself, to disseminate narratives and images that counter the accepted, oppressive, or inaccurate ones" (Gross and Woods 1999, 16). In this chapter, we will work through how such a praxis is occurring through the lives and work of these leading cases in the cultural politics of diversity in a commercializing online space.

Where Representation Meets Activism

Cultural theorist Larry Grossberg asserts, "'Hollywood' . . . its powers— not only economic and cultural, but also political—have haunted critics and intellectuals for at least a century" (Grossberg 2010, xiii). Over the past several decades, these concerns around the power of entertainment have contributed to the rise of new disciplines (critical cultural studies) and contending schools of thought feeding in from Frankfurt to Birmingham. The politics of representation has been a core concern: "The idea that all cultural representations are political is one of the major themes of media and cultural theory of the past several decades" (Kellner and Durham 2012, 16). The politics of representation includes not only media visibility but also invisibility. Allied to Pierre Bourdieu's notions of symbolic power and violence (1990), George Gerbner and Larry Gross (1976) are clear that the absence of media representation represents "symbolic annihilation" (Gerbner and Gross 1976, 182).

More precisely, concerns over media representation have focused on the margins—around minorities and diversity. These concerns are aligned with the goals of "a multiculturalist program that demonstrates how culture reproduces certain forms of racism, sexism, and biases against members of subordinate classes, social groups, or alternative lifestyles" (Kellner 2003, 3). As part of larger concerns with social movements and social justice on behalf of minorities, this struggle "serves as a means for minority groups to acquire cultural rights, and invariably, political rights as well" (Lopez 2016, 12). Media representations are political, and the struggle for more diverse and responsible media representations is a vital strategy towards securing full cultural citizenship (Miller 2006).

Debates on the cultural politics of representation have evolved from a focus on content, text, and image to questions of active audience and critical reception. These concerns have emphasized visibile diversity as well as more responsible and nuanced forms of representation that, for example, extend beyond stereotypes and feature those typically rendered passive more centrally in the narrative. We adopt more holistic, multiperspectival approaches such as those advocated by Douglas Kellner (2003), John Caldwell (2008), and Timothy Havens, Amanda Lotz, and Serra Tinic (2009). Combined, these approaches account for "critical industrial practices" that inform representational practices and, in some instances, forms of media activism conducted by practitioners operating within the cultures of media production.

Yet, even the most multiperspectival cultural and media studies approaches have not accounted for the distinctiveness of SME, where traditional hierarchies and divisions of creative media labor have either collapsed or are being replaced by new industrial and creative practices. As we saw in chapter 2, creators operate as producers, writers, actors, and directors, as well as marketing and distribution executives, business strategists, and entrepreneurs. SME intermediaries, whether firms or professionals, offer highly differentiated value propositions, from digital studios producing content to talent representatives brokering deals on behalf of creators to advertising-focused influencer marketing firms.

Media activism, along with media representation, has also been an established focus of concern in media and cultural studies. Robert Hackett and William Carroll (2006) offer a typical definition: "organized 'grassroots' efforts directed to creating or influencing media practices and strategies, whether as a primary objective, or as a byproduct of other campaigns (for example, efforts to change public opinion on environmental issues)" (Hackett and Carroll 2006, 28). "Grassroots" functions here to signal the way scholars have focused on alternative, usually nonprofit, media activism explicitly on behalf of social, cultural, or political movements. When seeking to understand the potential for activism within commercial media culture, scholars have been more muted. Roopali Mukherjee and Sarah Banet-Weiser (2012) employ the term "commodity activism" to describe the "promise and perils of consumer-based modes of resistance as they take shape within the dynamics of neoliberal power" (Mukherjee and Banet-Weiser 2012, 2). Lori Lopez (2016) acknowledges "the difficult and complex negotiations we must make in a neo-liberal moment in which the marketplaces have become the central site for rendering identities visible and allowing capitalist endeavors to be reframed as ethical or political" (Lopez 2016, 129). Beyond representation, however, she argues that "media activists must explicitly connect media representations to social realities" (Lopez 2016, 24).

Others are more sanguine about such potential. Kevin Howley (2014) proposes the term "media intervention" ("activities and projects that secure, exercise, challenge, or acquire media power for tactical and strategic action" (Howley 2014, 5) and suggests that it can account for "why commercial and corporate interests exercise media power to effect change" (Howley 2014, xiv). In his account of "political entertainment," Jeffery Jones (2010) challenges the traditional binary between entertainment and information, which "obscures the array of interactions that citizens have with political programming forms, engagements that cannot be captured in such limited categorization" (Jones 2010, 13). Jones argues that "popular culture is just as capable of shaping and supporting a culture of citizenship as it is of shaping and supporting a culture of consumption" (Jones 2010, 39).

Social media have amplified these concerns around representation and activism, commercialism, and entertainment, while also provoking engagement around their political and progressive potential. In his account of an emerging network society, Manuel Castells (2007) identifies how the means for *mass self-communication* represent potential for counterpower, which he defines as "the capacity of a social actor to resist and challenge power relations that are institutionalized" (Castells 2007, 237). In *Convergence Culture*, Henry Jenkins (2006) traces the influences of a participatory culture on education and media reform. More recently, Tim Highfield (2016) has described how social media may operate at the intersection of the political and the personal, of *everyday politics*. He studies how "social media afford the opportunity for different groups, including citizens, traditional political actors and journalists, to contribute to, discuss, challenge and participate in diverse aspects of politics in a public, shared context" (Highfield 2016, 19).

In *By Any Media Necessary*, Jenkins and his colleagues (2016) feature case studies of how youth are harnessing social media to engage in more overtly political forms of social media activism beyond the quotidian and the representational. According to Jenkins, "[W]e have seen an expansion of the communicative and organizational resources available to everyday people (and grassroots organizations) as we become more and more accustomed to using networked communications toward our collective interests" (Jenkins 2016, 3). (We have seen one of the best examples of this, SME creators Hank and John Green [aka Vlogbrothers], in chapter 4.)

In other accounts, the space for cultural progressivity in social media is more circumscribed. Alice Marwick (2013), for example, is unequivocal: social media promotes micro-celebrity and entrepreneurial self-branding, and "[t]aken as a whole, these themes of authenticity, meritocracy, and entrepreneurialism reinforce both a closed system of privilege and one centered around the core beliefs of neoliberal capitalism" (Marwick 2013, 247). Banet-Weiser (2011) provides a more nuanced approach in her account of YouTube videos produced by girls: "The fact that some girls produce media—and thus ostensibly produce themselves through their self-presentation—within the context of a commercially-driven technological space is not only evidence of a kind of empowering self-work but also a way to self-brand in an increasingly ubiquitous brand culture" (Banet-Weiser 2011, 284).

This scholarship acts as important analytical framing, but, as we have seen in previous chapters, SME represents distinct terrain to be mapped. Technological, communicative, and commercial affordances are different. In contrast to the scarcity and complex intermediation of traditional media, these affordances allow for the distribution of unlimited content without demanding ownership and with censorship essentially limited only by viewer age and commercial, especially brand, sensitivity. Social media platforms feature an array of precision analytical measurement. Cultural influence can be traced through comment streams. The collapsed division of labor constitutes creative producer, business developer, and political strategist in one fused agent. The normative discourses of authenticity and community, as we have discussed in chapter 4, determine what might appear to be formulaic but highly effective "rhetorical action." The platforms provide far more open access, although digital divides persist in various countries depending on regulation, affordability, and technology. Most important, as we have seen at the start of the chapter, SME is a far more diverse and open cultural space than traditional media.

In the light of these differences, the heightened visibility of diverse creators (that is, their representational politics) but also their influence (that is, their cultural activism) can be brought closer together. Google recently posted the results of a series of studies that account for the heightened cultural influence of YouTube creators (O'Neile-Hart and Blumenstein 2016). These studies indicated that 70% of teenage YouTube subscribers relate to creators more than to traditional celebrities, while 40% claim that their favorite creator understands them better than their friends do. They also indicated that 70% of YouTube subscribers believe the platform changes and shapes culture. These studies, to reiterate, were commissioned by Google, which clearly renders them tendentious. Nonetheless, these data are significant as part of broader trends in marketing developments, which consistently point to the rise of online creators as "influencers," while underlining that this means deepening cultural influence alongside their commercial value to advertisers and brands. These claims have been repeated by other press outlets conducting their own surveys, including those conducted by *Variety* (Ault 2014, 2015).

Asian American Creators

We look to account for the heightened visibility and influence of Asian Americans in SME—in stark contrast to their presence in traditional entertainment. We draw on the limited academic literature that has addressed the matter of Asian Americans online. Our account complements this research, featuring interviews with numerous Asian American creators and how they reflexively account for their heightened representational and activist strategies. Insights have been generated from interviews with creator Phillip Wang of Wong Fu Productions, musician David Choi, prominent Viner Zach King, LGBTQ Asian American web series creator Matt Palazzolo, LGBTQ Indian American Krishna Kumar, early YouTube star and creator Kim Evey, social media journalist and marketing expert Benny Luo, former YouTube executive, social media entrepreneur, and cofounder of Victorious, Bing Chen, and social media entrepreneur and partner in Social Edge, Vak Sambath.

According to the Pew Research Center (2013), there are twenty million Asian American US citizens, comprising nearly 6% of the population. They are not only the fastest-growing racial group in the population but also the "highest income, best-educated," and most satisfied of any group. They are also the largest group of immigrants coming to the United States, outnumbering Hispanics in the past decade. That said, they still represent significantly lower percentages of the population than other US racial groups, including Hispanic and Latino/a Americans (17%) and African Americans (12%). The Asian American population also embraces wide multilingual, ethnic, national, and subcultural diversity. The Pew report lists over twenty populations, from Chinese, Filipino, Indian, Vietnamese, Korean, and Japanese to those from Okinawa, Malaysia, and Indonesia.

Despite the history, embeddedness, and growth of this US community, Asian Americans are dramatically underrepresented in film and television entertainment. USC's "Comprehensive Annenberg Report on Diversity in Entertainment" (Smith, Choueiti, and Piper 2016) claims that only 1.4% of films feature Asian leads. In more than half of the films, television shows, and digital series covered in the report, not a single Asian character could be identified. A similar GLAAD report claimed that less than 4% of television roles feature Asian Americans. We could find little contemporary data on Asian Americans employed off-screen in Hollywood, which is telling in its own right.

Furthermore, the entertainment industry engages in a pernicious but time-honored practice of "whitewashing." Whitewashing refers to the practice of Caucasian actors playing minorities in films, especially Asian

Americans. This casting practice continues in recent films such as *The Prince of Persia*, *Aloha*, *The Martian*, *Ghost in the Shell*, and Marvel's *Doctor Strange*. These racist practices have contributed to a backlash from the community, as reflected by this headline from the *Hollywood Reporter*: "Where Are the Asian American Movie Stars?" (Sun and Ford 2016).

The now-notorious 2016 Oscars even featured a racist joke about Asians. The joke was made by the host, Chris Rock, who had spent the evening critiquing the lack of African American nominees and the backlash created by the #OscarsSoWhite campaign. Even when Hollywood offers an apology for its lack of diversity, it may only appear in black and white. The backlash generated letters from Asian members of the Academy and on social media. Comparable to the viral hashtag campaign of #OscarsSoWhite, the social media movement created by Asian American activist Jaya Sundrash urged "followers to use #onlyonepercent to reflect the fact that Asian Americans have rec'd only 1% of Oscar noms in its history" (Ryzik 2016).

In television, these racist conditions and practices persist. In 2015, the Asian-themed ABC sitcom *Fresh off the Boat* came under criticism, most notably from Eddie Huang, whose life and memoir serve as the basis for the series that he sold to ABC. Huang is a chef, comedian, and social media activist who took to Twitter to savage the series before the show even aired, complaining that "the network's approach was to tell a universal, ambiguous, cornstarch story about Asian-Americans resembling moo goo gai pan written by a Persian-American who cut her teeth on race relations writing for Seth MacFarlane. . . . And why isn't there a Taiwanese or Chinese person who can write this?" (Moraes 2015).

Sundrash's and Huang's activism underlines how social media has emboldened the community to respond to Hollywood's perceived indifference to their concerns. Lopez (2016) points to "the outpouring of Asian American voices in the blogosphere" that has contributed to online activism and the potential for a sustainable social movement (Lopez 2016, 421). Amanda Hess (2016) similarly noted how the backlash from the Asian American community has been fueled by "an imaginative, on-the-ground social media army," referring to the proliferation of criticism across Twitter, Facebook, and other platforms. These practices are informed by additional distinctions between this community and others around access and early adoption of digital technology. In a recent Pew Research Center report, Andrew Perrin and Maeve Duggan (2015) described how Asian Americans use the Internet, have broadband, and own a smartphone in higher percentages than any other racial group, including Whites.

The early adoption and prolific use of social media by Asian Americans, including for engaging in forms of media activism, underpin their widely acknowledged overindexing and influence within SME. Contrasting SME to Hollywood, Austin Considine (2011) noted that "it's an entirely different story on the democratized platform of YouTube, where a young generation of Asian-Americans has found a voice (and millions of eager fans)." At the time of Considine's overview, three of the top twenty channels on the platform featured Asian Americans, including beauty vlogger Michelle Phan and comedian personality Ryan Higa, aka Nigahiga. Considine argues that such creators are not only prolific and successful but are operating with distinction around concerns over representation. As Asian American YouTuber Kevin Wu, aka Kevin Jumba, claims, "I'll talk about things that Asians don't like to talk about. We're a new breed of Asian Americans and I'm representative of that" (Considine 2011).

Critical studies of the representational dynamics of multicultural content and creators online offer conflicting but evolving accounts. Lei Guo and Summer Harlow (2014) conducted content analysis of 150 popular videos featuring Blacks, Latinos, and Asians, to consider "whether the most popular videos on the site were citizen-generated or professionally generated, to what degree the videos challenged racist stereotypes, and how audiences responded" (Guo and Harlow 2014, 282). They conclude that "YouTube caters to representations of race and stereotypes as fodder more for entertainment than for any actual contestation of power" (Guo and Harlow 2014, 296). Varying the argument somewhat, Guo and Lorin Lee (2013) describe how Asian Americans creators have proliferated influentially on YouTube, securing large audiences as well as commercial endorsements and revenue. Two prominent creators are considered, Ryan Higa and Kevin Wu; their analysis concluded that these creators were *potentially* revolutionary because they cultivated more and "cooler" visibility for Asian Americans while also engaging with other forms of identity work around race, commercialization, and sexuality. Nonetheless, the potential was limited by reinforced stereotypes and essentialized Asian identity (Guo and Lee 2013, 404).

Lopez (2016) provides a deeper, more nuanced account of the cultural citizenship of Asian American media activism in the digital age. Her work focuses on the "sites where mediated cultural citizenships are being deliberately engaged, formed, and recreated through the body of the collective" (Lopez 2016, 14). Lopez's emphasis on the collective captures how SME offers arguably more community engagement and thus potential influence than mainstream entertainment does. In her chapter about Asian American YouTubers and celebrities, Lopez offers a mixed assessment of their representational practices and activism. On the one hand, she affirms that these creators have the critical agency to "voice their opinions, initiate conversations, create their own media, and increase the impact of their messages—tactics which act in concert with or contribute to the efforts of Asian American media activists" (Lopez 2016, 141). At the same time, Lopez criticizes these creators for generating content in which "racism becomes sublimated and there is no intentional engagement with the politics of representation for Asian Americans" (Lopez 2016, 156). She mentions that some creators regularly promote charitable causes, but these are not always overtly political or dedicated to concerns over racism. Nonetheless, Lopez affirms, "[T]his cultural work is arguably political because it renders Asian American identities legible and disseminates Asian American narratives and voice" (Lopez 2016, 151).

Lopez's work uses interviews with Wong Fu Productions, whom she describes as narrative storytellers. We also interviewed Philip Wang, one of the principals in Wong Fu Productions. WFP is one of the most popular Asian Americans creators on YouTube—it has been posting videos since the platform was launched. In addition to nearly three million subscribers and nearly half a billion views on its first YouTube channel (as of mid-2017), WFP has 300,000 subscribers on its MoreWongFu YouTube channel featuring behind-the-scenes, direct vlogging accounts of its upcoming productions, which it also features on its Snapchat channel. In addition, WFP has over 650,000 Facebook likes, 266,000 Instagram followers, and 217,000 Twitter followers, plus hundreds more on its individual channels, pages, and sites, as well as its WongFuProductions .com site.

For over a decade in SME, WFP has created a sustainable business, deriving revenue from programmatic advertising and influencer marketing. It also runs a live-events business called International Secret Agents (ISA), which brought together a community of Asian American talent, including other online creators, with their communities. This venture reflects WFP's cultural and commercial practices integrated with its online and platform brand. It also has one of the most successful SME merchandise lines, called Awkward Animals, featuring plush toys and apparel. Its feature film projects have been community and crowd funded through sites like Indie-a-gogo, including *Everything before Us*, which was released exclusively on Vimeo, where it can be viewed separately through Pay Per View.

On first glance, WFP may look like an SME outlier because its scripted content more closely emulates traditional media narratives. But the content posted across its platforms is actually more diverse, including content more native to SME, like sketch comedy and gameplay. Nonetheless, as Wang acknowledges, "We didn't start this to be famous or personalities. We just wanted to focus on content. We just happened to need to be personalities on top of it. . . . I'd rather make a story that is meaningful to me than ride this 'Gangnam Style' wave or release 'a Harlem Shake' video" (Wang 2015). Here, Wang alludes to the generally greater reluctance of Asian Americans to base their online presence around individuated personality, while acknowledging the distinctiveness of SME and the convergent creative and entrepreneurial practices demanded of creators in this industry.

Regarding content, Wang professes that WFP's videos are fundamentally meant for all audiences. "We didn't intend to represent Asian America; nonetheless, we do and take this responsibility seriously." In a demonstrably critical account of the importance of multicultural media representations, the cultural and progressive affordances of SME, and his own work, Wang said,

> For any culture that's becoming mainstream, there's a process. I think Black culture has had to go through that, though they've been in the US longer. The Latino/Hispanic demographic has been going through that as well. I feel like we're the newbies, and we're trying to get ours going. Social media and technology has helped our community. . . . I would

like to get to a point where more Americans are more tolerant of not just Asian Americans but everyone. That goes beyond media; that's education, politics, and government. But from our part, what we can contribute is through media. I'm not going to be a politician anytime soon. What I can do is give young people an image they can look up to. (Wang 2015)

Furthermore, although WFP's content may not be intended solely or even primarily for Asian American audiences, Wang agrees that the Asian American community has helped sustain the business. He claims WFP's content appeals to this audience because "there isn't anywhere else to see themselves" (Wang 2015).

Creator musician David Choi made similar responses to Wang's around critical concerns of Asian American diversity, representation, and community more broadly in popular culture as well as his own work. Like WFP, Choi is a prominent, veteran Asian American creator who has spent a decade building his community and brand on YouTube and, now, other platforms. This has allowed Choi to pursue a more traditional career as well, not in the United States but in Asia, where he tours and has signed with Warner Music's Asia division. His career reinforces the global reach of these platforms, which allow multicultural creators to cultivate global

Figure 5.2. Wong Fu Productions has successfully secured large audiences alongside commercial endorsements and revenue. Wong Fu Productions, https://www.youtube .com/user/WongFuProductions.

communities and whose cross-cultural appeal means they can develop careers outside their own country. Like Wang, Choi claims his romantic songs are meant to be universal but is "happy that Asian Americans support him" (Choi 2015). He also confirms that the appeal of his content is informed by the lack of Asian American visibility in entertainment.

> There was no platform for Asian Americans at all. There was an Asian Channel (on TV) but that's what our parents watched. There was nothing for the young kids. That's what YouTube was. There were enough Asian Americans in the United States who found it to be really interesting and entertaining, and they just watched it. I think a lot of things just kind of clicked. (Choi 2015)

WFP's Wang offers a paradoxical account of the stature and influence of Asian Americans in SME. On the one hand, he acknowledges that Asian Americans ruled this industry in the early years, in part because they had a "head start," which he claims is a result of Asian American culture:

> Asian people and entertainment don't mix. We don't go out to pursue these things because, from our immigrant background, it's not safe and our parents don't encourage it, because they want something secure. . . . But YouTube was an easy, casual, non-threatening way to just be like, "Hey, I'm in my living room. I'm just gonna put something online." (Wang 2015)

Yet, in a challenge to our own claims, Wang argues that the Asian American moment has already passed in SME, alternatively alluding to elements of hegemonic white racism operating within the industry, but also indicting the cultural inhibitions of Asian Americans.

> We are not part of the mainstream YouTube culture. Sometimes we get left out because we don't necessarily play with them. Or it's a race thing because we don't necessarily fit in. We are not whistleblowers for the platforms. That's definitely a cultural thing. Asian Americans are more modest and don't toot their own horn so they don't notice. (Wang 2015)

This perspective allows some reflection on the relatively high socioeconomic (and technological) positioning of Asian Americans alongside their (in this case, arguably self-imposed) cultural and social inhibitions, which online activity has assisted in alleviating. Choi, in counterpoint to Wang's claims, suggests that these cultural inhibitions have diminished over time, informed by the proliferation of Asian Americans on YouTube.

> These days, Asian Americans are a lot less shy than they used to be. I definitely think [there's been a transformation], based on looking at pop culture and YouTube. You see Asian kids playing in front of the camera, Snapchatting . . . getting more confidence as a community, as individuals. Seeing another Asian on-screen anywhere gives them more confidence. (Choi 2015)

Wang's and Choi's accounts suggest that Asian American commitment to online media is not motivated only by real or perceived white male hegemony within entertainment. Rather, this phenomenon could also operate as the result of cultural inhibitions within this community. On the one hand, their industrial aspirations conform to the stereotype of Asian American immigrants as a "model minority"; and yet these cultural inhibitions and aspirations exist at the level of their lived experience.

Benny Luo is a digital marketing expert and journalist, the founder of NextSharks.com and NewMediaRockstars.com, which prominently feature Asian American creators and professionals operating in SME. Luo supported the claims made by Wang that Asian Americans no longer dominate the industry. As he noted, "[B]efore 2012, Asian Americans dominated YouTube" but now, as YouTube "is more like Hollywood and white American males are succeeding . . . they [Asian American creators] are not depending on YouTube as much anymore" (Luo 2015).

Both Wang's and Luo's accounts of the shift in influence of Asian Americans in YouTube calls for some interpretation. On the one hand, these claims may suggest subcultural appropriation from the margins to the mainstream, as originally theorized by Dick Hebdige (1979). These creators have successfully harnessed these platforms "to construct an alternative identity which communicated a perceived difference: an Otherness" (Hebdige 1979, 88–89). On the other hand, their activism within a commercializing environment would change Hebdige's trajectory;

these creators are like the punk musicians, if they owned their clubs and released their music on their own record labels, and the street artists who sell their own prints in their own galleries along with their licensed merchandise.

As Luo notes, these creators may be migrating off YouTube and onto other platforms, including Vine, where Asian American Zach King was recognized as one of the premier "Viners." In fact, King had been on YouTube for years producing DIY video tutorials teaching others how to produce and edit videos featuring these effects. However, as King notes, "[D]ifferent platforms give you different rules and boundaries" (King 2015). King's Vine content works within the tight constraints and affordances of the six-second video format, producing extraordinary magic and visual effects to create "digital illusion" (King 2015). With the demise of Vine in late 2016, King returned to YouTube, where, as of mid-2017, he has nearly two million subscribers and one hundred million views and, more remarkably, twenty million followers on Instagram. King further expanded his SME success into traditional media, securing a three-book deal with HarperCollins based on his roman à clef children's novel, *My Magical Life*, which was simultaneously optioned by Steven Spielberg's Amblin Entertainment to be adapted as a feature film (McNary 2016b).

Other than in his on-screen presence, King's Asian American identity is never a feature of his content, which may confirm Lopez's concerns over sublimated racism. Nonetheless, like Choi's, King's identity has generated cross-cultural and transnational appeal, which has helped him grow his career and business in the Asian market. In addition to licensing his content to Asian platforms, he is producing commercials for Coca-Cola and Volkswagen in Asia. Similarly, Kumar, an openly gay Indian American comedian, actor, and vlogger, discounts his identity work in his project because he does not want to be defined by his identity. Nonetheless, as he stated in our interview, "[T]he biracial, gay, Kansan is there anyway, so why talk about it? That content is in my videos no matter what I do" (Kumar 2015).

Creator and activist Matt Palazzolo, like WFP, produces and stars in scripted web series that emulate traditional genres of entertainment. Like WFP and Choi, Palazzolo began posting on YouTube very early and as a hobby initially until the platform proved a viable means of building a career. His work, featuring content he made while studying film and television at UCLA, was "mostly about identity" because of its semi-autobiographical nature. "One video went viral really fast simply because of its title, 'Hapa,' which means half Asian, half something else. It was like a visual exploration of what it means to be half Asian growing up" (Palazzolo 2015). After UCLA, Palazzolo pursued a career in traditional media and also became an LGBTQ activist, before focusing more of his efforts on SME to pursue his cultural, political, and commercial ambitions.

Palazzolo's content articulates some of the complex intersectional identity work appearing in this industry. His web series, *Bloomers*, has over thirty million views on YouTube and has a presence on Facebook, Instagram, and Twitter as well as BloomersTheSeries.com. Inspired by his own life and friends, Palazzolo writes and stars in the series about seven friends living in Los Angeles pursuing careers and relationships. The series platforms numerous forms of identity, including biracial characters, multiple sexual orientations, and a progressive Muslim female surfer, who is one of the series' breakout characters. As Palazzolo mentioned to us, his inspiration for her character reflects the diversity of his hometown in Northern California:

> My town is the largest Afghan community outside of Afghanistan. I grew up all around it. My best friend growing up was Muslim. I lived in this world where Muslims and their families were accepting of my sexuality. Everyone got along, no one was really segregated. Then I came to LA, where everything was separate, and it kind of blew my mind. I feel as passionately about Muslim progress as I do about LGBT progress. (Palazzolo 2015)

Palazzolo's account informs the way creators, including in scripted content, are engaging in discourses of authenticity inspired by their own identities and experiences. His development of this character represents a conscious activist and interventionist strategy, and affirms that activist creator strategy can translate much more directly to representation on screen based on the affordances provided within this proto-industry. Reflecting Jones's (2010) claims, Palazzolo has high regard for the political potential of entertainment: "[E]ntertainment is what I like to do, and it's also what I think changes the world fastest" (Palazzolo 2015).

As part of the intent to foster multicultural communities like his hometown, Palazzolo posts compilation videos of *Bloomers* scenes defined by identity, including lesbians, gays, and Muslims. The videos attracted even larger audiences from around the world than the series alone. "Our Muslim videos brought millions upon millions of views and new subscribers. Over 50% of our views and subscribers are young Muslims from the Middle East. Overall, Muslim women are a lot more supportive of the storyline than Muslim men" (Palazzolo 2015).

Palazzolo's account of the response to his Muslim content led to a discussion of how his work has caught the attention of YouTube and the State Department. He was asked to attend a conference about how YouTube content may help counter Islamic extremism. Palazzolo told us, "I think what *Bloomers* has done successfully is provide platforms for Muslims to have these discussions with each other" (Palazzolo 2015). The same dynamics of cultural pedagogy and potential for dialogical progress would apply to the array of multicultural identity practices featured in *Bloomers*, as well the other Asian American creators we have profiled.

LGBTQ Creators

Like Asian American creators, LGBTQ creators have appeared prominently in SME, overindexing when compared to their counterparts in traditional media, whether LGBTQ professionals on screen or behind. In contrast to racial identity work, the cultural politics of LGBTQ citizenship are informed by the politics of LGBTQ visibility, particularly around the coming-out process and progressive identity formation. Some prominent LGBTQ creators debuted out online while others came out midcareer. Regardless, the *serialized* nature of their creator practices reflects their ongoing psychosexual development—repeatedly (be) coming out as they evolve as LGBTQ citizens. These visibility practices represent varying degrees of political activism and media interventions, but also come with risks to their commercial viability.

We situate ourselves in the debates about LGBTQ media representations in traditional and social media, including accounts of their identity work on YouTube. We then profile several LGBTQ creators, their content, and their community management strategies. We draw on our interviews with prominent and midlevel LGBTQ creators. These include gay vlogger Joey Graceffa, lesbian beauty vlogger Ingrid Nilsen, Canadian trans beauty vlogger Gigi Gorgeous, lesbian singing duo Bria Kam and Chrissy Chambers, aka BriaAndChrissy, and lesbian vlogger and educator Stephanie Frosch, "ElloSteph." For some of these creators, we also include content and discourse analysis of their videos along with some analysis of comments streams across platforms. ("LGBTQ" stands for lesbian, gay, bisexual, transgender, and questioning, while other terms may be used in the quoted sources.)

The history of LGBTQ scholarship around media representation has been decidedly negative. In his seminal account of gays in movies, Vito Russo (1987) traced their lack of visibility, which, as we have seen, Gerbner and Gross (1976) previously described as a form of "symbolic annihilation." Russo also illustrated through exhaustive content analysis that, when featured, these characters were often stereotypically sissified, portrayed as lecherous villains, or appear as frivolous comic sidekicks: "The history of the portrayal of lesbians and gay men in mainstream cinema is politically indefensible and aesthetically revolting" (Russo 1987, 326). In *Up from Invisibility*, openly gay communications scholar Larry Gross (2001) continues Russo's critique, analyzing LGBTQ representation through several forms of established media, including television and print, and entertainment and journalism content. As Gross claims, "[W]e are among the least permitted to speak for ourselves in public life, including in the mass media" (Gross 2001, 15). He particularly singles out network television, which he claims "remains the most insular and undemocratic of the media, largely unavailable to most minority groups" (Gross 2001, 20).

Contemporary LGBTQ media studies has offered a more mixed account. The evolution of LGBTQ media representation since the late 1990s includes *Will and Grace*, the coming out of television comedian Ellen DeGeneres, the rise of niche channels like Showtime, Logo, and Bravo that featured LGBTQ-themed programming, and the recent proliferation of online platforms such as Netflix and Amazon, which have produced a virtual rainbow wave of LGBTQ-themed programming and representations. Nonetheless, critical scholars continue to criticize LGBTQ media representation, shifting emphasis to concerns over the lack of diversity or the class privilege of coming out. Taking a middle position, Wendy Hilton-Morrow and Kathleen Battles (2015) argue that, while LGBTQ visibility "may not signal full sexual equality" (Hilton-Morrow and Battles 2015, 225), the proliferation of these media representations has contributed towards greater cultural citizenship for LGBT citizens.

Some queer scholars have seen potential for advancement of LGBTQ identity, representation, and participation in digital and social media. Katherine Sender (2011) writes that "as new media technologies and distribution practices emerge, they are peripheral to the media center and thus allow for more fluid sexual minority representations" (Sender 2011, 211). Focusing on the rise of LGBTQ bloggers engaging in self-representation and self-production, she claims, "[W]e have moved beyond shame and loss, bitterness and resentment, towards a future-orientation of positive self-production" (Sender 2011, 211). Paul Venzo and Kristy Hess (2013) examine how LGBTQ Australians have harnessed social media to renegotiate their representation and identity. Engaging with Gerbner and Gross (1976), they claim that LGBTQ social media users mitigate the "symbolic annihilation" that continues throughout traditional media.

Mary Gray's (2009) seminal scholarship mapped LGBTQ online lives in rural America and combines "gay and lesbian studies of community and identity, social theories of public spaces, and studies of media reception, particularly the role of new media in everyday life, to frame how sociality, location, and media shape the visibility of LGBTQ-identifying young people" (Gray 2009, 5). She concludes that LGBTQ rural youth use media and technologies to "manage the delicate calculus of gay visibility's benefits and risks" (Gray 2009, 165). Andre Cavalcanti (2016) showed how social media facilitate counterpublics and care support for transgender "netizens." The affordances of online platforms provide new resources as well as distinctive challenges for transgender netizens "managing the trials and complexities of everyday life" (Cavalcanti 2016, 110). Both scholars reflect on the affordances of social media facilitating supportive communities around marginalized identities.

Earlier queer scholarship was clear about coming out as "a public act that served as a type of 'identity announcement,' which directed an individual's conduct and influenced that of others" (Stein 1997, 83). Beyond mere representation, the "coming out process" operates as a vital site of political resistance and activism. In addition, LGBTQ identity is not a fixed point but an ongoing process of progressive identity formation—what Barbara Ponse (1978) refers to as a "gay trajectory" to account for the psycho-sexual development of LGBTQ identity. Throughout their lives, LGBTQ people are repeatedly coming out and typically progress from more shame-based self-recrimination towards greater affirmation and self-pride. This process continues online.

Jonathan Alexander and Elizabeth Losh (2010) mapped the "rhetorical action" of coming out on YouTube, which represents "a distinctive YouTube form, one that appropriates the site's dominant modes of personal confession and mutual surveillance and yet also affirms the existence of separate online communities of potential resistance" (Alexander and Losh 2010, 24). Such action reflects the way LGBTQ citizens manage their sexual identities online in an attempt "to negotiate the boundary between intensely personal desires and public lives" (Alexander and Losh 2010, 24). In *Out Online* (2016), Tobias Raun considers how trans YouTubers have harnessed YouTube to engage in self-representation and community building. While vital contextualization for our research, none of these studies focus on commercializing creators and their communities.

Critical scholarship has questioned the coming-out-online genre on a number of counts. Bryan Wuest (2014) appreciates that coming out on YouTube can help "reframe our understanding of queer youth agency" (Wuest 2014, 31) but warns that diversity and intersectionality are underrepresented in coming-out videos, as they have been throughout LGBTQ media. Samantha Allen (2016) questions the formulaic and normative one-size-fits-all rhetorical style many YouTube coming-out videos have adopted: "The more coming out videos YouTube creators produce, the more conventional the genre has become" (Allen 2016). The circumambient discourse, Allen asserts, "swallows and amplifies their stories, to the exclusion of other more important facets of LGBT experience" (Allen 2016). For Allen, the way in which coming out is championed online presents a "happily-ever-after" moment that "soothes us into believing that we always have the power to shape our circumstances, instead of the other way around" (Allen 2016). Allen wants more balanced accounts of the everyday lived experiences of LGBTQ people as a political project, designed to build empathy and lead to social change and legislative action.

These critiques of coming out online rarely extend to the *serialization* of content afforded social media platforms. Our approach was to follow creator careers well beyond the moment of coming out and identify how their content practices progress from representation to more overtly political forms of media activism. Ponse (1978) calls this a gay trajectory—the psycho-sexual development of LGBTQ identity formation. Throughout their lives, LGBTQ people are repeatedly coming out and typically progress from more shame-based self-recrimination towards greater affirmation and self-pride. They continue to do so online as well.

Nevertheless, overtly political advocacy work conducted online around LGBTQ themes can be problematized. Doug Meyer (2015) considers how LGBTQ advocacy work that attempts to undermine homophobia often does so at the expense of bolstering other systems of inequality, including racism and sexism. Furthermore, for Meyer, LGBTQ advocacy work typically serves the interests of relatively privileged LGBTQ people—predominantly, those who are white, male, and middle-class—at the expense of other minority LGBTQ communities. While attempting to challenge homophobia and heteronormativity, the generalized middle-class narrative of LGBTQ campaigns like "It Gets Better" reinforces a regressive social-class politics and privileges experiences that are themselves "deeply implicated in race, class, and gender norms," while failing to adequately document the long-term challenges, which, "rather than simply 'getting better' after high school, often intensify" (D. Meyer 2015, 6).

Michael Lovelock (2016) doubles down on this critique, positing that SME creators are "'proto-homonormative,' defined through the neoliberal ideals of authenticity, self-branding and individual enterprise—the expected narrative of contemporary gay life" (Lovelock 2016, 1). Lovelock recognizes their agency and advocacy, but suggests that their commercial impulses mitigate their cultural value as role models for the community:

Proto-homonormativity discursively draws a connecting line between the gay/lesbian self and the societal integration of sexual minority people. In this framework, a proud and accepting bearing upon the self becomes a means both of overcoming socially-produced marginalization and of securing one's integration within the normative institutions of labor and polity in the future. (Lovelock 2016, 11)

We now profile several LGBTQ creators, their content, and their community-management strategies, focusing on the gay trajectories they are on. LGBTQ creators are perpetually (be)coming out—and therefore must continuously navigate their progressive and political activism alongside their commercial and brand interests.

Starting Out

Numerous SME creators debuted on YouTube out of the closet or came out shortly thereafter, and have managed to foster relatively long-term and successful careers. One of these more prominent vlogger personalities and performers is Tyler Oakley, who never declared his sexuality by coming out because he was never closeted. He was openly gay from the outset and candid with his audience about his sexual orientation as well as his previous eating disorders during his teens. His aspirational videos espouse a philosophy of "it's okay to be you," which has helped him secure over eight million subscribers and 570 million views on YouTube alone. He also has millions of followers on Twitter, Tumblr, Facebook, Snapchat, Instagram, iTunes, and more. In addition to online, he appears often and openly on television, including season 28 in 2016 of *American Race*, and his own feature documentary, *Snervous*, which detailed his coming out to his family. Furthermore, Oakley has parlayed his LGBTQ following into activism, using crowd sourcing to raise over $500 million for the Trevor Project. On the gay activist trajectory, Oakley arrived online in the post position with little need for change, which is why GLAAD has already recognized him with a Davidson/Valentini award.

Other creators, like lesbian comedian vlogger Hannah Hart, came out relatively early in their YouTube careers. She joined the platform in 2009 with her channel MyHarto, which has secured almost 2.5 million subscribers, and her videos have been viewed over 235 million times. In 2011, she launched her second channel, yourharto, and in 2012, she released a series of "chapters" in her "coming out series." In her most recent installment ("Coming Out (Ch. 6) 'Sticking Around'" 2014), she emotionally describes her 2015 LGBTQ panel at Vidcon, describing how "this year it's really hitting me about how wonderful and significant this is . . . for kids who, maybe just ten years ago, didn't have this type of inclusivity and support." Her video ends with a plea for those still struggling with their identity to "stick" because "it gets better."

Hart illustrates a form of strategic social media impression management, in which she cultivated a number of online "personae" with varying degrees of authenticity. Her first channel focuses more on her comedy, including her "My Drunk Kitchen" series. Her second channel affords her the opportunity to express more candor about her sexuality, relationships, and advice on coming out, among other political topics like gun control. Her coming-out "series" format supports this notion of a gay activist trajectory, which, as mentioned in the chapter's introduction, contributed to her receiving the GLAAD Award.

Like Oakley and Hart, LGBTQ creators Bria Kam, Chrissy Chambers, and Stephanie Frosch debuted on SME platforms out of the closet, launching commercializing careers that consistently feature LGBTQ content, topics, and concerns for the community. Musical duo and longtime partners Bria Kam and Chrissy Chambers operate the BriaAndChrissy channels across multiple platforms with a midrange following of over seven hundred thousand subscribers on YouTube with nearly three hundred million views, along with a modest number of followers, fans, and likes on Twitter. In addition, they have original songs available for download on iTunes and have a fan subscriber account on the platform Patreon, where they reportedly garner over twenty-three hundred dollars in fees per month. Bria and Chrissy claim to have built a sustainable business that allows them to pursue their SME careers full-time.

Bria and Chrissy's content is diverse, initially composed of music videos intended to launch their music careers as a singing duo. However, over time, their videos have included vlogging that often features their relationship and open displays of affection. One of their most-viewed videos is "What a Lesbian Kiss Feels Like," which aired in 2013 and has been viewed over 7.5 million times. The video was used to launch their second YouTube channel, entitled "Lesbian Love." This channel includes not only videos about their relationship but also accounts of everyday homophobia that they encounter along with their fearful response to the election of President Trump.

Over time, Bria and Chrissy's music also assumed more overtly political themes, particularly on behalf of LGBTQ topics like marriage equality. One of their earlier protest songs, "Dear Chick-Fil-A," references the backlash against and boycott of Chick-Fil-A, which had helped fund numerous anti-LGBTQ organizations fighting against marriage equality. According to Chrissy, "[It was] probably the second-most hate that we've ever gotten for any video we've ever done" (Kam and Chambers 2015). The song was subsequently released on iTunes and a portion of the funds went towards the pro–marriage equality organization Freedom to Marry.

They have produced numerous satirical music videos against bullying as well as against a conservative politician's position regarding "legitimate rape." After Chrissy came out publicly as a victim, the couple has also raised awareness about the phenomenon of revenge porn. In June 2015, at a town hall forum for presidential candidate Hillary Clinton with online content creators, Chrissy raised the topic. Clinton's response was to pursue greater legal and political support to combat this issue along with other concerns that have arisen in this sphere. "Some of you have kept people alive, because you have been able to communicate with a person who was bullied," Clinton said, "or a young person who was struggling with their sexuality and feeling all alone. And you were able to give that person a sense of survival. And a feeling they weren't by themselves" ("Creator Town Hall with Hillary Clinton" 2016).

The duo argued in our interview that their commercial interests and political activism are strategically interrelated, claiming that "part of our brand is activism." According to Chrissy, they were not initially political until Bria's older brother convinced them that "helping these young people was something that meant a lot to us. So we started veering our channel to be more LGBTQ-themed." Bria further acknowledged that

[t]he more our viewers trust us and the more they love us, the more they want to look out for us and support us. And we find that what they're looking for is this sense of normalcy. They want to be able to grow up and have a relationship, to be accepted and live a normal life. I think that's one thing that we've been able to do, is be really transparent and say, "Look, this is what it's like to be just a normal person." (Kam and Chambers 2015)

Figure 5.3. LGBTQ creators Bria and Chrisy. BriaAndChrissy, https://www.youtube .com/user/BriaAndChrissy/.

ElloSteph, aka Stephanie Frosch, a midlevel lesbian vlogger, has over 350,000 subscribers and 25 million views on her YouTube channel. In addition to platforms Twitter, Facebook, Tumblr, and Instagram, she also promotes merchandise on e-commerce platforms that cater to creators, Districtlines.com and bigcartel.com. Featured are t-shirts that declare "No Homo(phobia) ellosteph," a "Create Positive Change" brace- let, and caps that say "gay and tired." Initially, Frosch launched a Tumblr channel that offered advice about numerous topics from LGBTQ issues to depression. Her advice was informed by her experience growing up in a religious home and feeling isolated, as well as by her volunteer work for LGBTQ nonprofits and homeless shelters. She launched on YouTube because of the potential to reach larger audiences.

Frosch described her content as both subversive and pedagogical. As she claimed in our interview, "I like to think of [my content] as educational with a twist. I like to trick people into learning." She ref- erences one of her most popular videos based on a party game called "Never Have I Ever": "It starts off with me, Bria, Chrissy, and other girls, daring one another to respond to 'Never have I ever kissed more than one person in a night,' 'Never have I ever had a boyfriend.'

But then it gets serious and it's, 'Never have I ever been catcalled'" (Frosch 2015).

Frosch claims that these strategies have helped her grow her audience, but were also risky:

> I was worried at first that if I only tried to educate people, they would be turned off. But I guess because of the way I do it, it actually [becomes] one of my most-viewed videos. Often I do just go down the entertainment field, but whenever I do have the chance to put something in there that's educational, those actually are my most successful videos. (Frosch 2015)

For midlevel creators like Stephanie Frosch and Bria and Chrissy, the commercial prospects for being openly gay and engaging in political and pedagogical fare on their channels are limited and precarious. As discussed in chapter 2, YouTube's Adpocalypse has compromised the commercial success of these creators. In addition to flawed machine learning and contradictory platform policies, YouTube's practices laid it open to charges of sexual discrimination. LGBTQ creators claimed to experience a greater level of demonetization as their content was marked as "sexual content" and therefore ad-unfriendly. Bria and Chrissy recounted how their YouTube advertising revenue has plummeted from thirty-five hundred dollars a month to between two and three hundred dollars (Kam and Chambers 2015).

YouTube further crippled the channels of LGBTQ creators after launching another feature entitled "restricted mode" that claimed to block "potentially objectionable" and non–family friendly fare. LGBTQ creators discovered that their videos were no longer able to be viewed by those watching in restricted mode, which produced an outcry from the community. As noted by Rowan Ellis, a queer and feminist vlogger, "Videos about LGBTQ+ life, love, history, friendships etc. are no more inappropriate than videos with straight couples or telling the history of straight figures. . . . Yet they are apparently being treated differently" (Voss 2017). Subsequent YouTube declarations that they have corrected both filtering systems did not assuage creator concerns. Comments from YouTube support staff posted publicly that "honestly we have no idea why decisions are made that way" (Parlock 2017) only exacerbated them.

Coming Out

As noted already, coming out on YouTube is definitely a thing. In a company blog post, YouTube (YouTube Trends 2015) declared that there were now more than thirty-six thousand videos related to the subject. Its statement further made claims about the platform's progressive politics, declaring that coming-out videos "are a large and important part of You-Tube culture," with every story shared contributing to the "growing role of YouTube as a platform for advocacy and connection for the LGBTQ community" (YouTube Trends 2015).

In the mid-2010s, a wave of prominent and successful creators came out of the closet midcareer. In late 2014, Connor Franta, a successful SME creator, musician, and entrepreneur, posted a confessional, teary YouTube video ("Coming Out" 2014), which garnered over 10.6 million views as of 2017. A month later, the Rhodes Brothers came out to their father in an online video ("Twins Come Out to Dad" 2015) that has been viewed over twenty-two million times. As featured in our case studies below, prominent creators Ingrid Nilsen and Joey Graceffa came out in this time frame in videos that cumulatively garnered over forty-five million views as of 2017. This phenomenon led *Vanity Fair* columnist Richard Lawson (2015) to declare that "everyone will come out on YouTube eventually."

Ingrid Nilsen, Joey Graceffa, and Gigi Gorgeous are prominent creators who came out midcareer. Nilsen has been on YouTube since 2012 and as of June 2017, she had garnered nearly four million YouTube subscribers and over 350 million video views on her main channel. She also produces content on another YouTube channel and has millions of followers, likes, and fans on Instagram, Twitter, Facebook, Tumblr, and Snapchat. Her content features mostly lifestyle and beauty tips and, in addition to multiple revenue streams, she has a multiyear partnership with Covergirl as a "glambassador."

Nilsen did not initially appear out online. Rather, she came out midcareer in a YouTube video entitled "Something I Want You to Know (Coming Out)" (2015). As Nilsen's assistant, Eileen, confirmed in our interview (Nilsen 2015), "There hasn't been a female with as big a community as Ingrid who has come out." In addition to millions of views, Nilsen's confession was featured in *Time* and *People* magazines, along with recognition by the LGBTQ press, including *Out* magazine and the *Advocate*.

Like most others (and as anatomized by Alexander and Losh 2010), Nilsen's video took the form of a tearful confession and fear of rejection by her fans. However, these fears proved largely unwarranted as her community has since continued to grow and her fans have lauded her for her declaration. Most of the comments posted have been positive: "congratz," "Ingrid is amazing," "good for you." She inspired other YouTubers like Carissa Thorne to come out on their own pages. In her comments on Nilsen's video, Carissa declared, "I was so inspired by this video so I want to say thank you so much for making it."

Some comments were less positive, alluding to Nilsen's coming out as a means of securing attention, while others claimed that she lied. On the one hand, these comments reflect more pervasive practices of trolling and cyberbullying across social media, but they also suggest that homophobia persists in YouTube spaces while also underlining the commercialized nature of SME, which subjects their identity work to heightened critique. However, these negative comments also generated a counterbacklash by her fan community. Sam A posted, "These comments are so fucking disgusting. She had millions of followers who believe it or not care about her life and who she is as a person so she has every right to inform them this news. If you don't care don't comment hate and accuse her of seeking attention" ("Something I Want You to Know [Coming Out]" 2015). Nilsen turned off all advertising on her coming-out video—YouTubers can opt to do this at any time—which means she generated no revenue from it.

Nonetheless, Nilsen's coming out still represented a risk to her career, especially her partnership with Covergirl and other advertisers. In our interview, Nilsen addressed these concerns, privileging her relationship to her community over her concerns around her revenue and commercial value.

> All I thought was, if anyone has a problem with this, I don't want to work with them anyway. My community was one of my biggest concerns, along with my well-being. I hadn't shared this huge aspect of myself with them. If I had been out when I started . . . or dating women privately . . . it would have been different. But I had publicly dated men, so I was terrified and

nervous. I didn't know anyone else in this situation or how to articulate it to people, other than how I had told my friends. (Nilsen 2015)

Since coming out, Nilsen continues to promote her lifestyle and beauty tutorials, and her relationship with Covergirl has continued while her audience has grown. But Nilsen has also featured numerous videos, often on her second YouTube channel, that feature more LGBTQ topics and her evolving lesbian identity. These videos include details about her relationships with her girlfriends, including Hannah Hart and Jules Kutner, a former contestant on Lifetime's reality series *Project Runway*. Nilsen has also contributed to videos with more explicit political content, including her experiences at both the Democratic and Republican conventions. Along with other prominent SME creators, Nilsen promoted her participation in the women's marches in January 2017 protesting the election of President Trump.

Harnessing her online appeal, Nilsen has also addressed topics of concern to the LGBTQ social movement in the press and across multiple platforms. In her online interview with President Obama, she described coming out as a lesbian and mentioned the ongoing discrimination experienced by the community. She then prompted the president to discuss whether the progress made by the community is "fleeting" and whether his support of marriage equality is "here to stay" (Bendix 2016). In an interview on a panel of creators at the Social Good conference, Nilsen stated, "My job is on the internet. And every single day, my identity is challenged, and people tell me that I'm lying, and that I'm not who I say I am. For me, it's really important to be my authentic self and to share that with people as a feminine-presenting biracial gay woman" (Hirsh 2016)

Appearing on YouTube two years earlier than Nilsen, Graceffa started out making music video parodies and sketch comedy on a channel called WinterSpringPro. Two years later, he launched his own channel where he featured daily vlogs about his life and, as of July 2017, has garnered nearly eight million subscribers and over 1.28 billion video views. On a second channel, Graceffa posts gameplay videos, a popular genre of content where creators record themselves playing video games that may be comedic but also indirectly instruct in gameplay. Like other creators, Graceffa also has millions of fans, followers, and likes on Twitter and Instagram. He also created and stars in two seasons of *Escape the*

Something I Want You To Know (Coming Out)
Ingrid Nilsen
1 year ago • 16,521,334 views
We all deserve our best chance. Here's a random, but meaningful assortment of things that have given me comfort on my path to ...

Coming Out: One Year Later ◆ Ingrid Nilsen
Ingrid Nilsen
10 months ago • 1,637,626 views
One year ago today I came out. Lots of thoughts. Lots of feelings. And I'm sharing them with you. -------- Listen to my new podcast ...

Ingrid Nilsen on Coming Out | Shay Talk
Shay Mitchell
1 year ago • 648,726 views
I have a new series! TALK TO ME! My first guest, Ingrid Nilsen, talks to me about her inspirational coming out story and how she ...

LESBIAN STUFF! ft. Ingrid Nilsen
lacigreen
2 months ago • 256,782 views
Ingrid came by to talk stereotypes, family ish, and finding yourself ♥ watch her vid! https://youtu.be/ya__OBvHa5M and her ...

REACTING TO INGRID NILSEN'S COMING OUT
Ash Hardell
1 year ago • 284,874 views
Click to Tweet to show Ingrid and others your support: http://ctt.ec/97g9R I actually had so much more to say, but I wanted to give ...

Figure 5.4. Since coming out on YouTube, Ingrid Nilsen continues to address LGBTQ topics. Ingrid Nilsen, https://www.youtube.com/user/missglamorazzi.

Night, a scripted horror series for the subscriber-based YouTube Red platform. On television, he has also appeared on multiple seasons of the US version of *The Amazing Race.*

Like Nilsen, Graceffa did not appear out online until midcareer. Unlike Nilsen and numerous other LGBTQ creators whose coming-out videos featured tearful confessions, Graceffa developed a more entertaining approach. In May 2015, Graceffa posted a fantasy-themed pop music video on YouTube that he wrote, produced, and starred in entitled "Don't Wait" ("Don't Wait: Official Music Video" 2015). In the video, Graceffa rescues and kisses his own Prince Charming. Graceffa's video has been seen twenty-five million times, and his confession generated a marked increase in his fan community. On the day the video premiered, Graceffa's YouTube channel garnered an additional twenty-five thousand subscriptions.

Graceffa's coming out, however, proved to be part of a much larger and conspicuous commercial and branding strategy. At the end of the video, Graceffa announced that his music video reflects "just a small portion" of what his fan community can discover in his memoir entitled *In Real Life: My Journey to a Pixelated World*, to be released the next day. The book subsequently became a bestseller on Amazon. Graceffa also released the song for download on iTunes, and it debuted in the top one hundred on iTunes charts in the United States, the UK, Australia, and Canada.

In addition to his commercial interests, Graceffa also affirmed his activist intentions, stating in the video's postscript that "I really just hope that it [his book] will be able to help some of you guys out there

Figure 5.5. Joey Graceffa, "Don't Wait" official music video. Joey Graceffa, https://www .youtube.com/watch?v=Kcwo_mhyqTw.

going through similar struggles I went through and do some good in the world." Graceffa later posted a more explicit and tearful video that confirmed, "I'm gay" ("Yes I'm Gay" 2015). In the video, Graceffa describes his motivation for coming out: that he wanted to express his sexuality in a creative way that "was true to me," and to express proudly, "that's who I am and I'm not going to hide that anymore." He further explained that, despite having been on YouTube since October 2009, he needed to wait until he was confident about his own life before he could "become a role model for others." This video has been viewed over seven million times.

Graceffa's coming out, following the pattern, was received positively and negatively. YouTube user Chase Sanity recognized Graceffa's act as a form of queer provocation, commenting, "I hope all the homophobes are offended. You just saw two men kissing, now you'll never get it out of your head. ;) mwahaha." But the video has also garnered over forty thousand dislikes, which one commenter, Emiza Koshy J, bet were "all the homophobes" ("Don't Wait: Official Music Video" 2015).

Like Nilsen, Graceffa initially turned off monetization on his "Don't Wait" video. As his publicist, Leila Marsh, claimed, "It's not that the advertisers don't want to be displayed on videos that are being viewed millions of times. It's that the creators turn off monetization. They don't want to be accused of using this personal moment to make money, i.e., sell out" (Marsh 2015). However, in late October 2015, the video featured a pre-roll ad for Fuse TV's new docuseries, *Transcendent*, about the lives of a group of transgender Americans.

Since 2015, Graceffa's content has featured more LGBTQ themes and more heightened expressions of his LGBTQ identity. These include videos entitled "When Did I Know I Was Gay?" and queer/gender-bending escapades, like shopping for and applying nail polish. As Graceffa acknowledged in his interview, "I feel more open, like I can paint my nails and not feel like I'm going to be called out for that. This is who I am. I'm more comfortable in my skin, to be myself" (Graceffa 2015). He eventually revealed that Prince Charming in his music video was his long-held-secret boyfriend, actor-model and SME creator Daniel Preda. Joey and Daniel ("Janiel" to their fans) are often seen in videos engaging in relatively chaste displays of affection.

Although his videos have featured more heightened representations of his gay identity and his relationship, Graceffa has not been as overtly political as his contemporaries, including Nilsen and Gorgeous. Nonetheless, he has been featured talking to GLAAD about coming out (GLAAD .org) and released a video for the Ad Council's "Love has no labels" campaign timed with National Coming Out Day (Brouwer 2015d). Otherwise, Graceffa has focused on expanding his commercial brand, including deals with the likes of Wayfair.com, Target, Oreo, and others, along with launching a jewelry line and signing with a prominent Hollywood talent agency. In 2017, Graceffa published a science fiction novel, *Children of Eden*, which debuted as number one on the *New York Times* bestseller list.

The psychosexual development of LGBTQ citizens varies according to the underlying nature and evolution of their sexual orientation and gender identity. This is clear for transgender creators, such as prominent transgender beauty vlogger Gigi Gorgeous, whose image on the Sunset Boulevard hoarding started the book. Gorgeous began her career on YouTube in August 2008, first appearing as Gregory Gorgeous, a Canadian teenage boy offering makeup tutorials. Over the course of the past decade, Gregory transitioned to Gigi Gorgeous, a transition she has shared with her online community. Her content has evolved from beauty tips to include comedic skits along with anecdotes about her life. On YouTube alone, as of June 2017, she has over 2.4 million subscribers, and her videos have been seen over 350 million times. She has another 2.2 million followers on Instagram, 2.1 million likes on Facebook, and nearly 300,000 followers on Twitter. Her life was also featured in a recent documentary entitled *This Is Everything*, produced by multiple-Oscar-winning filmmaker Barbara Koppel. In addition to winning numerous industry awards, including Streamys and a Shorty for her beauty tutorials, she has secured numerous brand deals with Revlon and Crest. Gorgeous has also been honored as a community leader and role model by OutWebFest 2017, sponsored by YouTube and queer online video site Revry.

In our interview, Gigi claimed she never saw herself as a role model although she "loves to change people's minds" (Gorgeous 2015). Nonetheless, by documenting her transition before her online community, Gorgeous's representational practice suggests an activist stance. Although this journey was visually apparent, she confirmed her trans status in her video "I Am Transgender" (2013), which has since garnered over 3.5 million views. Gorgeous's coming out, like Nilsen's, generated both celebratory and condemnatory remarks, as well as a counterback-lash. Her fan Gabi declared, "nice to see a TRANSGENDER role model that has what it takes to better the world for trans people WE NEED YOU GIGI keep it up XXX." Conversely, Alicia Gonzales declared that "transgender is wrong totally wrong." In turn, these comments gener-ated numerous counterresponses, like that of Jaice Krabs, who declared "so is your shitty opinion" ("I Am Transgender" 2013).

Since affirming her trans status, Gigi has initiated openly political discussions about LGBTQ topics and engaged in more overt social media activism. She expressed grief at the massacre of LGBTQ patrons at the gay nightclub Pulse in Orlando ("Orlando Shooting" 2016), she debated the differences between "being black and being gay" ("Being Trans vs. Being Black with Todrick!" 2016), and tearfully described her "thoughts on Bruce Jenner," who has transitioned into Caitlyn Jenner ("My Thoughts on Bruce Jenner" 2015). She also partnered with Miley Cyrus in her #InstaPride campaign, a campaign in partnership with Instagram to raise awareness and celebrate transgender and gender-expressive lives.

In addition, Gigi has repeatedly detailed the trans harassment she has encountered. In August 2016, Gigi posted a video announcing that she had been detained and denied entry into Dubai because she is transgen-der ("Detained in Dubai for Being Transgender" 2016). This announce-ment appeared right after these events, featuring Gigi in the airport without her usually glam makeup and hair, describing the events. She eventually made it out of Dubai and, in her video, mentioned the as-sistance she received from GLAAD, the UN, the White House, and the State Department. Their aid not only attests to her celebrity but under-lines her political and cultural influence as well.

(Be)Coming Out: Gay Activist Trajectories

These case studies of LGBTQ creators deepen our understanding of the stakes in the debates around LGBTQ representation and activism. Enduring issues of cultural politics join with the affordances of social media and the commercial environment in which SME operates to engage questions of coming out and gay activist trajectories, commu-nity management, and navigating the commercial environment. We identified how some creators were already out online while others came out midcareer. In both cases, we tracked their career arcs over time rather than just focusing on the coming-out process.

SME platforms provide the means for these creators to engage in a virtual real-time practice of evolving self-representation. As we have seen in chapter 4, this is a practice governed and disciplined by the imperative discourse of authenticity. Our career case studies reinforce the proposition that coming out pitches these online creator entrepreneurs into heightened representations of their evolving LGBTQ identities and engagement with increasingly overt political content. They are on a *gay activist trajectory.* Whether on their initial channels or on separate channels, these creators openly addressed diverse topics of concern to the LGBTQ community. Some described ongoing homophobia and bullying, advocated for marriage equality and progressive politics, and responded to the rise of President Trump and the ensuing peril to the advances of the LGBTQ community. These comprise critical media interventions, while their creators wrestled with the consequences of trying to maintain a career as a commercial creator and LGBTQ advocate.

The case studies outlined in this chapter render more complex the critical concerns around the commercialization of LGBTQ creators. For the likes of Nilsen, Gorgeous, and Graceffa, coming out midcareer poses as much risk to their commercial interests as they may have also helped promote authenticity and community engagement. For midlevel LGBTQ creators Stephanie Frosch and Bria and Chrissy, their appeals to community and expressions of LGBTQ identity, relationships, politics, and pedagogy are strategic but also precarious. These practices grow community but also inhibit commercial value, as witnessed by the instance of the YouTube "adpocalypse." But more fundamentally, we argue, online creator entrepreneurs, *precisely because* they are working in a commercializing environment, commit themselves to maximizing their cultural and community reach, and thus must position themselves between subcultural identity politics and brand culture. There is no question that the interests of brands with which creators identify benefit from this, but—in Lovelock's words—so do the interests of "sexual minority people" in "societal integration"—especially if, beyond *representation* of sexual minorities, there are real-world politics of social *change* on the agenda.

Outro

Cultural and media studies scholarship has provided frameworks for understanding the struggles for diverse media representation on screen and within media industries. These struggles have been associated with various social movements that have engaged over the past few decades to secure political and cultural citizenship from the margins. These struggles have employed strategies, such as media activism, advocacy, and interventionism, from actors operating outside as well as practitioners operating within the media industries. Representation and activism are as much concerns of entertainment as of any media form.

We have shown in this chapter that social media entertainment represents the potential for embracing a progressive cultural politics, even with, and perhaps with the assistance of, its framing within a commercializing environment. BD (before digital), it was a commonplace that dominant media like television performed the integrative role, in Horace Newcomb and Seymour Hirsch's (1983) words, of a "cultural forum": "A cultural basis for the analysis and criticism of television is, for us, the bridge between the concern for television as a communications medium, central to contemporary society, and television as aesthetic object, the expressive medium that, through its storytelling functions, unites and examines a culture" (Newcomb and Hirsch 1983, 561). Most recent media and cultural scholarship has moved far away from such claims. However, we suggest that SME not only may constitute the latest "forum" to engage with the cultural politics of media representation in a commercial environment but also has the potential to embrace greater diversity and promote a more progressive agenda than previously dominant media.

As David Halperin (1995) notes, "[T]he history of the ongoing struggles for homosexual emancipation and gay liberation has consisted largely in the story of how lesbians and gay men fought to wrest from non-gay-identified people control over such matters as who gets to speak for us, who gets to represent our experiences, who is authorized to pronounce knowledgeably about our lives" (Halperin 1995, 56–57). The same could be applied to all those operating from all margins, identities, and differences in media and culture. The creators profiled in this chapter have sought to wrestle control over their own lives and identities and crafted their own on-screen representations, while engaging with global communities who are invited to share their affinities, values, identities, and politics. In the process, they also left their day jobs and incubated their own media brands, while also managing to pay the rent.

6

Globalizing Social Media Entertainment

The state of Turkey takes a particularly strong interventionist stance against the potential disruption to the political, religious, and social order posed by the global-spanning digital platforms, including Facebook, Twitter, and YouTube, and has regularly blocked them around election periods, particularly during the major 2016 crisis in its political system (Coldewey 2016). Turkish Tourism, however, has had a YouTube channel since February 2014, and the national carrier, Turkish Airlines, has used YouTube content creators and multichannel networks to develop youth-oriented, social media–based engagement strategies in its attempt to build brand recognition in the ultra-competitive international airline market (Kerr 2012).

While operating on US-owned social media platforms, international SME content creators have proliferated and profited, representing marginal, alternative, subcultural, and subaltern voices rarely seen in the United States or, in many cases, in the traditional entertainment in their home countries. Musicians like Elissa from Lebanon, Iranian-Saudi Arabian a capella artist Alaa Wardi, and comedian Bader Sadeh, aka the "Saudi King of Comedy," have launched global careers and secured cross-cultural and diasporic Middle Eastern audiences less inhibited by local online platform or content censorship. ValleyArm, an Australian-based multichannel network, works with aspiring online musicians in their attempts to break into the booming Asian pop music scene. India has experienced "breakneck growth" (Weiss 2016b) of amateur content creation and is, according to Sangeet Kumar (2016), "gradually chipping away" at the structural dominance of institutions such as Bollywood, television networks, and the celebrity culture, which have remained hegemonic forces within the sphere of cultural production in India. And in the United States, as we have seen in chapter 5, AsianAmerican YouTubers overindex in SME, in stark contrast to their near invisibility in traditional US entertainment (Considine 2011).

This chapter investigates new forms of media globalization engendered by SME, the diverse cultural formations they must navigate, and some of the emerging policy issues for governments that they pose. Thus far, we have not brought the spatial dimension of SME into full focus, and yet it is one of its most distinctive features. The chapter first outlines the actual nature of the globality of SME, then considers the need to revise established theories of media imperialism in the light of SME globalization. It then looks at the irreducible specificity of major variants on what has been our de facto US-centricity thus far in the book. Featured here are India (where SME is building out against the hegemony of Bollywood film and music, and offering an alternative for educated urbanites underserved by the great wasteland of television), China (where SME, exemplifying early-stage capitalist modernism, sees Chinese platforms currently eclipsing the affordance innovation and e-commerce integrations of their Western counterparts), and Germany (where assertive cultural regulation of platforms is working, and where the state also looks to financially support local content creation). The chapter then focuses on the rationale and methods used by diverse state actors to support the emerging screen ecology of SME. The tensions that must be managed when online culture meets established film and broadcasting culture are examined in a case study of Australia. The international regulatory challenges confronting the platforms that carry SME are dealt with in the book's conclusion.

For the past two decades, the United States has continued its historic dominance of the global online entertainment scene as the corporate home of the largest digital television portals (HBO Go, Netflix, Amazon Prime) and social media platforms (YouTube, Facebook, Twitter) in the world. These portals and platforms have become familiar to and popular with populations around the planet with even greater ease and swiftness than previous epochs of Hollywood and the music industry's "cultural imperialism." By 2017, Netflix had close to one hundred million subscribers in all but a few countries on earth, and represents itself as "the birth of a new global Internet TV service." But these sheer numbers can be trumped by the social media platforms, like YouTube, which has 1.5 billion users and operates in seventy-six languages. It is notable that 80% of YouTube traffic comes from outside the United States, and 60% of creators' views come from outside their home country. In turn, YouTube is a distant second to Facebook with over two billion users, which represents more than half of the global online population. All the while, new US-owned platforms have scaled even more rapidly, like Snapchat, which secured over two hundred million users in half the time it took Facebook, YouTube, or Twitter to reach that milestone (Morrison 2015).

But this litany of warp-speed global reach needs to be framed as well against the great singularity of China, where state-based regulation has helped incubate, protect, censor, and build a parallel universe of digital and social media industries that in some respects are world-leading innovators. Parented by the Chinese BATs (Baidu, Alibaba, and Tencent), Chinese SME features an even more hypercompetitive landscape than in the West. The history and contours of this landscape are outlined by Michael Keane (2016) in his account of the rise of digital TV platforms (including iQiyi, Sohu, and LeTV) and by Elaine Zhao's (2016) survey of the proliferation of Chinese social media platforms (Youku Toudu, Weibo, and WeChat). And China is well ahead of the West in live-streaming mobile-app development. All of these portals and platforms are competing for some seven hundred million Chinese mobile web users, roughly twice the population of the United States "or, if you prefer, 28 Australias" (Scutt 2014).

Entering a further caveat on their frictionless global reach, US-owned distribution platforms and portals face constant concerns over access, content, and advertising and are subject to variegated and often inconsistent state, regional, and national Internet regulation and related interventions. These combine and collide with the popularity with which demotic take-up of platform affordances occurs below and around state action in numerous countries and regions of the world. And particularly in liberal democracies, state action regarding the platforms and portals can be not only regulatory in nature but also facilitative of local content and creators' participation in SME.

Despite what might appear to be the fulfillment of Thomas Friedman's (2005) notion of seamless globalization captured in his book *The World Is Flat*, this new world of online entertainment is far from flat. What we must account for is *both* qualitatively greater frictionlessness in SME media globalization *and* the unevenness or "lumpiness" consequent on regulatory and political difference territory by territory and on the immense industrial and cultural diversity embodied in SME.

Another Wave of Media Imperialism?

Media globalization has been an enduring topic in film, media, and communication studies. Traditionally centered on questions of US "cultural imperialism" through widespread dissemination and popularity of its film and television output, debates of this long-established vintage have been staged, for example, around whether global television traffic is a "one-way street" (Nordenstreng and Varis 1974) or a "patchwork quilt" (Tracey 1988). Influenced by cultural studies' emphasis on viewer and audience agency, versions of "weak" rather than "strong" globalization that have largely characterized recent discussion (Tomlinson 1999; Straubhaar 2007; Flew 2007) continue to contend with reassertions of "strong" cultural globalization (Boyd-Barrett 2015).

However, a reassessment of this debate is imperative in light of the global reach of YouTube and other major SME platforms, and the types of content they have spawned. On the one hand, it is possible to posit a new wave of media globalization based on the global availability and uptake of SME content, which is relatively frictionless compared with national broadcasting and systems of film and DVD licensing by territory. It needs to be emphasized that platforms perform constant and widespread self-regulation in response to takedown notices concerning copyright, as well as to avoid controversy over content offending community standards, by dealing with such blights as hate speech and revenge porn. It is estimated that Google alone handles seventy to eighty million takedown notices per month globally for copyright claims alone (Mills 2016). However, there is little or no imposed content regulation on the big social platforms—some of the world's largest information and communication companies—as their penetration proliferates globally. (But this, as we will see in our conclusion, is changing.)

On the other hand, the new professionalizing-amateur screen ecology embodies a huge step change in producer diversity, in terms of both amateur backgrounds and global locations. It is the differences that we stress between such content and platforms, on the one hand, and the system of national broadcasting, film, and DVD release and licensing by windowing and territory, on the other. The latter, established forms of media globalization, enter territories with IP-controlled content, whereas platforms such as YouTube facilitate rather than control content, and exhibit much greater content, creator, and language and cultural diversity than traditional global media hegemons.

The implications of social media entertainment for main academic accounts of media imperialism have hardly been broached. Mostly, the lead has been taken by exponents—for example, critical political economists Christian Fuchs (2014) and Dal Yong Jin (2013)—who insist on a strict continuity between earlier forms of media imperialism and today's version.

For Fuchs, social media is viewed entirely through the lens of its claims to democratize access to and participation in information exchange (rather than this book's focus on social media entertainment) while he refuses any and all claims that social media may extend participation and offer outlets for alternative voices:

> The Internet and social media are today stratified, non-participatory spaces and an alternative, non-corporate Internet is needed. Large corporations colonise social media and dominate its attention economy. . . . On corporate social media, the liberal freedom of association and assembly are suspended: big corporate and, to a lesser extent, political actors dominate and therefore centralise the formation of speech, association, assembly and opinion on social media. (Fuchs 2014, section 5.1)

For Jin, there is essential continuity across a century of imperialisms (Lenin's imperialism, cultural imperialism, information imperialism, and now platform imperialism). "The US, which had previously controlled non-Western countries with its military power, capital, and later cultural products," Jin argues, "now seems to dominate the world with platforms, benefitting from these platforms, mainly in terms of capital accumulation." He regards "the major role of intellectual property rights as the most significant form of capital accumulation in the digital age" (Jin 2013, 146). But there are critical distinctions to be made between information and cultural dominance, and, at least at the level of content, global social media entertainment must be critically differentiated from earlier stages of cultural imperialism because such content is initially primarily amateur and is generated under very different IP regimes than the strong copyright regimes through which traditional media hegemony has been exercised.

This point develops from our discussion of power in chapter 1. There, we distinguished among economic, political, and cultural/symbolic power and, using Michel Foucault, we distinguished between power and domination in advancing a critique of critical political economy's analysis of media, including platform, power. Power, for Foucault, is inherently relational and unstable, and resistance is a necessary corollary of, and inherent in the exercise of, power. Critical political economy's concept of power is what Foucault (1991) would call "domination," a subset of power, which emphasizes supervening, top-down control, assuming that economic power results in the ability to exercise political and cultural power. Here, we take this argument forward by stressing that the presumed alignment among economic, political, and cultural power can never be decided in advance when the diversity of SME cultural formation around the world—facilitated by the platforms *precisely because* of their lack of IP control over content—is considered. Nick Srnicek (2016) misses this lack of IP control in his models for the extraction of surplus value in "platform capitalism."

As we have said at various stages of this book, we take full account of structural conditions—in this instance, the power of the huge, globe-spanning platforms, the leaders of which are far bigger than the Hollywood majors that have had a dominating influence on global media—but we are driven by a commitment to new voices, the small businesses, and the amateurs developing what they hope may be sustainable careers. We are interested in tracking cultural progressivity where it carves out space within commercializing systems. In this chapter, we are looking at the spatial and sociocultural dispersal of those voices, businesses, and careers and the lumpiness of the global regulatory plane over which the hegemons seek to glide. Power, we find, is inherently relational and unstable, and resistance is localized and endemic and a necessary corollary of power.

The scale and significance of this industry posits continuities and discontinuities with established understandings of media globalization. While the relatively frictionless globality of such phenomena demands attention, we stress the differences between such platforms and the system of national broadcasting, film, and DVD release and licensing by windowing and territory. We therefore argue against the notion that SME provides a setting for new forms of cultural hegemony. The latter, established forms of media globalization enter territories with

IP-controlled content, whereas platforms such as YouTube exhibit facilitation rather than content control and much greater content, creator, service firm (MCN), and language and cultural diversity than traditional global media hegemons.

As we showed in chapter 1, a comparison of SME and the major PGC streaming services such as Netflix, Amazon Prime, Hulu, and iTunes brings out significant differences. Social media entertainment, we argue, is a more radical *cultural* and *content* challenge to established media and works on different IP and business models. For Netflix, its aggressive global expansion requires it to negotiate with preexisting rights holders in each new territory and often requires it to attempt to close down informal means of accessing its popular content, such as VPN workarounds in such territories. As such, and together with its levels of investment in original intellectual property around which it builds a strong IP-based global brand, Netflix is rapidly resembling a Hollywood studio. In contrast, SME content, once purged of infringing content, is largely born global and is created primarily to be "spreadable" (Jenkins, Ford, and Green 2013). This is the case because this content industry, in stark contrast to content industries in general (Hollywood and broadcast television industries in particular), is not primarily based on IP control. Rather, YouTube elected to avoid the legally cumbersome traditional media model of owned or shared IP. YouTube also avoided paying fees for content as well as offering backend residual or profit participation. Rather, YouTube entered into "partnership agreements" with its content creators based on a split of advertising revenue from first dollar.

YouTube talks of being primarily a facilitator of creator and content in the many international markets in which it operates. The key difference between traditional media operating multinationally and YouTube is that the former produces, owns, or licenses content for distribution, exhibition, or sale in multiple territories, while the latter seeks to avoid the conflation of YouTubers as the IP creators with YouTube as "platform" and "middleman" operating to facilitate linking of brands and advertisers with YouTube creators and MCNs. There are significant reasons for YouTube not taking an IP ownership position, which have to do with its continued status as a platform or online service provider rather than a content company. The US Digital Millennium Copyright Act 1998, in addition to criminalizing circumvention measures and heightening the penalties for copyright infringement on the Internet, created "safe harbor" provisions for online service providers (OSPs, including ISPs) against copyright infringement liability, provided they responsively block access to alleged infringing material on receipt of infringement claims from a rights holder.

YouTube's lack of conventional IP control has not, of course, inhibited its monetization strategies, which other SME platforms like Facebook, Twitter, and Snapchat are trying to emulate. These monetization strategies have exposed the faltering codependency between media and advertising, reflecting the inefficiencies of traditional media advertising while highlighting the affordances and targeted efficacy of online analytics. Throughout its AdSense and TruView technology, Google first initiated programmatic advertising—the automation of ad buying and ad placement through the deployment of big data analytics—which it simply extended onto YouTube upon acquisition. Facebook followed suit, although shifting from an open to a closed ecosystem with its Facebook Audience Network ad tech system (Sloan 2016). Programmatic ad sales enable platforms to generate great efficiencies in matching advertising to digital content as content travels virtually seamlessly across borders and regions.

Online social media entertainment content is being distributed globally in ways that radically depart from time-honored principles and practices of territorial rights and traditional IP control. We are witnessing the rise of a nascent media industry that represents nontraditional media ownership, disruptive platforms, and content innovation that challenge our prior conceptions of media globalization, including nationalized regulatory regimes. Having said all that, however, such relatively frictionless globality seen in the operations of the major digital platforms is decidedly uneven. SME platforms generally do not seek to create or own intellectual property and are subject to significant "lumpiness" in business cultures and regulatory frameworks across the globe.

YouTube reports that it is "localized" in multiple countries and numerous languages (i.e., it has a local presence, usually consisting of sales forces and government/public relations operatives). Of course, this is not a full index of the global reach—or limits—of YouTube. YouTube is accessed and used across much wider territory than localization data shows, while a number of countries block, or restrict access to, YouTube. Those that do so tend to also block access to Twitter and/or Facebook as well. North Korea (where Internet access itself is highly restricted) and China (with the exception of the Shanghai Free Trade Zone) block YouTube, Facebook, and Twitter. As we have seen, temporary blocking at a national level has always been an option used to deal with political and/or religious issues. Over the last few years, Pakistan has blocked YouTube on several occasions when it refused to remove an anti-Islamic video. Other nations, including Eritrea, Iran, Egypt, the Congo, Tajikistan, Syria, Iraq, Sudan, Bangladesh, Afghanistan, and Morocco, have also instituted temporary bans.[1]

In addition to the need to deal with global politico-cultural divergences of this order, localization is also a response to preexistent entertainment content being subject to "location-based filtering that results from the unevenness of content-licensing deals across national jurisdictions" (Burgess 2013, 53). "Location-based filtering" is usually geoblocking, which occurs when rights holders and/or content producers may not have the rights to show some content in different regions. We look later in the chapter at one of the most prominent cases of geoblocking, a long dispute between YouTube and GEMA, a performance rights organization in Germany, over payment of rights to performers of music, and this has resulted in music videos or videos containing music being hard to access or unavailable on YouTube in Germany.

Variegated media regulation and policy are helping to shape, restrict, censor, as well as assist this emergent industry. Europe, the Middle East, and Africa (dubbed "EMEA" in globalization dialect) are much more regulated in terms of community standards, sponsorship, and advertising than the United States. The relative free-for-all in branded content and sponsorship in the United States is by no means mirrored elsewhere. These are the same "glocalization" dynamics that have been scrutinized in multinational advertising debates for decades, with the difference being that the dollar-per-unit value is, at this stage of the monetization of digital content worldwide, much lower, and thus the "education" of brands and advertisers needs to be that much more strategic.

India

Outside the United States, in addition to outright, strategic, and temporary blocks on the digital platforms, national and regional regulation can sometimes create friction that challenges the globalizing imperatives of these platforms. In the case of India, Facebook's self-aggrandizing efforts to provide free, but limited, online access through the Facebook portal was rejected by the government despite the country suffering from limited, irregular, and expensive access. The Indian government's major interventions, such as the Digital India Program, have, nonetheless, facilitated the growth of an SME industry operating with cultural and subcultural distinction from Western versions.

India is a global incubator of information technology (IT) talent. As of 2016, the chief executives of Alphabet (Google), Microsoft, MasterCard, Adobe, and SanDisk were all Indian born, and this situation continued a tradition of Indian IT leadership. (One in three residents of Silicon Valley are first-generation migrants.) But, while nurturing the growth of US-owned platforms, the success of global Indians in IT abroad has further contributed to a growing Internet economy back home. Chennai-born and -raised Google chief executive Sundar Pichai's interest in India is obvious: there are already more Indian than American Internet users, with several hundred million still unconnected. And Indian Prime Minister Narendra Modi's interest in the digital platforms is equally clear: Digital India will have to be largely built on corporate investment.

It is estimated that India will become the youngest country in the world by 2020 and already has the world's largest population of ten- to twenty-four-year-olds. According to a KPMG (2017) report, the number of Internet users in India has expanded to around 389 million in 2016. There has been a 62% increase in the broadband speed India has experienced from a very low and slow base to an average of 4mbps. India is experiencing a proliferation of Internet-enabled mobile phones. It has already crossed three hundred million and is expected to reach seven hundred million by 2021. 4G connections are predicted to grow at 38% CAGR. About 80% of the connections are expected to be on 3G or 4G by 2021, which is a 55% increase from 25% in 2016. In addition to speed, the cost of mobile telephony and streaming plans remains prohibitively high, despite the rapid growth of the Indian middle class, limiting access to online video mainly to urban dwellers and cosmopolitan youth. The technological and economic limitations of the Indian mobile market may only temporarily inhibit the growth of Indian SME, whereas the lack of diversity and access to India's traditional film, television, and music industries may further accelerate it. Bollywood has been the dominant format for Indian film and music for decades, inhibiting new genres, stars, voices, and formats. Representing a limited form of vertical media integration, over 70% of all music released in Indian is filmed music, foreclosing alternative genres like Indian rap, pop, or hip hop. Despite 850 channels vying for attention and the advertising rupee, Indian television remains focused on older audiences and traditional formats and content, including primetime soap operas and political news discourse. In numerous instances, our interviewees derided hegemonic Indian popular discourse as "ABCD"—Astrology, Bollywood, Cricket, and Devotional. Kumar (2016) sees Indian SME as "gradually chipping away" at the structural dominance of institutions such as Bollywood, television networks, and celebrity culture, which have remained the hegemonic forces within the sphere of cultural production in India.

Figure 6.1. Old cotton mills of Mumbai—Now producing Indian SME. Photo by David Craig.

Figures 6.2 and 6.3 show the levels at which Indian engagement with SME compares with that of other Internet consumption categories, while figure 6.4 highlights how the proliferation of smartphones is accelerating the rapid growth of Indian SME.

As a consequence, Indian millennials have turned off television, migrated online, and begun to create content outside these national and indeed global stereotypes of Indianness, grounded in hyperlocal regionalism, millennial popular interests, and sharp satire. Indian SME has fostered a wave of new voices, genres, and formats, alternative to traditional Indian film, TV, and music. In many cases, these developments have seen the production online of scripted web series and satirical comedy that would be considered more mainstream in the West, but that have been radically underdeveloped in India.

The earliest creators in this space were stand-up comedians and alternative musicians, who first harnessed YouTube to promote their concerts and performances. In short order, these performers evolved into concert promoters and comedy tour agents, music labels and talent agents. Some of this energy has been directed into the creation of multichannel networks, like OML (Only Much Louder). OML produces India's largest circuit of weekender music festivals, while representing numerous pop, rap, and hip-hop music acts, and representing and producing content featuring India's most popular comedy troupes, All India Bakchod (AIB) and East India Comedy. Arjun Ravi of OML comments on the relationship between India's IT fame and emerging SME prowess:

> Essentially, when you think of startups in India, predominantly you're thinking of a tech startup, but over the last few years, we've seen this major proliferation of creative industry-based startups, whether that's music or film, gaming, journalism, publishing, content creation, makers. . . . This year our talent roster will expand out of just comedy, music, and storytellers. We might be managing talent as writers, directors. Literally any sort of creative field where we feel like we can invest in that talent. (Ravi 2016)

A growing Indian middle class seeking more diverse content with access and the means to afford online video has fueled a wave of online Indian

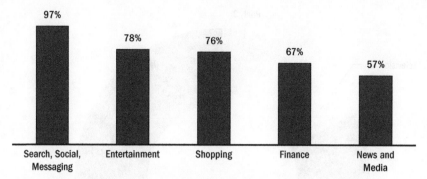

Figure 6.2. Reach of Top 5 Engagement Categories, India 2016.
Source: Kantar IMRB & MMA Smartphone Usage and Behaviour Report Overview—
India, Mobile Marketing Association, http://www.mmaglobal.com/files/documents
/kantar_imrb_mma_smartphone_usage_and_behaviour_report_india_2016-17_oct
-dec2016.pdf.

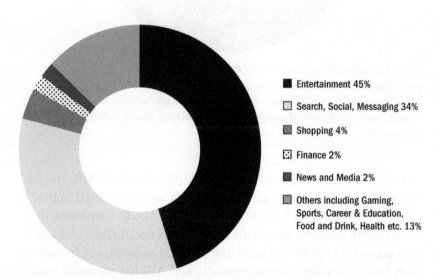

Figure 6.3. Percent of Time Spent on Smartphones, India 2016.
Source: Kantar IMRB & MMA Smartphone Usage and Behaviour Report Overview—
India, Mobile Marketing Association, http://www.mmaglobal.com/files/documents
/kantar_imrb_mma_smartphone_usage_and_behaviour_report_india_2016-17_oct
-dec2016.pdf.

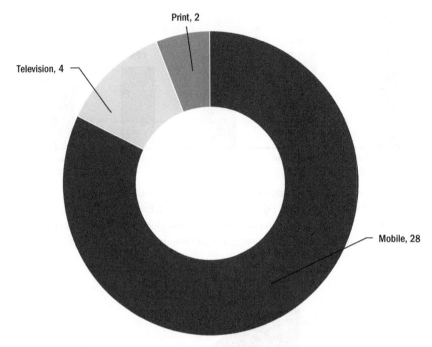

Figure 6.4. Indian Engagement Levels, Hours per Week, 2016.
Source: Kantar IMRB & MMA Smartphone Usage and Behaviour Report Overview—
India, Mobile Marketing Association, http://www.mmaglobal.com/files/documents
/kantar_imrb_mma_smartphone_usage_and_behaviour_report_india_2016-17_oct
-dec2016.pdf.

comedians and comedy troupes. Both All India Bakchod (AIB) and East
India Comedy (EIC) were launched in 2012 and specialized in prank,
satire, and sketch comedy that targeted Indian ABCD. Combined, these
troupes have garnered over half a billion views on YouTube and a presence across other platforms including Twitter, Facebook, and Instagram.
Both troupes are represented by OML, and AIB has morphed from a
group of SME creators to their own brand and set of businesses, including their own ad firm, Vigyapanti, a second YouTube channel, AIB
Doosra, and a writer's residency program designed to identify and nurture next-gen Indian comedians.

Even with the growing demand for comedy and non-ABCD fare, crossing over into Indian television has proven no more successful than in the
numerous failed efforts by US creators like Grace Helbig and Tyler Oakley.

Figure 6.5. East India Comedy. Indian SME creators offer hungry audiences greater diversity. Image: East India Comedy, https://www.youtube.com/watch?v =SF4vL8RNoKg.

AIB produced and starred in *On Air*, a parody news show on Star Network and, later, Hotstar; however, according to our interview with Atul Khatri from EIC, "The AIB show didn't do so well on television. They had a deal that they couldn't put in YouTube for a week or so after it aired. It just sort of lost its purpose, because when it comes to TV it's a ratings game." Khatri's comments affirm that the value of television (ratings) remains distinct from that of SME (community engagement). TV may elicit the siren call but these creators are beholden to a higher power, their fan community, many of whom have little interest in subscribing to traditional TV.

Operating in the less-regulated and -censored space of SME platforms has afforded these troupes the opportunity to engage in social critique, for which they have both benefited from recognition and suffered from comparable backlash. AIB's notorious satirical video "Rape: It's Your Fault" generated over six million views while other social-issue topics tackled by the troupe include gay rights, sexism, recent efforts at demonetization by the Modi government, and even net neutrality. AIB has been notoriously opposed to Facebook's Free Basics program, even as Facebook's growth would seem to benefit the troupe, which has 3.5 million likes on the platform.

Navigating politics and humor, speech and commerce proves a razor's edge for these comedians. As Khatri noted, "Ever since Facebook came out, it was the first platform where you could express your opinion or your views." Facebook helped him incubate and develop his unique brand of "observational comedy," which helped him give up his computer business to go full-time into comedy and join EIC. But, as he noticed, this freedom is not without peril. Even though, as a middle-aged comedian, he can focus on less political topics like marriage, children, school, and college, Khatri still warns, "We have to be very careful. In any country, there are politicians who are very sensitive."

Other genres that would be considered traditional in other television ecologies have made successful transitions online, notably, regional food culture. The Indian Food Network, fostered by the Mumbai-based Ping Network in partnership with Tastemade, a US-based food-themed multichannel network, is the key example. Ping Network creates premium high-end video content across genres like food, lifestyle, entertainment, and gaming. Ping also produces over seventy minutes of content on a daily basis. It is also a registered YouTube Partner. Starting only in 2013, it has more than one thousand channels, five hundred content creators, three hundred million monthly views, and more than nine million fan subscribers. Prashanto Das of the Ping Network speaks to the notion of amateur diversity and regionalism as core values of Ping in the way it goes about identifying chefs:

> That was the challenge. Pro-ams were interesting to discover. They were people who had won local competitions, but we didn't know if they would be camera ready. They weren't online, they had expertise. India Food Network started with them. We started with different languages and we started with Marathi. We had twenty-five thousand views in three months and now Ping Network has fifteen hundred channels. . . . People come to us because we speak a language that people understand. We're creators first. It's too early for people to be predatory. If you don't build communities and ecosystems, we will all die. (Das 2016)

In addition to the stand-up format, scripted online web comedy has also found a large audience in India among younger audiences seeking nontraditional fare. The Viral Fever (TVF) is composed of a group of twentysomethings with training in pharmacy, business, and engineering: as they noted in our interview, entertainment training is in short supply—"In India, there aren't a lot of options." However, founder Arunabh Kumar learned how to produce on the job while working as an assistant director in Bollywood. With his cofounder, Amit Golani, Kumar began pitching youth-oriented sitcoms to Indian MTV but was rejected. Instead, they launched their own series on YouTube. TVF became one of the first YouTube channels to reach a million subscribers in 2015, primarily due to the success of the scripted web series *Permanent Roommates*.

As the technological and market-based conditions of Indian SME are rapidly evolving, these creators are pursuing their own creative impulses informed by the willingness of their fan communities to remain engaged. According to Arunabh Kumar of The Viral Fever,

> We wanted to make stories with three acts. Yes, we were doing spoofs of celebrities, but we always wanted stories around them. We were genetically programmed to do that! Audiences kept demanding that we do longer and longer. Each episode just got longer and longer. . . . Some people work their whole life for a hit. Very low production budget to start with but now production budget is very comparable with TV, as TV is declining, as youth demographic departs for online in a mobile, small-screen medium, where you can turn off at any moment, every line has to move the plot forward, mini-cliffhanger every five minutes. (Kumar 2016)

OML and Ping represent a wave of highly differentiating media intermediaries, operating within this new ecosystem, jockeying not only for space, value, and brand equity but, more urgently, for creators, advertisers, and audiences. In turn, these conditions have further contributed to platform investment, enticing YouTube to launch another of its creator-focused YouTube Spaces in Mumbai in 2016. The space is dedicated to "democratizing access," according to Jigisha Mistry Iyengar, the head of the space, helping further professionalize creators operating out of their living rooms by offering them digital studios featuring state-of-the-art technology and postproduction support. Ironically, the space shares facilities with Whistling Woods International, one of India's most prestigious film schools. Mistry points to the homegrown nature of innovative content that meets direct needs: "A lot of moms at home are creating animated content. It's nursery rhymes. It's simple. YouTube is the world's best nanny. It's what you learn in school but you don't have to listen to your teacher, you can see nursery rhymes in animation" (Iyengar 2016). But she also underlines the major gap Indian SME is addressing for millennials:

> So the one big rise is scripted web series. I'm curious to see where it goes. There's no content for the likes of me to talk about. I have to rely on comedy guys or stand-up comedy or I'm watching American or British shows. There's a whole bunch of creators creating scripted drama comedies for my kind of audience. It's going to see traction. It's telenovelas and it's doing great and it's connecting with a huge audience. But, for the young audience, there isn't any content that is scripted that is on TV. (Iyengar 2016)

China

As with India, the contours and evolution of China's digital and social media industries have been fueled by the growth in China's economy and middle class. In the past thirty-five years, China has incubated, and cocooned, one of the largest experiments in autarkic development yet seen. In that period, China's per capita GDP has grown seventeen times over. Venture capital funds raised more than $320 billion in 2015. In the past two years, China has opened more than sixteen hundred start-up incubators. Many recent innovations in global online commerce (e.g. QR codes, digital wallets), messaging, and live-streaming have been incubated and popularized in China.

In many ways, China's singular and rapid development of its tech and online industries is due to the fact that

> it was able to fill a vacuum after the country essentially created much of its economy from scratch following the end of the Cultural Revolution. . . . Unlike in the United States, where banks and retailers already have strongholds on customers, China's state-run lenders are inefficient, and retailers never expanded broadly enough to serve a fast-growing middle class. (Mozur 2016)

For this reason, there is a much more sustainable basis to monetization, as China can be very much characterized as an early-stage consumer culture. Indeed, drawing on some of Satyananda Gabriel's (2006) work, we would characterize the zeal with which large populations have embraced the thorough commercialization of personalized social media as China's early-stage capitalist modernism. Outside the "first tier" cities on the east coast, there is significant fall-away of major branded brick-and-mortar consumer outlets, and thus e-commerce thrives. Competition among digital platforms is more intense than in the United States as they are more unilaterally focused on mobile applications in a country that leads the world by a long way in mobile phone ownership and where the installed base of standard computers per capita is low. Bryan Shao, vice president of corporate strategies and PGC operation at Youku, suggested that the fierce level of competition between the major platforms at times works like collaboration: "They can kill us, and we can kill them. So we need to stay together so we can both grow faster" (Shao 2016).

China has notoriously built an alternative online ecosystem based around state-based intervention, which includes not only banning YouTube, Facebook, Twitter, and Instagram but nurturing the growth of its own platforms (Keane 2016). The government's digital economic strategy incubated the massive tech giants, the so-called BATs (Baidu, Alibaba, and Tencent), which, in turn, either birthed or adopted multiple highly competitive online TV platforms. As a consequence of this highly charged, iterative, competing landscape, a number of online TV platforms have since been aborted, including Ku6, while other platforms have pivoted aggressively towards a subscription-based, PGC model (for example, iQiyi, LeTv, and Sohu). The latter platforms have not only engaged in a programming arms race over US and Chinese film and television content. Like Western SVOD platforms, China's iQiyi is distributing and producing ever more sophisticated fare, even partnering with Netflix to distribute content inside China (Brzeski 2017).

Zhao (2016) gives a sense of the rate of experiment and change in the short history of the online video space in China and its uneven professionalization. Initial enthusiasm for the possibilities of user-generated, amateur content saw a major correction when swathes of copyright-infringing content and platforms were closed down by the state in 2007–2008. Platforms swung, pendulum-like, to professionally generated content, but many struggled with the cost of licensing increasingly expensive licit content. Zhao focuses on the current period of "resurgence and revalidation" of UGC. Online video production has rapidly come to offer alternatives to officially sanctioned institutions in

Figure 6.6. Logos of Chinese Platforms and MCNs. *Clockwise from top left*: Youku, Weibo, WeChat, Xingzhan, Feidishuo, Baozoumanhua, and Xinpianchang.

cultural production, distribution, and consumption. Many online video platforms, she argues, have their roots in amateur practices, facilitating flows of content unavailable in the official marketplace.

Thus, platforms like Youku Tudou have moved away from the more expensive and competitive PGC portals to return to their original value proposition of user-generated content with social networking capabilities. Similarly to the West, multiple social media platforms have launched to compete with or offer diverse affordances with Youku. China's gameplay platforms like Duoyu and PandaTV have already outpaced Western equivalents like Twitch or YouTube Gaming, while accelerating China's booming e-game industry. The live-broadcasting affordances of these platforms supercharged the launch of over one hundred live mobile applications in the past few years, which, in turn, contributed to a swift backlash from China's censors (Custer 2016a). What the state incubates, it may also abort.

Despite rapid commercialization and expansion of the system, the state unrepentantly intervenes to censor content deemed "unhealthy" or "harmful" before production or to force offending content to be removed from screens. Qing Zhou of Feidieshou suggests that this causes online entrepreneurs, as much as mainstream broadcasters, to be agile and creative in the way they commission and produce content, trying to "think ahead of" Chinese media regulation in its guise as both censor and protector—not only in the production of original online content but in the repackaging of that content for traditional television audiences (Zhou 2016). One of our key Chinese informants, SME entrepreneur Heng Cai, forensically enumerates four ways the government seeks to manage online video: blocking the channel; licensing (to be a legal video distribution platform, one needs a permit called an "Internet broadcasting license"); censoring (which effectively means most video platforms self-censor); and subsidizing (the government hires "Internet commentators," who are paid by the propaganda department to write comments favoring the government). If one or more of these interventions fail, the final option is banning outright (Cai 2016).

Second-gen platforms like Tencent's WeChat, China's formidable messenger service, have reverse engineered platform development in the West. Facebook's purchase of WhatsApp messenger service for an exorbitant $19 billion may have represented a defensive effort by the West to block Chinese platform penetration outside its great firewall. In light of Chinese commitment to the soft power of media (Xi 2014), Zuckerberg barely thwarted the first salvo in the social media war rapidly looming on the digital horizon (Lunden 2014).

Micro-blogging platform Weibo makes an interesting contrast with its US-based counterpart Twitter. Like Twitter, Weibo is a text-based micro-blogging service that has been threatened repeatedly with demise from various competitors, not least of which is WeChat (Custer 2016b). Unlike Twitter, Weibo integrated photos and a video player into the platform from the beginning, which helped nurture key opinion leaders, Weibo personalities from throughout the public sphere, including entrepreneurs, politicians, and celebrities, engaging millions of Chinese netizens around the globe. With the proliferation of smartphones with 4G speed fostering seven hundred million subscriptions, leaping over Youku, Weibo has become the premier platform for short video content, helping foster the advertising-defined "influencer" (Wanghong 网红) economy (Zhou 2016). Table 6.1 shows the Chinese app market to be well populated by SME applications.

TABLE 6.1. China's Top 10 Mobile Apps, Monthly Active Users

App	MAU Millions, Sept. 2016	%YoY MAU Growth	Average Monthly Sessions per User
WeChat (Instant messaging)	817.8	32.80%	569.5
QQ/Tencent (Instant messaging)	565.4	0.10%	229
Taobao (Online shopping)	433.3	42.70%	63.3
Weibo (Micro-blogging)	390.6	79.00%	52
Tencent Video (Video streaming)	378.5	71.80%	36.2
Alipay (Mobile payment)	374.1	65.90%	21.3
Baidu (Search)	358.3	34.90%	53.7
iQiyi (Online video)	347.6	72.00%	35.4
Sogou (Search)	294.5	17.90%	1070.7
Youku (Online video)	292.5	54.90%	35.1

Source: "Top 2000 Apps in China: Autumn 2016 Review," *Quest*, http://www.questmobile.com.cn/blog/en/blog_63.html, accessed 18 May 2018.

The Chinese influencer economy shows how these platforms have helped create the technological and commercial conditions upon which an alternative Chinese social media entertainment industry has emerged. In an interview with Di Zhou, an executive with Xinpianchang, Zhou stressed how Chinese SME features rapidly professionalizing amateur Chinese content creators engaging in content innovation distinct from traditional Chinese film and television, like the aforementioned game players, food, fashion, and style vloggers, and a wave of social media celebrities. Bryan Shao at Youku also stressed the popularity of online content steeped in China's long history, particularly content that differs from that offered through traditional TV. Once again, the Chinese state has engaged in tandem actions, nursing and disciplining these upstart micro-celebrities, like the Chinese vlog queen Miss Papi (Jiang). Wrist-slapped by censors for foul language, Papi issued a message of contrition

Figure 6.7. Popular Chinese vlogger Miss Papi. Papi Jiang Official Channel, https://www.youtube.com/channel/UCgHXsynhD8GxbFcNlPEn-_w.

to her eleven million followers, while simultaneously securing multimillions in investment and brand integration (BBC 2016).

As in the West, the Chinese SME industry co-evolves alongside traditional Chinese media. In contrast to the United States, but comparable to India, the industry exploits the lack of diversity in traditional film and TV to embrace more professionally generated traditional content, albeit in more affordable formats than traditional scripted fare. One of the most popular shows on Youku is *The Luogic Show*, a history- and social-issue-themed talk show hosted by former CCTV producer Luo Zhen Yu. *Baozoudashijian* is an entertainment show hosted by Baozoumanhua, who remains anonymous, emerging onscreen solely in a *papier-mâché* mask, providing arguably a brilliant ploy to thwart state censorship.

As in the West, a new wave of intermediaries operating among platforms, creators, advertisers, and traditional media has emerged. Unlike in the West, these firms also function as digital production companies generating original IP content across multiple platforms. As Qing Zhou of Feidieshou stated, "As advertising is our major source of revenue, we seek to enlarge our influence. Our goal then is to put Feidieshou content across Youku, Weibo, iQiyi, Tencent, LeTV, Meipai, Miaopai, Baidu, Panda, and Douyu" (Zhou 2016). Playing off the continued decline of youth audiences across CCTV, Feidieshuo has developed original animation designed for millennials, or rather 1980s and 1990s *balinghous* and *jiulinghuos*, featuring mature topics missing on Chinese TV, such as relationships, sex, and social pressure (Zhou 2016). Cofounder of Xingzhan (StarStation) TV Heng Cai (2016) discusses his company's multipronged strategy of developing its own vertical brands around sports, food, antiques, and more, converting offline experts into online influencers, and engaging in content marketing with leading brands and advertisers. Operating as both influencer agency and multichannel network, Xinpianchang also features its own content as well as channels that it operates but does not own. Unlike their MCN counterparts that have been acquired by traditional media firms, these upstarts have accelerated through several rounds of investor financing, including courting Palo Alto–based VCs or, in the case of Xinpianchang, launching and securing an IPO in Beijing's New Market exchange.

However, investment, acquisition, or a successful IPO launch is not a guarantee of sustainability; Youku was recently bought back from the market and returned to the private sector. According to interviews with senior personnel at YouKu, this buyback affords the company greater leeway to pivot, innovate, disrupt, but mostly generate much-needed synergies with the e-commerce partners in the Alibaba corporation, including T-mall and Taobao stores. In contrast to the West, along with the lucrative fan-funding virtual-goods market fostered by the gameplay platforms, influencer-fueled e-commerce monetization represents one of the more sustainable revenue strategies of Chinese SME. In an interview with Matrix, an example was provided of an online game streamer who extended his revenue stream by opening a Taobao store to deliver snacks to hungry users, earning twenty million RMB (the Chinese currency) in one year on snack sales alone. Little surprise, then, that Amazon is trying to emulate Alibaba's YouKu Taobao synergies by launching its own UGC platform, Video Direct. As with Facebook's WhatsApp messenger play, Amazon is operating on the defensive, trying to thwart a potential incursion from the East.

As reflected by the strategic interplay between the US-based global platforms and China's emergent SME industries, China's "Great Firewall" has fostered a playing field comprised of numerous major teams, players, rules, and skirmishes operating at the level of the domestic and the global—many of which are larger and some of which are more innovative than US leaders in the field.

Germany

In Germany, the key characteristics we focus on are language and market limitation; strong cultural regulation; the stronger integration of MCNs/MPNs into main media companies and its implications; and the existence of significant public subvention for SME in Germany. We conclude with a short production case study, which illustrates many of these key structural features of German SME.

Despite the numerical size of the Eurozone (the European Union has a population of 510 million), it is for YouTube—as it is for all those dealing in global markets—a very localized, segmented market. One clear continuity with older versions of cultural imperialism is the dominance of the English language in SME. For English-language SME, the world is indeed flatter than for anyone else. Robert Vossen and Ralf Osteroth of Multiplatform Network Studio 71 (based in Berlin, London, and Vienna) emphasize the dialectical communicative politics even within the German language. High German is key to communicating within up to 80% of the online traffic in German. This means that Bavarians and Austrians have to break out of their dialects to become more commercially viable whereas those individuals who natively speak Swiss German, pronounced totally differently from High German, will have to translate their dialect into "virtually a different language" (Vossen and Osteroth 2016).

Germany, despite being one of the three largest, most viable linguistic markets in Europe, along with the UK and France, is fractured. (For Google/YouTube, Spain, Russia, and Turkey are the key second-tier EMEA markets to develop.) What makes this more significant for SME than other communication and media content is that SME's demotic, communitarian authenticity (see chapter 4) is in tension with its market viability in these linguistically fractured markets, and it is one possible reason why the standard fare in the United States of personality vlogging is not a main genre, or vertical, in Europe. It means that language and culture are "front stage" considerations for creator, intermediary, and platforms as marketers. But it also means that in Germany, most of the top online creators are local, which is unusual (although this is especially the case in European countries smaller than Germany).

For creators and MCNs/MPNs, the challenge is to be able to grow a sufficiently popular base in German and then expand with a second or subsequent English-language channel. Google is also seeking to address the language issue by bringing to bear some of its advanced simultaneous translation technologies on this very low-tech but popular SME content.

France is often cited as the most assertive Western defender of its cultural patrimony in the face of US cultural hegemony. But Germany has arguably been more consistently assertive in the area of cultural regulation in the online space. The stand-out example is the stand-off between YouTube and GEMA (Gesellschaft für musikalische Aufführungs und mechanische Vervielfältigungsrechte), the state-authorized collecting society and performing-rights organization. This dispute, which started in 2009 and was partially resolved as of late 2016, was fundamentally about a German court's refusal to apply principles enshrined in the US DMCA safe harbor provisions. The court held that YouTube could be liable when it hosts copyrighted videos without the copyright holder's permission. While the court was responding to an action taken by GEMA, the motivation for which was that copyrighted German music should receive appropriate "pay for play," the effect of the stand-off was much wider. Uniquely for YouTube globally, a study estimated that 61.5% of the thousand most-viewed YouTube clips were at one stage blocked in Germany. This compares to 0.9% blocked in the United States. A further study found that about 3% of all YouTube videos, and 10% of videos with over one million views, have been blocked (Kretschmer and Peukert 2014). The seven-year stand-off was partially resolved in late 2016 when YouTube agreed to an undisclosed rate at which GEMA members would be remunerated for video streams. YouTube may have been motivated to move to settlement given that the terms of the deal both included ad-supported free viewing and prepared the way for the European launch of YouTube Red.

The GEMA case is indicative of a broader predilection for intervention for cultural and social ends in the online environment. Gameplay is arguably the dominant vertical in Germany (Studio 71 says it is "huge" [Vossen and Osteroth 2016]) but, as in other countries, there are social concerns about the antisociability of gameplay, its gender segregation, and the reputation of game intermediaries signing gamers to exploitative contracts. Despite the fact that 70% of Germans play computer games (Siegismund 2016), gameplay struggles for social legitimacy and market acceptance. Fabian Siegismund contrasts the situation in the United States, where Nike, Coke, or Monster sponsors gameplay, whereas it struggles for any market support in Germany. This is further complicated by strict regulations about "youth protection," backed up by the operations of the Federal Review Board for Media Harmful to Minors (Bundesprüfstelle für jugendgefährdende Medien, or BPjM). The

BPjM is a German federal agency responsible for examining and censoring media works allegedly harmful to young people. One of Germany's leading gameplay exponents, Siegismund, who has also advised BPjM, warns that advanced shooter games represent a significant business risk for German YouTubers because YouTube does not have a compliant youth protection system for games ranked for ages sixteen or older. The usual recourse to gestures of self-regulation may not work in Germany because legally such protections need to be sanctioned by government agencies (Siegismund 2016).

German regulations regarding transparency in product placement, sponsorship, and advertising are strict, extensive, and have been in place for longer than in other major territories. Product-placement regulations stipulate that there must be a declaration of at least three seconds at the beginning and the end of the video and a watermark of "P." Branded entertainment, aka advertorials, must be watermarked as such through the entire video. The fundamental marketing regulation is the Declaration of Werbung ("Werbung" is translated as "advertising") that creators are legally required to mark on video content that they have been paid for, such as games they have been paid to play. Siegismund recalls that part of his job at Studio 71 was to find workarounds for the Werbung Declaration—such as product placement (Siegismund 2016).

A significant diversion of resources from broadcasting to online occurred in late 2016 with the establishment of FUNK, an annual €45 million investment in online content services for young viewers from the German public broadcasters ARD and ZDF. As far as we can ascertain, this is the largest public subvention of SME to this time (2017). While coverage of this initiative has suggested that it is in part motivated by the need to create efficiencies due to fixed high costs in broadcasting (it involved the closure of ARD's EinsPlus and ZDFkultur), it is more fundamentally a response to the demographic crisis in public service media and a decision to "offer formats on the net in which young people are interested and make them available on the platforms they use," in the words of ZDF general director Thomas Bellut (quoted in Krieger 2016). Indeed, a wide range of formats are supported, including news and critical analysis, satire, humor, and science fiction, balancing the preponderance of gaming, as well as a range of platforms, including Facebook, Snapchat, and Instagram and the FUNK app, as well as YouTube. For Annalina

Micus, program strategist at the YouTube Space Berlin, it is an opportunity to develop much more experimental web series: "formats YouTubers always wanted to do but didn't have the resources" (Micus 2016).

A significant structural feature consistent with our characterization of a firmly regulated SME environment with the very active oversight of state agencies and public broadcasters is the degree to which MCNs/MPNs are perforce integrated with established media institutions. Berlin-based MCN Divimove is now a subsidiary of Fremantle Media, a former UK production company that is now a division of Bertelsmann's RTL Group based in Germany. German media conglomerate ProSieben acquired Berlin-based Studio 71, which then acquired Los Angeles–based Collective Digital Studios. In early 2017, French-owned TF1 and Italian broadcasters MediaSet joined ProSieben as minority partners in Studio 71 (Tartaglione 2017). These Euro mergers and acquisitions signal the rise of regional intermediaries competing with the US and UK firms that benefit from English-language globality. Whereas joint ventures and partnerships with traditional media companies may increase economies of scale, foster synergies, and provide capital, these moves are fraught with complication. As divisions of multinational media conglomerates, these firms are forced to operate according to the structural, material, and regulatory conditions of their parent companies. According to Studio 71 executives, "We have to treat our content as TV content even though it airs online. We're selling advertising across both platforms and if it's seen that we are trying to get around content restrictions online, that could affect our sales and license" (Vossen and Osteroth 2017). For a key MPN like Studio 71, the operating environment is unlike most others for SME intermediaries. Influencer marketing is arguably the key SME revenue source, but it struggles in the context of the German regulatory tradition, which puts strong stress against "hidden persuasion" dating back to postwar reforms to combat the influence of propaganda, and the tendency to treat online as functionally equivalent to broadcast.

* * *

An intriguing project, which typifies contemporary European cosmopolitan culture and illustrates many of the issues for German online content is *The Great War* (https://www.youtube.com/user/TheGreatWar/about).

This is the ultimate online web series—producing episodes three times a week, fifty-two weeks a year, following in extreme detail the weekly events of the First World War exactly one hundred years later, starting in 2014 and finishing in 2019. As of early 2017, it had collected 578,000 subscribers and over 72 million views. Produced by a five-person team under contract to one of Germany's major hybrid MCN/media companies, Mediakraft Networks, it adopts, according to its researcher, writer, and main presenter, Indy Neidell, "as neutral position as possible." "[W]e have positions from all the different nations represented. . . . We present it in such a way that there are enemies . . . but no bad guys. Everybody was the bad guy" (Neidell 2016). The project sets itself firmly against what second producer and technician Tony Stellar says is "the problem of German content—that it is clickbait-y" (Stellar 2016).

The program concept allows the production to be highly planned, and the five-year time frame necessitates a much longer contract than usual in this start-up industry. Program producer and social media manager Florian Witteg says, "[T]he people appreciate German thoroughness," and the ability to plan long-term means "my work/life balance is great, it lets me concentrate more!" (Witteg 2016). Not only is the series significantly crowd funded but also its knowledge base is significantly crowd sourced. Neidell avers, "[T]his is global, free, interactive, real-time documentary" whose capacity to harness a global expert fan community generates a depth of knowledge that "even a Ken Burns documentary might not be able to achieve" (Neidell 2016).

Made in a corner of an old, unused factory in Kreuzberg, in suburban Berlin, with props, equipment, and costumes more basic than an elementary school drama production, the series taps into the enduring fascination with the twentieth-century industrialization of military mayhem. Yes, the core audience is eighteen to forty-four and 96% male, but there are lots of older people offering free research input, and Neidell claims there is a lot of couple viewing (Neidell 2016). The program concept would never find its way onto German television, in part because the average viewers of public television are in their sixties and unlikely to be sympathetic to the "no bad guys/everybody was the bad guy" standpoint. In our view, the program's ethos, outreach strategy, and innovation make it more exemplary of public service media than most official public service history programs.

Figure 6.8. *The Great War*, started in 2014, produces three episodes a week and will finish in 2019. Image: The Great War, https://www.youtube.com/user/TheGreatWar.

YouTube is the content hub for the series, but Facebook, Twitter, and Instagram provide backstage material for hard-core viewers. Programmatic advertising at $1 CPM produces negligible revenue, whereas Patreon crowd funding generates about $15,000 per month and is the key revenue source. Merchandising, subscription revenue on YouTube Red, and sponsors and branded content also contribute. These revenue sources have to be set against the costs of licensing a great deal of historical footage from British Pathé Film Library. German copyright law is strong enough, according to the producers, that even user-generated content, such as pictures of family members that viewers submit, is not used because the submitters would have to be compensated and the photos contracted for. Finally, it should be noted that the producers wanted to publish in German and Polish as well as English, but the program was not financially viable other than in English, with audiences comprised of 42% US, 10% UK, and 8% Canada, and EU countries registering a bare 2%.

State Support for SME

In this chapter, we have noted, despite the relatively frictionless movement of online content around the world, how culturally diverse SME is in numerous countries. Supporting this, and recognizing that increasingly especially young citizens are engaged online, government and state agencies have begun to shore up local capacity to participate in global online culture. We have seen this with Germany's FUNK initiative.

In 2015, the Arts Council England recognized that it needed to assess the kind of contemporary art production it funded and take steps to make sure it reached the places where audiences are more likely to be. For this reason, it awarded £1.8 million to online distribution company Rightster to deliver Canvas—an online digital arts hub or multichannel network. Canvas is a program designed specifically *not* to make art but to collate, curate, and showcase content from leading UK arts organizations alongside original content (Romer 2015). In Japan, YouTube partnered with Toei (a major Japanese producer and distributor of film and TV programs) in an initiative designed to help creators produce videos in the style of Japanese *jidaigeki*, or period drama (Byford 2015). Funding provided tutorials for sword fighting, styling, and special effects. Google Canada and Canada Media Fund have partnered to develop a YouTube channel dedicated to showcasing original Canadian films. The channel will be managed by BBTV (Canada Media Fund 2017).

In the United States, combining a YouTube sensibility with a PBS commitment to quality, PBS Digital Studios network has earned 9.4 million subscribers, generated 800 million lifetime views with 30 million monthly views, and won seven Webby Awards as of 2017. PBS Digital Studios reaches a community of gamers, filmmakers, and other creators with over fifty original web series from arts to sciences to lifestyle. Notably, Hank and John Green's Crash Course is featured as part of the studio's portfolio. The studio boasts that 70% of users are between the ages of eighteen and thirty-four and that the average user watches about thirty minutes of its content per month.

But what questions of state cultural and media policy does subsidizing SME content raise? Questions of government policy have been sotto voce in the book thus far; here, we bring them forward in a case study of the challenges faced by state actors as they navigate between online culture and established screen culture. In our conclusion we will examine the regulatory issues this clash of cultures raises.

Online Culture Meets Established Australian Screen Culture

The new dynamics of media globalization impact Australia's screen industries as they undergo shifts driven by digital disruption, convergence, and the new demographics of taste and consumption. Historically, numerous countries have developed elaborate cultural policy frameworks to protect their cultural patrimony, especially from the inroads of powerful cultural hegemons such as the United States. Countries like Australia have additional reasons based on the small size of their domestic markets (which make amortizing production costs in their local market much more difficult) and the ease with which US and UK product enters their markets (because English is the dominant language).

The first important point is that the presence of the global digital platforms in local jurisdictions is more than a matter for cultural and media policy. The Google/YouTube presence in Australia has a corporate, an R&D, as well as a cultural dimension. Figures from 2016 for Google show that the corporation now employs over 72,000 people worldwide. Some 38% (21,600) of its workforce was located outside of the United States, according to 2015 figures. Now with over 1300 employees in Australia, Google's Sydney office is one of its larger global engineering centers. There is a significant research and development presence in Australia, employing about five hundred engineers. Google Maps started in Australia, and Sydney also contributes to Google Drive, and the Chrome web browser. Sydney also makes an important contribution to developing apps for the Next Billion Users project.

Google positions itself publicly as a major contributor to Australian science and technology innovation. But the bulk of its work, like the bulk of its work globally, is developing relationships with significant brands and advertisers in order to grow revenue and educate brands and advertisers in the new digital marketing dynamics. Indeed, the 2016 Google annual filing documents the generation of 88% of Google's total revenues from advertising.

In the last several years, Google Australia has heightened its public policy presence, contributing to public inquiries and debates and defending its tax-minimization practices as many jurisdictions put pressure on Google (together with Microsoft, Apple, and other major software and entertainment multinationals) by profiling its investment of about $1 billion in Australia over the three years to 2015 (then Google Australia managing director Maile Carnegie, cited in Lehmann 2015). In addition to these policy touchpoints, Google Australia also engages with the main government screen support body Screen Australia to promote career development for Australian YouTubers.

Google's voice in the Australian cultural policy space is provocatively orthogonal to the established mindset. Its business model for SME entrepreneurship challenges content makers to move beyond the old dichotomy between cultural address to the domestic market and entertainment address to international markets, while beginning to embrace new revenue streams in addition to, and sometimes completely independent of, public subvention and broadcaster and distributor licensing. Australian screen content culture and policy have been historically structured by what Susan Dermody and Elizabeth Jacka (1987) termed "Industry 1" (culturally specific, domestic market–oriented production) and "Industry 2" (internationally oriented entertainment product), with a normative bias toward the former over the latter, conditioned by cultural policy–based state subvention and regulatory support. Cultural policy influence also treats long-form narrative fiction and social documentary as privileged genres for the purposes of subsidy as they are uniquely vulnerable to market failure.

As the screen sector has globalized, some of the normative weight in these dualisms has eroded. Deb Verhoeven (2014) identifies a now established "Industry 3," which is comfortably ensconced across both domestic and international vectors, but focuses on an "Industry 4," which "is characterized by the adoption of new methodologies for producing and distributing content afforded by the digitization of the screen industries," including such tactics as data mining to identify audiences, different labor practices such as a twenty-four-hour work cycle, and an opportunistic approach to finance (Verhoeven 2014, 163). In many respects, "Industry 4" characterizes emergent SME culture in Australia.

The point at which YouTube culture meets Australian screen culture most directly is Skip Ahead. (There is also a Skip Ahead program in New Zealand, which sees Google partnering with the principal funding body NZ on Air.) In 2013, Google and Screen Australia launched this program, aimed to provide local talent with the resources necessary to develop episodic scripted content for distribution via YouTube, by providing funding and production resources. There were three rounds of Skip Ahead between 2014 and 2016. Screen Australia selected creators for the program, and those selected received a share of jointly contributed seed funding—initially, for round one, AU$400,000, growing to $500,000 for round two and AU$725,000 for round three—along with access to local production resources, and an opportunity to network at the YouTube Space in Los Angeles. Australian creators who were actively engaged in creating new original content on YouTube and had built a substantial following (for round one, a minimum subscriber base of 100,000 or a combined subscriber base of 120,000 for collaborative projects) were eligible to apply for funding. Screen Australia promoted the program as one that aimed to cultivate original Australian narrative-based content made specifically for global online audiences.

First-round awards went to *Axis All Areas* (Axis of Awesome), a musical comedy about a rock band; *Across Australia* (Mighty Car Mods), a documentary about journeying across Australia in a budget modified car; *Neighbours—Zombie Edition* (Neighbours Official and Louna Maroun collaboration), a scripted web series that saw the soap opera inundated with zombified ex-characters; *Fernando's Legitimate Business Enterprise* (Sexual Lobster), an animated story about a singer and his shifty business partner; and *Reinventing Education* (Veritasium), a documentary exploring the future of education. Funding for the second round went to *The Tale Teller* (Draw with Jazza), a documentary animation about animated storytelling; *Traffic Jam—The Musical* (SketchShe), a musical comedy about road rage; *1999* (Aunty Donna), a comedy about the dreaded Y2K bug; *The Sweetest Thing* (How to Cook That), a documentary about extreme desserts and family; and *The Australiana Hostel* (Frenchy SungaAttack and The Roundabout Crew), a comedy about a rundown Sydney hostel. Third-round winners were *RackaRacka: LIVE*, a live-action one-off special featuring the filmmakers on a rampage (RackaRacka); *The Superwog Show* (Brothers Theo and Nathan Saidden); *Crafty Kingdom* animated series (Charli's Crafty Kitchen); and *Mutant Menu*, a forty-five-minute documentary that explored genetic manipulation to create superheroes (science communication channel BrainCraft).

We have commented already on Google's provocations to the established mindset. But the "established mindset" is certainly not static and is evolving with responsive intent. Contemporary cultural policy can no longer rely only on market failure as a justification for action, but must also focus on policies to support emerging new practices and markets. Skip Ahead is a good example of a small experiment in meeting these challenges. Mike Cowap, Screen Australia development manager for Skip Ahead, backgrounds the program:

> We were talking to Google probably for two years prior to Skip Ahead happening about doing a joint initiative. Our approach was "you have

global ubiquitous platform, we have talented content creators." The interest for us is how can we offer an opportunity for our filmmakers to make the best of the platform for finding an audience, monetizing an audience, and building a loyal fan base. And that fitted with what YouTube has endeavored to do also. They wanted to show that YouTube is about more than funny cat videos, and that there is quality content available, and also to show that they do support Australian content creators. (Cowap 2015)

Cowap emphasizes that Australia has had online creators who have been a success for their target audience for much longer than the broader film and TV industry generally gives them credit for. Cowap argues that Screen Australia has long recognized two camps of online content creators. On the one hand, there are people from a traditional media background who have acted to engage with the new platforms, while on the other hand there is a range of SME talent that has been creating content as professionalizing amateurs for many years without the support or even understanding of screen industry associations or government agencies. Many in this latter group may not have even felt any particular or pressing need for such understanding.

Cowap suggests that the greater change is that people in the wider film and TV industry are now coming to realize something that YouTubers have known for years—that SME is not a springboard for a post-YouTube film or television career but a viable platform for monetization and professionalization itself, and that any new online talent that is successfully courted will not disappear from YouTube and migrate exclusively to film or TV. Rather, such talent will aim to be successful across the platforms, with the most savvy using the logics of traditional screen outlets while continuing to build their own monetization opportunities online. The aim of the Skip Ahead program, he suggests, is to actively engage with new content creators in order to show them that there are organizations able to provide funding and support that do not only deal with old media.

The outcomes from the first round—taking creators who already had a level of success on YouTube and funding them to create more ambitious content, challenge themselves and their audiences, and build their subscriber base—show that the strategy was, Cowap claims, by and large achieved. This confidence was underlined in late 2015 when Google and

Screen Australia took the very unusual move of placing a series of main media advertisements for select recipients of second-round funding in the national press: "*1999* was looking for funding. So we helped give it a future." "They needed funding for *The Australiana Hostel*. We couldn't help but accommodate." "*Traffic Jam—The Musical* needed funding. We helped get it moving."

Viewing Skip Ahead as a professional development exercise, equal parts business model improvement and content innovation, justifies Screen Australia in making qualitative distinctions between what they will and will not support:

> One of the values that we were judging Skip Ahead on was "what difference is this going to make to you as a content creator, what does this allow you to do that you're not already doing?" I would say, for example, if an unboxing creator came in and wanted to do more unboxing videos, I think that whilst it would be eligible, I'm not sure it would be making that much of a difference to what they're already doing, we wouldn't want to see them doing more of the same. It may give them the capacity to be even more popular, but we want to see an improvement in craft as well. (Cowap 2015)

Cowap argues that through programs like Skip Ahead, Screen Australia has developed a very strong understanding of YouTube and social media ecosystems:

> The broader industry has to understand where audiences are consuming content now. We can't keep our heads in the sand and keep pumping things out on the normal channels, even though they are still viable platforms. And even where colleagues assume they don't know much, they generally know a lot more than they think they do. All of them these days are active and literate in social media, they just assume that there is more to it than there actually is. Most of us have become hardwired with an understanding of how online behavior and communities work. A lot of people at Screen Australia also come from a script editing or screen development background, and understand the building blocks necessary to tell an engaging story or pull an audience in. These skills are as valuable for creating online content as they are for traditional film or TV.

Even in the most simple and seemingly innocuous or superficial videos, an understanding of basic beginning, middle, and end is still valuable. (Cowap 2015)

When pressed about how far the cultural remit of the national screen agency needs to be stretched to accommodate cooking shows, car modification, and low-end Flash animation, Cowap argued that Screen Australia is prepared to defend what it sees as an important development for cultural products:

> One thing that Screen Australia really liked is that there are whole new genres of programming on YouTube . . . and while some of these new genres would be easy for a film or television professional to sneer at— production values are low, generally no narrative—they are captivating. And if you're prepared to measure the worth of a show on the volume and appreciation of its audience, that stuff is brilliant. (Cowap 2015)

The content selected for first-round funding by Screen Australia is indicative of the main YouTube verticals, with the inclusion of sketch comedy, "how-to" science and car-modification videos, animation for a hipster audience, and a prominent Melbourne vlogger. Screen Australia was looking to further professionalization and generic legibility: rather than support already-successful YouTubers to produce more of the same, Screen Australia promoted the program as an initiative to cultivate native Australian "storytelling" online. Content supported through the Skip Ahead program could be factual or have factual elements, but it also had to carry a substantial narrative capable of selling Australian culture in a way that was appealing and accessible to a particular global audience no longer defined by the limitations of cinema and television.

So, for example, rather than producing more videos that perform and discuss DIY car modifications with fellow car enthusiasts, Mighty Car Mod-ers Marty (Martin Mulholland) and Moog (Blair Joscelyne) journey from Sydney to Alice Springs on an epic road trip, borrowing an impressive range of cars from enthusiasts, willing locals, and their YouTube channel fans. The result is six twenty-minute films that invoke key elements of iconic Australiana, riffing on classic and recent film and television content such as John Heyer's *The Back of Beyond* (1954), Mike and

Mal Leyland's *Ask the Leyland Brothers* (1976–1984), and David Batty's *Bush Mechanics* (2001).

The initiative literally seeks to have YouTube culture meet Australian screen culture. Prominent Melbourne vlogger and YouTube personality Louna Maroun takes her craft "to another level" by collaborating with an established Australian media company (Freemantle) to deliver a fresh take on an iconic Australian TV show. The resulting *Neighbours— Zombie Edition* exposes Louna Maroun to *Neighbours* fans even as it brings *Neighbours* to Louna's large global audience—notably in the United States and Brazil—and the wider YouTube community. For someone completely outside the industry environment who, inspired by other YouTubers, "began recording performances to share with family, friends and peers" without "really realizing that it was a way to access an audience" to find herself collaborating with and directing "people I have watched on TV since I was a kid" was, undoubtedly, "a huge experience" (Maroun 2015).

Australia is deeply enmeshed in the major transformations in the political economy and modes of production and consumption of media content. The dramatic flow of advertising revenue to the major platforms has seen the then head of the major public service media organization, the ABC, warn that "the era of profitable Australian media companies was over and the power now lay with digital players like Google, Facebook, Amazon and Apple" (Mark Scott in Meade 2015). Google Australia's policy objectives are clear enough. YouTube (along with other streaming platforms) offers global, emerging-market opportunities. However, legacy regulatory and support frameworks are not technology neutral, and have not geared sufficiently to support the new waves of online production, while legacy licensing by territory inhibits internationalized streaming. Policy makers and film, television, streaming, and ISP industries impacted by such change will be unable to avoid the increasing impetus of these issues, especially as the consumption preferences of young online viewers meet increasingly effective digital marketing. It is highly likely that demographic and consumption trends in Australia will reflect US data indicating that children, adolescents, and young adults coalesce around interest in online personalities almost to the complete exclusion of "mainstream" celebrities populating the "main" media. As we have seen throughout this chapter, SME represents a different level and type of globalized media, with every content creator and every aggregator, of whatever scale and level of success, involved in multiple markets and communities.

Outro

This chapter has analyzed the global dynamics of SME, suggesting the need for a revision to accounts of media, cultural, and platform imperialism that insist on strict continuity between twentieth- and twenty-first-century media. This is based on two fundamental arguments. First, such "continuity" versions of US domination focus exclusively on the news and the infosphere whereas, in the realm of entertainment and culture, notions of domination are much harder to maintain. Second, the fact that SME content on the big digital platforms is able to circle the globe completely independently of standard windowing and territorial licensing, and without standard IP control, suggests a fundamentally different model of extreme spreadability without domination.

Having asserted the relative frictionlessness of SME globally based on "facilitation" rather than IP control, we have been careful to stress that it is mitigated by irreducible national cultural, market, and regulatory specificity. Indian SME has been shaped nationally as an alternative to the longstanding hegemony of Bollywood. Protected as well as censored by the state and fueled by China's transition to a consumption-based economy, the Chinese platforms and the SME industry based on them are well advanced and may, as we discuss in the next chapter, look to go global themselves. Germany's heightened regulatory constraint, coupled with public funding of homegrown creators, provides evidence of government policy and strategy, which we will also pursue further in the next chapter. The partnership between Screen Australia and Google evidences the challenges and opportunities of how productively to engage SME from the standpoint of cultural and industry development policy.

Globalizing SME is now beginning to attract some scholars' attention. For example, Yomna Elsayed (2016) and Mohamed El Marzouki (2017) have focused on the cultural politics and commercialization practices of Middle Eastern creators in Egypt and Morocco, respectively. Carlos Scolari and Damián Fraticelli (2017) examine the discursive practices of

Spanish YouTubers and their influence on traditional Spanish media. These national case studies further highlight the multivariance of global SME on national, transcultural, and language axes. This new "geo-linguistic market" (Sinclair, Jacka, and Cunningham 1996) has already nurtured the success of HolaSoyGerman, second only to PewDiePie in subscribers on YouTube; the El Smosh, the Spanish-dubbed channel by prominent US SME comedian Smosh; beauty vlogger Yula with more subscribers than Bethany Mota and Michelle Phan combined; and MiTú, a well-funded SME intermediary that is "changing the way Latino creators and communities connect" (Kozlowski 2014).

Due to their vintage, debates in media and communication studies about media and cultural imperialism and globalization can develop a shop-worn quality. Due to the depth with which it studies cultural specificity, anthropology may offer a fresh, and perhaps more nuanced grasp of cultural globalization. Anthropologist Richard Wilk, for example, in a study of beauty pageants in Belize, captures both weak and strong cultural globalization while seeing the global cultural system promoting cultural differences by organizing diversity rather than replicating uniformity. Cultural diversity is communicated through formalized conventions (such as youth-oriented genres) that are increasingly global. Cultural power and influence is gained to the extent that institutions engage with and amplify such formalized conventions. "We are not all becoming the same," he says, "but we are portraying, dramatizing, and communicating our differences to each other in ways that are more widely intelligible" (Wilk 2003, 118).

Conclusion

Media historian Michelle Hilmes (2009) claims that media industry historiography is "a bold and iconoclastic task"—the equivalent of "nailing mercury." "Mercury is, after all, the messenger, the symbol of human communication; as a substance, it is difficult to pin down but very good at escaping from arbitrary restraints" (Hilmes 2009, 30). Historiography studies the "structuring frameworks" (Hilmes 2009, 31) through which we make sense of this "new and indeterminate" field (Hilmes 2009, 21). In words that have uncanny resemblance to this book's project, she writes that media "refuse to conform to comfortable analytical paradigms. They refute essentialization, require many components and participants, blur creative lines, stretch the boundaries of expressive forms, transgress aesthetic standards, cross over cultural borders, break down disciplined reception, muddy meanings, pervade public and private spaces, and generally make a mess of our accepted ways of doing scholarship" (Hilmes 2009, 21–22).

We have sought to deal with the problem of writing a history of the present—of an industry whose shape can change mercurially—by first historicizing the industry. The temporal dynamics are traced through differentiating between more and less fundamental changes between SME 1 and SME 2. Later in this concluding chapter, we also describe key underlying trends that signal further change in the accelerated evolution of this industry. Second, we look to nail mercury by adopting an "ecological" view of SME: mapping the multiple dimensions of this industry, showing how these operate interdependently and with distinction from Hollywood. Our multidimensional strategy demanded a multiperspectival approach, drawing on, and often proposing revisions to, theories and frameworks in political economy, network economics, production cultures, critical studies of labor and management, content, genre, and representation analysis, and globalization debates. Fundamentally, we situate ourselves in critical media industry studies, which draws on, and is in dialogue with, the disciplinary contexts of cultural, media, and communication studies.

Overview

In chapter 1, we framed the political economy of this new proto-industry from the point of view of the extremely volatile interdependent clash of cultures between Hollywood (entertainment IP-driven content industries) and Silicon Valley (iterative tech experimentation), rather than as capitalist hegemons conducting business as usual. There is nothing unitary about the challenge to established screen industries by digital TV-like content portals or community-driven social media platforms. These sites are as much competing against each other as they are posing challenges to established screen media industries. There are clear dividing lines between Netflix and Amazon, committed to professional content and competing directly against cable and broadcast, and those sites that, though iterating content strategies and monetizing through advertising, remain firmly on the social media side of social media entertainment (Facebook, Vine, Snapchat, Instagram). YouTube sits somewhere in the middle. Driven by constant iteration (permanent beta) and competitive experimentation, these platforms have framed the structural and material conditions for our creator-centric focus. Looking to "nail mercury," we argue that the first phase of the history of SME is characterized by platforms, centrally YouTube, providing open access to share content and foster community, thus distinguishing themselves from digital TV portals. SME 2.0 is a distinct second phase marked by the increased competition from second-generation platforms and the rise of multiplatforming.

In chapter 2, we argued that the conditions of creator labor in social media entertainment are empowering at the same time as they are precarious. The diverse practices of media labor include content production, vertically integrated throughout the supply chain from conception to circulation, with little division of traditional media labor and complicated by demands of spreadability across increasingly numerous and differentiating platform features. Less well understood, but operating with even greater distinction to, and lesser comparison with, traditional media labor, are the high-touch practices of creator communities.

The entrepreneurialism of creators keeps exploring avenues by which to remain viable. This is a form of risk management in pursuit of sustainability that has helped foster a number of, by now, very high-profile careers, but is overwhelmingly characterized by creators' modest earnings due to the activity of committed, globally scaling communities. Creators foster both traditional and innovative revenue streams. They harness the commercial platform features and user affordances available on and across multiple platforms through programmatic advertising and influencer marketing, in concert with traditional media through performance fees and generation of traditional IP, as well as through ancillary platforms that offer fan funding and merchandise. Newer platforms fall into line, introducing partner schemes with split revenue coupled with new technological and commercial features, like e-commerce and virtual goods.

Because intermediaries operate across, if they are not also trapped between, platforms and creator, advertising and traditional media, we treat them as potentially as precarious as creator careers—perhaps even more so. Chapter 3 explores the waves of firms and professionals, less surfing across than bobbing and weaving among opportunism, subsidization, diversification, and acquisition strategies. For some of these organizations, formerly known as multichannel networks, their precarity has proven paradigmatic of the perilous waters this entire industry is navigating.

While some of the evidence in chapter 3 reminds us that the profile of SME intermediaries overlaps that of intermediaries in traditional media, chapter 4, perhaps more than any other, illustrates how different this industry is from traditional content industries. Here, we attempt to interpose into the often dualistic rendering of the relationship between cultural authenticity and commerce a revisionist analysis of the management and disciplining of brand culture through the twinned discourses of authenticity and community in SME content.

In chapter 5, we consider evidence that SME is much more racially plural, multicultural, and gender diverse than mainstream screen media. Focusing on representation and activism around Asian American and LGBTQ creator-communities, we explore the potential of SME to foster progressivism capable of crossing geographic, cultural, linguistic, and national boundaries. In chapter 6, we have treated SME's relatively frictionless globality, not as another instance of Western cultural impe-rialism but as facilitated by content not governed by standard copyright industry high-control regimes. While the book has been US-centric, as that is where SME has built out from, it is impossible not to acknowl-edge the rise, but also the leap forward over their Western counterparts, of a Chinese SME industry nurtured by world-leading platform growth and innovation and protected but also disciplined by an ever-present state. We have sought to account for qualitatively greater frictionlessness in SME media globalization, the unevenness consequent on regulatory and political difference territory by territory, as well as the immense cul-tural diversity embodied in SME.

In the following sections, we identify two recent industrial currents that potentially signal further change and perhaps a new phase in the history of SME. We proceed with caution because multiplying stake-holders and multilateral pressures exerted within and upon this highly unstable industry make broad projections contentious and unreliable. Nevertheless, we identify the rise of both more heightened and distinctly new regulatory action, along with the industrial disruption caused by the proliferation of live-streaming platforms and the latest and most dis-tinct of creators, live-streamers, as potentially powerful change agents.

A New Regulatory Era

One of the defining features of a potential new phase in SME globally is that the platforms are entering a regulatory era in which public policy and regulation will impact them to a far greater extent than hitherto. This regulation features both state-based intervention and preemptive self-regulatory practices around the fundamental status of the platforms as "intermediaries" (Gillespie 2018) (not to be confused with our use of the term in chapter 3). Platform regulation is advancing at the state and suprastate level, with notable and contentious faultlines between US and European frameworks. It is becoming increasingly unavoidable to con-sider the implications of the platforms morphing into media companies (Napoli and Caplan 2017).

But it is also important to distinguish between such public regulatory in-tervention, self-regulation, and the kind of regulation (or, better, dramatic influence) that can be brought to bear by commercial interests. We analyze this new regulatory era by parsing these differences. The potential in such an experimental commercial environment for advertisers and brands to be jittery, and for business models therefore to be vulnerable, is ever present. Decades-old regulatory concerns about children and commercial disclosure are also endemic to platform and SME culture but are now significantly heightened. And then there are the profound implications to be considered if platforms were to be regulated as media companies.

These are interrelated. Even as there is considerable governance, moderation, and curation of content on these platforms—Google deals with eighty million takedown notices per month, covering not just copyright claims but also revenge porn, cyberbullying, and fake news—the pressures to regulate online content have been growing in recent years. Tarleton Gillespie (2018) observes that

> social media platforms have increasingly taken on the responsibility of curating the content and policing the activity of their users: not simply to meet legal requirements, or to avoid having additional policies imposed, but also to avoid losing offended or harassed users, to placate advertisers eager to associate their brands with a healthy online community, to protect their corporate image, and to honor their own personal and institutional ethics.

We have seen how the Adpocalypse represents one form of "regulatory" pressure on SME platforms brought powerfully to bear by brands and advertisers. This saw Google and Facebook move extremely rapidly to establish brand safety measures and filtering systems to thwart advertising on ad-offensive content. Yet, like the overcorrection by platforms around IP control, YouTube's intervention on programmatic advertising has crippled that as a source of revenue upon which creators depend. In the case of LGBTQ creators, their political, gendered, and sexual content challenges the platforms' filtering systems. These overindex in platform responses to the Adpocalypse.

Heightened Endemic Concerns

Preexisting policy formulations against "false and misleading advertising" well predate, and have been a consistent feature of, the commercial

Internet. We have seen instances of the effects of such frameworks with respect to PewDiePie in chapter 4 and for German creators (the Werbung Declaration) in chapter 6. In 2015, the US Federal Trade Commission (FTC) issued an Enforcement Policy Statement on Deceptively Formatted Advertisements, including "advertorials," "online advertising," or "sponsored content." The UK Advertising Standards Association (ASA) has recently set forth one of the most onerous sets of guidelines for online advertising in the world: the Code of Non-Broadcast Advertising, Sales, Promotion, and Direct Marketing (or CAP Code) was passed in 2014, requiring that creators disclose when they are being paid to promote products, brands, or services.

Similarly, regulatory concern that sees special protection measures for children also well predates the online era and has been a strong focus of attention in that era. For decades, moral panics over new technologies for children's media have contributed to substantial regulatory response. In 1930, the National Legion of Decency began reviewing movies for objectionable content for audiences including children. In the 1970s, the Action for Children's Television campaign persuaded the FTC to ban advertising directed at children. Since then, the videogame industry has been repeatedly targeted for regulation out of concerns over children and violence.

With the advent of convergent and participatory media, these concerns around children's media have been both contested and further heightened. Henry Jenkins (2006, 3) struck this chord early: "Rather than talking about media producers and consumers as occupying separate roles, we might now see them as participants who interact with each other according to a new set of rules that none of us fully understands." According to Chester (2015), "[T]here is a 'digital gold rush' underway to cash in on young people's passion for interactive media."

The rise of SME has seen multiple government agencies engaging in sometimes contradictory policies designed for children of varying age limits that target platforms and advertisers. Both the Federal Communications Commission (FCC) and the FTC are charged with regulating for children. In 1998, the Children's Online Privacy Protection Act (COPPA) required that the FTC issue and enforce regulation concerning children's online privacy. This rule limits platforms, websites, and applications from collecting personal data about children under thirteen years of age, which could be made available to third parties like advertisers.

Such regulations apply within the US's national borders, but the big digital platforms operate near-globally. As a result, other countries have begun to issue similar forms of online regulation, which has resulted in inevitable inconsistencies. The European Union has implemented many measures, including Safer Internet Action (1999–2004), the Safer Internet Plus Programme (2005–2008), the Safer Internet Programme (2009–2013), and the Audiovisual Media Services Directive, which replaced Television without Frontiers in 2010 and has been updated repeatedly. Most recently, the European Union issued the General Data Protection Regulation (2016), which demands that platforms protect the private data of users under the age of sixteen, whereas COPPA's age limit is thirteen.

In addition, most countries see self-regulatory efforts promoted by advertising trade organizations designed to thwart further government regulation. In the United States, the Council of Better Business Bureaus launched the National Advertising Review Council (the ingeniously titled NARC) in 1974 to oversee advertising directed towards children. Today, NARC provides prescreening for advertisers to ensure COPPA compliance.

In response to these heightened concerns, YouTube has self-regulated regarding children's access, privacy, and advertising. Google users are restricted to ages thirteen and over in the United States and most countries, although Spain's and South Korea's limit is fourteen and the Netherlands' is sixteen. In addition, videos may be age restricted by YouTube's review board to users over eighteen, particularly if the videos feature vulgar language, nudity, violence, or harmful or dangerous activities. As for advertising, YouTube issues a complex list of "community and technical guidelines" and advertising policies well beyond legal requirements. Although YouTube allows product placement and endorsements, it requires that creators be transparent about these partnerships, and also cautions creators that different jurisdictions have various requirements.

In a further self-regulatory initiative, as well as preemptive move to thwart further regulatory intervention around their kids programming, YouTube launched YouTube Kids (YTK) in 2015. In 2017, it was available in twenty-six countries for those with late-model smart devices and has garnered more than thirty billion views and over eight million weekly active viewers. According to YouTube, the app provides a safer and easier environment for children to find videos on topics they want to explore. This move reflected the massive shift in viewing habits by children from television to online, including YouTube, Amazon, and Netflix (Alba 2015). The app features curated content, including unboxing, designed for children and parental control, while also blocking children from posting videos and viewing targeted ads, and thereby helping to avoid regulatory scrutiny (Grande 2015). The app is ad-supported, although numerous categories of advertising are restricted (e.g. beauty and fitness, food and beverage, dating sites, and political ads). In addition, all branding must be transparent, with clear distinction between advertising/branding content and general YouTube content.

Nonetheless, advocates continue to demand greater regulation and accountability, claiming platforms are in violation of state rules, and the YTK app has done little to assuage their concerns. Within six months of the launch, a coterie of children's media watchdog organizations filed a complaint, claiming that the app targets children with deceptive and unfair advertisements, that Google markets YTK to parents in a deceptive manner, and that sponsored videos shown on YTK violate the FTC's Endorsement Guide (Greenberg 2015). The consequence of such sustained and heightened concerns has been emerging fissures between stakeholders in the industry, whether regulators and corporate owners, platforms and advertisers, or creators and communities, including parents and children.

Of particular concern for advocates is the kid's toy unboxing genre, which often features children creators-as-hosts. Advocates repeatedly complain about these videos, which they regard solely as marketing and for which even the most obvious disclosures of promotion were insufficient. Against this, educationist Jackie Marsh (2016) argues that there is no evidence that children only watch these to develop interest in a new product; rather, "the children already have an interest in the product." Marsh (2016) thought that "the whole issue of how commercial [unboxing videos] are and how far they drive children or their parents' buying practices isn't much researched."

Regulatory panic over unboxing obscures the agency and opportunities presented to unboxing creators, including children, and the parents and carers building their own branded content business around this genre. Our interviews with unboxing creators or their parents—all adults—revealed entrepreneurial aspiration and the ethos of a family-run business. Their accounts also belied activists' claims that these videos were merely corporate advertisements with creators operating as guileless shills for big toy firms. Their businesses were imperiled by programmatic claims that unboxing amounts to nothing more than commercialized exploitation of children.

Crossing the Content Rubicon

Social media platforms have often walked on both sides of the street when it comes to their intermediary status. On the one hand, they have long positioned themselves as "open, impartial, and nonintervention-ist" (Gillespie 2018), reflecting in part the desire to avoid regulation but also a "Silicon Valley ethos" (Vaidhyanathan 2012) that prides itself on a commitment to free speech, open culture, and individual autonomy. In the US platforms were extended legal protections under the "safe harbor" provisions of Section 230 of the Telecommunications Act 1996 (Mueller 2015).

In chapter 1, we described how YouTube and Facebook, informed by these provisions that predate their arrival, protected themselves against copyright infringement liability through automated self-regulatory mechanisms, such as Content ID. Platforms were liberated from prior constraint provided they responsively block access to alleged infringing material on receipt of infringement claims from a rights holder. However, we also described the unintended consequences, if not deliberate overcorrection, by the platforms that inhibit users and creators borrowing from or referencing these cultural products. Fair use provisions, even liberally applied, may not prevent perceived content violators from having their content removed. In best-case scenarios, creators retain their content but lose monetization to underlying IP holders.

Chapter 6 outlined the implications of safe harbor and DMCA regulation, coupled with the self-regulatory platform features of automated ditigial rights management (DRM), which have allowed major tech firms and their SME platforms to scale globally at rapid pace. Factored here is the regulatory principle that treats the platforms like ISPs—as like carriage services in telecommunications law, which cannot be held directly responsible for the content carried on such services. Indeed, the DMCA treated the platforms as online service providers (a category that included ISPs), creating near frictionless expansion, albeit constrained by national and supranational regulation around other concerns, whether advertising disclosure, children's protection, or digital privacy.

The fine line being trod by the platforms is captured in this perspective, offered in an interview by SME professional and analyst Sarah Ullman:

> Facebook isn't creating original content yet, and YouTube, for legal reasons, is not officially pushing play on the record button on the camera. But they are doing everything but that. The second that YouTube becomes an actual content creator itself, the legal definition changes and the ramifications of that for copyright on its platform are pretty huge. In terms of content creation, while YouTube is financing content, they're not producing. It's a copyright question. Right now they have a platform, they clean up content for others, but production changes the definition. It is the IP defense. YouTube can finance content but won't own the IP. (Ullman 2015)

Beyond curation of content and IP control, as described in our history of SME platforms, as these platforms reach global scale, they have turned to the SoCal practices of content to create scarcity and value. This began with the convergence of integrated video players and extends into original content production appearing on separate subscription-driven, ad-free platforms (YouTube Red) integrated alongside multiple YouTube platforms. In August 2017, Facebook launched Watch, a separate video platform to compete with YouTube Red and Netflix and circumvent DMCA regulatory restraint over its social media mothership (Silver 2017).

As a consequence, the platforms are now increasingly close to being considered media companies. Napoli and Caplan (2017) forensically examine the implications of these tech companies being treated as media companies—it is "no mere semantic distinction." They point to the increasingly dominant position that Facebook and Google have in both advertising revenue and the "marketplace of ideas." The fact that this has rarely "sparked a conversation" in US policy discourse can at least in part be attributed to "the success thus far of the tech-company-not-media-company rhetoric." But these platforms "inevitably evolve in ways that make the technology-company-not-media-company distinction even more invalid": for example, vertical integration into content creation and more interventionist curation. And what we have called the information catastrophe that unfolded around the 2016 US presidential election has accelerated high-level US policy concerns focused on how the digital platforms might be either pressured into much more effective self-regulation or threatened with state-imposed intervention to ensure that news values are preserved given that they are now the prime sources of news for most US citizens.

In Europe, state and suprastate actors have moved beyond sparking a conversation, acting to regulate, and to fine substantially, US platforms based on concerns about a wide array of their impacts and influence. These initiatives relate to tax, privacy, competition, and also content. All of these have potential to impact the future environment in which SME operates, and the latter—content regulation—is of direct relevance to SME.

The Atlantic Faultlines

The fundamental faultline driving this new regulatory phase is the increased distance between US and European regulatory frameworks and practice. The US regulatory model is one based on competition, innovation, and national champions (antitrust principles of competition within the United States, state support for industry outside the United States—following time-honored principles established for Hollywood from the 1920s, as Thomas Guback [1969] and Kristin Thompson [1985] showed). This is underlined in the exquisite symmetry of the Digital Millennium Copyright Act—shoring up the ability of established media hegemons to continue to extract copyright rents while further criminalizing attempts to circumvent strong copyright control, while at the same time, through the safe harbor provisions, curating the conditions for the new generation of US digital hegemons operating on quite distinct principles of aggregation and spreadability rather than control.

In contrast, the EU has been escalating its regulatory responses to the digital platforms over almost a decade now. The first major intervention was the "right to be forgotten," a controversial EU regulation that forces Google and other companies to purge inaccurate or outdated personal information from their search results. The "GAFA" (Google, Amazon, Facebook, Apple) are also being pursued over the use of low-tax havens to minimize their tax burdens in higher-taxing countries. This is now the subject of high-level international coordination.

The most recent evidence of a concerted crackdown on US-based technology companies in Europe has been catalogued by Klint Finley (2017): France fined Facebook 150,000 euros for alleged privacy violations, and several other EU countries are investigating the company's privacy practices. In 2016, the EU ordered Apple to pay 13 billion euros—about $US14.5 billion at the time, plus interest in back taxes, saying that Ireland had given the company preferential tax treatment. The EU also filed a formal antitrust complaint against Google over its Android operating system in 2016, arguing that requiring handset makers to include Google's apps on Android phones was unfair to competitors. The European Union fined Google $2.7 billion in 2017, ruling that its preferential treatment of its own content (Google Shopping) was illegal and anticompetitive. "Not only was this a very large fine," says Finley; "it also was an order for Google to essentially change how it handles search." This has the potential to impact Google's NoCal imperative for iterative innovation.

For all this pushback from across the Atlantic, domestically, the platforms are seen as national champions and drivers of innovation, seeding US business and innovation principles globally. President Barack Obama called the EU actions against US platforms protectionism. "[Americans] have owned the Internet. Our companies have created it, expanded it, perfected it in ways that [European companies] can't compete," Obama said in an interview with *Recode* in 2015. "And oftentimes what is portrayed as high-minded positions on issues sometimes is just designed to carve out some of their commercial interests" (quoted in Finley 2017).

Google has largely escaped antitrust scrutiny for anticompetitive behavior in the United States. Finley (2017) submits that Federal Trade Commission staffers recommended a lawsuit against Google over unfair business practices back in 2012, according to documents acquired by the *Wall Street Journal* in 2015. But, ultimately, FTC commissioners decided not to pursue a lawsuit after Google made a few changes, such as allowing companies like TripAdvisor and Yelp to opt out of having their content used in Google's own services. Google's Android policies may also have come into the FTC's regulatory frame in 2016, but the agency has not taken action.

There is an argument that regulators should only seek action against anticompetitive behavior where there is clear harm to consumers, for example, through rising prices. In contrast to this scenario, most of Google's and Facebook's online services are free. This, together with a policy priority placed on innovation (backgrounded by a governing ideology of support for national champions), may help to explain the FCC having a largely hands-off approach to platform regulation (except, as we have seen, for COPPA) and the FTC concerning itself principally with disclosure rules around online commercial interests (Gutelle 2017b).

Because of a lack of government action around platforms and antitrust, the news publishing industry has attempted to take action.

> A group of news organizations will begin an effort to win the right to negotiate collectively with the big online platforms and will ask for a limited antitrust exemption from Congress in order to do so. It's an extreme measure with long odds. But the industry considers it worth a shot, given its view that Google and Facebook, regardless of their intentions, are posing a bigger threat economically than President Trump is (so far) with his rhetoric. (Rutenberg 2017)

A more direct potential impact on SME (although these measures are directed more toward PGC content makers) may be felt through European lawmakers' attempts to sequester a portion of platform revenue to support European creators and to enact a minimum quota for local content on streaming platforms. A nationally specific attempt, consistent with previous practice, is the French legislature passing a bill to levy a 2% tax on the advertising revenues of online video platforms, including YouTube, to help finance local content. However, local content in this instance is not SME but French filmmaking.

Similarly, the European Commission, in proposing to update the 2010 Audiovisual Media Services Directive (AVMSD), is seeking to develop a "targeted" approach to online platforms. Under the banner of "More European creativity," it states,

> Currently, European TV broadcasters invest around 20% of their revenues in original content and on-demand providers less than 1%. The Commission wants TV broadcasters to continue to dedicate at least half of viewing time to European works and will oblige on-demand providers to ensure at least 20% share of European content in their catalogues. The proposal also clarifies that Member States are able to ask on-demand services available in their country to contribute financially to Europeans works. (European Commission 2016)

The year 2017 saw further refinement of the AVMSD, with members of the European Parliament calling for a 30% quota for European works in VOD catalogues, instead of the 20% proposed by the commission, and a widening of the scope of what could come under the regulation, to "include social media services" (European Parliament 2017).

The emerging shape of this new regulatory era has the potential to protect the cultural interests of national media industries and, possibly, SME creators. Policies and regulations canvased here may thwart misleading advertising practices and prevent labor exploitation, and may foster competition and diversity. However, the history of particularly US media regulation is dotted with instances of capture by corporate players, serving commercial interests first and public interests second. Moreover, if legacy regulatory policy dedicated to normative media copyright and IP control is extended into this space, platforms may be held more accountable, but at the risk of suppressing creator agency, innovation, and entrepreneurialism.

A Live Era

We view technological innovation and platform competition as distinguishing features when historicizing SME. These features, in turn, intersect with creator labor, intermediary management, and global dimensions of SME. Live broadcasting—synchronous interactivity between social media users appearing in and commenting on video—may be driving change sufficient to posit the possibility of a new phase of SME. Largely, our analysis to this point has been predicated on SME content as uploaded, archivable video content coupled with asynchronous interaction, including commenting, liking, and sharing.

Live SME is emerging as live features are integrated on preexisting SME platforms, as well as seeing the development of dedicated live platforms. But live SME's immediacy and popularity have also provoked a backlash from Chinese censors to live-streamers. China's Live SME industry figures prominently, exemplifying elements of a more advanced and accelerated system, which we outlined in chapter 6. Chinese interests have taken strategic ownership positions in the most successful live platforms in the West.

Live: Features and Affordances

Live-streaming is not new. Some platforms are as old as YouTube, Facebook, and Twitter. Justin.TV, later renamed Twitch and bought by Amazon, features live-streaming. Another early streaming platform includes Ustream, not to mention lucrative porn-streaming sites, which are part of an industry that dare not speak its name (Simpson 2011). In the mid-2010s, due to advancing speeds and mobile access, a wave of live-streaming platforms scaled while others died. Market reports already predict that this sector, including platforms, advertising, and other stakeholders, will comprise a $70 billion industry by 2021 (Swant 2016).

The battle between live-streaming platforms Periscope and Meerkat is yet another story of acceleration and precariousness, shaped within the NoCal/SoCal sashay. Periscope was acquired before launch by Twitter (as was the now-shuttered Vine). Live-streaming has since been added to the Twitter platform itself as it morphs into a media content company including recent deals for live sports content like NFL football. Nonetheless, Kayvon Beykpour, Periscope's CEO and cofounder, claims that Periscope remains vital to Twitter's multiplatform strategy: "Having a dedicated space for watching and creating live video, having a dedicated space [where] you can go and discover those communities, where you can search the map, those are things that power the ecosystem. The ecosystem wouldn't exist without those things" (Flynn 2017b).

In contrast, Meerkat went from "hypeball to pivot" (Flynn 2016) in less than one year. Launched in March 2015, the live-streaming platform was created by tech wizards and deep funded by a mix of venture capitalists and traditional Hollywood firms, including Universal Music Group, talent agencies Creative Artists and United Talent, Comcast, and celebrities Ashton Kutcher and Jared Leto (Griffith 2015). By fall 2016, the platform disappeared from the app market and was rumored to be relaunched as a "video social network" (Wagner 2016a).

Contributing to Meerkat's demise was the incorporation of live features on the dominant platforms, including Facebook and YouTube in addition to Twitter. Facebook founder, Mark Zuckerberg, has been described as "obsessed with live-streaming, making live a top priority at Facebook" (Wagner 2016b). Concurrently, a second wave of Chinese-owned live-streaming platforms aggressively entered the market, including Live.ly and Live.me, which are claimed to be "taking the US by storm" (Soo 2016).

Live technology offers new communicative and commercial affordances for platforms, advertisers, users, and creators. In contrast to archived content-on-demand, liveness fosters heightened interactivity through simultaneous on-screen commenting.

> Digital video has been a preferred means for many brands to communicate with and entertain consumers for some time, with the ultimate goal of going viral. Live streaming takes digital video one step further, letting marketers have a two-way conversation with consumers. A Facebook Live video is watched three times longer than a video that isn't live. Live videos on the platform also receive 10 times more comments than regular videos. (Poggi 2016)

Liveness offers competitive advantages and disadvantages for brands. For platforms pivoting towards a traditional media play, live allows them to compete with television for expensively licensed live professional content, e.g. sports and concerts that, in turn, attract premium advertisers and viewers. However, brands and advertisers are struggling to develop strategies for live-streaming influencer marketing. In a background interview with two Chinese executives at Procter & Gamble in China, they pointed out that live content does not provide the same return on investment and conversion rates as video on demand. In addition, brands find live creator brand integration campaigns harder to co-create, manage, and supervise for quality control.

The Creator-Streamers

Live has enabled another wave of creators, sometimes referred to as "live-streamers," or "live showroom hosts" in China, or "BJs (broadcast jockeys)" in Korea. Third-party data sites such as Tubular Labs included numerous live platforms and began posting ratings for live creators in early 2016. In 2017, trade site Tubefilter started reposting the ratings for Live.me creators, noting how

> Live.me, born out of the Beijing-based Cheetah Mobile, first started letting users broadcast themselves and watch the broadcasts of other individuals around the world in April 2016. In the short nine months since, the live broadcasting platform has been embraced by mainstream celebrities, established online creators, musicians, fans, and a brand new crop of homegrown talent that's very good at getting the attention of its peers. The app now features hundreds of thousands of hours of live broadcasts daily and reported it processed over $1 million in payouts to creators as of October 2016 by way of its gifting economy. That number has only increased, providing a lucrative opportunity for a handful of Live.me stars to leave their regularly scheduled jobs and focus on the platform full time to the tune of solid five and six-figure annual salaries. (Cohen 2017)

Live-streamers embrace a range of distinctive SME screen aesthetics, including even lower production values: a single set controlled for optimal lighting and sound, or in situ live appearances with compromised lighting and sound. Live creation practices introduce programming and scheduling demands on both creators and communities. For example, to optimize the most available watch times, creators must stream before and after typical school and work hours.

Without editing, live creators engage the appearance of more improvisational performativity. Facebook live magician Julius Dein "makes his audiences at home part of the event, asking them what pranks he should play next. This is how to make the most of the interaction that live video offers" (C. Johnson 2017). Experienced VOD creators have introduced live into their practice in experimental and strategic ways. Many creators we interviewed had replaced their secondary YouTube channels, Facebook or Twitter updates, or Snapchat posts with live chats, channels, and platforms. Live provides easier and continuous interaction with their community in between developing, producing, editing, and "spreading" their asynchronous content. Premier creators Rhett and Link engage in a slightly different strategy, appearing once a week live on their main channel to engage in Q&A sessions with their fans, fostering even more interactivity and co-creation between creators and their community.

As we have noted, live SME platforms tend to generate less lucrative influencer marketing opportunities. But these platforms have revenue-sharing partnership agreements through virtual goods and tip jars. In addition to these fan-funding strategies, live platforms such as Twitch have introduced sponsorship and subscriptions. As a Twitch game player notes, these "become a base salary for streamers, instead of just relying on tips, which one month could be $100, which next month could be $4,000—you never know" (Convery 2017). Meanwhile, platforms continue to introduce new commercial features that may help creators secure more revenue, like Facebook Live's in-stream video ads play (Boland and Angelidou-Smith 2017). This pattern replicates the program break structure of traditional television—a decidedly retrograde strategy that may prove as short-lived as New Coke.

The Live Wild West and East

Like all social media, live platforms and features have the potential to amplify the best and worst of people and culture. Facebook Live has been particularly singled out for allowing users to air criminal activity, including a spate of live murders. Such grotesque criminality rightfully demands platform accountability. But liveness has also allowed victims to identify their harassers, as evidenced by the use of live cameras to record police brutality in the United States. In 2016, when the congressional cable television network C-Span was shut down, Democrats used Periscope and Facebook Live to stream their sit-in protest in support of gun control. The attempted coup in Turkey in mid-2016 was notably communicated across live-streaming platforms. To update the adage, the revolution may not be televised, but it may be live-streamed.

The implications of live for the future of SME are best exemplified by the Chinese industry. This industry has accelerated at a rate that has put it months, if not years, ahead of its Western counterparts. Twitter's live-streaming platform Periscope claims only around ten million users worldwide while the top five Chinese live-stream apps have more than eighty-five million active users (NextShark.com 2016). The Chinese live SME industry is valued even more highly than its Western counterpart, further bolstering the commercial success of their "live stream queens—They are young, narcissistic, and getting rich" (Birtles 2016). Chinese "[l]ive streaming has also bolstered the growth of ancillary businesses, including agencies looking to find the next live-streaming star, consumer loans, and even cosmetic surgery" (Zhang and Miller 2017). CNBC's Qian Chen (2016) refers to this phenomenon as "a game changer for all," referring to platforms, investors, advertisers, users, and creator-streamers. There has been an explosion of live users, faced with the limited array of television content, on digital portals (Iqiyi), and even the slow emergence of native SME creators on first- and second-generation recorded platforms (Youku and Weibo). "The lure is some 344 million Chinese netizens—more than the population of every country on the planet bar China and India" (Zhang and Miller 2017) and a live-streaming market that grew 180% in 2016 (Xiang 2017).

Figures C.1 and C.2 show the rapid growth in China's live-streaming sector. PC-based Chinese live gameplay platforms like Douyu and PandaTv

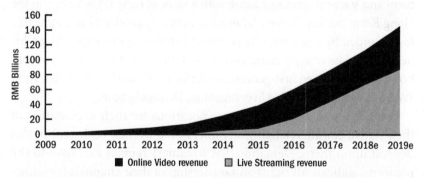

Figure C.1. Revenue of China's Online Video Sector and Live-Streaming Sector, 2009–2019e.

Source: Report: China's live streaming market grew 180% in 2016, Technode, http://technode.com/2017/03/31/chinas-live-video-streaming-market-grew-180-2016-report/; Revenue of China's Online Video Sector Topped 60 Bn Yuan in 2016, iResearch Global, http://www.iresearchchina.com/content/details7_30535.html.

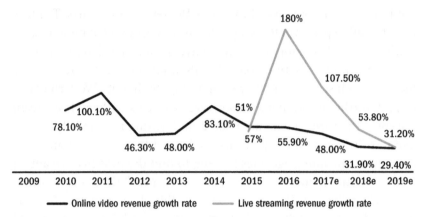

Figure C.2. Revenue Growth in China's Online Video Sector and Live-Streaming Sector, 2009–2019e.
Source: Report: China's live streaming market grew 180% in 2016, Technode, http://technode.com/2017/03/31/chinas-live-video-streaming-market-grew-180-2016-report/; Revenue of China's Online Video Sector Topped 60 Bn Yuan in 2016, iResearch Global, http://www.iresearchchina.com/content/details7_30535.html.

have scaled rapidly while competing for premier e-gamers since 2015. In contrast, Amazon-owned Twitch has experienced limited competition from YouTube Gaming, launched in 2015. By mid-2016, there were three hundred Chinese live mobile apps, fostered by an aggressive private venture investment and start-up economy along with a wave of early IPOs listing on the Hong Kong market. These platforms are cheaply produced and run, able to be funded by a few wealthy patrons from the rapidly expanding Chinese upper class who purchase virtual goods to support the "live showroom hosts." Like US-based first-generation platforms, Youku (YouTube-like) and Weibo (Twitter-like) added live-streaming features in 2016.

Some Chinese live platforms are notorious for their exploitation of their native commercializing streamers even as their scale and profits depend upon them. Demands that streamers remain exclusive to the platform, abdicate all rights and ownership of their channels (or showrooms) in exchange for PPV rates, and foster only brand-safe strategies at peak streaming hours are common.

Mitigating these conditions, Chinese live creators are experiencing commercial success. Like Twitch, Chinese live SME platforms offer integrated commercial features and provide revenue sharing:

> In China, where live-streaming has taken off rapidly, apps such as YY, by far the market leader with 80 million viewing hours in April, allow viewers to reward their hosts with virtual gifts, including flowers or sports cars in the form of emoticon-like symbols that move across the screen. These can be traded for real money. Other services let users buy digital tokens to tip performers. (The Economist 2016)

The cultural and market conditions of Chinese live SME are underscored by insistent gendering of live creators and their communities. Numerous accounts describe how attractive Chinese young women dominate this space, appealing to the "lonely hearts" of rural Chinese men (Yang 2017a). Live showroom hosts operate as socially mediated surrogates in the wake of the fewer dating and marriage options due to the Chinese one-child policy and the migration of women to urban centers for employment in the emerging service-based economy.

Such cultural politics do not escape the surveillance of the state. Labeling the material as too "seductive" and "inappropriately erotic," China clamped down on live-streamers engaging in "erotic" banana eating (Phillips 2016). China has also cracked down on political and subversive speech across video and streaming sites, threatening to shutter three major platforms—Sina Weibo, iFang, and AcFUN. This crackdown extends to LGBTQ content, deemed "abnormal sexual behaviors" and "unhealthy" (Yang 2017b). These regressive moves are simply extensions of prohibitions already in place in Chinese film and television. The Chinese LGBT magazine *Gay Voice* said in a statement, "The false information in these regulations has already caused harm to the Chinese LGBT community—who are already subjected to prejudice and discrimination" (Wang 2017).

Chinese-owned live SME platforms' ability to attract Western audiences may presage impending battles between the Chinese and US players. Live.Me is owned by Cheetah Mobile, a Beijing-based tech firm that specializes in creating apps that the firm claims reach more than 620 million monthly users of its twenty-plus services, with around 80% of that figure located outside of China (Russell 2017). Based on the success of its music-niched, mobile VOD platform, Musical.ly, its Shanghai-based owners have launched a live-streaming counterpart, Live.ly: "Three months after its launch, Live.ly, the live-streaming video app from Musical.ly, has captured nearly 4.6 million monthly active users on Apple's iOS platform in the US—making the teen-girl-skewing service bigger today on iPhones than Twitter's Periscope, which has about 4.3 million on iOS, according to data from SurveyMonkey Intelligence" (Spangler 2016e).

China has incubated a live SME industry with more advanced technological innovation and multiplatform competition than the West, conditions that provide for more sustainable returns for Chinese creators. As we have seen throughout the book, SME has been marked by an interdependency yet clashing of cultures between NoCal tech and SoCal content industries, requiring deft management, experimentation, and constant pivoting. Fueled by live technology, these battles may be overtaken in importance by the impending battles over platform supremacy between East and West.

A Closing Bid for Creator Advocacy

In this conclusion, in addition to overviewing the book, we have highlighted some of the underlying currents that may point to the future of the industry. These include platform evolution oscillating between the NoCal tech-based scalability of social media and the premium-value, higher-touch practices fostered by a century of SoCal content industry strategies. The extraordinary growth and now global dominance of Google and Facebook are provoking increased regulatory concern and oversight, led by indomitable actions taken by particularly the European Union. Concerns continue to heighten around children and SME commercialization. SME in live-streaming mode underscores that SME is a communication as much as a content industry and may give rise to significant areas of Chinese, as distinct from US, supremacy.

These trends may suggest advancing industrial formalization. However, online "formalization," if that is the right word, has taken a different tack to that contemplated by the critics we encountered in chapter 1 (for example, Kim 2012; van Dijck 2013). We are not witnessing the subsumption of SME into main media and the iteration of traditional media history: amateur innovation and experimentation leading to conglomeration and consolidation, the horizontal and vertical integration throughout the media supply chain, the exploitation of entertainment IP across film, television, music, and publishing industries, and the advancement and convergences of media technology from analogue to digital, broadcast to broadband, mobile, and beyond.

Rather, from the creator-centric position we have declared from the start, we anticipate something new—not media business as usual. Creators have proven more agile, responding nimbly and innovatively to platform imperiousness and advertising impulses. Viable creator careers have continued to grow globally, even as algorithmic twists and social, political, and cultural turns have played havoc with revenue models. For the most part, creators have been nurtured, if not emboldened, by their fellow creators, in contrast to the competitive, often-toxic environment of traditional media producers and professionals. Creator communities comprise vital partners lending their cultural and commercial support, not media audiences to be tolerated or sold to the highest bidder through automated and nontransparent platform practices.

Government and suprastate intervention towards platforms and advertisers may provide some security and recognition for creator practice through increasing subsidy and support in the present, and regional and local content regulation in the future. Other forms of intervention may contribute to preemptive self-regulation, if not overcorrection, by these players. As reflected in our earlier comments on unboxing, regulatory intervention often neglects the creators who harness these platforms for commercial and cultural value and the communities that support them. These stakeholders arguably have the most to lose and, ironically, comprise the publics and citizenry that regulators claim to protect. Yet, who will advocate for them?

A small band of nonprofit organizations has answered the call—dedicated to promoting the commercial and cultural interests of creators. One such example is the Re-Create Coalition, comprised of "innovators, creators, and consumers united for balanced copyright." Their agenda states,

> Online platforms that enable creativity and free expression rely partly on the exclusive rights granted by the Copyright Act, but also on the Act's flexible limitations and exceptions to copyright such as fair use and the Digital Millennium Copyright Act's (DMCA) safe harbors. It is this balanced approach that makes possible the online platforms that generate

revenue streams for creators, small businesses, entrepreneurs, application developers, startups and large content producers. Consumers have more choice and the public has greater access to information. (Re-Create Coalition 2017)

Public-interest advocate Joshua Lamel (2017), who operates inside the public policy Beltway for the Re-Create Coalition, reminded us in an interview of the importance also of the Organization for Transformative Works (OTW), an online platform and advocacy community for fan-creators, and the Electronic Frontier Foundation (EFF), which has litigated a lot of cases defending SME creators against platforms and rights-holding corporations.

A key development is the Internet Creators Guild (ICG), launched in late 2016 to "support, represent, and connect online creators" (https://internetcreatorsguild.com/). The ICG was conceived by Hank Green and is yet another venture generated by the Vlogbrothers, mentioned repeatedly throughout this book as thought leaders and advocates for SME creators and their communities. In addition to their own content, these intrepid midwestern educators-turned-influencers have launched a series of commercial ventures like Vidcon, dedicated to the promotion of heightened community engagement as well as a forum for identifying the best practices for industrial tradecraft. Their nonprofit ventures, like Project for Awesome, champion a civic imagination, advocating for creators to harness their cultural power for progressive media interventionism. The formation of this organization, backed by leading creators, suggests a call to collective arms, self-defense on behalf of creators from the peril of capricious platform practices, advertiser exploitation, traditional media backlash, and regulatory backsliding, such as the threats to net neutrality.

After numerous attempts, in 2015, the FCC adopted the rule for an open Internet (commonly known as net neutrality). The rule is designed to protect access to legal online content without access providers being allowed to block, impair, or establish fast/slow lanes to lawful content. In this ruling, the Internet was deemed comparable to a utility, like water or electricity, and therefore a service that should be made available to all citizens without limitation. The Trump administration, through new leadership of the Federal Communications Commission, followed through on a campaign promise to eliminate net neutrality in 2017. The ICG has entered the battle to save this ruling, unsuccessfully, arguing that its windback could have a "huge effect" on creators (Internet Creators Guild 2017).

Whatever else happens to change the landscape of social media entertainment, battles like these will go on having to be fought. As we have gone about our research, we have witnessed the thirst for knowledge about this emerging industry and the need for thorough, independent accounts of its shape, size, challenges, and prospects. Most of our interlocutors believe that making this knowledge widely available may help this proto-industry survive. We trust this book contributes to meeting this need.

ACKNOWLEDGMENTS

The logistical magnitude of the research entailed in the preparation of this book has meant that we have incurred lasting debts of gratitude to numerous people and organizations for their assistance. The fundamental funding assistance that underpinned the project was provided by the Australian Research Council (ARC) Discovery Project 160100086, "The New Screen Ecology and Opportunities for Innovation in Production and Distribution," awarded to Stuart Cunningham in 2016. Cunningham was also awarded a Fulbright Senior Scholarship, "The Emerging New Global TV Networks and Opportunities for Innovation in Screen Production and Distribution," by the Australian-American Fulbright Commission, which was conducted in 2014–2015 at the University of California–Santa Barbara and the University of Southern California.

When it comes to the research team that supported us, thanks first and foremost goes to Dr. Adam Swift, who has worked from the start on this project and has contributed not only expert research assistance but great knowledge and insight into social media entertainment. The work would not be what it is without him. We would also like to thank Jarrod Walczer, Guy Healy, Andrew Golledge, Nicki Hall, Molly Kossoff, Yuqi Liang, Junyi Lv, Heng Cai, Catherine Zhang, Jiya Jaisingh, Vibish Sivakumar, and Joyee Chatterjee for research and logistical assistance at various stages and in various countries.

When it came to approaching series editors and publishers for a book of this nature, we could not have imagined a better advocate than Henry Jenkins, series editor for Postmillennial Pop, and the expert advice and support of Eric Zinner, publisher at NYU Press, and assistant editors Lisha Nadkarni and Dolma Ombadykow. We also thank the anonymous reviewers who provided searching but affirmative commentary on the manuscript.

Cunningham's Fulbright was enormously influential in accelerating the research on which this book is based. It enabled critical engagement with leading US colleagues (Michael Curtin, Jennifer Holt, and Karen Petruska, at UCSB; Kevin Sanson, then at UCSB, now at Queensland University of Technology; and Henry Jenkins, Gabriel Kahn, and the then Annenberg Dean Ernest Wilson at USC) while at the same time creating the opportunity for the collaboration between Cunningham and Craig on which the whole project has pivoted.

The scholarly environment of the Digital Media Research Centre in the Creative Industries Faculty at Queensland University of Technology (QUT) is seriously stimulating, as is the Annenberg School for Communication and Journalism at the University of Southern California. The funding and project support, from both the ARC and the Australian-American Fulbright Commission, has allowed Cunningham to spend time at USC and Craig to spend time at QUT, which has enhanced our collaboration significantly.

Most important of all for Stuart is eternal thanks to family: Jo, Vivien, Ben, and Hugo. Stuart acknowledges and thanks Terry Flew, Jean Burgess, Jon Silver, Patrick Wikstrom, Michael Keane, Stephanie Duguay, and QUT Creative Industries Executive Dean Mandy Thomas for their support and collegiality. David acknowledges the support from his USC Annenberg colleagues, including Dean Willow Bay, Larry Gross, Sarah Banet-Weiser, Rebecca Weintraub, Ben Lee, Daniella Baroffio, Colin Miles Maclay, Andrea Hollingshead, and Arlene Luck, along with Annenberg support staff.

We have greatly benefited from discussions with colleagues, including Crystal Abidin, Nancy Baym, Jean Burgess, John Caldwell, Aymar Jean Christian, Donna Chu, Brooke Erin Duffy, Jonathan Gray, Tim Highfield, Jeffrey Jones, Michael Keane, Neta Kligler-Vilenchik, Sangeet Kumar, Ramon Lobato, Lori Kiddo Lopez, Amanda Lotz, Denise Mann, Kate Miltner, Sheri Ortner, Erika Pearson, Aswin Punathambekar, Violaine Roussel, Ralph Schroeder, Ellen Seiter, Limor Shiffman, Jeremy Shtern, Julian Thomas, Patrick Vonderau, Jing Elaine Zhao, and Ying Zhu.

Preliminary findings from the research have been presented at a wide variety of venues as keynotes and papers, and in panels and workshops. We would like to thank the receptive audiences, institutions, and organizers at the following: Queensland University of Technology Digital Media Research Centre (May 2014, June 2016, July 2017), University of California–Santa Barbara Carsey Wolf Research Center (November 2014, thanks to Jennifer Holt), University of Southern California Annenberg School for Communication and Journalism (April 2015), Swinburne University of Technology Institute for Social Research (October 2015), USC-SJTU Institute of Cultural and Creative Industry in Shanghai (November 2015), International Communication Association Fukuoka (June 2016) and San Diego (May 2017), Tsukuba University Japan (May 2016, thanks to Aki Yamada), India Culture Lab at Godrej Industries, (May 2016, thanks to Parmesh Shahani and his team), Soochow University, Suzhou University (June 2016), Association of Internet Researchers conference Berlin (October 2016, thanks to Nancy Baym and Jean Burgess) and Tartu (October 2017, thanks to Thomas Poell and David Nieborg), YouTube conference Middlesex University London (September 2016, thanks to Jane Arthurs), King's College London Department of Media and Communications (September 2016, thanks to Paul McDonald), SMIT at Vrije Univeriteit Brussels (October 2016, thanks to Katharina Hoelck), VIDCON Anaheim (June 2017, thanks to Internet Creators Guild and Executive Director Laura Chernikoff, as well as panel host and creator, Akilah Hughes).

* * *

This book includes material fully revised from previous articles and chapters: Stuart Cunningham and David Craig (2017), "The Emerging Global Screen Ecology of Social Media Entertainment," in *The Routledge Companion to World Cinema*, edited by Rob Stone, Paul Cooke, Stephanie Dennison, and Alex Marlow-Mann; Stuart Cunningham, David Craig, and Jon Silver (2016), "YouTube, Multichannel Networks, and the Accelerated Evolution of the New Screen Ecology," *Convergence: The International Journal of Research into New Media Technologies* 22(4): 376–91; Stuart Cunningham and David Craig (2016), "Online Entertainment: A New Wave of Media Globalization?" *International Journal of Communication* 10: 5409–25; Stuart Cunningham and David Craig (2017), "Being 'Really Real' on YouTube: Authenticity, Community, and Brand Culture in Social Media Entertainment," *Media International Australia* 164(1), August; David Craig and Stuart Cunningham (2017), "'Unboxing': Living in a(n Unregulated) Material World," *Media International Australia* 163(1), May.

All reasonable efforts were made to secure permission for illustrative material used, but the publishers would be glad to hear from anyone we have been unable to contact.

* * *

A significant amount of the primary research for this book has been based on substantial interviews—over 150 in total—with a wide range of participants in the emerging and rapidly evolving field of social media entertainment. We would like to thank every one of these interviewees who gave up their time to provide us with the rich insights that have greatly enhanced the texture of the book. We list here the positions and institutional affiliations, where appropriate, that were current at the time of interview. Direct citation of interview sources are given full references in the text.

In Australia
Stephen Baker, Director, Hit Record; Mike Cowap, Development Management, Screen Australia; Steve Crombie, Managing Director, Totem; Matthew Hancock, Strategy and Operations, Screen Producers Association; Mike Jones, Writer, Wastelander Panda; Simone Kelly, Manager, Charlie's Crafty Kitchen; Sasha Kouvchinov, Sales Executive, Boom Video; Lucy Tullet, Community Manager, Valleyarm Digital; and the following creators: Rachel Anderson (Rachelleea); Charlie Aspinal and Daly Pearson (Ludo Studios); Nick Bertke (Pogomix); Kodi Brown (Kodi); Eyasu Church (Eya5u); Sharon Farrell (Sharon Farrell); Sarah Grimstone (Sarah Stone); Wendy Huang (Wengie); Luna Maroun (LunaMaroun); Derek Muller (Veritasium); Lee Naimo (Axis of Awesome); Jason Pinder (SimpleCookingChannel).

In Brazil
Ekaterine Karageorgiadis, Lawyer, Instituto Alana.

In China
Heng Cai, Cofounder, Star Station TV; Nan Huang, Management for Series Programs; Dan Li, Content Cooperation and Distribution, Yang Li, Producer, Xingliang Yin, Cofounder and CEO, and Di Zhou, Social Media Accounts Manager, Xinpianchang; Rick Myers, Chief Executive Officer, Youya; Bryan Shao, Vice President Corporate Strategies, Youku;

Huadong Wang, Partner, Matrixx Partners China; Catherine Zhang, Director, International Department, Youku; Hao Zhang, Manager of Strategic Planning, Weibo; Qing Zhou, Chief Communication Officer, Feidieshou Communication and Technology Company.

In Germany
Anna Lena Micus, Programs Strategist, YouTube Space (Germany); Indiana Neidell, Lead Writer, Toni Stellar, Producer, Florien Witteg, Producer and Social Media Manager, Mediakraft Networks (*The Great War*); Ralf Osteroth, Senior Vice President of Sales and Marketing, and Robert Vossen, Senior Manager of Business Development, Studio 71 GmbH; Fabian Siegismund, Creator, Battle Bros.

In India
Samir Bangara, Cofounder and Managing Director, Qyuki; Das Prashanto, Cofounder, Ping Network; Pratik Gupta, Cofounder, Foxy Moron; Ali Hussein, Entrepreneur; Jigisha Mistry, Head of Operations, YouTube Space (India); Sameer Pitawalla, Founder, Culture Machine; Mansi Poddar, Founder, Brown Paper Bag; Arjun Ravi, Director and Cofounder, NH7; Neeraj Roy, Managing Director and Chief Executive Officer, Hungama Digital Media Entertainment; Roopesh Shah, Founder, Web Chutney; Gurpreet Singh, Cofounder and Chief Executive Officer, One Digital Entertainment; Aditya Wasudeo, Growth Partnerships, Facebook; and the following creators: Malini Agarwal (MissMalini); Atul Khatri (Atul Khatri); Aditi Mittal (Aditi Mittal).

In Japan
Alan Swartz, Cofounder and CEO, Breaker Media.

In New Zealand
Ralph Sanchez, Senior TV Producer, Mechanic Animation Limited; David White, Founder and Chief Executive Officer, IndieReign.

In the United Kingdom
Adam Watson Brown, Principal Administrator, Digital Futures Task Force, European Commission; Greg Dray, Head of Kids and Learning Partnerships, Google EMEA; Kelly Greaves, Senior Strategist, Creative Development, and Marc Joynes, Manager, YouTube Space (London);

Matt Heiman, Founder, and David Jackson, Head of Audience Development, Diagonal View; Andrew Lindenmayer, Head of Business Development, Zoomin.TV; Jackie Marsh, Professor of Education, University of Sheffield; Haas Mosa, Head of Content and Strategy, and Bryan Randel, Managing Director, Endemol Shine Beyond UK; Brad Taylor, Audience Development and Social Media Executive, Channel Flip/Endemol Shine Beyond UK.

In the United States
Greg Benson, Producer, Mediocre Films; Jeff Cohen, Attorney, and Bradley Garrett, Attorney, Cohen Gardener; Jessie Albert, Agent (Digital), and Keyvan Peymani, ICM Partners; Byron Austin Ashley, Talent Manager, Big Frame/Awesomeness; Barry Blumberg, Chief Content Officer, and Jordan Levin, Executive Vice President, Defy Media; Gary Bryman, Vice Chairman, Producers Guild of America New Media Council; Jay Bushman, Chief Content Officer and Transmedia Producer, Pemberley Digital; Jamie Byrne, Head of Talent, Lance Podell, Global Head of Studios, and Michelle Beaver, Content Partnerships Manager at YouTube; Bing Chen, Chief Creative Officer, Victorious; Dimitri Cherner, Influencer Operations Manager, Scott Pollack, Executive Vice President and Managing Director, and Ryan Yudell, Chief Operating Officer, Thoughtful Media; Laura Chernikoff, Executive Director, Internet Creators Guild; Josh Cohen, Chief Information Officer, TubeFilter; Leisl Copland, Agent, William Morris Endeavour (WME); James Creech, Senior Vice President of Growth, Bent Pixels; Vanessa DelMuro, Vice President of Talent Management, and Christine Train, Vice President of Communications, StyleHaul; Derek Dressler, Director of Content Acquisition, Vimeo; Kim Evey, Producer and Writer, Geek and Sundry; Lisa Filipelli, Vice President of Talent, Big Frame; Tess Finkle, Publicist, Metro Public Relations; Laura Allen Fischer, Head of Production, and Ian Moffit, Senior Vice President of Original Programming, Yahoo!; Emily Barclay Ford, Senior Director, Brett Lemick, Vice President of Talent Management, Li Peiyu, Director of Audience Development, Maker Studios; Brian Forester, Manager (Gabe and Garrett); Oliver Gers, Global President, Liquid Thread; Matthew Goldfine, Content Architect, and Tamara Kruger, Global Branded Content, Google; Adam Goldstein, Director of Business Development, ZEFR; Josh Golin, Executive Director, Campaign for a Commercial-Free

Childhood; Joe Hodorowicz, Manager, and Evan Weiss, Executive Vice President of Strategic Alliances, Collective Digital Studios; Gabrielle Kahn, Professor of Journalism, University of Southern California; Charlotte Koh, Head of Originals, Hulu/Whipclip; Lori Kozlowski, Editorial Director, Atom Factory; Varun Lella, Agent, Paradigm; Max Levine, Talent Management, Shimmur; Meredith Levine, Fanthroplogist, ZEFR; Benny Luo, Founder, New Media Rockstars; Denise Mann, Head of School of Theater, Film, and Television's Producers Program, University of California–Los Angeles; Leila Marsh, Vice President Talent, Addition Management; Mickey Meyer, Cofounder, JASH; P. J. Miele, Mobile Solutions and Strategies, AOL; Leslie Morgan, Executive Director, Endemol Beyond; Sharon Mussalli, US Industry Manager Entertainment, Facebook; Joe Orlando, Vice President Digital Development, Crackle; Matt Palazzolo, Writer, Star, and Producer, *Bloomers*; Jen Robinson, Chief Technology Officer, Awesomeness; Vak Sambath, Business Development, Social Edge; Jon Skogmo, Chief Executive Officer, Jukin Media; Alison Stern, Cofounder and Vice President of Marketing, Tubular Labs; Kelly Summers, Chief Executive Officer, Bella Raffe Media; Amanda Taylor, Chief Executive Officer, DanceOn; Sarah Ullman, Founder, The Jungle; James Veraldi, Senior Vice President Strategy and Business Development, Fullscreen; Phil Wang, Partner, Wong Fu Productions; Brett Weinstein, Agent, UTA Digital; Larry Weintraub, Chief Innovation Officer, Fanscape; Jed Weintrob, Vice President of Production, Conde Naste Entertainment; Adam Wescott, Manager, Select Management; Freddie Wong, Creative Director, RocketJump: and the following creators: Seth Bling (SethBling); Chrissy Chambers and Bria Kam (BriaandChrissy); David Choi (David Choi); Anthony D'Angelo (Anthony D'Angelo); Stephanie Frosch (Ello-Steph); Gigi Gorgeous (GigiGorgeous); Joey Graceffa (JoeyGraceffa); Hank Green (Vlogbrothers); Zach King (Zach King); Krishna Kumar (Krishna the Kumar); Boone Langston (Toy Replay); Rhett McLaughlin and Charles Lincoln Neal (Rhett & Link); Ingrid Nilsen (IngridNilsen); Brett Rivera (Mr Rivera); Ashley and Chris Veit (The Toy Bunker); Tati Westbrook (Tati [GlamLifeGuru]).

NOTES

CHAPTER 1. PLATFORM STRATEGY

1 A Deloitte report predicts that declining growth and increased cable cutting will result in a decrease in US households with pay-TV services from 100.9 million in 2011 to 90 million in 2016, while the CAGR (compound annual growth rate) in monthly subscriptions costs is 3.5–5% over the same period.

2 We draw here on Cunningham, Flew, and Swift (2015), 54–55.

CHAPTER 6. GLOBALIZING SOCIAL MEDIA ENTERTAINMENT

1 Data on these matters vary; however, Google posts traffic disruptions to their site: http://www.google.com/transparencyreport/traffic/disruptions/#expand=Y2015,Y 2014,Y2013,Y2012.

REFERENCES

Abidin, C. (2015). "Communicative Intimacies: Influencers and Perceived Interconnectedness." *Ada: A Journal of Gender, New Media, and Technology*, 8. http://adanewmedia.org/2015/11/issue8-abidin/, accessed 22 August 2017.

Abidin, C. (2016a). "Visibility Labour: Engaging with Influencers' Fashion Brands and #OOTD Advertorial Campaigns on Instagram." *Media International Australia* 161(1): 86–100.

Abidin, C. (2016b). "'Aren't These Just Young, Rich Women Doing Vain Things Online?': Influencer Selfies as Subversive Frivolity." *Social Media + Society*, 2(2): 1–17.

Aisch, G., and Giratikanon, T. (2014). "Charting the Rise of Twitch." *New York Times*, 27 August. http://www.nytimes.com/interactive/2014/08/26/technology/charting-the-rise-of-twitch.html, accessed 26 March 2017.

Alba, D. (2015). "Google Launches 'YouTube Kids,' a New Family Friendly App." *Wired.com*, 23 February. http://www.wired.com/2015/02/youtube-kids/, accessed 29 July 2016.

Albarran, A. (2008). "Defining Media Management." *International Journal of Media Management*, 10(4): 184–86.

Albarran, A. (2010). *The Media Economy.* New York: Routledge.

Alexander, J., and Losh, E. (2010). "A YouTube of One's Own? Coming Out Videos as Rhetorical Action." In *LGBT Identity and Online New Media*, edited by C. Pullen and M. Cooper, 37–50. New York: Routledge.

Allen, S. (2016). "Young Hollywood's Public Coming Out." *Daily Beast*, 16 January. http://www.thedailybeast.com/articles/2016/01/16/young-hollywood-s-public-coming-out.html, accessed 16 January 2016.

Anderson, C. (2006). *The Long Tail: Why the Future of Business Is Selling Less of More.* New York: Hyperion.

Anderson, R. (2015). Creator, Rachelleea, 23 March, interview with Stuart Cunningham, Australia.

Appadurai, A. (1990). "Disjuncture and Difference in the Global Cultural Economy." *Theory, Culture, and Society*, 7 (1990): 295–310.

Arvidsson, A., Malossi, G., and Naro, S. (2010). "Passionate Work? Labour Conditions in the Milan Fashion Industry." *Journal for Cultural Research*, 14(3): 295–309.

Ashley, B. A. (2015). Talent Manager, Big Frame/Awesomeness, 11 June, interview with David Craig, United States.

Ault, S. (2014). "Survey: YouTube Stars More Popular Than Mainstream Celebs among U.S. Teens." *Variety*, 5 August. http://variety.com/2014/digital/news

/survey-youtube-stars-more-popular-than-mainstream-celebs-among-u-s -teens-1201275245/, accessed 20 July 2017.

Ault, S. (2015). "Digital Star Popularity Grows versus Mainstream Celebrities." *Variety*, 23 July. http://variety.com/2015/digital/news/youtubers-teen-survey-ksi -pewdiepie-1201544882/, accessed 20 July 2017.

Bach, S. (1985). *Final Cut: Dreams and Disaster in the Making of Heaven's Gate.* New York: William Morrow.

Bagdikian, B. (1983). *The Media Monopoly.* Boston: Beacon.

Bagdikian, B. (2004). *The New Media Monopoly.* Boston: Beacon.

Baker, G. (2014). "Meet PewDiePie's First Subscriber Ever!" *Baker Brother TV*, 6 June. http://bakerbrothertv.com/2014/06/06/pewdiepies-first-subscriber/, accessed 15 May 2017.

Ballon, P. (2014). "Old and New Issues in Media Economics." In *The Palgrave Handbook of European Media Policy*, edited by K. Donders, C. Pauwels, and J Loisen, 70–95. Basingstoke: Palgrave.

Banet-Weiser, S. (2011). "Branding the Post-Feminist Self: Girls' Video Production and YouTube." In *Mediated Girlhoods*, edited by M. Kearney, 277–94. New York: Peter Lang.

Banet-Weiser, S. (2012). *AuthenticTM: The Politics of Ambivalence in a Brand Culture.* New York: NYU Press.

Banks, J., and Deuze, M. (2009). "Co-creative Labour." *International Journal of Cultural Studies*, 12(5): 419–31.

Banks, M. (2010). "Autonomy Guarantee? Cultural Work in the 'Art-Commerce' Relation." *Journal for Cultural Research*, 14(3): 251–69.

Banks, M., and Hesmondhalgh, D. (2009). "Looking for Work in Creative Industries Policy." *International Journal of Cultural Policy*, 15(4): 415–30.

Baym, N. (2015). "Connect with Your Audience! The Relational Labor of Connection." *Communication Review*, 18(1): 14–22.

BBC (2016). "China Internet Star Papi Jiang Promises 'Corrections' after Reprimand." *BBC News*, 20 April. http://www.bbc.com/news/world-asia-china-36089057, accessed 16 June 2017.

Beale, T. (2016). "Why Scott Disick's Instagram Fail Is Everything Wrong with Influencer Marketing." *Traackr*, 20 May. http://wp.traackr.com/blog/2016/05/why-scott-disicks -instagram-fail-is-everything-wrong-with-influencer-marketing/, accessed 11 July 2017.

"Being Trans vs. Being Black with Todrick!" YouTube video, 8:40. Posted by "Gigi Gorgeous," 2 February 2016. https://youtu.be/HU7XCpdDyz4, accessed 7 November 2016.

Bendix, T. (2016). "President Obama Tells Ingrid Nilsen LGBT Rights Are 'Here to Stay.'" *AfterEllen*, January 21. http://www.afterellen.com/people/470609-president -obama-tells-ingrid-nilsen-lgbt-rights-stay, accessed 19 June 2017.

Birtles, B. (2016). "Chinese Social Media 'Stream Queens' Getting Rich by Broadcasting Their Lives Online." *ABC News Lateline*, 27 July. http://www.abc.net.au/news/2016 -07-26/chinas-narcissistic-social-media-stars-making-$20k-per-month/7661118, accessed 27 July 2016.

Bloom, D. (2014). "Fullscreen Launches First Live Event for Its Digital Stars." *Deadline Hollywood*, July 18. http://deadline.com/2014/07/fullscreen-intour-live-event-you tube-vine-kevin-lyman-jennxpenn-806125/, accessed 4 August 2015.

Blumberg, B. (2015). Chief Content Officer, Defy Media, 13 May, interview with Stuart Cunningham and David Craig, United States.

Boland, B., and Angelidou-Smith, M. (2017). "An Update on Video Monetization." *Facebook Media*, 23 February. https://media.fb.com/2017/02/23/update-on-video -monetization/, accessed 23 February 2017.

Bourdieu, P. (1984). *Distinction: A Social Critique of the Judgement of Taste*. Cambridge, MA: Harvard University Press.

Bourdieu, P. (1990). *Language and Symbolic Violence*. Cambridge, MA: Harvard University Press.

boyd, d. (2010). "Social Network Sites as Networked Publics: Affordances, Dynamics, and Implications." In *Networked Self: Identity, Community, and Culture on Social Network Sites*, edited by Z. Papacharissi, 39–58. London: Routledge.

boyd, d., and Ellison, N. (2007). "Social Network Sites: Definition, History, and Scholarship." *Journal of Computer-Mediated Communication*, 13(1): 210–30.

Boyd-Barrett, O. (2015). *Media Imperialism*. London: Sage.

"Brand Deal Rant." YouTube video, 4:08. Posted by "doodlevoggle," 27 August 2015. https://www.youtube.com/watch?v=PPChNyCwMEo, accessed 11 July 2017.

Brouwer, B. (2015a). "Digital Advertising Will Overtake TV Ad Spend Globally by 2017, in the U.S. by 2016." *Tubefilter*, 7 December. http://www.tubefilter.com/2015/12/07 /digital-advertising-will-take-over-tv-ad-spend-globally-by-2017-in-the-u-s-by -2016/, accessed 26 March 2017.

Brouwer, B. (2015b). "Twitch Claims 43% of Revenue from \$3.8 Billion Gaming Content Industry." *Tubefilter*, 10 July. http://www.tubefilter.com/2015/07/10/twitch -global-gaming-content-revenue-3-billion/, accessed 17 July 2017.

Brouwer, B. (2015c). "Vlogbrothers Open Sponsorship for Educationally Minded Online Video Channels, Projects." *Tubefilter*, 11 November. http://www.tubefilter .com/2015/11/11/vlogbrothers-sponsorship-applications/, accessed 29 November 2016.

Brouwer, B. (2015d). "Joey Graceffa Tells His Candid Coming Out Story as Part of Ad Council's 'Love Has No Labels' Campaign." *Tubefilter*, 9 October. http://www .tubefilter.com/2015/10/09/joey-graceffa-ad-council-love-has-no-labels-coming -out-video/, accessed 9 October 2015.

Bruell, A. (2016). "The Ad Agency of the Future Is Coming. Are You Ready?" *Advertising Age*, 2 May. http://adage.com/article/print-edition/agency-future/303798/, accessed 18 July 2017.

Bruns, A. (2008). *Blogs, Wikipedia, Second Life, and Beyond: From Production to Produsage*. New York: Peter Lang.

Brzeski, P. (2017). "Netflix Signs Licensing Deal with China's iQiyi." *Hollywood Reporter*, 24 April. http://www.hollywoodreporter.com/news/netflix-signs-licensing -deal-chinas-iqiyi-997071, accessed 4 September 2017.

Bucher, T. (2015). "Networking; or, What the Social Means in Social Media." *Social Media + Society*, 1(1): 1–2.

Buckman, R. (2008). "Lonelygirl Gets Popular with Investors." *Wall Street Journal*, 17 April. https://www.wsj.com/article/SB120840403372722269.html, accessed 15 May 2017.

"Build Your YouTube Community—Featuring Kalista Elaine." YouTube video, 3:53. Uploaded by "YouTube Creator Academy," 19 June 2017. https://www.youtube.com /watch?v=G6guP7dMs3s, accessed 17 July 2017.

Burch, S. (2017). "YouTube Star Tyler Oakley's Deal with Ellen DeGeneres Has Dissolved (Exclusive)." *Wrap*, 19 July. http://www.thewrap.com/youtube-star-tyler-oakleys-deal -with-ellen-degeneres-has-dissolved-exclusive/, accessed 29 August 2017.

Burgess, J. (2006). "Hearing Ordinary Voices: Cultural Studies, Vernacular Creativity, and Digital Storytelling." *Continuum: Journal of Media & Cultural Studies*, 20(2): 201–14.

Burgess, J. (2013). "YouTube and the Formalisation of Amateur Media." In *Amateur Media: Social, Cultural, and Legal Perspectives*, edited by D. Hunter, R. Lobato, M. Richardson, and J. Thomas, 53–58. London: Routledge.

Burgess, J. (2014). "From 'Broadcast Yourself' to 'Follow Your Interests': Making Over Social Media." *International Journal of Cultural Studies*, 18(3): 281–85.

Burgess, J., and Green, J. (2008). "Agency and Controversy in the YouTube Community." In IR 9.0: Rethinking Communities, Rethinking Place—Association of Internet Researchers (AoIR) Conference, 15–18 October 2008, IT University of Copenhagen, Denmark.

Burgess, J., and Green, J. (2009). *YouTube*. Cambridge: Polity Press.

Byford, S. (2015). "Google Is Helping Japanese YouTubers Shoot Samurai Dramas." *Verge*, 7 April. https://www.theverge.com/2015/4/7/8359063/youtube-toei-samurai -drama-jidaigeki, accessed 6 June 2017.

Cai, H. (2016). Cofounder, Star Station TV, 31 May, interview with Stuart Cunningham and David Craig, China.

Caldwell, J. (2008). *Production Culture: Industrial Reflexivity and Critical Practice in Film and Television*. Durham, NC: Duke University Press.

Caldwell, J. (2009). "How Producers 'Theorize': Shoot-Outs, Bake-Offs, and Speed-Dating." In *Media/Cultural Studies: Critical Approaches*, edited by R. Hammer and D. Kellner, 68–87. New York: Peter Lang.

Canada Media Fund (2017). "CMF and Google Canada Announce Partnership for Iconic Canadian Content." *Canada Media Fund*, 26 January. http://cmf-fmc .ca/en-ca/news-events/news/january-2017/cmf-and-google-canada-announce -partnership-for-ico, accessed 6 June 2017.

Castells, M. (2007). "Communication, Power, and Counter-Power in the Network Society." *International Journal of Communication*, 1: 238–66.

"Catch My Heart." YouTube video, 9:01. Posted by "Michelle Phan," 25 August 2011. https://www.youtube.com/watch?v=jzi4nDZldNk, accessed 5 July 2017.

"Catering to Your Audience—PewDiePie." YouTube video, 5:39. Posted by "PewDiePie," 2 February 2016. https://www.youtube.com/watch?v=oL_FwiJX8go, accessed 5 July 2017.

Cavalcanti, A. (2016). "'I Did It All Online': Transgender Identity and the Management of Everyday Life." *Critical Studies in Media Communication*, 33: 109–22.

Caves, R. (2000). *Creative Industries: Contracts between Art and Commerce*. Cambridge, MA: Harvard University Press.

Chen, Q. (2016). "China's Live-Streaming Explosion: A Game Changer for All?" *CNBC*, 1 December. https://www.cnbc.com/2016/12/01/chinas-live-streaming-explosion-a -game-changer-for-all.html, accessed 3 August 2017.

Chen, Y. (2016). "Swinging from Vine: More Than Half of Top Vine Influencers Have Left the Platform." *Digiday*, 17 May. https://digiday.com/media/swinging-vine-half -top-influencers-left-platform/, accessed 24 August 2017.

Chen, Y. (2017). "'A Dicey Situation': Snapchat Gives Influencers the Cold Shoulder." *Digiday*, 5 July. https://digiday.com/marketing/dicey-situation-snapchat-gives -influencers-cold-shoulder/, accessed 27 August 2017.

Chernikoff, L. (2016). Executive Director, Internet Creators Guild, 4 February, interview with David Craig, United States.

Chester, J. (2015). "How YouTube, Big Data, and Big Brands Mean Trouble for Kids and Parents." *Alternet.com*, 6 April. http://www.alternet.org/media/how -youtube-big-data-and-big-brands-mean-trouble-kidsand-parents, accessed 29 July 2016.

Choi, D. (2015). Creator, David Choi, 17 June, interview with David Craig, United States.

Choudary, S. (2014). "Reverse Network Effects: Why Today's Social Networks Can Fail as They Grow Larger." *Wired*, 1 March. https://www.wired.com/insights/2014/03 /reverse-network-effects-todays-social-networks-can-fail-grow-larger/, accessed 26 March 2017.

Christensen, C. (2000). *The Innovator's Dilemma*. Boston: Harvard Business School Press.

Cohen, H. (2014). "Are You Ready for Multi-Platform Social Media Use?" *Heidi Cohen: Actionable Marketing Guide*, 23 June. http://heidicohen.com/multi-platform-social -media-use/, accessed 26 March 2017.

Cohen, J. (2012). "YouTube's Next Goal: Catapulting 16 Vloggers to More Than 125M Views." *Tubefilter*, 9 May. http://www.tubefilter.com/2012/05/09/youtube-next -vloggers/, accessed 30 January 2017.

Cohen, J. (2014). "At 24 Million YouTube Subscribers, PewDiePie Decides to Scale Back." *Tubefilter*, 4 March. http://www.tubefilter.com/2014/03/04/pewdiepie -youtube-subscribers-scale-back/, accessed 11 May 2017.

Cohen, J. (2017). "Introducing the Tubefilter Live.me Top Broadcaster Rankings." *Tubefilter*, 9 January. http://www.tubefilter.com/2017/01/09/tubefilter-liveme-top -broadcaster-rankings/, accessed 3 August 2017.

Coldewey, D. (2016). "Facebook, Twitter, and YouTube Blocked in Turkey during Reported Coup Attempt." *TechCrunch*, 15 July. https://techcrunch.com/2016/07/15 /facebook-twitter-and-youtube-blocked-in-turkey-during-reported-coup-attempt/, accessed 16 June 2017.

"Coming Out." YouTube video, 6:27. Posted by "ConnorFranta," 8 December 2014. https://www.youtube.com/watch?v=WYodBfRxKWI, accessed 24 October 2016.

"Coming Out (Ch. 6). 'Sticking Around.'" YouTube video, 1:07. Posted by "yourharto," 10 July 2014. https://www.youtube.com/watch?v=iazrQYZZxM4, accessed 15 June 2017.

Considine, A. (2011). "For Asian-American Stars, Many Web Fans." *New York Times*, 29 July. http://www.nytimes.com/2011/07/31/fashion/for-asian-stars-many-web-fans.html, accessed 16 June 2017.

Constine, J. (2016). "Facebook Launches Video Rights Manager to Combat Freebooting." *TechCrunch*, 12 April. https://techcrunch.com/2016/04/12/content-fb/, accessed 24 August 2017.

Constine, J. (2017a). "Instagram's Growth Speeds Up as It Hits 700 Million Users." *TechCrunch*, 26 April. https://techcrunch.com/2017/04/26/instagram-700-million-users/, accessed 24 August 2017.

Constine, J. (2017b). "Patreon Doubles in a Year to 1M Paying Patrons and 50K Creators." *TechCrunch*, 18 May. https://techcrunch.com/2017/05/18/patreon-pushes-as-youtube-stutters/, accessed 18 May 2017.

Convery, S. (2017). "The Women Who Make a Living Gaming on Twitch." *Guardian*, 3 January. https://www.theguardian.com/technology/2017/jan/03/women-make-living-gaming-twitch, accessed 3 January 2017.

Covington, P., Adams, J., and Sargin, E. (2016). "Deep Neural Networks for YouTube Recommendations." Proceedings of the Tenth ACM Conference on Recommender Systems, ACM, New York, NY.

Cowap, M. (2015). Development Management, Screen Australia, 4 March and 4 September, interview with Stuart Cunningham and Adam Swift, Australia.

Craig, D., and Cunningham, S. (2017). "How Social Media Stars Are Fighting for the Left." *Conversation*, February 21. https://theconversation.com/how-social-media-stars-are-fighting-for-the-left-71691, accessed 4 September 2017.

Cravo, C. (2016). "9 Micro-Influencer Statistics (No. 4 Will Seriously Surprise You!)." *Contevo*, 23 November. https://contevo.com.au/micro-influencers-statistics-2016/, accessed 16 December 2017.

"Creator Town Hall with Hillary Clinton." YouTube video, 1:00:13. Posted by "Hillary Clinton," 28 June 2016. https://www.youtube.com/watch?v=3FITPKRwaVw, accessed 1 November 2016.

Cresci, E. (2016). "Lonelygirl15: How One Mysterious Vlogger Changed the Internet." *Guardian*, 16 June. https://www.theguardian.com/technology/2016/jun/16/lonelygirl15-bree-video-blog-YouTube, accessed 22 August 2017.

Csathy, P. (2016). "Whatever Happened to MCNs?" *TechCrunch*, 10 June. https://techcrunch.com/2016/06/10/whatever-happened-to-mcns/, accessed 16 December 2017.

Cunningham, S., and Craig, D. (2016). "Online Entertainment: A New Wave of Media Globalization?" *International Journal of Communication*, 10: 5409–25.

Cunningham, S., Craig, D., and Silver, J. (2016). "YouTube, Multichannel Networks, and the Accelerated Evolution of the New Screen Ecology." *Convergence: The International Journal of Research into New Media Technologies*, 22(4): 376–91.

Cunningham, S., Flew, T., and Swift, A. (2015). *Media Economics*. London: Palgrave.

Cunningham, S., and Silver, J. (2013). *Screen Distribution and the New King Kongs of the Online World*. London: Palgrave MacMillan.

Curtin, M., and Sanson, K. (eds.). (2016). *Precarious Creativity: Global Media, Local Labor*. Berkeley: University of California Press.

Curtin, M., and Sanson, K. (eds.). (2017). *Voices of Labor: Creativity, Craft, and Conflict in Global Hollywood*. Berkeley: University of California Press.

Custer, C. (2016a). "China's Live-Streaming Platforms Are All under Investigation for Sex, Violence, and Crime." *Tech in Asia*, 15 April. https://www.techinasia.com/chinas -livestreaming-platforms-investigation-sex-violence-crime, accessed 16 June 2016.

Custer, C. (2016b). "WeChat May Be King, but Weibo Isn't as Dead as You Think." *Tech in Asia*, 28 June. https://www.techinasia.com/wechat-king-weibo-dead-data-shows, accessed 16 June 2016.

Cyk, J. (2015). "Cracking the Code of Beauty Vloggers' Authenticity." *WWD*, 16 January. http://wwd.com/beauty-industry-news/beauty-features/cracking-the-code-of-b eauty-vloggers-authenticity-8093143/, accessed 21 November 2016.

Das, P. (2016). Co-founder, Ping Network, 26 May, interview with Stuart Cunningham and David Craig, India.

Defy Media (2015). "Millennials Ages 13–24 Declare It's Not Just the Cord, TV Content Doesn't Cut It." *Defy Media*, 3 March. http://www.defymedia.com/2015/03/03/mille nnials-ages-13-24-declare-just-cord-tv-content-doesnt-cut/, accessed 15 May 2017.

Dermody, S., and Jacka, E. (1987). *The Screening of Australia*: Volume 1, *Anatomy of a Film Industry*. Sydney, NSW: Currency Press.

"Detained in Dubai for Being Transgender." YouTube video, 8:02. Posted by "Gigi Gorgeous," 11 August 2016. https://youtu.be/J_gGZpPEB9Q, accessed 7 November 2016.

Deuze, M. (2007). *Media Work*. Cambridge: Polity Press.

Deuze, M., and Steward, B. (2011). "Managing Media Work." In *Managing Media Work*, edited by M. Deuze, 1–11. Thousand Oaks: Sage.

"Don't Wait: Official Music Video." YouTube video, 4:32. Posted by "Joey Graceffa," 16 May 2015. https://www.youtube.com/watch?v=Kcwo_mhyqTw, accessed 24 October 2016.

"Draw My Life." YouTube video, 11:24. Posted by "Michelle Phan," 19 May 2013. https:// www.youtube.com/watch?v=05KqZEqQJ4o, accessed 26 November 2016.

Dredge, S. (2015a). "YouTube Star Attacks 'Theft, Lies, and Facebook Video.'" *Guardian*, 4 August. https://www.theguardian.com/technology/2015/aug/04/youtube -facebook-video-vlogbrothers-hank-green, accessed 26 March 2017.

Dredge, S. (2015b). "YouTube: Hank Green Tells Fellow Creators to Aim for '$1 Per View.'" *Guardian*, 8 April. https://www.theguardian.com/technology/2015/apr/08 /hank-green-youtube-1000-cpm-vlogbrothers, accessed 20 November 2015.

Duffy, B. (2015a). "The Romance of Work: Gender and Aspirational Labour in the Digital Culture Industries." *International Journal of Cultural Studies*, 19(4): 441–57.

Duffy, B. (2015b). "Amateur, Autonomous, and Collaborative: Myths of Aspiring Female Cultural Producers in Web 2.0." *Critical Studies in Media Communication*, 32(1): 48–64.

Duffy, B. (2017). *(Not) Getting Paid to Do What You Love: Gender, Social Media, and Aspirational Work*. New Haven, CT: Yale University Press.

Dunn, G. (2015). "Get Rich or Die Vlogging: The Sad Economics of Internet Fame." *Fusion*, 14 December. http://fusion.net/story/244545/famous-and-broke-on-youtube-instagram-social-media/, accessed 13 July 2017.

Elmer, G., Langlois, G., Powell, A., and Renzi, A. (2015). "Call for Papers: International Communication Association Preconference Big Data; Critiques and Alternatives." Fukuoka, 9 June 2016. http://www.icahdq.org/conf/2016/bigdataCFP.asp, accessed 10 December 2015.

Elsayed, Y. (2016). "Laughing through Change: Subversive Humor in Online Videos of Arab Youth." *International Journal of Communication*, 10(2016): 5102–22.

Eördögh, F. (2014). "Why the Outrage over Daily Grace and My Damn Channel Matters." *Medium*, 13 January. https://medium.com/@fruzse/why-the-outrage-over-daily-grace-and-my-damn-channel-matters-3bac86166b62, accessed 18 July 2017.

European Commission (2016). "Commission Updates EU Audiovisual Rules and Presents Targeted Approach to Online Platforms Brussels." European Commission, 25 May. http://europa.eu/rapid/press-release_IP-16-1873_en.htm, accessed 3 August 2017.

European Parliament (2017). "The Audiovisual Media Services Directive." *Briefing: EU Legislation in Progress*, 25 April. http://www.europarl.europa.eu/RegData/etudes/BRIE/2016/583859/EPRS_BRI%282016%29583859_EN.pdf, accessed 4 September 2017.

Evey, K. (2015). Producer and Writer, Geek and Sundry, 12 May, interview with Stuart Cunningham and David Craig, United States.

Finkle, T. (2015). Publicist, Metro Public Relations, 11 June, interview with David Craig, United States.

Finley, K. (2017). "Google's Big EU Fine Isn't Just about the Money." *Wired*, 27 June. https://www.wired.com/story/google-big-eu-fine/, accessed 28 June 2017.

Fish, A., and Srinivasan, R. (2011). "Digital Labor Is the New Killer App." *New Media & Society*, 14(1): 137–52.

Flew, T. (2007). *Understanding Global Media*. Basingstoke: Palgrave Macmillan.

Florida, R. (2002). *The Rise of the Creative Class: And How It's Transforming Work, Leisure, Community, and Everyday Life*. New York: Basic Books.

Flynn, K. (2016). "What Happened to Meerkat? From Hype-Ball to Pivot in Just One Year." *International Business Times*, 9 March. http://www.ibtimes.com/what-happened-meerkat-hype-ball-pivot-just-one-year-2333379, accessed 3 August 2017.

Flynn, K. (2017a). "Instagram Adds 'Paid Partnership' Feature, the Formal Alternative to #ad or #spon." *Mashable*, 14 June. http://mashable.com/2017/06/14/instagram-paid-partnership-ad-spon/#JTETAq_HBkqg, accessed 15 December 2017.

Flynn, K. (2017b). "Inside Twitter's Decision to Keep Periscope and Abandon Everything Else." *Mashable Australia*, 1 March. http://mashable.com/2017/02/28/periscope-ceo-kayvon/, accessed 3 August 2017.

Forde, E. (2016). "Is YouTube Wrecking the Music Industry—or Putting New Artists in the Spotlight?" *Guardian*, 18 July. https://www.theguardian.com/business/2016/jul/18/youtube-music-industry-artists-spotlight, accessed 26 March 2017.

Foucault, M. (1991). *Discipline and Punish: The Birth of a Prison*. London: Penguin.

Foxx, C. (2016). "Fine Brothers Spark Fury with YouTube Trademark Attempt." *BBC*, 1 February. http://www.bbc.com/news/technology-35459805, accessed 2 February 2016.

Friedman, T. (2005). *The World Is Flat: A Brief History of the Twenty-First Century*. New York: Farrar, Straus, and Giroux.

Frosch, S. (2015). Creator, ElloSteph, 7 July, interview with David Craig, United States.

Fuchs, C. (2010). "Labour in Informational Capitalism and on the Internet." *Information Society*, 26(3): 179–96.

Fuchs, C. (2014). *Social Media: A Critical Introduction*. London: Sage.

Gabe and Garret channel (2016). Manager, Gabe and Garrett, 24 June, interview with Jarrod Walczer, United States.

Gabriel, S. (2006). *Chinese Capitalism and the Modernist Vision*. London: Routledge.

Gambino, L. (2016). "Hillary Clinton Warns Fake News Can Have 'Real World Consequences.'" *Guardian*, 9 December. https://www.theguardian.com/us-news/2016/dec/08/hillary-clinton-fake-news-consequences-pizzagate, accessed 4 September 2017.

Garrahan, M. (2017). "Disrupting Hollywood: Amazon Goes to the Oscars." *Financial Times*, 17 February. https://www.ft.com/content/d4784afe-f432-11e6-95ee-f14e55513608, accessed 4 September 2017.

Gelles, D. (2014). "Citigroup Says Instagram Is Worth $35 Billion." *New York Times*, 19 December. https://dealbook.nytimes.com/2014/12/19/citigroup-says-instagram-is-worth-35-billion/, accessed 15 December 2017.

Gerbner, G., and Gross, L. (1976). "Living with Television: The Violence Profile." *Journal of Communication*, 26: 172–99.

Gibson, J. (1977). "The Theory of Affordances." In *Perceiving, Acting, and Knowing: Toward an Ecological Psychology*, edited by R. Shar and J. Bransford, 67–82, Hillsdale, NJ: Lawrence Erlbaum.

Gill, R. (2007). "Technobohemians or the New Cybertariat? New Media Work in Amsterdam a Decade after the Web." Institute of Network Cultures. http://www.networkcultures.org/_uploads/17.pdf, accessed 13 July 2017.

Gill, R., and Pratt, A. (2008). "The Social Factory? Immaterial Labour, Precariousness, and Cultural Work." *Theory, Culture, and Society*, 25(7–8): 1–30.

Gillespie, T. (2018). "Regulation of and by Platforms." In *The Sage Handbook of Social Media*, edited by J. Burgess, T. Poell, and A. Marwick, 254–78. Thousand Oaks, CA: Sage.

Gillespie, T., and Seaver, N. (2016). "Critical Algorithm Studies: A Reading List." *Social Media Collective Research Blog*, 15 December. https://socialmediacollective.org/reading-lists/critical-algorithm-studies/, accessed 13 July 2017.

Glamour (2013). "YouTube Makeup Guru Michelle Phan on Becoming a Beauty Superstar: 'My Only Goal Was to Help My Family.'" *Glamour*, 3 September. http://www.glamour.com/story/michelle-phan-youtube-beauty-glamour-october-2013, accessed 15 May 2017.

Goffman, E. (1959). *The Presentation of Self in Everyday Life*. New York: Doubleday.

Goldman, W. (1989). *Adventures in the Screen Trade*. New York: Grand Central Publishing.

Gorgeous, G. (2015). Creator, GigiGorgeous, 9 July, interview with David Craig, United States.

Graceffa, J. (2015). Creator, JoeyGraceffa, 6 July, interview with David Craig, United States.

Grande, A. (2015). "Google Launches YouTube Kids App as Privacy Issues Linger." *Law360.com*, 23 February. http://www.law360.com/articles/624055/google-launches-youtube-kids-app-as-privacy-issues-linger, accessed 29 July 2016.

Gray, M. (2009). *Out in the Country: Youth, Media, and Queer Visibility*. New York: NYU Press.

Green, H. (2014). "The $1,000 CPM: Advertising Is a Kinda Shitty Model; It's Very Exciting That We're Moving beyond It." *Medium.com*, 15 April. https://medium.com/@hankgreen/the-1-000-cpm-f92717506a4b, accessed 5 July 2017.

Green, H. (2015a). Creator, VlogBrothers, 5 July, interview with David Craig, United States.

Green, H. (2015b). "A Decade Later, YouTube Remains a Mystery, Especially to Itself." *Medium*, 23 February. https://medium.com/@hankgreen/a-decade-later-youtube-remains-a-mystery-especially-to-itself-80a1c38feeaf, accessed 31 August 2017.

Green, H. (2015c). "Theft, Lies, and Facebook Video." *Medium*, 3 August. https://medium.com/@hankgreen/theft-lies-and-facebook-video-656b0ffed369#.k2uj8hh8l, accessed 31 January 2017.

Greenberg, J. (2015). "Exposing the Murky World of Online Ads Aimed at Kids." *Wired*, 7 April. https://www.wired.com/2015/04/exposing-murky-world-online-ads-aimed-kids/, accessed 17 August 2017.

Griffith, E. (2015). "Meerkat Raises Cash from Greylock and Hollywood." *Fortune*, 26 March. http://fortune.com/2015/03/26/meerkat-funding/, accessed 3 August 2017.

Grimstone, S. (2015). Creator, Sarah Stone, 25 March, interview with Stuart Cunningham and Andrew Golledge, Australia.

Gross, L. (2001). *Up from Invisibility: Lesbians, Gay Men, and the Media in America*. New York: Columbia University Press.

Gross, L., and Woods, J. (1999). "Being Gay in American Media and Society." In *The Columbia Reader: On Lesbians and Gay Men in Media, Society, and Politics*, edited by L. Gross and J. Woods, 297–301. New York: Columbia University Press.

Grossberg, L. (2010). "Forward." In *Hollywood's Exploited: Public Pedagogy, Corporate Movies, and Cultural Crisis*, edited by B. Frymer, T. Kashani, A. Nocella, R. Van Heertum, xii–xv. New York: Palgrave Macmillan.

Grubb, J. (2016). "PewDiePie Denies Wrongdoing in Warner Bros.–YouTube Game Scandal." *Venture Beat*, 13 July. https://venturebeat.com/2016/07/13/pewdiepie -denies-wrongdoing-in-warner-bros-youtube-game-scandal/, accessed 10 May 2017.

Guback, T. (1969). *The International Film Industry: Western Europe and America since 1945* (Indiana University international studies). Bloomington: Indiana University Press.

Guerrero, D. (2017). "Gigi Gorgeous: Trans, Lesbian, and the Face of an Online Move-ment." *Advocate*, 1 May. https://www.advocate.com/advocate50/2017/5/01/shes-all -gigi-gorgeous, accessed 4 September 2017.

Guo, L., and Harlow, S. (2014). "User-Generated Racism: An Analysis of Stereotypes of African Americans, Latinos, and Asians in YouTube Videos." *Howard Journal of Communications*, 3(1): 281–302.

Guo, L., and Lee, L. (2013). "The Critique of YouTube-based Vernacular Discourse: A Case Study of YouTube's Asian Community." *Critical Studies in Media Communica-tion*, 30(5): 391–406.

Gutelle, S. (2013). "YouTube Has Removed All References to Its Original Channels Initiative." *Tubefilter* 12 November. http://www.tubefilter.com/2013/11/12/youtube -original-channels-initiative-experiment-end/, accessed 18 July 2017.

Gutelle, S. (2017a). "Casey Neistat's Airport Protest Vlog Gets Three Million Views in One Day." *Tubefilter*, 30 January. http://www.tubefilter.com/2017/01/30/casey -neistat-jfk-protest-vlog/, accessed 4 September 2017.

Gutelle, S. (2017b). "'Anti-Haul' Videos Provide Fresh Perspective in YouTube's Beauty Scene." *Tubefilter*, 17 May. http://www.tubefilter.com/2017/05/17/anti-haul-videos -beauty-youtube/, accessed 22 August 2017.

Gutelle, S. (2017c). "FTC Pushes for More Disclosure of Sponsored Content on Instagram." *Tubefilter*, 19 April. http://www.tubefilter.com/2017/04/19/ftc-guidelines -sponsored-posts-instagram/, accessed 20 April 2017.

Hackett, R., and Carroll, W. (2006). *Remaking Media: The Struggle to Democratize Public Communication*. New York: Routledge.

Hallinan, B., and Striphas, T. (2016). "Recommended for You: The Netflix Prize and the Production of Algorithmic Culture." *New Media & Society*, 18(1): 117–37.

Halperin, D. (1995). *Saint Foucault: Towards a Gay Hagiography*. London: Oxford University Press.

Hamedy, J. (2015). "Diversity Report Card: YouTubers Get the Only 'A' Grade of 2015." *Mashable*, 30 December. http://mashable.com/2015/12/29/diversity-report-card -online-video-2015/#78l8wVn3BGqR, accessed 30 December 2015.

Hamedy, S. (2015). "E!'s Grace Helbig Experiment: Does YouTube Stardom Equal Rat-ings?" *Los Angeles Times*, 1 May. http://www.latimes.com/entertainment/envelope /cotown/la-et-ct-grace-helbig-show-20150502-story.html, accessed 17 July 2017.

Hart, P. (2013). "Bob McChesney on Internet Giants and the National Security State." *Fair: Fairness & Accuracy in Reporting*, 7 June. http://fair.org/home/bob-mcchesney -on-internet-giants-and-the-national-security-state/, accessed 24 August 2017.

Hartley, J., Potts, J., Cunningham, S., Flew, T., Keane, M., and Banks, J. (2013). *Key Concepts in Creative Industries*. London: Sage.

Havens, T. (2014). "Towards a Structuration Theory of Media Intermediaries." In *Making Media Work: Cultures of Management in the Entertainment Industries*, edited by D. Johnson, D. Kompare, and A. Santo, 39–63. New York: NYU Press.

Havens, T., and Lotz, A. (2011). *Understanding Media Industries*. Oxford: Oxford University Press.

Havens, T., Lotz, A., and Tinic, S. (2009). "Critical Media Industry Studies: A Research Approach." *Communication, Culture & Critique*, 2(2): 234–53.

Heath, A. (2017). "Facebook and Google Completely Dominate the US Digital Ad Industry." *Business Insider Australia*, 27 April. https://www.businessinsider.com.au/facebook-and-google-dominate-ad-industry-with-a-combined-99-of-growth-2017-4, accessed 27 April 2017.

Hebdige, D. (1979). *Subculture: The Meaning of Style*. London: Routledge.

Hechter, S. (2013). "Amateur Creative Digital Content and Proportional Commerce Type Equation Here." In *Amateur Media: Social, Cultural, and Legal Perspectives*, edited by D. Hunter, R. Lobato, M. Richardson, and J. Thomas, 35–52. London: Routledge.

Hesmondhalgh, D., and Baker, S. (2010). "'A Very Complicated Version of Freedom': Conditions and Experiences of Creative Labour in Three Cultural Industries." *Poetics*, 38(1): 4–20.

Hesmondhalgh, D., and Baker, S. (2011). *Creative Labour: Media Work in Three Cultural Industries*. London: Routledge.

Hess, A. (2016). "Asian-American Actors Are Fighting for Visibility: They Will Not Be Ignored." *New York Times*, 25 May. http://www.nytimes.com/2016/05/29/movies/asian-american-actors-are-fighting-for-visibility-they-will-not-be-ignored.html, accessed 25 May 2016.

Hetcher, S. (2013). "Amateur Creative Digital Content and Proportional Commerce." In *Amateur Media: Social, Cultural and Legal Perspectives*, edited by D. Hunter, R. Lobato, M. Richardson, and J. Thomas, 35–52. London: Routledge.

Higgins, S. (2014). "List of YouTube Multi-Channel Networks." *Play Square*, 31 August. http://www.playsquare.co/blog/list-of-youtube-multi-channel-networks/, accessed 18 July 2017.

Highfield, T. (2016). *Social Media and Everyday Politics*. Malden, MA: Polity.

Hilmes, M. (1997). *Radio Voices: American Broadcasting, 1922 to 1952*. Minneapolis: University of Minnesota Press.

Hilmes, M. (2009). "Nailing Mercury: The Problem of Media Industry Historiography." In *Media Industries: History, Theory, and Method*, edited by J. Holt and A. Perren, 21–34. Malden: Blackwell.

Hilmes, M. (2010). "Cinema and the Age of Television, 1945–1975." In *The Wiley-Blackwell's History of American Film*, edited by C. Lucia, R. Grundmann, and A. Simon. Oxford: Wiley-Blackwell.

Hilton-Morrow, W., and Battles, K. (2015). *Sexual Identities and the Media: An Introduction*. New York: Routledge.

Hipes, P. (2016). "Amazon Taking on YouTube with User-Generated Hub." *Deadline Hollywood*, 10 May. http://deadline.com/2016/05/amazon-video-direct-user-generated-platform-launch-avd-1201752405/, accessed 26 March 2017.

Hirsh, S. (2016). "How Activists like Jazz Jennings, Ingrid Nilsen See LGBTQ Media Representation." *Mashable*, September 19. http://mashable.com/2016/09/19/lgbtq-media-social-good-summit-2016, accessed 19 June 2017.

Hodorowicz, J. (2015). Manager, Collective Digital Studios, 12 May, interview with Stuart Cunningham and David Craig, United States.

Holt, J., and Perren, A. (eds.). (2009). *Media Industries: History, Theory, and Method.* Malden, MA: Wiley-Blackwell.

Holt, J., and Sanson, K. (eds.). (2013). *Connected Viewing: Selling, Streaming, and Sharing Media in the Digital Age.* London: Routledge.

Hough, J. (2015). "Why YouTube Is Twice as Valuable as Netflix." *Barron's*, 26 December. http://www.barrons.com/articles/why-youtube-is-twice-as-valuable-as-netflix-1451108321, accessed 26 March 2017.

"How Collaboration Can Help Your YouTube Channel Grow (ft. LaToya Forever & King of Random)." YouTube video, 1:48. Uploaded by "YouTube Creator Academy," 5 January 2017. https://www.youtube.com/watch?v=wWjV_axRHNo, accessed 17 July 2017.

"How to Be a Nerdfighter: A Vlogbrothers FAQ." YouTube video, 3:58. Posted by "vlogbrothers," 27 December 2009. https://www.youtube.com/watch?v=FyQi79aYfxU, accessed 5 July 2017.

"How to Vote in Every State." YouTube Channel. 12 July 2016. https://www.youtube.com/channel/UC7SMwipBlDwBPEwxq8QD8sw, accessed 4 September 2017.

Howkins, J. (2001). *The Creative Economy: How People Make Money from Ideas.* London: Penguin.

Howley, K. (2014). *Media Interventions.* New York: Peter Lang.

Hsieh, Y. (2012). "Online Social Networking Skills: The Social Affordances Approach to Digital Inequality." *First Monday*, March. http://firstmonday.org/ojs/index.php/fm/article/view/3893/3192, accessed 26 March 2017.

Huang, W. (2015). Creator, Wengie, 23 March, interview with Stuart Cunningham, Australia.

Hudson, D. (2017). "This Is What Disclosing Paid Partnerships Means for Brands." *Medium*, 28 June. https://medium.com/@DashHudson/this-is-what-disclosing-paid-partnerships-means-for-brands-d81b59eafd42, accessed 14 December 2017.

Huet, E. (2014). "Google Finally Shuts Down Orkut, Its First Social Network." *Forbes*, 30 June. https://www.forbes.com/sites/ellenhuet/2014/06/30/google-kills-orkut/, accessed 24 August 2017.

Humphreys, S. (2009). "The Economies within an Online Social Network Market: A Case Study of Ravelry." In: ANZCA 09 annual conference: Communication, Creativity, and Global Citizenship, 8–10 July 2009, QUT Brisbane.

Hunter, D., Lobato, R., Richardson, M., and Thomas, J. (eds.). (2013). *Amateur Media: Social, Cultural, and Legal Perspectives.* London: Routledge.

Hutchby, I. (2001). "Technologies, Texts, and Affordances." *Sociology*, 35(2): 441–56.

"I Am Transgender." YouTube video, 4:08. Posted by "Gigi Gorgeous," 16 December 2013. https://youtu.be/srOsrIC9Gj8, accessed 7 November 2016.

Ifeanyi, K. (2017). "Gigi Gorgeous Ups Her Brand with 'This Is Everything' (but 'This' Is Just the Start)." *Fast Company*, 15 February. https://www.fastcompany.com/3068121/gigi-gorgeous-ups-her-brand-with-this-is-everything-but-this-is-just-the-start, accessed 4 September 2017.

"I'm Banned . . ." YouTube video, 14:53. Posted by "PewDiePie," 22 January 2015. https://www.youtube.com/watch?v=61686cq6s7c&t=8s, accessed 13 January 2017.

"I'm Sorry [VOSTFR]." YouTube video, 8:51. Posted by "PewDiePie," 8 January 2013. https://www.youtube.com/watch?v=Ws4kb1wMeUU, accessed 7 November 2016.

Internet Creators Guild (2017). "Creators Fighting for Net Neutrality." 25 May. https://docs.google.com/document/d/1HAkMxxKuU2vZRSqIeiI-5b9TJt7GC-Jhoz4Q2xA3gos/edit, accessed 17 August 2017.

"I've Discovered the Greatest Thing Online. . . ." YouTube video, 13:08. Posted by "PewDiePie," 11 January 2017. https://www.youtube.com/watch?v=KtxXKezbQ9w, accessed 13 January 2017.

Iyengar, J. M. (2016). Head of Operations, YouTube Spaces (India), 21 May, interview with Stuart Cunningham and David Craig, India.

Jacewicz, N. (2017). "Social Media Star Has a 'Crazy Idea' to Help Somalia." *NPR*, 22 March. http://www.npr.org/sections/goatsandsoda/2017/03/22/521097218/social-media-star-has-a-crazy-idea-to-help-somalia, accessed 4 September 2017.

James, E. (2015). "Facebook Video Is Now Bigger Than YouTube for Brands." *Social Bakers*, 15 January. http://www.socialbakers.com/blog/2335-facebook-video-is-now-bigger-than-youtube-for-brands, accessed 26 March 2017.

Jarvey, N. (2017a). "Web Video Star Casey Neistat Reveals His Plans at CNN." *Hollywood Reporter*, 3 January. http://www.hollywoodreporter.com/news/web-video-star-casey-neistat-reveals-his-plans-at-cnn-981501, accessed 4 September 2017.

Jarvey, N. (2017b). "What's Next for Maker Studios amid Disney's Digital Downsizing." *Hollywood Reporter*, 3 March. http://www.hollywoodreporter.com/news/what-maker-studios-pewdiepie-fallout-downsizing-means-disney-981433, accessed 3 March 2017.

Jenkins, H. (1992). *Textual Poachers: Television Fans and Participatory Culture: Studies in Culture and Communication*. New York: Routledge.

Jenkins, H. (2006). *Convergence Culture: Where Old and New Media Collide*. New York: NYU Press.

Jenkins, H. (2016). "Youth Voice, Media, and Political Engagement: Introducing the Core Concepts." In *By Any Media Necessary: The New Youth Activism*, edited by H. Jenkins, S. Shresthova, L. Gamber-Thompson, N. Kligler-Vilenchik and A. Zimmerman, 1–60. New York: NYU Press.

Jenkins, H., Ford, S., and Green, J. (2013). *Spreadable Media: Creating Value and Meaning in a Networked Culture*. New York: NYU Press.

Jerslev, A. (2016). "In the Time of the Microcelebrity: Celebrification and the YouTuber Zoella." *International Journal of Communication*, 10: 5233–51.

Jin, D. Y. (2013). "The Construction of Platform Imperialism in the Globalization Era." *tripleC*, 11(1): 145–72.

Johnson, C. (2017). "10 Top Live Video Influencers to Follow." *Entrepreneur*, 21 March. https://www.entrepreneur.com/article/290400, accessed 3 August 2017.

Johnson, D., Kompare, D., and Santo, A. (eds.). (2014). *Making Media Work: Cultures of Management in the Entertainment Industries*. New York: NYU Press.

Johnson, J. (2017). "Is Facebook's Rights Manager Really Protecting Video Creators from Freebooting? Short Answer: Not Quite." *Video Link*, 17 January. https://thevideoink.com/is-facebooks-rights-manager-really-protecting-video-creators-from-freebooting-9dcc18963734, accessed 24 August 2017.

Jones, J. (2010). *Entertaining Politics: Satiric Television and Political Engagement*. New York: Rowman & Littlefield.

Kain, E. (2017). "YouTube Wants Content Creators to Appeal Demonetization, but It's Not Always That Easy." *Forbes*, 18 September. https://www.forbes.com/sites/erikkain/2017/09/18/adpocalypse-2017-heres-what-you-need-to-know-about-youtubes-demonetization-troubles/#7734a4fc6c26, accessed 16 December 2017.

Kam, B., and Chambers, C. (2015). Creators, BriaandChrissy, 7 July, interview with David Craig, United States.

Kantrowitz, A. (2017). "Frustrated Snap Social Influencers Leaving for Rival Platforms." *Buzzfeed*, 2 March. https://www.buzzfeed.com/alexkantrowitz/frustrated-snap-social-influencers-leaving-for-rival-platfor?utm_term=.pawOkYAWD#.endLKzlrx, accessed 17 July 2017.

Keane, M. (2016). "Disconnecting, Connecting, and Reconnecting: How Chinese Television Found Its Way out of the Box." *International Journal of Communication*, 10(2016): 5426–43.

Kellner, D. (2003). "Cultural Studies, Multiculturalism, and Media Culture." In *Gender, Race, and Class in Media*, edited by G. Dines and J. M. Humez, 9–20. Thousand Oaks, CA: Sage.

Kellner, D. (2009). "Media Industries, Political Economy, and Media/Cultural Studies: An Articulation." In *Media Industries: History, Theory, and Method*, edited by J. Holt and A. Perren, 95–107. Malden, MA: Blackwell.

Kellner, D., and Durham, M. (2012). "Adventures in Media and Cultural Studies: Introducing the Keywords." In *Media and Cultural Studies: Keywords*, edited by M. Durham and D. Kellner, ix–xxxviii. Oxford: Blackwell.

Kellogg, C. (2015). "Can YouTube Stars Save Publishing?" *Los Angeles Times*, 11 June. http://www.latimes.com/books/jacketcopy/la-et-jc-can-youtube-stars-save-publishing-20150611-story.html, accessed 4 August 2015.

Kelly, S. (2015). Manager, Charlis Crafty Kitchen, 23 March, interview with Stuart Cunningham, Australia.

Kemper, T. (2009). *Hidden Talent: The Emergence of Hollywood Agents*. Berkeley: University of California Press.

Kerr, D. (2012). "YouTube Cedes to Turkey and Uses Local Web Domain." *CNET*, 2 October. https://www.cnet.com/news/youtube-cedes-to-turkey-and-uses-local -web-domain/, accessed 16 June 2017.

Khadem, N. (2015). "Google Paid $11.7M Tax in 2014, but Says 'There's More We Can Do.'" *Sydney Morning Herald*, May 1. http://www.smh.com.au/business/google -paid-117m-tax-in-2014-but-says-theres-more-we-can-do-20150430-1mxbx7. html#ixzz3rcFMTXnX, accessed 16 November 2015.

Khatri, A. (2016). Creator, Atul Khatri, 24 May, interview with Stuart Cunningham and David Craig, India.

Kim, J. (2012). "The Institutionalization of YouTube: From User-Generated Content to Professionally Generated Content." *Media, Culture & Society*, 34(1): 53–67.

King, Z. (2015). Creator, Zach King, 15 July, interview with David Craig, United States.

Kligler-Vilenchik, N. (2016). "Mechanisms of Translation: From Online Participatory Cultures to Participatory Politics." *Journal of Digital and Media Literacy*, 4(1–2). http://www.jodml.org/2016/06/27/mechanisms-of-translation-from-online -participatory-cultures-to-participatory-politics/, accessed 10 May 2017.

Kouvchinov, S. (2015). Sales Executive, Boom Video, 2 March, interview with Stuart Cunningham, Australia.

Kozlowski, L. (2014). "MiTu, a YouTube Network Changing How Latino Content Creators and Audiences Connect." *Forbes*, 27 June. https://www.forbes.com/sites /lorikozlowski/2014/06/27/mitu-a-youtube-network-changing-how-latino-content -creators-and-audiences-connect/, accessed 7 August 2017.

KPMG (2017). *Media for the Masses: The Promise Unfolds*, Media and Entertainment Industry Report. https://assets.kpmg.com/content/dam/kpmg/in/pdf/2017/04 /FICCI-Frames-2017.pdf, accessed 21 August 2017.

Kretschmer, T., and Peukert, C. (2014). "Video Killed the Radio Star? Online Music Videos and Digital Music Sales." *CEP Discussion Papers dp1265*, Centre for Economic Performance, London School of Economics, http://cep.lse.ac.uk/pubs /download/dp1265.pdf, accessed 28 June 2018.

Krieger, J. (2016). "ARD and ZDF Unveil Youth Service 'Funk.'" *Broadband TV News*, 29 September. http://www.broadbandtvnews.com/2016/09/29/ard-zdf-unveil -youth-service-funk/, accessed 19 July 2017.

Kücklich, J. (2005). Precarious Playbour: Modders and the Digital Games Industry." *Fibreculture*, 5. http://five.fibreculturejournal.org/fcj-025-precarious-playbour -modders-and-the-digital-games-industry/, accessed 25 June 2018.

Kuehn, K., and Corrigan, T. (2013). "Hope Labour: The Role of Employment Prospects in Online Social Production." *Political Economy of Communication*, 1(1): 9–25.

Kumar, A. (2016). Founder, Viral Fever, 24 May, interview with Stuart Cunningham and David Craig, India.

Kumar, K. (2015). Creator, Krishna the Kumar, 22 May, interview with Stuart Cunningham and David Craig, United States.

Kumar, S. (2016). "YouTube Nation: Precarity and Agency in India's Online Video Scene." *International Journal of Communication*, 10(2016): 5608–25.

Küng, L. (2008). *Strategic Management in the Media: From Theory to Practice*. Thousand Oaks, CA: Sage.

Küng, L. (2017). *Strategic Management in the Media: From Theory to Practice*, 2nd ed. Thousand Oaks, CA: Sage.

Lamel, J. (2017). Executive Director, Re:Create Coalition, 24 July, interview with David Craig and Stuart Cunningham, United States.

Langston, B. (2016). Creator, Toy Replay, 24 August, interview with Jarrod Walczer, United States.

Lash, S., and Urry, J. (1987). *The End of Organised Capital*. Madison: University of Wisconsin Press.

Lawler, R. (2013). "Maker Studios Co-Founder Danny Zappin Sues the Company over His Ouster." *TechCrunch*, 26 June. https://techcrunch.com/2013/06/26/maker -studios-co-founder-danny-zappin-sues-the-company-over-his-ouster/, accessed 17 July 2017.

Lawson, R. (2015). "Everyone Will Come Out on YouTube Eventually." *Vanity Fair*, June 12. http://www.vanityfair.com/culture/2015/06/youtube-digest-june-12, accessed 24 October 2016.

Le, K. (2016). "Monetization in Livestreaming: 2015 & 2016." *StreamLabs*, 24 January. https://blog.streamlabs.com/monetization-in-livestreaming-2015-2016 -c08835ca2331, accessed 17 July 2017.

Leadbeater, C. (1999). *Living on Thin Air: The New Economy*. London: Penguin.

Lehmann, M. (2015). "Eyes Wide Open: Google Australia's Maile Carnegie." *Weekend Australian*, 27–28 June, 12–16.

Levin, J. (2015). Executive Vice President, Defy Media, 17 April, interview with Stuart Cunningham and David Craig, United States.

Levine, M. (2015). Fanthropologist, ZEFR, 11 May, interview with Stuart Cunningham and David Craig, United States.

Linqia (2017). *The Value of Influencer Content 2017: A Look into How Brands and Agencies Value Influencer Content in 2017*. http://www.linqia.com/wp-content /uploads/2017/04/The-Value-of-Influencer-Content-2017_Final_Report.pdf, accessed 13 July 2017.

Lobato, R. (2016). "The Cultural Logic of Digital Intermediaries: YouTube Multichannel Networks." *Convergence: The International Journal of Research into New Media Technologies*, 22(4): 348–60.

Lobato, R., and Thomas, J. (2015). *The Informal Media Economy*. Cambridge: Polity.

Lopez, L. K. (2014). "Blogging While Angry: The Sustainability of Emotional Labor in the Asian American Blogosphere." *Media, Culture & Society*, 36(4): 421–36.

Lopez, L. K. (2016). *Asian American Media Activism*. New York: NYU Press.

Lotz, A. (2017). *Portals: A Treatise on Internet-Distributed Television*. Ann Arbor: Michigan Publishing, University of Michigan Library.

Lovelock, M. (2016). "'Is Every YouTuber Going to Make a Coming Out Video Eventually?': YouTube Celebrity Video Bloggers and Lesbian and Gay Identity." *Celebrity Studies* 8(1): 1–17.

Lunden, I. (2014). "If WhatsApp Is Worth $19B, Then WeChat's Worth 'At Least $60B' Says CLSA." *TechCrunch*, 11 March. https://techcrunch.com/2014/03/11/if-whatsapp -is-worth-19b-then-wechats-worth-at-least-60b-says-clsa/, accessed 16 June 2017.

Luo, B. (2015). Founder, New Media Rockstars, 11 May, interview with Stuart Cunningham and David Craig, United States.

Madrigal, A. (2014). "How Netflix Reverse Engineered Hollywood." *Atlantic*, 2 January. http://www.theatlantic.com/technology/archive/2014/01/how-netflix-reverse -engineered-hollywood/282679/, accessed 26 March 2017.

Maheshawri, S. (2016). "Endorsed on Instagram by a Kardashian, but Is It Love or Just an Ad?" *New York Times*, 30 August. https://www.nytimes.com/2016/08/30 /business/media/instagram-ads-marketing-kardashian.html, accessed 14 December 2017.

Main, S. (2017). "Micro-Influencers Are More Effective with Marketing Campaigns Than Highly Popular Accounts." *Adweek*, 30 March. http://www.adweek.com /digital/micro-influencers-are-more-effective-with-marketing-campaigns-than -highly-popular-accounts/, accessed 30 March 2017.

Mann, D. (2014). "Welcome to the Unregulated Wild, Wild, Digital West." *Media Industries*, 1(2). http://dx.doi.org/10.3998/mij.15031809.0001.206, accessed 27 April 2018.

Marotta, J. (2015). "After a Billion Views on YouTube, Michelle Phan Shows a New Side of Herself." *Cosmopolitan*, 8 June. http://www.cosmopolitan.com/style-beauty /beauty/a39944/michelle-phan-internets-most-fascinating/, accessed 21 November 2016.

Maroun, L. (2015). Creator, LunaMaroun, 23 March, interview with Stuart Cunningham, Australia.

Marsh, J. (2016). Professor of Education, University of Sheffield, 5 July, interview with Jarrod Walczer, United Kingdom.

Marsh, L. (2015). Vice President Talent, Addition Management, 6 July, interview with Stuart Cunningham and David Craig, United States.

Marshall, P. D. (2009). "New Media as Transformed Media Industry." In *Media Industries: History, Theory, and Method*, edited by J. Holt and A. Perren, 81–89. Malden MA: Wiley-Blackwell.

Marwick, A. (2013). *Status Update: Celebrity, Publicity, and Branding in the Social Media Age*. New Haven, CT: Yale University Press.

Marwick, A., and boyd, d. (2014). "Networked Privacy: How Teenagers Negotiate Context in Social Media." *New Media & Society*, 16(7): 1051–67.

Marzouki, M. E. (2017). "Commerce, Creativity, and Youth Participation on YouTube Morocco." Paper presented at the 67th Annual Conference of the International Communication Association, Interventions: Communication Research and Practice, 25–29 May, San Diego, California.

Mau, D. (2014). "How the Fastest-Rising Beauty Bloggers Found YouTube Success." *Fashionista*, 30 January. http://fashionista.com/2014/01/beauty-vloggers, accessed 21 November 2016.

Mayer, V., Banks, M., and Caldwell, J. (eds.). (2010). *Production Studies: Cultural Studies of Media Industries*. New York: Routledge.

Mayes, J. (2017). "YouTube Hate Videos Haunt Advertisers on Google." *Bloomberg*, 24 March. https://www.bloomberg.com/news/articles/2017-03-23/youtube-hate-videos-snare-ikea-ads-as-google-crisis-spans-europe, accessed 16 December 2017.

McChesney, R., and Schiller, D. (2003). *The Political Economy of International Communication: Foundations for the Emerging Global Debate about Media Ownership and Regulation*. United Nations Research Institute for Social Development, Technology, Business, and Society Program.

McCormick, R. (2016). "PewDiePie and Other YouTubers Took Money from Warner Bros. for Positive Game Reviews." *Verge*, 12 July. https://www.theverge.com/2016/7/12/12157310/pewdiepie-youtubers-sponsored-videos-ftc-warner-bros, accessed 10 May 2017.

McLaughlin, R., and Neal, C. L. (2015). Creators, Rhett & Link, 3 September, interview with David Craig, United States.

McNab, J. (2016). "Netflix Is on F***ing Fire," *Medium*, 3 January. https://medium.com/swlh/netflix-is-on-f-ing-fire-1675d47e722, accessed 4 September 2017.

McNary, D. (2016a). "Minority Coalition Pushes Movie Studios for More Diversity." *Variety*, 4 February. http://variety.com/2016/film/news/oscars-diversity-minority-coalition-movie-studios-1201697518/, accessed 20 July 2017.

McNary, D. (2016b). "Steven Spielberg's Amblin Developing Digital Star Zach King's 'My Magical Life.'" *Variety*, 27 October. http://variety.com/2016/film/news/steven-spielberg-amblin-zach-king-my-magical-life-1201902957/, accessed 24 July 2017.

McRobbie, A. (2002). "Clubs to Companies: Notes on the Decline of Political Culture in Speeded Up Creative Worlds." *Cultural Studies*, 16(4): 517–31.

Meade, A. (2015). "ABC's Mark Scott Calls for New Funding Model to Keep Australian Content Alive." *Guardian*, 15 September. https://www.theguardian.com/media/2015/sep/15/abcs-mark-scott-calls-for-new-funding-model-to-keep-australian-content-alive, accessed 16 June 2017.

Mediakix (2015). "Influencer Marketing to Be a $5–$10 Billion Market within Next 5 Years." *Mediakix*, 21 December. http://mediakix.com/2015/12/influencer-marketing-5-10-billion-dollar-market/#gs.bEQ4mvc, accessed 18 July 2017.

Mediakix (2017). "Instagram Influencer Marketing Is a $1 Billion Dollar Industry." *Medikix*, 5 May. http://mediakix.com/2017/03/instagram-influencer-marketing-industry-size-how-big/#gs.OtSPVhw, accessed 14 December 2017.

"Meeting Future Madam President (ft. Hillary Clinton)." YouTube video, 2:44. Posted by "Tyler Oakley," 7 November 2016. https://www.youtube.com/watch?v=NwY74h3Mujk, accessed 4 September 2017.

Meyer, D. (2015). "'One Day I'm Going to Be Really Successful': The Social Class Politics of Videos Made for the 'It Gets Better' Anti-Gay Bullying Project." *Critical Sociology*, 43(1): 113–27.

Meyer, M. (2015). Cofounder, JASH, 19 May, interview with Stuart Cunningham and David Craig, United States.

Meyer, R. (2015). "The Decay of Twitter." *Atlantic*, 2 November. http://www.theatlantic
.com/technology/archive/2015/11/conversation-smoosh-twitter-decay/412867/,
accessed 26 March 2017.

Micus, A. L. (2016). Programs Strategist, YouTube Space (Germany), 7 October, interview with Stuart Cunningham and David Craig, Germany.

Miller, T. (2006). *Cultural Citizenship: Cosmopolitanism, Consumerism, and Television
in a Neoliberal Age*. Philadelphia: Temple University Press.

Miller, T. (2010). "A Future for Media Studies: Cultural Labour, Cultural Relations,
Cultural Politics." In *How Canadians Communicate*. Volume 3, *Contexts of Cana-
dian Popular Culture*, edited by B. Beaty, D. Briton, G. Filax, and R. Sullivan, 35–53.
Athabasca: Athabasca University Press.

Mills, C. (2016). "Google's Copyright Takedowns Have Grown by a Gazillion Per Cent
in Ten Years." *Gizmodo*, 8 March. https://www.gizmodo.com.au/2016/03/googles
-copyright-takedowns-have-grownby-a-trillion-percent-in-ten-years/, accessed 21
August 2017.

Miltner, K., and Highfield, T. (2017). "Never Gonna GIF You Up: Analyzing the
Cultural Significance of the Animated GIF." *Social Media + Society*, 3(3): https://doi
.org/10.1177/2056305117725223.

"Minecraft Multiplayer Fun." YouTube video, 2:03. Posted by "PewDiePie," 2 October
2010. https://www.youtube.com/watch?v=9jeJbdVl2jI, accessed 7 November 2016.

Mittal, A. (2016). Creator, Aditi Mittal, 24 May, interview with Stuart Cunningham and
David Craig, India.

Mittell, J. (2015). *Complex TV: The Politics of Contemporary Television Storytelling*. New
York: NYU Press.

Mittell, J. (2016). "Why Netflix Doesn't Release Its Ratings." *Atlantic*, 23 February.
http://www.theatlantic.com/entertainment/archive/2016/02/netflix-ratings/462447/,
accessed 26 March 2017.

Moe, H., Poell, T., and van Djick, J. (2016). "Rearticulating Audience Engagement."
Television & New Media, 17(2): 99–107.

Moraes, L. (2015). "'Fresh off the Boat' Creator Eddie Huang Continues to Trash His
ABC Show." *Deadline Hollywood*, 8 April. http://deadline.com/2015/04/eddie-huang
-fresh-off-the-boat-tweets-1201406604/, accessed 24 July 2017.

Morrison, K. (2015). "Snapchat Is the Fastest Growing Social Network." *Social Times*,
July 28. http://www.adweek.com/socialtimes/snapchat-is-the-fastest-growing-social
-network-infographic/624116, accessed 16 June 2017.

Moses, L. (2017). "Publishers Are Switching Affections from Snapchat to Instagram."
Digiday, 14 July. https://digiday.com/media/publishers-switching-affections
-snapchat-instagram/, accessed 24 August 2017.

Mozur, P. (2016). "China, Not Silicon Valley, Is Cutting Edge in Mobile Tech." *New York
Times*, 2 August. http://www.nytimes.com/2016/08/03/technology/china-mobile
-tech-innovation-silicon-valley.html, accessed 16 June 2017.

Mueller, M. (2015). "Hyper-transparency and Social Control: Social Media as Magnets
for Regulation." *Telecommunications Policy*, 39(9): 804–10.

Mukherjee, R., and Banet-Weiser, S. (2012). *Commodity Activism: Cultural Resistance in Neoliberal Times*. New York: NYU Press.

"My Thoughts on Bruce Jenner." YouTube video, 3:16. Posted by "Gigi Gorgeous," 24 April 2015. https://youtu.be/YSmBKqhqXUE, accessed 7 November 2016.

Nagy, P., and Neff, G. (2015). "Imagined Affordance: Reconstructing a Keyword for Communication Theory." *Media + Society*, 1(2): 1–9.

Napoli, P., and Caplan, R. (2017). "Why Media Companies Insist They're Not Media Companies, Why They're Wrong, and Why It Matters." *First Monday*, 22(5). http://firstmonday.org/ojs/index.php/fm/article/view/7051/6124.

"Natural Looking Makeup Tutorial." YouTube video, 7:09. Posted by "Michelle Phan," 20 May 2007. https://www.youtube.com/watch?v=OB8nfJCOIeE, accessed 26 November 2016.

Neff, G. (2012). *Venture Labour: Work and the Burden of Risk in Innovative Industries*. Cambridge, MA: MIT Press.

Neff, G., Wissinger, E., and Zukin, S. (2005). "Entrepreneurial Labor among Cultural Producers: 'Cool' Jobs in 'Hot' Industries." *Social Semiotics*, 15(3): 307–34.

Neidell, I. (2016). Lead Writer, Mediakraft Networks (The Great War), 6 October, interview with Stuart Cunningham and David Craig, Germany.

Newcomb, H., and Alley, R. (1983). *The Producer's Medium: Conversations with Creators of American TV*. Oxford: Oxford University Press.

Newcomb, H., and Hirsch, P. (1983). "Television as a Cultural Forum: Implications for Research." *Quarterly Review of Film & Video*, 8(3): 45–55.

Newton, C. (2016a). "Is Twitter Doomed?" *Verge*, 26 January. http://www.theverge.com/2016/1/26/10833024/is-twitter-doomed, accessed 26 March 2017.

Newton, C. (2016b). "Why Vine Died." *Verge*, 28 October. https://www.theverge.com/2016/10/28/13456208/why-vine-died-twitter-shutdown, accessed 24 August 2017.

NextShark.com (2016). "Girls in China Are Making up to $20,000 a Month Live Streaming Their Lives Online." *Nextshark.com*, 27 July. https://nextshark.com/china-live-streaming-cam-girls/, accessed 3 August 2017.

Nilsen, I. (2015). Creator, IngridNilsen, 23 September, interview with David Craig, United States.

Nordenstreng, K., and Varis, T. (1974). "Television Traffic: A One-Way Street." *UNESCO Reports and Papers on Mass Communication No. 70*, UNESCO, Paris.

O'Connor, C. (2017). "Forbes Top Influencers: Meet the 30 Social Media Stars of Fashion, Parenting, and Pets (Yes, Pets)." *Forbes*, 26 September. https://www.forbes.com/sites/clareoconnor/2017/09/26/forbes-top-influencers-fashion-pets-parenting/#647fced27683, accessed 16 December 2017.

O'Neil-Hart, C., and Blumenstein, H. (2016). "Why YouTube Stars Are More Influential Than Traditional Celebrities." *thinkwithgoogle.com*, July. https://www.thinkwithgoogle.com/infographics/youtube-stars-influence.html, accessed 16 July 2017.

O'Reilly, L. (2015). "Google Just Told Advertisers That If They Want to Reach Young People YouTube Will Need to Take 24% of Their TV Budgets." *Business Insider*,

14 October. http://www.businessinsider.com/at-brandcast-google-tells-advertisers
-to-shift-tv-money-to-video-youtube-2015-10, accessed 26 March 2017.

"Orlando Shooting." YouTube video, 1:58. Posted by "Gigi Gorgeous," 12 June 2016. https://youtu.be/9HUvzqNknD8, accessed 7 November 2016.

Palazzolo, M. (2015). Writer and Producer, Bloomers, 16 May, interview with Stuart Cunningham and David Craig, United States.

Papacharissi, Z. (2015). *Affective Publics: Sentiment, Technology, and Politics*. Oxford: Oxford University Press.

Parker, G., Alstyne, M., and Choudary, S. (2016). *Platform Revolution: How Networked Markets Are Transforming the Economy—and How to Make Them Work for You*. New York: Norton.

Parlock, J. (2017). "YouTube Has 'No Idea' Why Queer Gaming Videos Are Being Barred from Monetisation." *Let's Play Video Games*, 18 September. http://letsplay videogames.com/2017/09/youtube-has-no-idea-why-queer-gaming-videos-are -being-barred-from-monetisation/, accessed 16 December 2017.

Patel, S. (2017). "Inside Disney's troubled $675 Mil. Maker Studios Acquisition." *Digiday*, 22 February. https://digiday.com/media/disney-maker-studios/, accessed 23 February 2017.

Pathak, S. (2017). "Brands Are Using Influencers like Ad Agencies." *Digiday*, 24 May. https://digiday.com/marketing/brands-using-influencers-like-ad-agencies/, accessed 24 May 2017.

"Peanut Butter Face (while discussing the Georgia-Russia War)." YouTube video, 3:58. Posted by "vlogbrothers," 12 August 2008. https://youtu.be/v_p3hLtr5Ok, accessed 5 July 2017.

Perez, S. (2016a). "YouTube Expands Creator Outreach with New Features, Better Support." *TechCrunch*, 24 June. https://techcrunch.com/2016/06/24/youtube -expands-creator-outreach-with-new-features-better-support/, accessed 26 March 2017.

Perez, S. (2016b). "YouTube Gets Its Own Social Network with the Launch of YouTube Community." *TechCrunch*, 13 September. https://techcrunch.com/2016/09/13 /youtube-gets-its-own-social-network-with-the-launch-of-youtube-community/, accessed 26 March 2017.

Perrin, A., and Duggan, M. (2015). "Americans' Internet Access: 2000–2015: As Internet Use Nears Saturation for Some Groups, a Look at Patterns of Adoption." *Pew Research Center*, 26 June. http://www.pewinternet.org/2015/06/26/americans -internet-access-2000-2015/, accessed 27 June 2016.

Pew Research Center (2013). "The Rise of Asian Americans." *Pew Research Center*. http://www.pewsocialtrends.org/2012/06/19/the-rise-of-asian-americans/, accessed 24 July 2017.

PewDiePie (2012). "No More Rape Jokes." *PewDiePie*, 25 October. http://pewdie.tumblr .com/post/34309686617/no-more-rape-jokes, accessed 5 July 2017.

PewDiePie (2015). "Nintendo 'Sharing' YouTube Ad Revenue." *PewDiePie*, 30 January. http://pewdie.tumblr.com/post/109571543425/nintendo-sharing-youtube-ad -revenue, accessed 5 July 2017.

PewDiePie (2017). "Just to Clear Some Things Up . . ." *PewDiePie*, 12 February. http://pewdie.tumblr.com/post/157160889655/just-to-clear-some-things-up, accessed 5 July 2017.

Phillips, T. (2016). "Gone Bananas: China Bans 'Erotic' Eating of the Fruit on Live Streams." *Guardian*, 9 May. https://www.theguardian.com/world/2016/may/09/gone-bananas-china-bans-erotic-eating-live-streams, accessed 3 August 2017.

Pinder, J. (2015). Creator, SimpleCookingChannel, 23 March, interview with Stuart Cunningham, Australia.

Pittman, T. (2015). "How YouTubers Became a New Breed of Celebrity That Hollywood Stars Can't Touch." *Huffington Post*, 3 March. http://www.huffingtonpost.com.au/entry/teens-prefer-youtubers-over-celebrities_n_6801792.html?section=australia, accessed 30 January 2017.

Podell, L. (2016). Global Head Studios, YouTube, 8 February, interview with Stuart Cunningham and David Craig, United States.

Poggi, J. (2016). "CMO's Guide to Live Video." *Advertising Age*, 18 July. http://adage.com/article/media/cmo-s-guide-live-video/304978/, accessed 3 August 2017.

Poggi, J. (2017). "Digital Advertising Tops TV in the U.S. for the First Time." *Advertising Age*, 29 March. http://adage.com/article/advertising/magna-u-s-digital-ad-sales-top-tv-time-2016/308468/, accessed 31 August 2017.

Ponse, B. (1978). *Identities in the Lesbian World: The Social Construction of Self*. Westport, CT: Greenwood.

Popper, B. (2017). "YouTube Will No Longer Allow Creators to Make Money until They Reach 10,000 Views." *Verge*, 6 April. https://www.theverge.com/2017/4/6/15209220/youtube-partner-program-rule-change-monetize-ads-10000-views, accessed 7 April 2017.

Postigo, H. (2009). "America Online Volunteers: Lessons from an Early Co-production Community." *International Journal of Cultural Studies*, 12(5): 451–69.

Postigo, H. (2014). "Playing for Work Independence as Promise in Gameplay Commentary on YouTube." In *Media Independence: Working with Freedom or Working for Free?* edited by J. Bennett and N. Strange, 202–22. New York: Routledge.

Postigo, H. (2016). "The Socio-technical Architecture of Digital Labor: Converting Play into YouTube Money." *New Media & Society*, 18(2): 332–49.

PRWeb (2012). "Michelle Phan Launches FAWN (For All Women Network)." *PRWeb*, 4 April. http://www.prweb.com/releases/youtube/fawn/prweb9368622.htm, accessed 15 May 2017.

Rao, L. (2016). "YouTube CEO Says There's 'No Timetable' for Profitability." *Fortune*, 19 October. http://fortune.com/2016/10/18/youtube-profits-ceo-susan-wojcicki/, accessed 24 August 2017.

Raun, T. (2016). *Out Online: Trans Self-Representation and Community Building on YouTube (Gender, Bodies, and Transformation)*. New York: Routledge.

Ravi, A. (2016). Director and Cofounder, NH7, 23 May, interview with Stuart Cunningham and David Craig, India.

"Reacting to Old Videos (45 Mil Subs) (Fridays with PewDiePie—Part 118)." YouTube video, 9:08. Posted by "PewDiePie," 18 June 2016. https://www.youtube.com/watch?v=dtAuAu3nI_0, accessed 5 July 2017.

Re-Create Coalition (2017). "Re-Create Coalition Letter to 115th Congress and White House: Supporting a Pro-Innovation, Pro-Creator, Pro-Consumer Copyright Agenda." Re-Create Coalition Blog, 3 April. http://www.recreatecoalition.org/recreate-coalition-letter-115th-congress-supporting-pro-innovation-pro-creator-pro-consumer-copyright-agenda/, accessed 3 August 2017.

Reddit.com (2015). "I Miss the Old PewDiePie." Reddit.com—PewDiePie, 2 March. https://www.reddit.com/r/pewdiepie/comments/2xn6tp/i_miss_the_old_pewdiepie/, accessed 4 July 2017.

Rivera, B. (2015). Vine creator (Mr Rivera), 3 September, e-mail interview with David Craig, United States.

Robehmed, N. (2015). "How Michelle Phan Built a $500 Million Company." Forbes, 5 October. https://www.forbes.com/sites/natalierobehmed/2015/10/05/how-michelle-phan-built-a-500-million-company/#77050fe8c4a, accessed 15 May 2017.

Robertson, M. (2015). "500 Hours of Video Uploaded to YouTube Every Minute [Forecast]." http://tubularinsights.com/hours-minute-uploaded-youtube/, accessed 10 July 2017.

Robinson, J. (2015). Chief Technology Officer, Awesomeness, 17 April, interview with Stuart Cunningham and David Craig, United States.

Roettgers, J. (2017). "Disney's Maker Studios Drops PewDiePie Because of Anti-Semitic Videos." Variety, 13 February. http://variety.com/2017/digital/news/disney-pewdiepie-anti-semitic-videos-1201987380/, accessed 14 February 2017.

Romer, C. (2015). "Big Exposure." Arts Professional, 18 June. https://www.artsprofessional.co.uk/magazine/285/article/big-exposure, accessed 18 July 2017.

Ross, A. (2002). No-Collar: The Humane Workplace and Its Hidden Costs. New York: Basic Books.

Ross, A. (2007). Fast Boat to China: Corporate Flight and the Consequences of Free Trade; Lessons from Shanghai. New York: Vintage.

Ross, A. (2009). Nice Work If You Can Get It: Life and Labor in Precarious Times. New York: NYU Press.

Rossiter, N. (2007). Organized Networks: Media Theory, Creative Labour, New Institutions. Rotterdam: NAi Publishers.

Roussel, V. (2015). "'It's Not the Network, It's the Relationship': The Relational Work of Hollywood Talent Agents." In Brokerage and Production in the American and French Entertainment Industries: Invisible Hands in Cultural Markets, edited by V. Roussel and D. Bielby, 103–22. London: Lexington Books.

Roussel, V. (2016). "Talent Agenting in the Age of Conglomerates." In Precarious Creativity: Global Media, Local Labor, edited by M. Curtin and K. Sanson, 74–87. Berkeley: University of California Press.

Roussel, V., and Bielby, D. (eds.). (2015). Brokerage and Production in the American and French Entertainment Industries: Invisible Hands in Cultural Markets. London: Lexington Books.

Rushe, D. (2011). "Myspace Sold for $35M in Spectacular Fall from $12B Heyday." *Guardian*, 30 June. https://www.theguardian.com/technology/2011/jun/30/myspace -sold-35-million-news, accessed 24 August 2017.

Russell, J. (2017). "Cheetah Mobile's Live.me Streaming Service Raises $60M from Chinese Investors." *TechCrunch*, 2 May. https://techcrunch.com/2017/05/02/cheetah -mobile-live-me-60-million/, accessed 3 August 2017.

Russo, V. (1987). *The Celluloid Closet: Homosexuality in the Movies*. 2nd ed. New York: HarperCollins.

Rutenberg, J. (2017). "News Outlets to Seek Bargaining Rights against Google and Facebook." *New York Times*, 9 July. https://www.nytimes.com/2017/07/09/business /media/google-facebook-news-media-alliance.html, accessed 10 July 2017.

Ryzik, M. (2016). "Chris Rock's Asian Joke at Oscars Provokes Backlash." *New York Times*, 29 February. http://www.nytimes.com/2016/03/01/movies/chris-rocks-asian -joke-at-oscars-provokes-backlash.html?_r=0, accessed 29 February 2017.

Sambath, V. (2015). Business Development, Social Edge, 16 April, interview with Stuart Cunningham and David Craig, United States.

Samuelson, K. (2014). "25 Vloggers under 25 Who Are Owning YouTube." *Huffington Post*, 26 October. http://www.huffingtonpost.co.uk/2014/12/17/25-vloggers -under-25-who-are-owning-the-world-of-youtube_n_6340280.html, accessed 27 December 2016.

Sanchez, R. (2015). Former Vice President Production, Machinima, 11 April, interview with Stuart Cunningham, New Zealand.

Scholz, T. (2008). "Market Ideology and the Myths of Web 2.0." *First Monday*, 13(3). http://firstmonday.org/article/view/2138/1945, accessed 13 July 2017.

Scholz, T. (ed.). (2013). *Digital Labour: The Internet as Playground and Factory*. New York: Routledge.

Schumpeter, J. A. (1975 [1942]). *Capitalism, Socialism, and Democracy*. New York: Harper Perennial.

Scolari, C., and Fraticelli, D. (2017). "The Case of the Top Spanish YouTubers: Emerging Media Subjects and Discourse Practices in the New Media Ecology." *Convergence: The International Journal of Research into New Media Technologies*, 10.1177/1354856517721807.

Scutt, D. (2014). "The Growth of China's Mobile Use Is Mind-Blowing." *Business Insider Australia*, July 24. https://www.businessinsider.com.au/china-mobile-growth -2015-7, accessed 16 June 2017.

Seetharaman, D., and Perlberg, S. (2016). "Facebook to Pay Internet Stars for Live Video." *Wall Street Journal*, 19 July. https://www.wsj.com/articles/facebook-to-pay -internet-stars-for-live-video-1468920602, accessed 18 July 2017.

Sender, K. (2011). "No Hard Feelings: Reflexivity and Queer Affect in the New Media Landscape." In *The Handbook of Gender, Sex, and Media*, edited by K. Ross, 207–25. Oxford: Wiley-Blackwell.

Senft, T. (2008). *Camgirls: Celebrity and Community in the Age of Social Networks*. New York: Peter Lang.

Shao, B. (2016). Vice President Corporate Strategies and PGC Operation, Youku, 31 May, interview with David Craig, China.

Shaughnessy, H. (2011). "Who Are the Top 10 Influencers in Social Media?" *Forbes*, 2 December. https://www.forbes.com/sites/haydnshaughnessy/2011/12/02/who-are -the-top-10-influencers-in-social-media/#754d98f260b7, accessed 16 December 2017.

Sherman, L. (2013). "Want to Make $5 Million a Year? Become a Beauty Vlogger." *Cosmopolitan*, 22 November. http://www.cosmopolitan.com/style-beauty/beauty /how-to/a16610/beauty-vloggers/, accessed 15 May 2017.

Shifman, L. (2013). *Memes in Digital Culture*. Cambridge, MA: MIT Press.

Shinal, J. (2017a). "Meet the Man Who Helped Facebook Bring Snapchat to Its Knees." *CNBC*, 15 July. https://www.cnbc.com/2017/07/15/instagram-kevin-weil-helped -facebook-beat-snapchat.html, accessed 24 August 2017.

Shinal, J. (2017b). "Facebook Plans to Launch Its Own TV-Like Shows in June, Says Report." *CNBC*, 5 May. https://www.cnbc.com/2017/05/05/facebook-plans-to -launch-its-own-tv-shows-in-june-says-report.html, accessed 24 August 2017.

Siegel, T. (2016). "Sundance: How Amazon, Netflix turned the Market on Its Head." *Hollywood Reporter*, 27 January. http://www.hollywoodreporter.com/news /sundance-how-amazon-netflix-turned-859372, accessed 27 January 2016.

Siegismund, F. (2016). Creator, Battle Bros, 6 October, interview with Stuart Cunning- ham and David Craig, Germany.

Silver, C. (2017). "Facebook Watch Is Here to Quench Our Undying Thirst for Online Video Content." *Forbes*, 11 August. https://www.forbes.com/sites/curtissilver /2017/08/11/facebook-watch-online-video-content, accessed 17 August 2017.

Simpson, A. (2011). "X-Rated Ethics: Socially Sustainable Sex Could Save the Economy, the Environment, and Our Society." *Utne Reader*, September. http://www.utne.com /mind-and-body/sustainable-sex-industry-corporate-social-responsibility, accessed 3 August 2017.

Sinclair, J., Jacka, E., and Cunningham, S. (eds.). (1996). *New Patterns in Global Televi- sion: Peripheral Vision*. London: Oxford University Press.

Slefo, G. (2017). "Desktop and Mobile Ad Revenue Surpasses TV for the First Time." *Advertising Age*, 26 April. http://adage.com/article/digital/digital-ad-revenue -surpasses-tv-desktop-iab/308808/, accessed 31 August 2017.

Sloan, G. (2016). "Facebook's Using Its Muscle to Remake the Ad Tech World." *Digiday*, 31 May. http://digiday.com/platforms/facebooks-using-muscle-remake-ad-tech/, accessed 16 June 2017.

Smith, S., Choueiti, M., and Piper, K. (2016). "Inclusion or Invisibility? Comprehen- sive Annenberg Report on Diversity in Entertainment." University of Southern California. http://annenberg.usc.edu/pages/~/media/MDSCI/CARDReport%20 FINAL%2022216.ashx, accessed 20 July 2017.

Snell, T. (2017). "The #Adpocalypse Is Here to Stay." *Tubefilter*, 11 May. http://www .tubefilter.com/2017/05/11/the-adpocalypse-is-here-to-stay/, accessed 11 May 2017.

Social Blade (2017). "Broadband TV." *Social Blade*. https://socialblade.com/youtube /network/broadbandtv, accessed 18 July 2017.

Solomon, F. (2017). "YouTube Could Be About to Overtake TV as America's Most Watched Platform." *Fortune*, 28 February. http://fortune.com/2017/02/28/youtube -1-billion-hours-television/, accessed 14 December 2017.

Somaney, J. (2016). "2015 Was a Year to Forget from Every Aspect for Tim Cook and Apple." *Forbes*, 3 January. https://www.forbes.com/sites/jaysomaney/2016/01/03/2015 -was-a-year-to-forget-from-every-aspect-for-tim-cook-and-apple/, accessed 26 March 2017.

"Something I Want You to Know." YouTube video, 19:12. Posted by "Ingrid Nilsen," 9 June 2015. https://www.youtube.com/watch?v=Eh7WRYXVh9M, accessed 9 June 2015.

Soo, Z. (2016). "Meet the Chinese Live-Streaming App Live.me That's Taking the US by Storm." *South China Morning Post*, 23 November. http://www.scmp.com/tech /enterprises/article/2048354/cheetah-mobiles-live-streaming-app-liveme-showed -us-users-will, accessed 3 August 2017.

Spangler, T. (2014a). "Facebook Adds YouTube-Like Video Features, as It Tops 1 Billion Daily Views." *Variety*, 7 September. http://variety.com/2014/digital/news/facebook -expands-video-features-now-tops-1-billion-views-daily-exclusive-1201300064/, accessed 26 March 2017.

Spangler, T. (2014b). "Zefr Buys Social-Marketing Startup Engodo to Expand beyond YouTube." *Variety*, 24 September. http://variety.com/2014/digital/news/zefr-buys -social-marketing-startup-engodo-to-expand-beyond-youtube-1201312727/, accessed 18 July 2017.

Spangler, T. (2016a). "Amazon Takes on YouTube and Others, Opening Video Platform to All Creators." *Variety*, 10 May. http://variety.com/2016/digital/news/amazon -video-direct-youtube-creators-1201770058/, accessed 26 March 2017.

Spangler, T. (2016b). "Tyler Oakley Talk Show Launches on Ellen DeGeneres' Digital Network." *Variety*, 21 September. http://variety.com/2016/digital/news/tyler-oakley -talk-show-ellen-degeneres-1201866708/, accessed 21 September 2016.

Spangler, T. (2016c). "Warner Bros. Settles FTC Charges over Payments to PewDiePie, Other Influencers to Promote Game." *Variety*, 11 July. http://variety.com/2016 /digital/games/warner-bros-pewdiepie-ftc-1201811908/, accessed 10 May 2017.

Spangler, T. (2016d). "PewDiePie Responds to Warner Bros. Pay-for-Play 'Scandal': 'It's Kind of Bulls—.'" *Variety*, 13 July. http://variety.com/2016/digital/news/pewdiepie -warner-bros-video-game-scandal-response-1201813386/, accessed 10 May 2017.

Spangler, T. (2016e). "Musical.ly's Live.ly Is Now Bigger Than Twitter's Periscope on iOS (Study)." *Variety*, 30 September. http://variety.com/2016/digital/news/musically -lively-bigger-than-periscope-1201875105/, accessed 3 August 2017.

Spangler, T. (2017). "Disney's Maker Studios Set for Round of Big Layoffs." *Variety*, 15 February. http://variety.com/2017/digital/news/maker-2017-layoffs -disney-1201989473/, accessed 17 July 2017.

Spector, L. (2015). "How Social Authenticity Creates Community and Customers." *Linkedin*, 29 May. https://www.linkedin.com/pulse/show-tell-how-social-authenticity-creates-community-leah-spector, accessed 5 July 2017.

Srauy, S. (2015). "The Limits of Social Media: What Social Media Can Be, and What We Should Hope They Never Become." *Social Media + Society*, 1(1): 1–3.

Srnicek, N. (2016). *Platform Capitalism*. Oxford: Polity.

Stein, A. (1997). *Sex and Sensibility: Stories of a Lesbian Generation*. Berkeley: University of California Press.

Stellar, T. (2016). Producer, Mediakraft Networks (*The Great War*), 6 October, interview with Stuart Cunningham and David Craig, Germany.

Stern, A. (2017). "In 2017, Every Brand Needs to Have an Influencer Strategy." *Tubular Insights*, 31 May. http://tubularinsights.com/influencer-strategy/, accessed 13 July 2017.

Strangler, D., and Arbesman, S. (2012). "What Does Fortune 500 Turnover Mean?" *Ewing Marion Kauffman Foundation*, June 17. http://www.kauffman.org/what-we-do/research/2012/06/what-does-fortune-500-turnover-mean, accessed 26 March 2017.

Straubhaar, J. (2007). *World Television: From Global to Local*. Thousand Oaks, CA: Sage.

Streeter, T. (1996). *Selling the Air: A Critique of the Policy of Commercial Broadcasting in the United States*. Chicago: University of Chicago Press.

Streeter, T. (2011). *The Net Effect: Romanticism, Capitalism, and the Internet*. New York: NYU Press.

Sun, R., and Ford, R. (2016). "Where Are the Asian-American Movie Stars?" *Hollywood Reporter*, 9 May. http://www.hollywoodreporter.com/features/are-asian-american-movie-stars-890755, accessed 15 June 2017.

Swant, M. (2016). "As Social Platforms and Brands Turn to Live Video, Will Viewers Keep Tuning In?" *Adweek*, 4 December. http://www.adweek.com/digital/social-platforms-and-brands-turn-live-video-will-viewers-keep-tuning-174876/, accessed 3 August 2017.

"Take Your Pants Off! (Update Vlog)." YouTube video, 5:01. Posted by "PewDiePie," 3 March 2014. https://www.youtube.com/watch?v=kCjboXbqiLE, accessed 4 July 2017.

Talavera, M. (2015). "Making the Market for Influencer Marketing." *Adweek*, 19 May. http://www.adweek.com/digital/making-the-market-for-influencer-marketing/, accessed 13 July 2017.

Taplin, J. (2017). *Move Fast and Break Things: How Facebook, Google, and Amazon Cornered Culture and Undermined Democracy*. Boston: Little, Brown.

Tartaglione, N. (2017). "TF1, Mediaset Take Stakes in ProSieben's Studio71 with 53M Euro Investment." *Deadline|Hollywood*, 12 January. http://deadline.com/2017/01/tf1-mediaset-investment-53-million-euros-studio71-1201883942/, accessed 3 September 2017.

Tassi, P. (2013). "Google Plus Creates Uproar over Forced YouTube Integration." *Forbes*, 9 November. https://www.forbes.com/sites/insertcoin/2013/11/09/google-plus-creates-uproar-over-forced-youtube-integration, accessed 24 August 2017.

Tassi, P. (2014). "YouTube's PewDiePie Details Machinima's Disinterest, May Create His Own Video Network." *Forbes,* 5 October. https://www.forbes.com/sites/insertcoin/2014/10/05/youtubes-pewdiepie-details-machinimas-disinterest-may-create-his-own-video-network/#2ea7c21b4079, accessed 18 July 2017.

Tate, R. (2014). "Disney's $1B YouTube Channel Investment Is the Future of TV." *Wired,* 1 April. https://www.wired.com/2014/04/disney-maker-studios/, accessed 17 July 2017.

Taylor, A. (2015). Chief Executive Officer, DanceOn, 12 May, interview with Stuart Cunningham and David Craig, United States.

Terranova, T. (2004). *Network Culture: Politics for the Information Age.* London: Pluto Press.

The Economist (2016). "Live Streaming: Amateur's Hour." *Economist,* 11 April. https://www.economist.com/news/business/21704850-amateurs-hour, accessed 3 August 2017.

The Hollywood Reporter (2014). "Silicon Beach Power 25: A Ranking of L.A.'s Top Digital Media Players." *Hollywood Reporter,* 28 May. http://www.hollywoodreporter.com/person/ynon-kreiz, accessed 18 July 2017.

"The PewDiePie 'Scandal'!!" YouTube video, 5:16. Posted by "PewDiePie," 13 July 2016. https://www.youtube.com/watch?v=9JqJDRkKlt8, accessed 14 July 2016.

"The YouTube Heroes!" YouTube video, 4:12. Posted by "PewDiePie," 24 September 2016. https://www.youtube.com/watch?v=OkcdKKVuLg4, accessed 13 January 2017.

Thompson, K. (1985). *Exporting Entertainment: America in the World Film Market, 1907–1934.* London: British Film Institute.

Toffler, A. (1980). *The Third Wave: The Classic Study of Tomorrow.* New York: Bantam.

Tomlinson, J. (1999). *Globalization and Culture.* Chicago: University of Chicago Press.

Topolsky, J. (2016). "The End of Twitter." *New Yorker,* 29 January. http://www.newyorker.com/tech/elements/the-end-of-twitter, accessed 26 March 2017.

Tracey, M. (1988). "Popular Culture and the Economics of Global Television." *Intermedia,* 16(2): 19–25.

Tsoi, G. (2016). "Wang Hong: China's Online Stars Making Real Cash." *BBC News,* 1 August. http://www.bbc.com/news/world-asia-china-36802769, accessed 17 July 2017.

Tully, S. (2017). "How Snapchat's IPO Became One of Wall Street's Biggest Flops." *Fortune,* 21 March, http://fortune.com/2017/03/21/snapchat-snap-ipo-wall-street/, accessed 24 August 2017.

"Twins Come Out to Dad." YouTube video, 8:36. Posted by "The Rhodes Bros," 14 January 2015. https://www.youtube.com/watch?v=L3KoCJ8usPU, accessed 24 October 2016.

Ullman, S. (2015). Founder and Creator, the Jungle, 16 December, interview with Stuart Cunningham, United States.

"Underneath Your Love." YouTube video, 22:24. Posted by "Michelle Phan," 12 January 2012. https://www.youtube.com/watch?v=nDtcsooJq40, accessed 5 July 2017.

Vaidhyanathan, S. (2012). *The Googlization of Everything (and Why We Should Worry).* Berkeley: University of California Press.

van Dijck, J. (2013). *The Culture of Connectivity: A Critical History of Social Media*. New York: Oxford University Press.

van Dijck, J., and Poell, T. (2013). "Understanding Social Media Logic." *Media and Communication*, 1(1): 2–14.

Vardhan, J. (2015). "The Startups behind the Ultimate Rise of Multi-channel Networks (MCN)." *Your Story*, 16 February. https://yourstory.com/2015/02/rise-of-multi-channel-networks-mcn, accessed 18 July 2017.

Varley, S. (2016). "Did Casey Neistat Just Commit the Ultimate YouTube Sin?" *BBC*, 5 December. http://www.bbc.co.uk/bbcthree/item/24f75660-01bb-45b6-8e67-98115115bc57, accessed 4 September 2017.

VAST Media (2014). "34 Multi-channel Networks That Matter—Exclusive VAST MEDIA White Paper." *MIP Blog*, March 17. http://blog.mipworld.com/2014/03/34-multi-channel-networks-that-matter---vast-media-exclusive-white-paper/#.U3FU2hYRCik, accessed 4 August 2015.

Vaynerchuk, G. (2016). "The Snap Generation: A Guide to Snapchat's History." *Gary Vaynerchuk*, 28 January. https://www.garyvaynerchuk.com/the-snap-generation-a-guide-to-snapchats-history/, accessed 26 March 2017.

Venzo, P., and Hess, K. (2013). "'Honk against Homophobia': Rethinking Relations between Media and Sexual Minorities." *Journal of Homosexuality*, 60(11): 1539–56.

Verhoeven, D. (2014). "Film, Video, DVD, and Online Delivery." In *The Media and Communications in Australia*, 4th ed, edited by S. Cunningham and S. Turnbull, 151–71. Crows Nest, NSW: Allen & Unwin.

Vonderau, P. (2016). "The Video Bubble: Multichannel Networks and the Transformation of YouTube." *Convergence: The International Journal of Research into New Media Technologies*, 22(4): 361–75.

Voss, B. (2017). "YouTube's Restricted Mode Is Blocking LGBT Content." *NewNowNext*, 19 March. http://www.newnownext.com/youtube-is-blocking-lgbt-videos-in-restricted-mode/03/2017/, accessed 16 December 2017.

Vossen, R., and Osteroth, R. (2016). Senior Manager of Business Development and Senior Vice President of Sales and Marketing, Studio 71 GmbH, 4 October, interview with Stuart Cunningham and David Craig, Germany.

Votta, R. (2015). "The Definitive Guide to YouTube Stars with Book Deals." *Daily Dot*, 13 April. https://www.dailydot.com/upstream/youtube-celebrity-book-deals/, accessed 17 July 2017.

Vranica, S., and Marshall, J. (2016). "Facebook Overestimated Key Video Metric for Two Years." *Wall Street Journal*, 22 September. https://www.wsj.com/articles/facebook-overestimated-key-video-metric-for-two-years-1474586951, accessed 24 August 2017.

Wagner, K. (2016a). "Meerkat Is Ditching the Livestream—and Chasing a Video Social Network Instead." *Recode*, 4 March. https://www.recode.net/2016/3/4/11586696/meerkat-is-ditching-the-livestream-and-chasing-a-video-social-network, accessed 3 August 2017.

Wagner, K. (2016b). "Mark Zuckerberg Is 'Obsessed' with Livestreaming, Making Live a Top Priority at Facebook." *Recode*, 26 February. https://www.recode.net/2016/2/26/11588264/mark-zuckerberg-is-obsessed-with-livestreaming-making-live-a-top, accessed 3 August 2017.

Wagner, K. (2017). "Here's Why Facebook's $1 Billion Instagram Acquisition Was Such a Great Deal." *Recode*, 9 April. https://www.recode.net/2017/4/9/15235940/facebook-instagram-acquisition-anniversary, accessed 15 December 2017.

Wallenstein, A. (2017). "YouTube Unveils New Streaming Features at Vidcon." *Variety*, 22 June. http://variety.com/2017/digital/news/youtube-unveils-new-streaming-features-at-vidcon-1202476251/, accessed 24 August 2017.

Wang, P. (2015). Partner, Wong Fu Productions, 12 June, interview with David Craig, United States.

Wang, Y. (2017). "Chinese Regulator Calls Homosexuality 'Abnormal' and Bans Gay Content from the Internet." *Fortune*, 1 July. http://fortune.com/2017/06/30/china-homosexuality-internet-weibo-censorship/, accessed 3 August 2017.

Weinstein, B. (2015). Agent, UTA Digital, 13 May, interview with Stuart Cunningham and David Craig, United States.

Weintraub, L. (2015). Chief Innovation Officer, Fanscape, 28 April, interview with Stuart Cunningham and David Craig, United States.

Weiss, E. (2015). Executive Vice President Strategic Alliances, Collective Digital Studios, 19 May, interview with Stuart Cunningham and David Craig, United States.

Weiss, G. (2016a). "Warner Bros. Has Agreed to Acquire Gamer Video Network Machinima." *Tubefilter*, 17 November. http://www.tubefilter.com/2016/11/17/warner-bros-acquires-gamer-network-machinima/, accessed 18 July 2017.

Weiss, G. (2016b). "YouTube Announces 'Breakneck Growth' in India, Slate of New Shows from Local Content Partners." *Tubefilter*, 17 March. http://www.tubefilter.com/2016/03/17/youtube-announces-breakneck-growth-in-india-slate-of-new-shows-from-local-content-partners/, accessed 16 June 2017.

Weiss, G. (2016c). "Hannah Hart to Be Honored at Annual GLAAD Gala for Promoting LGBT Equality." *Tubefilter*, 3 August. http://www.tubefilter.com/2016/08/03/hannah-hart-honored-glaad-gala-lgbt-equality/, accessed 4 August 2016.

Weiss, G. (2017). "Here's How the YouTube 'Adpocalypse' Is Affecting Top Creators." *Tubefilter*, 4 May. http://www.tubefilter.com/2017/05/04/how-youtube-adpocalypse-affected-top-creators/, accessed 4 May 2017.

Weiß, M. (2016). "Is Amazon Video, Now at 4.26% of U.S. Prime Time Downstream, Growing Fast Enough?" *Early Moves*, 24 June. https://earlymoves.com/2016/06/24/is-amazon-video-now-at-4-26-of-u-s-prime-time-downstream-growing-fast-enough/, accessed 10 July 2017.

Welch, C. (2015). "Google+ and YouTube Are Finally Splitting Up." *Verge*, 27 July. https://www.theverge.com/2015/7/27/9047785/youtube-ditching-google-plus-requirement, accessed 24 August 2017.

Westbrook, T. (2015). Creator, Tati (GlamLifeGuru), 4 September, interview with Stuart Cunningham and David Craig, United States.

Whitaker, B. (2016). "The Influencers." *60 Minutes*, 23 October. http://www.cbsnews .com/news/60-minutes-kim-kardashian-logan-paul-social-media-influencers/, accessed 23 October 2016.

"Why I Left." YouTube video, 11:11. Posted by "Michelle Phan," 1 June 2017. https://www .youtube.com/watch?v=UuGpm01SPcA, accessed 22 August 2017.

"Why I'm a Sell Out." YouTube video, 2:15. Posted by "Anna Akana," 1 June 2015. https:// www.youtube.com/watch?v=Rgd30_JiK24, accessed 11 July 2017.

Wilk, R. (2003). "Learning to Be Local in Belize: Global Systems of Common Difference." In *Worlds Apart: Modernity through the Prism of the Local*, edited by D. Miller, 110–33. New York: Routledge.

Willey, C. (2016). Vice President of Development, DEFY Media, 29 October, personal communication with David Craig, United States.

Williams, R. (1981). *Culture*. London: Fontana.

Willman, K. (2016). "10 Reasons PewDiePie Is YouTube's Most Subscribed Channel." *Turbo Future*, 25 November. https://turbofuture.com/internet/10-Reasons -PewDiePie-Is-Most-Subscribed-on-YouTube, accessed 10 May 2017.

Winkler, R. (2015). "YouTube: 1 Billion Viewers, No Profit: Revenue Growing at Google Video Site, but Still Limited by Narrow Audience." *Wall Street Journal*, 25 February. http://www.wsj.com/articles/viewers-dont-add-up-to-profit-for -youtube-1424897967, accessed 26 March 2017.

Winokur, J. (2004). *The War between the State: Northern California vs. Southern California*. Seattle: Sasquatch Books.

Winter, D. (2011). "Adsense, No Sense at All: What It's Like Being Sacked by a Computer . . ." *Ducksworth Magazine*, January. http://www.duckworksmagazine.com/11 /columns/guest/winter/index.htm, accessed 13 July 2017.

Witteg, F. (2016). Producer and Social Media Manager, Mediakraft Networks (The Great War), 6 October, interview with Stuart Cunningham and David Craig, Germany.

Wolff, M. (2015). *Television Is the New Television*. New York: Portfolio/Penguin.

Wong, F. (2015). Creative Director, RocketJump, 9 July. Personal interview with David Craig, United States.

Woolley, E. (2014). "PewDiePie: YouTube's Biggest Star Is a Profane Swede You've Never Heard Of." *Globe and Mail*, 25 February. https://www.theglobeandmail.com /technology/digital-culture/pewdiepie-this-profane-bro-you-never-heard-of-is -youtubes-biggest-star/article17079452/, accessed 5 July 2017.

Wuest, B. (2014). "Stories like Mine: Coming Out Videos and Queer Identities on YouTube." In *Queer Youth and Media Culture*, edited by C. Pullen, 19–33. Basingstoke: Palgrave Macmillan.

Xi, J. (2014). *The Governance of China*. Beijing: Foreign Languages Press.

Xiang, T. (2017). "Report: China's Live Streaming Market Grew 180% in 2016." *Techcrunch*, 31 March. http://technode.com/2017/03/31/chinas-live-video-streaming -market-grew-180-2016-report/, accessed 3 August 2017.

Yang, Y. (2017a). "In China, Live-Streaming Apps Soothe Lonely Souls and Create Fortunes." *Los Angeles Times*, 5 January. http://www.latimes.com/world/asia/la-fg -china-live-streaming-20161128-story.html, accessed 3 August 2017.

Yang, Y. (2017b). "China Bans Homosexuality, Luxurious Lifestyles from Online Videos." *Financial Times*, 2 July. https://www.ft.com/content/7da123ac-5ed8-11e7-8814 -0ac7eb84e5f1, accessed 3 August 2017.

"Yes I'm Gay." YouTube video, 11:58. Posted by "Joey Graceffa," 18 May 2015. https:// www.youtube.com/watch?v=z1PoNhYb3K4, accessed 24 October 2016.

Yi, D. (2016). "Michelle Phan Is Starting Over." *Mashable*, 13 February. http://mashable .com/2016/02/13/michelle-phan-starting-over/, accessed 21 November 2016.

YouTube Help (2017). "Multi-Channel Network (MCN) Overview for YouTube Creators." *YouTube Help*. https://support.google.com/youtube/answer/2737059?hl=en, accessed 18 July 2017.

YouTube Help. (2018). "Policies and Safety." *YouTube Help*, https://www.youtube.com /intl/en-GB/yt/about/policies/#community-guidelines, accessed 26 June 2018.

YouTube Trends. (2015). "YouTube Trends Explainer: Coming Out on YouTube." *YouTube Trends*, 19 February, http://youtube-trends.blogspot.com/2015/02/youtube -trends-explainer-coming-out-on.html, accessed 3 August 2017.

"YouTube's New Thing (and a New Thing of Our Own)." YouTube video, 3:52. Posted by "vlogbrothers," 13 September 2016. https://www.youtube.com/watch?v=K9Vop29u _UE, accessed 5 July 2017.

Zapata-Kim, L. (2016). "Should YouTube's Content ID Be Liable for Misrepresentation under the Digital Millennium Copyright Act?" *Boston College Law Review*, 57(5): 1847–74.

Zhang, S., and Miller, M. (2017). "China Live Streaming: Would-Be Internet Stars Boost Billion-Dollar Market." *Reuters*, 12 April. http://www.reuters.com/article/us -china-internet-livestreaming-idUSKBN17E0EV, accessed 3 August 2017.

Zhao, E. (2016). "Professionalization of Amateur Production in Online Screen Entertainment in China: Hopes, Frustrations, and Uncertainties." *International Journal of Communication*, 10(2016): 5444–62.

Zhou, Q. (2016). Chief Communication Officer, Feidieshou Communication and Technology Company, 16 June, interview with Stuart Cunningham and David Craig, China.

INDEX

ABOUT THE AUTHORS

Stuart Cunningham is Distinguished Professor of Media and Communication, Queensland University of Technology. His most recent books include *Media Economics* (with Terry Flew and Adam Swift, 2015), *Screen Distribution and the New King Kongs of the Online World* (with Jon Silver, 2013), and *Hidden Innovation: Policy, Industry, and the Creative Sector* (2013).

David Craig is Clinical Assistant Professor at USC Annenberg's School for Communication and Journalism and a Fellow at the Peabody Media Center. Craig is also a veteran media producer and executive nominated for many Emmy Awards and responsible for over thirty critically acclaimed films, TV programs, and stage productions.

Printed and bound by CPI Group (UK) Ltd, Croydon, CR0 4YY

16/04/2025

14658443-0003